AF560247

PUNJAB POLITICS, 1940-1943: STRAINS OF WAR

Governors' Fortnightly Reports and other Key Documents

Punjab Politics, 1940-1943: Strains of War

Governors' Fortnightly Reports and other Key Documents

compiled and edited by
LIONEL CARTER
Former Librarian, Centre of South Asian Studies, University of Cambridge

MANOHAR
2005

First published 2005

ISBN 81-7304-626-3

Published by
Ajay Kumar Jain for
Manohar Publishers & Distributors
4753/23 Ansari Road, Daryaganj
New Delhi 110 002

Printed at
Lordson Publishers Pvt Ltd
Delhi 110 007

Distributed in South Asia by

4381/4, Ansari Road
Daryaganj, New Delhi 110 002
and its branches at Mumbai, Hyderabad,
Bangalore, Chennai, Kolkata

To the memory of Sir Penderel Moon,

1905-1987

Contents

Editor's Introduction

This volume is a continuation of my *Punjab Politics, 1936-1939: The Start of Provincial Autonomy* which Manohar published in 2004.[1] As with that volume the principal aim is to reproduce in full the Fortnightly Reports of the Governor of the Punjab to the Viceroy. Considerations of space do not allow the inclusion of the Viceroy's replies and enclosures to Governors' Reports are only reproduced when they are of significance. In addition to the Reports, other key documents sent by the Governor or his Secretary to the Viceroy have also been included. The introduction to the previous volume provides an account of the origins of the series of Fortnightly Reports.

The narrative of the present volume takes place against a background of war, constitutional discussions and food grain and other supply shortages. In all these matters the Punjab was at the forefront of attention. It was the major supplier of troops to the Indian Army; its communal balance gave rise to much anxiety; and, as the 'granary of India', it was an important source for Delhi and eastern India of wheat and other food products.

The start of the Second World War in September 1939 triggered off a constitutional bargaining process in India and all the problems which were to bedevil the last years of the Raj now became apparent. We have already noted in the previous volume the Viceroy's October 1939 Statement on 'India and the War' as well as the unfavourable reactions of the parties to it. In the present volume there are successively the Muslim League's Lahore Resolution of March 1940 calling for the creation of sovereign Muslim states; the 1940 'August Offer' of the British Government and its rejection by both Congress and the League; the expansion of the Viceroy's Executive Council in July 1941 (with the inclusion of non-official members) and the creation of a National Defence Council; the Cripps' Offer and Mission to India in March and April 1942 which was to be unsuccessful; and finally the passing by the All-India Committee of Congress of the August 1942 'Quit India' resolution accompanied by the internment of the principal Congress leaders. This last event was to lead to Mahatma Gandhi's epic 21 days' fast which took place between 10 February and 3 March 1943.

The Muslim Unionist Premier of the Punjab, Sir Sikander Hyat Khan, played an important part in these developments commensurate with his standing as both a Provincial and a national leader. He was a staunch supporter of the war believing it was not merely Britain's war but the Punjab's too (see Enclosure 2 to No. 129, effectively drafted by him). Initially he stood out in support of the 'August Offer' saying that 'shorn of superfluous diplomatic verbiage, the declaration contains a substantial concession to Indian opinion.' (No. 44, note 16 – the verbiage was mainly Churchill's.[2]) At this stage Sikander indicated that he and his party would withdraw from the League since their constitutional object had been fully secured by the terms of the Offer (No. 42). This stance of Sikander's must, however, be seen against the background of exchanges that were taking place between him and Congress (Nos. 44 and 46). When, against his urgings, Congress rejected the Offer, Sikander went along with the League's eventual rejection. In a letter of 16 October 1940 (No. 52), the Governor of the Punjab, Sir Henry Craik, gave Sikander's explanations for his changed outlook. They included the argument that 'Muslims might find themselves in a very difficult position if after sending their representatives to the Executive Council and thus assuming their share in the responsibility for a policy of repression towards Congress, should that become necessary, the Congress should at some subsequent date reconsider their attitude and themselves decide to accept [the] offer.' Sikander also felt that the communal situation would steadily become more and more bitter if the Muslims joined the Executive Council while Congress and the Mahasabha held aloof – an argument which the Governor felt possibly had some force.

Sikander's equivocal stand on the 'August Offer' was symptomatic of a weakening of his position with respect to Jinnah and the Muslim League which occurred in the years 1940-2. His decision to support the Lahore Pakistan resolution in March 1940 and his resignation from the new National Defence Council in August 1941 (following discussions with Jinnah and the League in Bombay) caused dismay amongst non-Muslim communities and a potential weakening of the Unionist cause in the Punjab (see, for example, No. 91). Yet despite all the uncertainty which these manoeuvrings caused, Sikander's sudden death, aged 50, on 26 December 1942 was felt at the time to be a major loss (No. 131). From the perspective of history, however, we can see this event less dramatically. As Sir Penderel Moon has written, Sikander 'died at the height of his power and reputation and escaped a future which seemed to threaten both. The truth is that the demand for Pakistan had put him in a quandry from which there was no obvious way out.'[3] Indeed the record presented here suggests that Sikander's power and standing were already starting to decline by the time of his death.[4]

* * *

There is a clear division in the documentation of this volume caused by the change in Governors which took place in April 1941. In his last Report Craik wrote that he was: 'glad that I am handing over to [Glancy] at a moment when the Province is in a strong financial position and its war effort is at the apex of enthusiasm and confidence; and particularly when the communal outlook – always our main anxiety here – is not darkened by any imminent cloud' (No. 69). This might almost have been a elegy for the old Punjab.

The new Governor, Sir Bertrand Glancy, was widely regarded as one of the ablest administrators in the India of his day.[5] He possessed a clear, analytical mind and a powerful strategic grasp to which was coupled a slightly cynical approach towards men and events. As his Governorship progressed Glancy was not averse to the odd tactical gamble.[6] For our present purposes it is important to note that, unlike his immediate predecessors, Glancy's working life had not centred on the Punjab. For more than 30 years, Glancy had been involved with the affairs of the Princely States. He had had two spells helping in Jammu and Kashmir and had ended up as Political Adviser to the Crown Representative between 1938 and 1941.[7]

Although, therefore, Glancy shared with Craik a desire that the Punjab Ministry should adopt a broad, non-communal approach, he had not been brought up in what has been described as the 'Punjab tradition'[8] – the outlook which held that the first concern of the Punjab Government should be to preserve a stable rural base and which stressed the fundamental importance of the Punjab Land Alienation Act of 1901. This was an approach that was particularly concerned with the welfare of the peasant proprietor and was anxious to limit the rapacious activities of some moneylenders. Glancy's differing approach becomes apparent soon after his assumption of the Governorship. He places a greater emphasis on the well-being of townspeople and their relations with the countryside. He is anxious about the position of the Sikhs as the political and constitutional situation evolves. He appears to have much less sympathy for some of the economic legislation which the Unionist Government had undertaken, primarily in the interests of rural communities and peasant proprietors, and he is particularly critical of the speed with which it was rushed through (see No. 90, paragraph 8). At the conclusion of a *hartal* by shopkeepers against a new sales tax, Glancy wrote: 'Let us hope that one good result will come out of the affair – and that is that the Provincial Government will feel less temptation to press forward further legislation of an anti-urban variety' (No. 100).[9] No doubt Glancy's differing emphasis helps partly to explain why his relations with Sikander became noticeably less close than Craik's. A clear distance between the Governor and the Ministry grew up. One suspects that the Ministry's threats of resignation in July 1941 would not have helped its relations with Glancy (No 82).

Glancy's greater distance from Sikander means that we have less information on the Premier's activities and thinking during the Glancy years. Our knowledge of events is also affected by the fact that Glancy did not produce his Reports with the required frequency. Although his Reports are of great interest for their perceptive analysis, very often a month or more elapsed between the dates when they were written and they sometimes lack detailed accounts of developments. One may cite, as an example of this lack of information, the rather sketchy details provided of the circumstances under which the Sikander-Baldev Singh Pact was concluded. (See Appendix for the text of the Pact.) The Pact was of great importance as it brought Sardar Baldev Singh, a moderate Akali representative, into the Unionist Ministry. It is difficult to believe that in securing this success, Sikander did not receive help from concerned intermediaries. One writer has suggested that Major John Short (an Army Liaison Officer with the Sikhs) and Penderel Moon (then Deputy Commissioner in Amritsar) had decided to detach the Akalis from the Congress and bring them into a coalition with the Unionists.[10]

During 1943, following Sikander's death, Glancy's relationship with his Ministry was to become closer. There were a number of reasons for this. Firstly, he was evidently more in sympathy with the new Premier, Malik Khizar Hyat Khan. 'There is no denying', Glancy wrote of Khizar in July 1943, that he 'lacks the experience and political agility of his predecessor, but he is in many respects a firmer character. He has a most attractive personality and he is very pleasant to work with. He is shrewd, even-tempered and blessed with a sense of humour. Though he is at heart an aristocrat and something of a reactionary, he keeps his prejudices in the background and is in my opinion essentially fair-minded. He has shown no signs of communal bias.' (Enclosure to No. 157.) Secondly, events forced Glancy to defend his Ministers. Jinnah was propagating the Pakistan doctrine which was widely being taken up and the Qaid-i-Azam was attempting to exercise his authority over Khizar and control the Punjab Ministry. (See particularly No. 163.) In these moves Jinnah was to gain the support of Sikander's eldest son, Major Shaukat Hyat Khan, who had entered the Ministry in February 1943 (see Enclosure to No. 157). In addition to problems with Jinnah, the Ministry came under attack because of its actions with regard to food grain supplies. It was alleged that Ministers were encouraging growers to withhold supplies (with a view to higher prices) and were helping to starve Bengal. Whilst severely reprimanding the Jat leader and Revenue Minister, Sir Chhotu Ram, for some of his speeches (Nos. 146 and 151), Glancy came strongly to the support of the Punjab Ministry and opposed Linlithgow's threats to impose a Section 93 administration. One particular letter of Glancy's is notable for its strength of argument (No. 164). On this occasion one suspects that Glancy could not have been far from resignation himself. The volume ends with the Ministry agreeing to the imposition of price control on food (No. 169). It is clear that through this action, Glancy's relations had got off to a good start with the new Viceroy, Lord Wavell.

* * *

This volume is dedicated to the memory of Sir Penderel Moon whom I had the privilege of working for between 1972 and 1980 and with whom I remained in contact until the end of his life. Moon joined the Indian Civil Service in 1929 and contributions from him appeared in the previous volume (see, particularly, *P.P., 1936-1939*, Enclosure to No. 89). In the present volume Moon appears as both Governor's Secretary and Deputy Commissioner, Amritsar. (See, particularly, Enclosure to No. 20 and its note 55.) The present volume also includes documentation on Moon's resignation in 1943 (Nos. 129 and 132) – an event which impressed a number of British District Officers elsewhere in India.[11] Moon's contributions in these volumes, and his *Strangers in India*[12] published in 1944 and based on the experiences of his first Indian years, show how far ahead of much contemporary thinking his mind was. Fortunately Leo Amery (Secretary of State for India) sent Wavell a copy of *Strangers in India* and the Viceroy, while disputing Moon's more fundamental conclusions, hoped that it might be possible to offer Moon employment in India later on.[13] This in fact happened in 1946 when, at the suggestion of Sir Evan Jenkins, Wavell gave Moon a contract to act as Secretary of the Development Board and Planning Advisory Board.[14] Thereafter, with only a brief absence, Moon was to remain until 1961 in senior government posts in India and

Bahawalpur (which acceded to Pakistan). He was truly a great servant and friend of India and Pakistan.

The documents in this volume are British Crown Copyright. Most are reproduced from a series of prints made in the Viceroy's Secretariat in New Delhi.[15] In the India Office Records these prints are given the following references:

R/3/1/62	January-December 1940
R/3/1/63	January-December 1941
R/3/1/64	January-December 1942
R/3/1/65	January-October 1943

If no reference is given to a document in the present volume, it may be assumed that the document is taken from the above prints. When a document is printed from a different source, that source is indicated in a footnote. All references in this volume are to items in the India Office Records.

In conclusion, I would like once again to express my thanks for help and advice received from Anthony Farrington, formerly head of the India Office Records at the British Library. I would also like to thank Graham Shaw, Director of the Asia, Pacific and Africa Collections at the British Library, for his interest. I again owe a special debt to Ram Advani and to Ramesh Dogra, M.B.E. and Urmila Dogra for advice on a wide range of issues. My publisher, Ramesh Jain, has, as ever, extended many kindnesses to me. None of the foregoing bears any responsibility for errors and omissions in the book. The responsibility for these rests solely with me.

Harrow, February 2004 LIONEL CARTER

NOTES

1. In the present work references to the previous volume are given the abbreviation '*P.P., 1936-1939*'.
2. See Wm. Roger Louis, *In the name of God, go! Leo Amery and the British Empire in the age of Churchill*, New York: W.W. Norton, 1992, pp. 134-5.
3. Penderel Moon, *Divide and quit,* London: Chatto & Windus, 1964, p. 37.
4. Sikander's standing in the autumn of 1942 is reflected in some remarks Linlithgow made to Amery while supporting Glancy's recommendation that Sikander be made a K.C.S.I. Linlithgow wrote: 'The Punjab's war performance is outstanding and none can doubt Sikander's large part in it. His failures have been in the field of party politics and not in the handling of his charge, or in

the lead he has given to the Province and to India in the war effort.' Linlithgow to Amery, 21 September 1942, MSS. EUR. F 125/11.

5. When he was told that Glancy would succeed him, Craik wrote: 'I think the choice of Glancy is a very wise one, if I may say so. There is no one in India who is his superior in capacity or experience, and I have no doubt that he will soon gain the confidence of the Ministers and people. His lack of recent experience of the Province, and perhaps the fact that his career has been wholly in the Political Department, will doubtless be at the start slight handicaps, but his capacity and personality should soon overcome these.' Craik to Linlithgow, 31 March 1940, MSS. EUR. F 125/62.
6. The episode I have in mind here is Glancy's dismissal of Major Shaukat Hyat Khan from the Punjab Ministry in April 1944. Muslim League had been returned as the largest party.
7. Information from Glancy's obituary in *The Times*, 18 March 1953. After retirement Glancy settled in Kenya where he headed at least one Commission. He died in Kenya.
8. P.H.M. van den Durgen, *The Punjab Tradition: Influence and Authority in Nineteenth-century India*, London: Allen & Unwin, 1972. See also: David Gilmartin, *Empire and Islam: Punjab and the Making of Pakistan*, London: I.B. Tauris, 1988, Chapter 1, 'The British Imperial State', pp. 11-38.
9. It is only fair to record that Craik was also doubtful of the wisdom of the sales tax but he did not express himself with Glancy's vehemence. See No. 63, paragraph 7.
10. Stephen Oren: 'The Sikhs, Congress, and the Unionists in British Punjab, 1937-1945', in *Modern Asian Studies* (Cambridge), Vol. 8, No. 3 (1974), p. 405.
11. Mr W.G. Archer (a District Officer in Bihar at the time) once said to me that he and other I.C.S. Officers felt the same way as Moon on the treatment of Congress in 1942 but, as they had young families to support, they were not able to make the demonstration of resigning.
12. Penderel Moon, *Strangers in India*, London: Faber and Faber, 1944.
13. See N. Mansergh and E.W.R. Lumby (eds.), *The Transfer of Power*, London: H.M.S.O., 1973, Vol. IV, Nos. 537, 552 and 565.
14. Information given by Philip Mason in his article on Moon in C.S. Nicholls (ed.), *The Dictionary of National Biography 1986–1990*, Oxford: OUP, 1996, pp. 308-9.
15. Identical copies of these prints are held in the Linlithgow Papers under the references MSS. EUR. F 125/89-92.

Abbreviations

A.C.	Assistant Commissioner.
A.D.C.	Aide-de-Camp.
A.G.	Adjutant-General.
A.H.Q.	Army Headquarters.
A.P.I.	Associated Press of India.
A.R.P.	Air Raid Precautions.
B.Os.	British Officers.
C.-in-C.	Commander-in-Chief.
C.I.D.	Criminal Investigation Department.
C.I.H.	Central India Horse.
C.I.O.	Central Intelligence Officer.
C.O.	Commanding Officer.
C.P.	Central Provinces.
D.C.	Deputy Commissioner.
D.I.B.	Director of the Intelligence Bureau.
D.I.G.	Deputy Inspector General.
D.M.	District Magistrate.
D.-O.	Demi-Official.
E.A.C.	Extra Assistant Commissioner.
F.L.	Fortnightly Letter.
F.O.R.	Free on Rail.
G. of I.	Government of India.
G.S.	Governor's Secretary.
H.E.	His Excellency.
H.M.G.	His Majesty's Government.
H.Q.	Headquarters.
I.A.	Indian Army.
I.C.S.	Indian Civil Service.
I.G.	Inspector General.
I.M.S.	Indian Medical Service.
I.N.A.	Indian National Army.
I.N.C.	Indian National Congress.

I.P.	Indian Police.
I.P.S.	Indian Political Service.
K.C.S.I.	Knight Commander of the Star of India.
M.C.S.	Member of the Council of State.
M.L.A.	Member of the Legislative Assembly.
M.L.C.	Member of the Legislative Council.
M.T.	Military Transport.
N.-W.	North-West.
N.-W.F.P.	North-West Frontier Province.
P.C.S.	Punjab Civil Service.
P.P., 1936-1939.	Lionel Carter (ed.), *Punjab Politics, 1936-1939: The Start of Provincial Autonomy.* (New Delhi: Manohar, 2004.)
P.S.C.	Public Services Commission.
P.S.V.	Private Secretary to the Viceroy.
Rs.	Rupees.
S.G.P.C.	Shiromani Gurdwara Parbandhak Committee.
S. of S.	Secretary of State.
U.P.	United Provinces.
Y.E.	Your Excellency.

Glossary

Akali	Particularly strict devotee of the Sikh faith; in modern usage a member of the extreme Sikh nationalist party.
Anna	One-sixteenth of a rupee.
Ayah	Nurse, governess, woman who looks after young children.
Bania	Trader, moneylender.
Bearer	A domestic servant who has charge of the master's clothes, household furniture and often his ready money; valet.
Belcha	Spade, often sharpened at the edges.
Burqa	A long enveloping garment worn in public places by Muslim women to screen them from the view of men and strangers.
Charpoy	The standard Indian bedstead with string webbing in place of springs.
Chaudhuri	Headman of village or caste.
Crore	One hundred lakhs or ten million.
Dacoity	Robbery with violence committed by a gang.
Daffadar	Cavalry sergeant.
Dal	Organization, association.
Diwali	Hindu festival: the festival of lights, held on the fourteenth day of the waning moon of Kartika (September-October).
Durbar	Royal court or levee.
Ghee, *ghi*	Clarified butter.
Giani	One who possesses knowledge; among Sikhs, a person well-versed in the scriptures.
Goonda	Hooligan, hired rascal.
Gur	Molasses, treacle, raw sugar.
Gurdwara	A Sikh temple, generally also the centre of Sikh social activity.

Gurmukhi	A script adopted by the first successor to Guru Nanak for recording his compositions and used subsequently by the Sikhs for writing Punjabi.
Hartal	Shopkeepers' strike; strike.
Holi	Hindu spring festival celebrated on the full-moon day of Phalguna (February-March). Participants throw coloured waters and powders on one another.
Id	A Muslim holy festival. Bakr-Id commemorates Abraham's sacrifice; Id-ul-fitr the feast on breaking the *Ramzan* fast.
Imam	Head of Muslims in religious matters; the functionary of a mosque who leads the daily prayers of the congregation.
Jagirdar	Holder of a *jagir*, a tenure under which public revenues of the land were assigned to the tenant either in return for services or unconditionally.
Jatha	An armed band or procession; a procession of religious or political protest.
Jhatka	Sudden death, when the animal is killed with one stroke, in contrast to *halal* meat of Muslims.
Khaksars	*Lit.*: like the earth, humble; semi-military organization of Muslims armed with spades, under the leadership of Inayatullah Khan.
Khalsa	The Sikh brotherhood instituted by Guru Gobind Singh; used for an individual as well as for the collective body.
Khan	A title borne by Muslim nobles especially when of Persian or Pathan descent.
Kharif	Grain crops sown in summer and reaped by early winter.
Kisan	Peasant, cultivator, tenant.
Lakh	One hundred thousand.
Lashkar	A body of armed men, especially of tribal Afghans.
Lathi	Thick stick, usually bamboo, sometimes bound with iron rings.
Maharaja	A sovereign prince.
Malik	A Muslim title inferior to Khan and Amir.

Mandi	Market (grain-market).
Masjid	Muslim place of worship, Mosque.
Maulana	The title of a person of learning or respectability; teacher, doctor.
Maulvi	Muslim religious teacher.
Maund	A measure of weight. The standard maund is 37.32 kilograms.
Mian	A term of respectful address to an old or respectable person; sir; master.
Mochi	Worker in leather, shoemaker, saddler, upholsterer.
Mohalla	Urban residential neighbourhood.
Morcha	Procession, protest march, generally for political or industrial purposes.
Muharram	First month of the year in the Islamic calendar; a Muslim festival held during Muharram. The festival commemorates the martyrdom of Ali, son-in-law of the Holy Prophet, and of Ali's two sons, Husain and Hassan.
Murdabad	Death to.
Mutwalli	Guardian, trustee.
Nawab	Originally a Governor under the Mughal Empire; thence a title or rank conferred on Muslim nobles.
Nawabzada	Son of a Nawab.
Paisa	One-fourth of an *anna*.
Pandal	Marquee.
Panth	A path, a sect, a religious order.
Pir	A Sufi saint or master.
Qaid-i-Azam	The supreme leader.
Rabi	Principal grain harvest sown after the rains and reaped in the spring season.
Raja	Chief, king.
Ramzan	The ninth Muslim lunar month observed as a 30 days' fast during daylight hours by all Muslims.
Sahukar	Hindu banker.
Sardar	*Lit.*: a chief, leader. Title borne by all Sikhs and also by some Hindus and Muslims.
Sarkar (Sirkar)	District, Government.

Satyagraha	*Lit.:* holding on to truth. Total self-giving; integral to Mahatma Gandhi's concept of victory achieved through non-violent resistance.
Satyagrahi	Participant in satyagraha.
Seer	One-fortieth of a maund (q.v.).
Sepoy	Native soldier employed in the Indian Army.
Shamiana	An awning or flat tent-roof, with or without sides, stretched from top to top of poles and with no centre pole.
Shia	One of the two main branches of Islam (cf. Sunni); followers of Ali, the son-in-law of Muhammad.
Sri	Sanskrit title used by Hindus.
Sunni	The majority in Indian Islam, who regard Caliphs Abu Bakr, Omar and Osman as spiritual descendants of Muhammad.
Swaraj	Self-rule, independence.
Tahsil	Revenue sub-division of a District.
Tazia	Tall, pagoda-like structures of wood or cardboard representing the mausoleums of Husain and Hassan. *Tazias* were carried during the Muharram (q.v.) festival procession. In Lahore some *tazias* were elaborately carved and gilded all over.
Ulama	The learned in Muslim law and religion.
Zaildar	Chief man in a circle of villages.
Zamindar	Landed proprietor paying land revenue to Government, revenue farmer.
Zindabad	Long live.

Principal Holders of Office, January 1940-December 1943

UNITED KINGDOM

Secretary of State for India	The Marquess of Zetland Mr L.S. Amery (from 15 May 1940)

INDIA

Viceroy, Governor-General and Crown Representative	The Marquess of Linlithgow Field Marshal Viscount Wavell (from 20 October 1943)
Private Secretary to the Viceroy	Mr Gilbert Laithwaite (KCIE, January 1941) Mr Evan Jenkins (from 20 October 1943)
Commander-in-Chief, India	General Sir Robert Cassels General Sir Claude Auchinleck (from 27 January 1941) General Sir Archibald Wavell[1] (from 11 July 1941) General Sir Claude Auchinleck (from 21 June 1943)

THE PUNJAB

Governor	Sir Henry Craik Sir Bertrand Glancy (from 7 April 1940)
Secretary to Governor	Mr E.P. Moon Mr G.E.B. Abell (from 18 September 1941)

	Mr G.M. Brander (from 15 March 1943)
Chief Secretary to Government	Mr J.D. Penny (KCIE, January 1943)
	Mr F.C. Bourne (from 1 October 1941)
Joint Chief Secretary to Government	Mr J.D. Anderson (until 20 October 1941; office then abolished)

MEMBERS OF THE COUNCIL OF MINISTERS

Premier	Sir Sikander Hyat Khan
	Malik Khizar Hyat Khan (from 30 December 1942)
Minister of Revenue	Sir Sundar Singh Majithia
	Sir Chhotu Ram (from 8 April 1941)
Minister of Development	Sir Chhotu Ram
	Sardar Dasaundha Singh (from 8 April 1941)
	Sardar Baldev Singh (from 26 June 1942)
Finance Minister	Sir Manohar Lal
Minister of Public Works	Malik Khizar Hyat Khan
	Major Shaukat Hyat Khan (from 6 February 1943)
Minister of Education	Mian Abdul Haye

PUNJAB LEGISLATIVE ASSEMBLY

Speaker	Sir Shahab-ud-Din
Deputy Speaker	Sardar Dasaundha Singh
	Sardar Gurbachan Singh (from April 1941)

NOTE

1. General Wavell was promoted to a Field Marshal in January 1943 and was made a Viscount on his appointment as Viceroy.

Summaries of Documents

CHAPTER 1 – DOCUMENTS FOR JANUARY-JUNE 1940

	Name and Number	*Date*	*Main subject or subjects*
		Jan.	
1	Craik to Linlithgow Letter 205	1	Explains position of Maharaja of Patiala in Sikh affairs; sees no objection to his taking prominent part in encouraging Sikh recruitment to Army but he should not become involved in more controversial issues
2	Moon to Laithwaite Letter G.S. 11	5	Sends note by Craik appraising various Punjab ministers
3	Craik to Linlithgow Letter 206	8	Reports that Sikander has received requests that he visit U.K. to represent cases of States and minorities; seeks Viceroy's advice; informs him of Sikander's discussion with Nehru on political situation; Enclosure: Letter from Nawanagar to Sikander about requested visit to U.K.
4	Craik to Linlithgow Report 207-F.L.	14	Nehru's visit to Amritsar and Lahore; forthcoming conference on food price control; serious health problems in Hissar famine area; 1940-1 budget; incident in Shahidganj Gurdwara; Craik would be unable to sanction (as it stands) proposed Bill to prevent situations similar to Shahidganj; Viceroy's Bombay speech

5	Craik to Linlithgow Letter 208	16	Suggested visit of Sikander to U.K.; corrects his account of Sikander's discussion with Nehru given in No. 3
6	Craik to Linlithgow Letter 209	19	Will keep him informed of developments following the issue of orders prohibiting drilling and carrying of arms in processions
7	Craik to Linlithgow Report 210-F.L.	28	Excellent rainfall helps standing *rabi* crops; charitable appeals; inter-Provincial food conference at Lahore; talk with Sant Singh on Sikhs' attitude to Army recruitment and the reported break between Patiala and Tara Singh; developments within Punjab Congress party; 'Independence Day' marked by more enthusiasm and larger processions that in preceding years; dinner at Punjab Club in honour of Ministry; Sikander's forthcoming visit to Delhi
		Feb.	
8	Craik to Linlithgow Tel. 3-G	8	Summarises Provincial and press reactions to failure of Linlithgow's discussions with Gandhi.
9	Craik to Linlithgow Report 211-F.L.	19	Craik's tour of Gujranwala and Sialkot; Maulana Azad's visit to the Punjab; Iftikhar-ud-Din replaces Gopi Chand as Punjab Congress President; case of police officer alleged to have been suborned to give false evidence against an Ahrar agitator; Moharram problems in Amritsar; attacks by raiders on Isakhel town; Sikh anxieties on the wearing of steel helmets in the Army; war propaganda work by students;

			improvement in medical condition of people in Hissar suffering from effects of famine
		Mar.	
10	Craik to Linlithgow Report 215-F.L.	4	Craik's visits to Montgomery, Multan, Muzaffargarh and Dera Ghazi Khan; orders issued banning drilling by private armies; they also ban carrying of arms or implements in processions in three larger towns; likelihood of agitation against orders from Khaksars and perhaps Akalis; Moharram passes without incident but communal situation remains acute; no further raids on Isakhel; Provincial budget; Patna resolution of Congress Working Committee; strains on Ministers from lengthy Assembly session; large audience for Sikh saint on day he said he would die
11	Craik to Linlithgow Letter 220	18	Khaksar problem; Jinnah understood to be anxious there should be no clash between Khaksars and Govt.; emissary of Sikander's sent to see Inayatullah in Delhi; Patiala's attitude to the wearing of steel helmets by Sikhs in Army; Bhatnagar given leave to become Director of Board of Scientific and Industrial Research
12	Craik to Linlithgow Letter 221	20	Gives details of Khaksar outrage in Lahore previous day; Inayatullah arrested in Delhi; attempt to persuade Jinnah to postpone League session in Lahore is unsuccessful
13	Craik to Linlithgow Letter 222	21	Khaksar situation; Jinnah's arrival at Lahore; Sikander presses for

			enquiry into Khaksar outrage; he is to tell Jinnah that he and his supporters would leave League if any resolution is discussed which condemns Ministry's action; anxieties that Khaksars might invade League meetings
14	Craik to Linlithgow Letter 223	22	Eight armed Khaksars arrested through use of tear-gas; League's Subjects Committee to consider possible resolution on Khaksars later that day; Craik visits injured in hospital; Khaksar photograph album; doubtful they will be able to convict Inayatullah; press attitudes
15	Craik to Linlithgow Letter 224	23	Jinnah has acted correctly over Khaksars; measures to save senior police officers from risks of serious injuries; publicity against Khaksars; some hostile demonstrations against Sikander; possible Khaksar resolution during League session; committee of enquiry
16	Craik to Linlithgow Letter 225	24	Sikander's speech at League's Subjects Committee; Khaksar resolution to be confined to expressing regret at incident and calling for enquiry; latest developments concerning Khaksars
17	Craik to Linlithgow Letter 226	25	Little exception can be taken to League's Khaksar resolution; talk with Pir Akbar Ali on Ahmadis' attitude to Khaksars; talk with Jinnah; Jinnah appears to visualise using reformed Khaksar movement as League's propaganda agency; he feels personnel of proposed enquiry should not be

			too closely connected with Govt.; Craik hopes any damage to Ministry from Khaksar episode will not be permanent; his opinion of Sikander is greatly enhanced
18	Craik to Linlithgow Letter 228	31	Jinnah's able handling of Khaksar resolution means no other Muslim leader (for a considerable time) will be able to criticise or oppose League's constitutional position; Yar Jang attempting to induce Ministers to rescind order declaring Khaksars unlawful
19	Craik to Linlithgow Report 229-F.L.	31	Long assembly session and recent events have caused Sikander serious strain; moderate Hindu opinion seriously dismayed by Congress resolutions; League session has greatly enhanced Jinnah's influence and League's authority; much loyal support shown during Craik's tours of Lyallpur and Shahpur; situation in famine districts remains serious and entails heavy expenditure; gratitude of inhabitants of Isakhel
		April	
20	Moon to Laithwaite Letter G.S.-226	1	Encloses tel. from Craik giving a general outline of his views on the political and constitutional situation in the light of recent developments
21	Craik to Linlithgow Letter 230	3	Informs him that Sikander has asked about possibility of rescinding order against Khaksars; precautionary measures Craik has taken to cover situation while he is away from Lahore; has seen report that Khaksar headquarters have been moved to Aligarh

22	Craik to Linlithgow Letter 232	6	Arrests of two Khaksar leaders; press reports that order against Khaksars will be lifted soon; situation in Rawalpindi similar to that in Lahore; Enclosure: Letter from Craik to Sikander stating that Governor could not agree to Khaksar order being rescinded until listed conditions are fulfilled
23	Craik to Linlithgow Letter 233	8	Reports interview in which Sikander denied that press articles on Khaksars were officially inspired; Craik assures Sikander that he retains his confidence and is satisfied with measures Govt. has taken; other Khaksar developments; Enclosure: Letter from Sikander replying to Enclosure to No. 22; Sikander would resign if he lacked Governor's confidence
24	Craik to Linlithgow Report 236-F.L.	14	Possible press communiqué on Khaksars; Lahore and Rawalpindi quiet; Young Committee begins recording evidence; police find bomb alleged to have been intended to be thrown at Ministerial benches in Assembly; murder of Karam Singh; reactions to League's partition resolution; Assembly session makes better progress; Craik's visits to Rawalpindi and Attock
25	Craik to Linlithgow Letter 239	22	Khaksar situation; press communiqué issued; Craik's meeting with senior police officers; Sikander urges that Govts. of N.-W.F.P. and U.P. should be pressed to declare Khaksars unlawful associations; Craik supports Sikander

26	Craik to Linlithgow Letter 240	23	Tel. from man assumed to be *Tribune* correspondent in Peshawar adds force to suggestion that action should be taken against Khaksars in other Provinces; sends two further pieces of evidence
27	Craik to Linlithgow Tel. 7-G	23	Ordinary prudence requires them to be prepared for very early declaration of civil disobedience by Congress; discusses tactics
28	Craik to Linlithgow Report 243-F.L.	30	One of Karam Singh's murderers arrested; 'Pakistan Day' celebration a failure in Lahore; League's Lahore resolution; Congress preparations for *Satyagraha*; Gandhi's pronouncement; Sikander still looking very strained and depressed; Khaksar situation; progress of Young Committee; Gainsford flies to England
		May	
29	Craik to Linlithgow Letter 244	5	Continuing concern on possible influx of Khaksars from N.-W.F.P.; police measures tightened up in Lahore; Privy Council's decision in Shahidganj case
30	Craik to Linlithgow Report 246-F.L.	15	Khaksar developments; Muslims generally receive Shahidganj judgement with commendable restraint; tension between rival groups in Punjab Congress Party remains acute; German invasion of Norway causes alarm and despondency together with criticism of H.M.G.; statements by Gandhi and Nehru; Relief of Indebtedness (Amendment) Bill
31	Craik to Linlithgow Report 248-F.L.	29	No signs of panic over German invasion of Belgium, Holland and

			France but heavy withdrawals reported from savings banks in a few districts; tone of press satisfactory; Khaksar situation – continuing infiltration from other Provinces; no further developments on Shahidganj judgement
		June	
32	Craik to Linlithgow Report 252-F.L.	14	Successful round-up of Khaksars in Lahore and Rawalpindi mosques; 500 additional police for Lahore City; general press approval for Govt.'s action; feels morale has slightly improved despite German advances and Italy's entry into the war; formation of Provincial War Board and Civic Guard; attendance small at Lahore *Satyagraha* Training Camp
33	Craik to Linlithgow Letter 256	19	Hindu press reactions to French request for an armistice are despairing but Muslim papers take stouter line; local English press is quite steady; first meeting of Provincial War Board has instilled greater confidence; slight lessening in financial panic
34	Craik to Linlithgow Letter 257	20	Nothing material to report on public reactions to war situation; gives details of interviews he has held and offers of help made to him; Narendra Nath's 'misgivings'; five Muslim M.L.As. attack Govt. policy on Khaksars; Sikander, Mamdot and other Punjab Muslims have not complied with League resolution prohibiting members from joining District War Committees; final

split between Jinnah and Sikander cannot long be delayed

CHAPTER 2 – DOCUMENTS FOR JULY-DECEMBER 1940

		July	
35	Craik to Linlithgow Express Letter	4	Agrees that some of Jinnah's terms for co-operation in Govt. are quite unacceptable; suggests representatives from Provinces not under Section 93 might be taken into Viceroy's Council; argues case for further public declaration of policy
36	Moon to Laithwaite Letter	6	Sikander and Fazlul Haq have met recently in Simla; reports Sikander's talk with Craik that morning; the two Premiers have written to Jinnah reminding of terms which League had authorised him to discuss with Viceroy; they were anxious Jinnah should soon make statement that League would offer co-operation to Govt.; Craik feels there was clear hint that Premiers might break with Jinnah; Sikander has considerable doubts whether Akalis will break with Congress and co-operate
37	Craik to Linlithgow Report 278-F.L.	16	Panic and defeatism less apparent; Gandhi's pronouncements on non-violence in the War have provoked much unfavourable comment; special secret session of Assembly discusses arrests of communists; Sikander's visits to Jullundur and Jhelum; two serious incidents between Muslims and Sikhs; Jinnah agrees to open negotiations

			between Khaksars and Punjab Govt.; Craik feels few Muslims will resign from War Committees despite League's ban; rupture between Jinnah and Sikander cannot long be delayed
38	Craik to Linlithgow Report 283-F.L.	31	Continued restoration of confidence on war situation; valuable work of War Boards; village in Lahore District delays paying land revenue and says it will pay Germans later; communal tension between Muslims and Sikhs remains high; measures taken by Govt. to deal with situation; attitude of the Punjab Congress to holding of next Indian National Congress session in the Punjab; Khaksar situation; excellent rainfall throughout Province
39	Craik to Linlithgow Letter	31	Sends note by Anderson on meeting with Adjutant-General which considered mutiny of Sikhs in Central India Horse; essential that no general orders are passed regarding Sikh recruitment to army without consulting Punjab Govt or receiving Viceroy's approval; Sikander suggests meeting with Sikh leaders
		Aug.	
40	Craik to Linlithgow Letter 284	6	Refers to No. 36 and sends message from Sikander; Abdul Aziz has told Jinnah of unease in League circles that negotiations with Viceroy were being unnecessarily prolonged; Sikander restates points of principle on which Working Committee had insisted; if Viceroy concedes these and

			Jinnah remains obdurate, Sikander would be prepared to call on Muslims to co-operate actively in War
41	Craik to Linlithgow Tel. 12-G	9	Discusses possible members from the Punjab for War Advisory Council
42	Craik to Linlithgow Tel. 13-G	12	Sikander to attend League Working Committee meeting on 17 Aug.; he intends, around that date, to announce that he and his party will withdraw from League having secured objects for which they had joined it; Sikander considers it almost certain that Jinnah will offer Viceroy full co-operation
43	Craik to Linlithgow Tel. G-15-C	17	Sikander will do all he can to expedite League meeting; he thinks Jinnah will stiffen his terms if Congress decide on attitude of uncompromising opposition
44	Craik to Linlithgow Letter 286-Camp	17	Amplifies Sikander's answer in No. 43; Sikander has urged Azad to see Viceroy; Rajagopalachariar has asked Sikander (through Shiva Rao) to go to Wardha to convince Gandhi but Sikander has been unable to accept
45	Craik to Linlithgow Tel. 16-G	18	Sikander thinks it would be a mistake in the Punjab at that stage to act against League National Guards for possible defiance of ban on drilling; he has urged main Congress leaders to see Viceroy and hopes Congress may co-operate; Jinnah says he is not yet in a position to fix date for Working Committee meeting

46	Craik to Linlithgow Letter 287	19	Sends text of tel. Sikander has received from Azad saying 'door seems to be closed to Congress'; also sends text of Sikander's reply; measures which Sikander feels might persuade Congress to participate in Executive Council
47	Craik to Linlithgow Letter 289	22	Encloses express letter giving his explanations of recent mutiny by Sikh soldiers of the Central India Horse
48	Craik to Linlithgow Report 290-F.L.	27	Relations between Muslims and Sikhs have somewhat improved; panic and defeatism almost completely subsided; commercial and industrial classes not supporting war loans as generously as Craik wishes; Muslim satisfaction that 'August Offer' recognises obligations to minorities; no tendency to illegal drilling or wearing of uniforms; Shah anxious to see Sikander; next session of Indian National Congress to be held in Punjab; difficult to see how Akalis can remain in Congress; Ministerial suggestion of a cut in civil servants' salaries
49	Craik to Linlithgow Letter 291	28	Reports meeting between Sikander and Shah after which Sikander agreed to rescind Punjab notification declaring Khaksars unlawful and to release those Khaksars not convicted for offences involving violence
		Sept.	
50	Craik to Laithwaite Letter	11	Sends: (1) letter from Sethi informing Craik that Tara Singh had resigned from Congress; (2) prefatory note by Tara Singh; (3) Tara Singh's resignation letter

51	Craik to Linlithgow Report 297-F.L.	24	Press almost unanimous in condemning idea of civil disobedience; Tara Singh's resignation from Congress; no bad reactions from Sikhs to punishments handed out to Army mutineers; problems with communist detenus; War Purposes Fund; release of certain Khaksar prisoners delayed; talk with Mamdot over his request to re-join Provincial War Board; arrests for illegal arms trafficking; Ministers' speaking tours
		Oct.	
52	Craik to Linlithgow Letter 301	16	Reports talks with Maqbool and Sikander himself on Sikander's role at League meetings where decision was taken not to join Executive Council; Sikander and Jinnah on much better terms than for some time past; Sikander explains his position on leaving League
53	Craik to Linlithgow Report 302-F.L.	16	Press reactions to Gandhi's views on the War; Congress decision that civil disobedience should be undertaken by individuals; Gandhi reported to have asked for suspension of preparations for I.N.C. session; Craik's visit to Amritsar; he is told insufficient number of Jat Sikhs offering themselves for recruitment; deaths of Yar Khan Daultana and Hasnie; some imprisoned Khaksars released; suggested pay cuts for civil servants; likely crop failure in Hissar; illegal arms trafficking
54	Craik to Linlithgow Letter 304	28	Explains why he thinks Punjab Congress were asked to proceed

No.	Document	Date	Subject
			with preparations for I.N.C. session
		Nov.	
55	Craik to Linlithgow Report 305-F.L.	1	Public opinion in rural areas is sound on war and no evidence of panic in towns; visit of Tahsin Rustu Bey; little interest in Punjab in non-co-operation campaign; press surprisingly critical of Gandhi; police seize circular sent to Congress primary committees; Craik's visit to Shaikhupura; preparations for I.N.C. session; relations between Sikhs and Congress; new taxation Bills; recovery of illicit arms
56	Craik to Linlithgow Report 309-F.L.	15	Quiet fortnight; Craik's visits to Gujrat, Kalabagh, Mianwali and Jehlum; he receives explanation for insufficient Sikh recruitment to Army; Sikh relations with Congress; Nehru's arrest and conviction arouses little interest; reactions to suggestion Gandhi might fast; likely numbers of Congress prisoners; arrests of communists
57	Moon to Laithwaite Letter	24	No important reaction in the Punjab to Viceroy's announcement that certain measures contained in 'August Offer' would be held in abeyance
58	Craik to Linlithgow Report 311-F.L.	30	Little enthusiasm for civil disobedience movement outside Lahore and Amritsar; press reactions; estimated number of prospective *Satyagrahis* in Punjab; crowd of 10,000 at arrest of Iftikharuddin; Gopi Chand also

			arrested; little chance of I.N.C. session being held; annual student conference; Sundar Singh's serious illness – Craik's talk with his son; Assembly session; donations to war funds; police campaign against illicit arms
		Dec.	
59	Craik to Linlithgow Tel. 19-G	11	Does not favour suggestion that imprisoned Provincial ex-Ministers should be held outside their own Provinces; Punjab Ministers would object to having to find accommodation
60	Craik to Linlithgow Report 317-F.L.	29	Sikander visiting Egypt; talk with Sundar Singh; Sampuran Singh's trial; civil disobedience campaign in Punjab; jailing of two students; Craik feared demonstration at University Convocation; Assembly passes a taxation and a primary education Bill; total amounts collected for war funds; condition of Gainsford; Craik refuses to see Ahmad Shah; visit of Turkish military mission

CHAPTER 3 – DOCUMENTS FOR 1941

61	Craik to Linlithgow Report 319-F.L.	13	Sikander's visit to Egypt; he tells Craik time has come when he should be relieved of Premiership; interest in *Satyagrahi* movement seems to be rapidly waning; a section of the Ahrars is identifying itself with Congress; Sikh recruitment to Army remains unsatisfactory; war propaganda;

			Primary Education Bill does not alter existing language position
62	Craik to Linlithgow Letter 320	21	Conveys Sikander's suggestion that Viceroy should set up machinery to work out general scheme of future constitution
		Feb.	
63	Craik to Linlithgow Report 321-F.L.	10	Craik's visits to Rohtak and Hissar; excellent rainfall throughout Province; public attitude towards war remains good but continued deficiency in Sikh recruitment; receipts by war funds; Saadat Ali Khan's benefactions; *Satyagraha* situation; communists; Assembly passes Sales Tax Bill; Sikh politics; League expels three prominent Punjab members; slight attempt to revive Khaksar movement
64	Craik to Linlithgow Report 323-F.L.	28	Arrests of *Satyagrahis*; Akali 'ultimatum' to Ministry; deterioration in Sikh-Muslim relations; Sikh recruitment; no development on Khaksars; Craik assents to Sales Tax Bill; traffic in illicit arms; Manohar Lal's budget
		Mar.	
65	Craik to Linlithgow Letter 324	3	Sends (1) letter from Tara Singh asking Craik to use his special powers to protect Sikhs; (2) resolution of S.G.P.C. asking for certain demands to be met by 1 April 1941; comments on Sikander's declared intention of resigning from League Working Committee
66	Craik to Linlithgow Letter 325	4	Continues No. 65; sends account of talk with Sikander on Sikh

			politics, Pakistan and Sikander's attitude to League; feels Sikander has thought out consequences of his proposed action and Craik did not feel he could advise him to reconsider this
67	Craik to Linlithgow Letter 329	13	Informs him of apparent plot to murder Sikander
68	Craik to Linlthgow Report 330-F.L.	17	Opinion on war remains optimistic; numbers of *Satyagrahis* arrested; communal situation gives ground for uneasiness; census returns in certain towns are unreliable; conversation with Sikander and Tara Singh; Sikander's attitude most reasonable; Sikh recruitment; Craik's conversation with Ujjal Singh; this sheds light on Patiala's position; Khaksar prosecutions withdrawn in Rawalpindi
		April	
69	Craik to Linlithgow Report 333-F.L.	2	Confidence in war victory grows stronger; few arrests at start of third phase of *Satyagraha*; threatened Sikh *morcha* will not take place; Sikander's statement in Assembly on Sikh demands; considers Sikander has managed question with considerable skill; Khaksar celebrations; death of Sundar Singh; Craik feels he hands over Punjab in strong financial position, at apex of enthusiasm for war effort, and not darkened by imminent communal cloud
70	Glancy to Linlithgow Report 336-F.L.	11	Appointment of Dasaundha Singh to Ministry

71	Glancy to Linlithgow Letter 341	18	Favours amendment to Govt. of India Act empowering suitable authority to prolong life of a Provincial Assembly; does not favour any rigid provision barring general elections for duration of war
72	Glancy to Linlithgow Report 343-F.L.	28	Widespread movement by trading classes to defeat recent economic legislation; Ministry adopting conciliatory attitude and has agreed modifications to Markets Act; many believe Ministry has 'rushed' economic legislation; despondency on war situation; Sikh recruitment still much below par; Glancy's interview with Patiala
		May	
73	Glancy to Linlithgow Report 344-F.L.	17	*Hartal* against General Sales Taxs Act has ended but *hartal* in grain markets continues; war news from Iraq depresses; Sikander's press conference on war situation; tone of press commendable but no sign of popular movement to sink domestic quarrels; communal situation has not improved – minor clash in Hissar; signs of revival of Khaksar activity; rulings of High Court which would affect some detenus
74	Glancy to Linlithgow Tel. 4-G	23	Would favour restricting changes at Centre to creation of War Advisory Council; doubts whether suitable persons would be available for expanded Executive Council
75	Glancy to Linlithgow Report 346-F.L.	30	*Hartal* in grain markets called off; public attitude to war much

			the same; no material change in communal situation – initiative made by Iftikharuddin; Sikh scheme for providing armed support for Hindus
		June	
76	Glancy to Linlithgow Letter 347	10	Sikander fully agrees that provision should be made for postponement of Provincial elections; they are both agreed it is preferable this should be until twelve months after conclusion of war
77	Glancy to Linlithgow Report 349-F.L.	23	Declaration by Govt. of India that Khaksars were unlawful has averted serious menace; reactions of some Muslim newspapers; Glancy's interview with deputation of Khalsa Defence League; points he is making to Sikh visitors; Iftikharuddin's attempts to promoted communal harmony; Glancy feels they should take public into confidence on A.R.P. and tentative evacuation plans
78	Glancy to Linlithgow Letter 350	26	Sends his views on certain matters connected with composition and working of proposed National Defence Council
		July	
79	Glancy to Linlithgow Letter 352	1	Sikander willing to serve on National Defence Council; sends and discusses Sikander's recommendations for Punjab representatives on Council
80	Glancy to Linlithgow Letter 354	6	Sikander asks Viceroy to defer final decision on National Defence Council until after Sikander's return from tour

81	Moon to Laithwaite Letter (unnumbered)	8	Sends note by Glancy appraising various Punjab ministers
82	Glancy to Laithwaite Letter (unnumbered)	13	Sends: (1) lengthy letter from Sikander explaining his misgivings on Viceroy's forthcoming statement in particular failure to consult him and rumoured absence of a Punjab representative on Executive Council; (2) letter conveying Sikander's resignation as Premier; (3) letter conveying resignation of the other Punjab Ministers
83	Glancy to Linlithgow Tel. 6-G	23	No notable reactions to Viceroy's statement in the Punjab except that Sikhs clamour that they have been slighted because they do not have representative on expanded Executive Council
		Aug.	
84	Glancy to Linlithgow Report 359-F.L.	2	Province quiet on the whole; arrangement likely with Nihang Sikhs; war situation – recruiting has been encouraging; Sikh criticisms of Viceroy's announcements; Ministerial unease at Jinnah's likely action towards Muslim Premiers; *Satyagraha* campaign languishing; rain needed in S.E. Punjab
85	Moon to Laithwaite Tel. 7-G	7	Sikander holding party meeting in Lahore with view to strengthening his position against Jinnah
86	Glancy to Linlithgow Tel. 9-G	16	Sikander's party meeting most successful; over 60 Muslim members of Unionist Party have handed him resignations from League to be used if necessary
87	Moon to Laithwaite Letter	26	Sends copy of letter from Sikander to Glancy conveying Sikander's

			resignation from National Defence Council; gives account of Sikander's stand at League Working Committee meeting; Viceroy's letter to Jinnah had made it impossible for Sikander to continue to serve on Council
		Sept.	
88	Glancy to Linlithgow Tel. 363	8	Action he feels they should take with respect to vacant places on National Defence Council
89	Glancy to Linlithgow Report 364-F.L.	10	Sikander's resignation from National Defence Council; Unionist Party, to all appearance, retains unity and cohesion; Sikh issues; danger from Nihangs has subsided; communal tension shows little sign of improving; *Satyagraha* campaign appears to be on its last legs in Punjab; Press attitudes to Iran; demands for controls on foodgrains; shortages of textile materials
90	Glancy to Linlithgow Letter 365	20	Sends details of Punjab legislation challenged in the courts
		Oct.	
91	Glancy to Linlithgow Report 368-F.L.	21	Sikander's attempt to re-establish his position; more intelligent Muslims are doubtful whether Unionist Party can remain indefinitely in the ascendant; non-Muslims form vigilance society; Sikh recruitment improved; war exercises; Congress activities in a trough
		Nov.	
92	Glancy to Linlithgow Letter	10	Punjab Govt. ready to fall in with Govt of India on release of *Satyagraha* prisoners

93	Glancy to Linlithgow Report 372-F.L.	22	Sikh grievances; some Sikhs dislike prospect of closer union with Congress; a number are exploring possibility of weaning Sikander and colleagues from Muslim League; Jat Sikh recruitment flags again; Khalsa Defence League; Begum Shah Nawaz and Nau Nihal Singh report on first meeting of National Defence Council; Muslim attitudes to events in Iran and Iraq; Congress activity scarcely noticeable

CHAPTER 4 – DOCUMENTS FOR 1942

		Jan.	
94	Glancy to Linlithgow Report 377-F.L.	1	Japanese successes have produced no profound impression; price control imposed on wheat; *hartal* against Marketing Act to be cancelled; Congress' reactions to release of *Satyagrahis*; possible meeting between Sikander and Baldev Singh
95	Abell to Laithwaite Letter	11	Encloses note by Glancy giving further appraisal of the Punjab Ministers
		Feb.	
96	Glancy to Linlithgow Report 382	5	Japanese successes give rise to uneasiness; wheat control working effectively enough; *hartal* against Sales Tax Act continues; Sikh politics much confused; *rabi* prospects promising
97	Glancy to Linlithgow Letter 387	23	Passes on Sikander's suggestions of points H.M.G. should make in any constitutional announcement

	Mar.	
98 Glancy to Linlithgow Tel. 14-G	4	Sends his reactions to first draft of 'Cripps' Offer'; believes it would affect war effort and would cause intensification of bitterness between Muslims and Sikhs; League would gain greatly in strength and most or all of Ministry would resign; considers Punjab would not accede to new constitution
99 Glancy to Linlithgow Tel. 15-G	4	Elaborates views in No. 98; suggests holding of Governors' meeting before decision; idea of possible role for Dominions or U.S.
100 Glancy to Linlithgow Report 388	5	Public morale has seriously deteriorated because of war news; relations between Muslims and Sikhs more and more strained; recruiting continues to be good; *hartal* against Sales Tax Act ends; *rabi* prospects encouraging
101 Glancy to Linlithgow Letter	7	Punjab arrangements for the National War Front
102 Glancy to Linlithgow Tel. 16-G	9	Revised version of 'Cripps' Offer' appears less disturbing but Glancy still anticipates strong protest from League and possible collapse of Ministry; repeats a suggestion in No. 99
103 Glancy to Linlithgow Tel. 17-G	10	Is still gravely apprehensive about proposed announcement; Congress is unlikely to be satisfied and effect on minorities and on Punjab will be disastrous; lists guarantees they should announce
104 Glancy to Linlithgow Tel. 18-G	11	Punjab will do what it can to assist with all-India wheat supplies but local situation is extremely serious

105	Glancy to Linlithgow Tel 19-G	16	Sends names of Sikhs he suggests Cripps should meet
		April	
106	Glancy to Linlithgow Letter 390	14	Failure of Cripps' Mission; feels it is essential to avoid giving impression that ultimate constitutional solution will follow formula of 'Cripps' Offer'
		May	
107	Glancy to Linlithgow Report 393	1	Less defeatism and despondency; Govt. taking measures to enhance war effectiveness; Press and political meetings causing concern; Sikh politics; objections to Khalistan are greater even than those that apply to Pakistan; possibility of Baldev Singh entering Punjab Ministry; traders' revolt against Sales Tax Act appears to have spent itself; favourable agricultural situation
108	Glancy to Linlithgow Report 396	26	Communal tensions show some signs of abatement; negotiations between Sikander and Baldev Singh going well; allegation European soldiers had manhandled girl in Lahore; Nehru's visit to Punjab; common belief that Gandhi will resort to some adventure; proposal for relaxing restrictions on Khaksars; move to Simla
109	Glancy to Linlithgow Letter 397	28	Possible candidates for office of Chief Justice of the Punjab
		June	
110	Glancy to Linlithgow Report 399-F.L.	10	Morale in towns growing steadier and tone of Press more satisfactory; concern at activities of Gandhi and Nehru; negotiations

			between Sikander and Baldev Singh make further progress; release of communists; Guerrilla War Training Camp going well
111	Glancy to Linlithgow Letter 399	25	Sikander-Baldev Singh Pact appears to have gone through; Dasaundha Singh has resigned; question of a job for him
112	Glancy to Linlithgow Report 400-F.L.	30	Set-backs in Libya and Egypt exercise disheartening effect; concern with Gandhi's activities; anxiety over proposal to partially lift ban on Khaksars; reactions to Sikander-Baldev Singh Pact; attack on Simla-Kalka Rail Motor
		July	
113	Abell to Laithwaite Letter G.S.-573	4	Encloses appraisal by Glancy of Baldev Singh
114	Glancy to Linlithgow Letter 401	10	Sends and comments on Sikander's formula for the solution of the communal problem in the Punjab; is very doubtful as to effect on Jinnah
115	Glancy to Linlithgow Tel. 33-G	15	Feels situation on Congress 'Quit India' resolution is becoming increasingly dangerous; suggests pre-censorship and intensive counter-propaganda
116	Glancy to Linlithgow Letter 402	17	Sends further suggestion from Sikander on procedure for appointment to Executive Council in interim period; Glancy doubts this would have any substantial effect; conveys Sikander's anxieties on situation
117	Glancy to Linlithgow Letter 403	18	Reactions of Muslim and Sikh press to Congress policy; will try to contact Jogendra Singh
118	Glancy to Linlithgow Letter 404	26	Detailed account of Provincial reactions to 'Quit India' resolution

119	Glancy to Linlithgow Tel. 36-G	29	Favours deportation of Congress leaders
120	Glancy to Linlithgow Tel. 37-G	29	Is satisfied police can tackle a Congress mass movement providing no other large-scale security measures are required at the same time
		Aug.	
121	Glancy to Linlithgow Tel. 40-G	5	Measures being taken to explain to public reasons for Govt.'s action against Congress
122	Glancy to Linlithgow Report 407	21	Punjab reactions to 'Quit India' movement have been mild with no serious outbreaks of violence; attitudes of the communities; coal supplies running dangerously short; Army recruitment going well; abundant rainfall
123	Glancy to Linlithgow Letter (unnumbered)	27	Chhotu Ram and Baldev Singh urge H.M.G. not to make any declaration on Pakistan following League resolution
		Sept.	
124	Glancy to Linlithgow Letter 408	1	Sends accounts from agents and other sources of attitude of Congress and Gandhi to terrorism and violence
125	Glancy to Linlithgow Report 411-F.L.	30	Student agitation; Sikh politics; Baldev Singh showing signs of taking independent line; Army recruitment going admirably; *rabi* prospects favourable
		Oct.	
126	Glancy to Linlithgow Tel. 75-G	1	Line Amery should take in Commons' debate
		Nov.	
127	Glancy to Linlithgow Report 417-F.L.	13	Communal relations less strained but fears effect of Jinnah's forthcoming visit; reactions to

			Sikander's scheme (Enclosure to No. 114); proposed removal of ban on Khaksars; Army recruitment declines markedly
128	Glancy to Linlithgow Report 419-F.L.	28	Jinnah's tour of Punjab; Sikander makes obeisance to him; effect of this on other communities; Communal Reunion Party; War Front rally at Chakwal; Punjab Govt's position on removal of ban on Khaksars; morale in urban areas improving
		Dec.	
129	Glancy to Linlithgow Letter 420	22	Sends intercepted letter from Moon to Shamsher Singh (Enclosure 1) which forwarded a copy of letter from Bourne to Moon on treatment of detenus (Enclosure 2); Glancy and Sikander feel that Moon must leave I.C.S. quickly and quietly
130	Glancy to Linlithgow Letter 422	28	Death of Sikander; procedure to be followed in appointment of new ministry
131	Glancy to Linlithgow Report 423-F.L.	29	Sikander's death overshadows all; Baldev Singh unlikely to break with Ministry but Akalis restive; appointment of Kirpal Singh as President of Khalsa College Council; hopes rainfall will bring down grain price; Sikh member for Public Service Commission; morale on war remains high
132	Glancy to Linlithgow Letter 424	30	Sends Moon's original protest on treatment of detenus; comments on this and describes treatment that detenus have received; policy towards Moon

CHAPTER 5 – DOCUMENTS FOR 1943

No.	Document	Date	Subject
		Jan.	
133	Glancy to Linlithgow Letter 425	2	Account of his discussions prior to offering Premiership to Khizar; re-appointment of remaining members of Ministry
134	Glancy to Linlithgow Letter 430	24	Background to decision to offer vacant seat in Cabinet to Shaukat
		Feb.	
135	Glancy to Linlithgow Letter (unnumbered)	12	Gravity of food situation has been stressed to officials; Punjab will do all it can to spare surplus grains from 1942 harvest and to increase production
136	Glancy to Linlithgow Report 432	13	Wheat shortages – action taken to help deserving; salt and sugar situations; visit of William Phillips; Shaukat takes charge as a Minister; Akalis focussing on Kapurthala
137	Abell to Laithwaite Letter G.S.-118	15	Encloses appraisal by Glancy on Shaukat and Baldev Singh
138	Glancy to Linlithgow Tel. 11-G	19	Punjab is taking appropriate precautions to deal with situation should Gandhi die while fasting
139	Glancy to Linlithgow Tel. 12-G	20	Is strongly opposed to closure of public offices and relaxation of orders on processions and meetings should Gandhi die
		Mar.	
140	Glancy to Linlithgow Report 442	15	Provincial reactions to Gandhi's fast; removal of price control on wheat – prices fall; decrease in serious crime; Khizar's attendance at League meeting and his relations with Jinnah
		Apr.	
141	Glancy to Linlithgow Report 444	17	Gandhi's fast recedes into background; Shaukat's interview with

No.	From/To	Date	Subject
			Jinnah; Shaukat applies for a League 'ticket' to fight bye-election; League-Unionist relations; Glancy's interview with Tara Singh; further release of communists; wheat, sugar and cloth situations
142	Glancy to Linlithgow Letter (unnumbered)	26	Punjab fully appreciates its responsibility and will do all it can to reach or exceed targets for export of foodgrains
		May	
143	Glancy to Linlithgow Letter 448	15	Reactions to proposal that Punjab and Delhi should be treated as one territory for purpose of grain movement
144	Glancy to Linlithgow Tel. 17-G	18	Will speak severely to Chhotu Ram about his speech to Chamars
145	Glancy to Linlithgow Letter 449	20	Comments on proposals for treatment of those guilty of pro-Japanese activities, particularly in Services
146	Glancy to Linlithgow Tel. 19-G	23	Refers to No. 144; in interview, Chhotu Ram said his remarks had been misrepresented by Press
147	Glancy to Linlithgow Report 451	29	General confidence in war; bumper *rabi* crop harvested but wheat price rises; difficulties of poor in urban areas; Muslim League situation; resurgence of Khaksars; Alalis giving some trouble; police successes in rounding up dacoits
148	Glancy to Linlithgow Tel. 21-G	31	Little unfavourable reaction in the Punjab to the withholding of Gandhi's letter to Jinnah
		June	
149	Glancy to Linlithgow Letter 453	8	Khaksar situation; is strongly in favour of firm action without delay

150	Glancy to Linlithgow Letter 455	18	Shares Viceroy's concern regarding Chhotu Ram's activities on food question; Enclosure: Cutting from *Inqilab* giving Chhotu Ram's statement on 'Import of wheat, prices and control'
151	Glancy to Linlithgow Letter 456	19	In talk with Glancy and Khizar, Chhotu Ram has explained his position on food question
		July	
152	Glancy to Linlithgow Letter (unnumbered)	3	Khaksar activities have increased in Punjab; feels all-India ban should be re-imposed without delay; important Provinces present united front
153	Glancy to Linlithgow Report 457	6	Foodgrain transport difficulties; other shortages; proposal to increase dearness allowances of provincial civil servants; unrest in Akali circles; Army recruitment declining; Police successes against dacoits; reactions to appointment of Auchinleck and Wavell
154	Glancy to Linlithgow Letter 458	16	Shaukat's interview with Linlithgow
155	Glancy to Linlithgow Letter (unnumbered)	19	Policy they should adopt if Gandhi fasts again; feels radio bulletins on his health should be omitted
156	Glancy to Linlithgow Letter 460	20	Rebuts suggestion that Punjab Govt. is inclined to give preferential treatment to Muslims; Shaukat's tour
157	Brander to Laithwaite Letter G.S.-441	21	Encloses appraisal by Glancy of Punjab Ministers
158	Glancy to Linlithgow Letter 462	23	With reference to No. 154, Glancy and Khizar have spoken to Shaukat very severely
159	Glancy to Linlithgow Letter (unnumbered)	29	Points arising from record of July 1943 Delhi Food Conference

		Aug.	
160	Glancy to Linlithgow Report 465	6	Khizar's relations with Jinnah – possibility of Section 93 situation; unlikely Congress will stage serious disturbances on anniversary of 'Quit India' movement but precautions taken; Glancy's talk with Tara Singh and Kartar Singh; proposed action against Khaksars is unlikely to arouse much resentment; widespread belief Punjab is cause of Indian food shortages; cloth and fuel shortages; decrease in serious crime; favourable agricultural prospects
161	Glancy to Linlithgow Letter 467	25	Says Punjab will do its best to help set right food situation; elaborates two concerns
		Sept.	
162	Glancy to Linlithgow Report 468	7	Punjab's assistance for Bengal; foodgrain procurement situation; Standard Cloth; Khizar hopes to make contact with Jinnah; Khaksar situation – possibility of Inayatullah's resignation; confusion in Sikh politics; Congress inactive; further release of communists
163	Glancy to Linlithgow Letter 469	16	Khizar's meeting with Jinnah; Khizar, Chhotu Ram and Baldev Singh are about to leave for discussion on food situation with Viceroy
164	Glancy to Linlithgow Letter 470	30	Measures which would help in the procurement of foodgrains; defends Ministry against charge it is blackmailing Bengal's starving population; Glancy's criticism of U.P. Govt.

165	Glancy to Linlithgow Letter 471	30	Sends answers to two questions Linlithgow had raised on Punjab Govt.'s actions with respect to wheat supplies
		Oct.	
166	Glancy to Linlithgow Letter (unnumbered)	12	Ministry has agreed to co-operate with the 'freezing' order relating to stocks of foodgrains pledged to banks
167	Glancy to Linlithgow Report (unnumbered)	12	Foodgrain procurement position; other shortages; *kharif* harvest patchy; All-India Muslim League meeting awaited; Hindu and Sikh politics
168	Glancy to Wavell Report 472-F.L.	30	Fooodgrain procurement position; Punjab Ministers not very easy to handle; Glancy's warning to them; particular problems with Chhotu Ram; Standard Cloth; Muslim League, Hindu and Sikh politics
		Nov.	
169	Glancy to Wavell Letter 474	30	Ministry has agreed to issue announcement on price control; Ministers feel extremely strongly that no requisitioning should be contemplated from the grower; they all regard it as essential that simultaneous announcements should be made by other provinces; Enclosure: Draft announcement by Punjab Govt.
		Dec.	
170	Glancy to Wavell Report 475	8	Announcement on food control; Khizar to issue statement of his own; League Committee wishes to visit Lahore; Akalis' approach to Jinnah; communists active; culprits behind Kalka Rail-Motor outrage; serious coal shortage

APPENDIX

	1942	
	June	
Sikander-Baldev Singh Pact	15	Terms of Pact as published

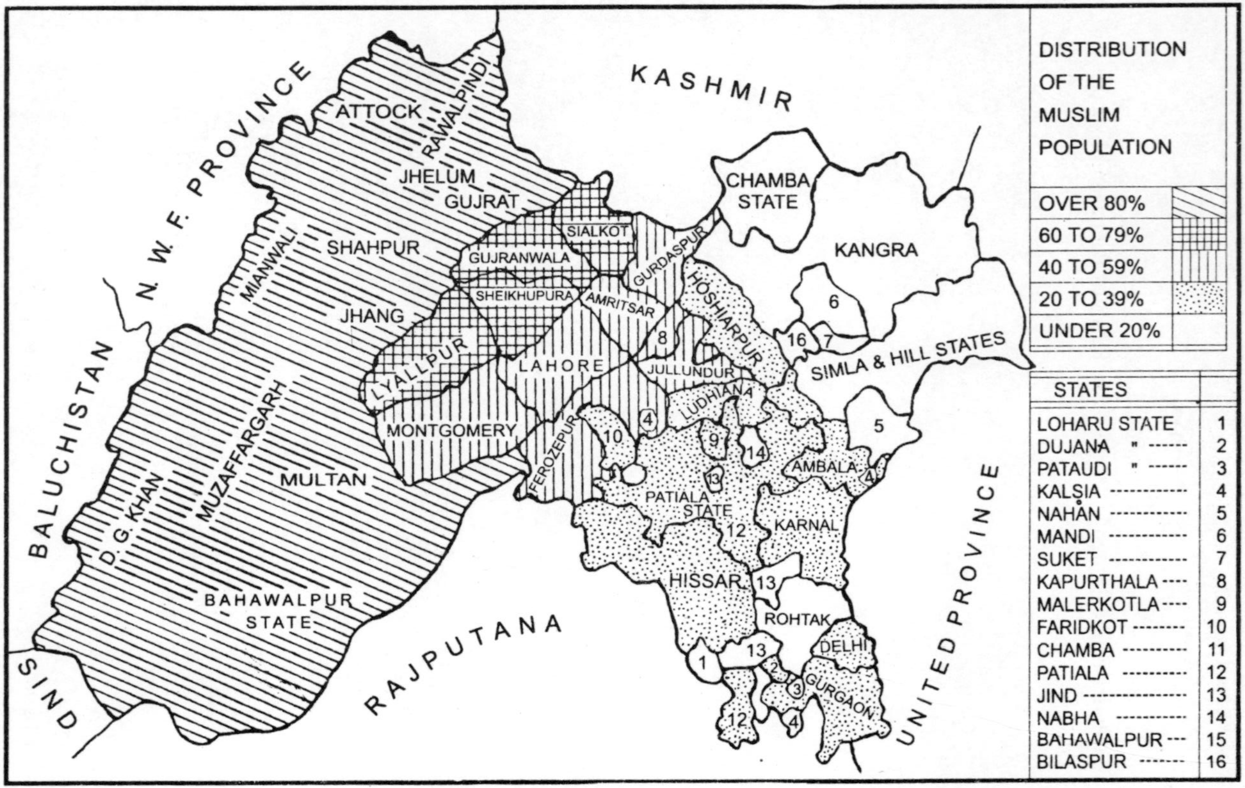

MAP OF PRE-PARTITION PUNJAB

CHAPTER 1

Documents for January-June 1940

1

CRAIK TO LINLITHGOW

Secret
D.-O. No. 205

Government House, Lahore,
January 1st, 1940

Dear Lord Linlithgow,

I am replying at once to your secret letter of the 28th of December[1] received last night, in which you gave me an account of the interview which you had granted that day to the Maharaja of Patiala.

2. As regards the question to what extent Patiala's position in regard to the Sikhs outside his own State is recognised in any way, I think it would be correct to say that as the Ruler of the premier Sikh State he is generally regarded by the whole Sikh community, with the exception only of certain extreme Left Wing elements such as communists, as its premier personage. To give one example of this feeling, I believe there is a fairly closely-defined ceremonial for the visits of important personages such as Viceroys, Provincial Governors and Ruling Chiefs to the Golden Temple at Amritsar, and I understand that the ceremonial to be observed would be more elaborate in the case of a visit from the Patiala Ruler than for any other personage with the single exception of the Viceroy. Whenever he pays such a visit convention demands that he should give a contribution of, I believe, Rs. 50,000 to the Temple funds (and for this reason he naturally hardly ever goes there!). Similarly tradition demands that he should be generous in the financial support he gives to Sikh denominational institutions, such as the Khalsa College, in British India – an incident which illustrates his position happened a few years ago when it became necessary to clear the accumulated silt in the sacred tank at the Golden Temple, and an appeal was made to religious-minded Sikhs to help

personally in carrying out this sacred duty. The present Maharaja's father on that occasion himself went to Amritsar and worked with a spade on this pious task, an incident which created a profound impression and great enthusiasm in the Sikh world. I should say that if the Patiala Maharaja were to take up any movement in which the Sikh community were interested, he would be in a position to exert a greater influence than any other adherent of the Sikh faith.

3. Ever since I have been in the Punjab any representation which the Patiala Ruler has made to the head of the Provincial Government in regard to Sikh matters has been treated with the greatest consideration and respect. This perhaps applied with greater force to the period before the Punjab States came into direct relations with the Central Government; but even since then the relations of the Ruler and his State with the Punjab have always been very close and friendly. A proportion of his high officials, for example, are usually officers lent by the Punjab Government or have retired from service under that Government. My recollection is that when the Akali movement first became troublesome about 1921, the late Maharaja was confidentially consulted on questions of policy arising out of this movement; but I am not absolutely certain of this. There has never, so far as I am aware, been any sort of *official* recognition of the Patiala Ruler as the head or spokesman of the Sikh community. But broadly speaking his position as the premier Sikh Prince places him in much the same relation to the Sikh community generally as that of the Nizam to the Muslim community.

4. I believe it is true that the Maharaja has since the outbreak of war been approached by the Khalsa National Party, i.e. the more conservative Sikhs who recognise Sir Sundar Singh Majithia as their leader, and also by the Akali leaders. On the 10th of December a representative meeting of the Sikhs was held at Amritsar under the auspices of the Khalsa National Party, with Sir Sundar Singh in the chair, and the resolution passed "noted with satisfaction that there has been a generous and almost unanimous response by the Sikhs to the appeal of His Highness the Maharajadhiraja Bahadur of Patiala for giving unstinted support to the Government for the successful prosecution of the present war". I know also that the Akalis have been in consultation with the Maharaja on the subject of Sikh recruitment to the Army. In this connection I would refer you to paragraph 8 of my personal and secret letter of November the 15th last to the Commander-in-Chief, a copy of which I sent you under cover of my letter No. 193 of the same date.[2] In writing to the Commander-in-Chief I mentioned that the Maharaja had been approached to speak in public on

the question of Sikh recruitment at a meeting of the Malwa Sikhs to be held at Ambala and that Sikander had signified his readiness to attend that meeting,. This meeting has not actually taken place, but I can personally see no objection to the Maharaja speaking on this subject at a meeting in British India, provided of course that he was careful to refrain from any reference to controversial political questions of the day.

5. While, therefore, I entirely agree with the conclusion stated in your letter of the 28th of December that Patiala would be exceedingly unwise from his own point of view to involve himself in the least degree in the British Indian aspects of Sikh controversies, I do not see any objection to his taking a prominent part in a movement to encourage Sikh recruitment to the Army in British India, if and when there is a demand for a considerable increase in such recruitment. I would regard his participation in such a movement as purely patriotic gesture, which he as the leading personage in the Sikh community and as head of a house with a great tradition of loyalty to the British Raj should not be discouraged from making. But he must of course be careful not to introduce into any pronouncement he may make on this subject any reference to more controversial issues such as the claim of Sikhs for greater representation in the legislatures or in the services, and he should also scrupulously refrain from giving colour to any suggestion that he is in favour of any particular political party in the Punjab.

6. There is possibly some foundation for your apprehension that the Maharaja may be anxious to turn the opportunity of the war to advantage in order to secure some strengthening of his own position in the community or of the decree of recognition which we extend to his present position. He is, I should say, an ambitious and shrewd young man and some plan of this kind may be at the back of his mind or of the minds of his advisers. Similarly, it is possible that the approaches which the two principal Sikh parties have made to him may have as an underlying motive a desire to secure his powerful support in the next elections for the Assembly. But this is pure speculation, and as I have indicated above, I am inclined to think that Patiala should not be discouraged from continuing to give a lead to his community in offering its co-operation in any war effort.

7. As requested by you, I am sending a copy of this letter direct to Glancy.[3]

Yours sincerely,
H.D. CRAIK

2

MOON TO LAITHWAITE

Confidential
D.-O. No. G.S.-11

Government House, Lahore,
January 5th, 1940

My dear Laithwaite,

With reference to your confidential D.-O. No. 2448-G.G., dated the 17th June 1938, I forward a note recorded by His Excellency the Governor on the Punjab Ministers.

Yours sincerely,
PENDEREL MOON

ENCLOSURE TO NO. 2

NOTE BY CRAIK

Government House, Lahore,
January 5th, 1940

There has been no change in the personnel of the Ministry since I last reported[4] and the Cabinet continues to work most harmoniously.

The prestige and popularity of the Premier, Sir Sikander Hyat Khan, stand higher than ever before. His call to the Province on the outbreak of war to give whole-hearted co-operation to the Empire was welcomed and endorsed by the vast majority of Punjabis and was the signal for a manifestation of enthusiastic loyalty. There have been no further defections or rumours of defection from the Unionist Party, and throughout the Autumn Session of the Assembly the Ministry was never in the slightest danger of defeat.

The appointment of an English I.C.S. Official[5] as Private Secretary to the Premier has given him substantial relief in the disposal of his ordinary Secretariat cases. He has also found some relief by making over one or two minor departments to his colleagues. Nevertheless the burden of work falling on him is extremely heavy, especially during the Assembly Sessions, and Sir Sikander would be all the better if he could get two or three months' complete holiday.

I have recently felt some anxiety about the health of the Revenue Minister, Sir Sundar Singh Majithia. He is now aged 68 and has frequently complained to me that he finds his official work a great burden, and has told me that he has occasional attacks of vertigo. He has never, however, given any indication of a desire to resign. I recently suggested to the Premier that Sir Sundar Singh might possibly like to be relieved of the burden of office and that it would be well to consider possible successors. The difficulty, however, is to find a Sikh who will command general confidence and respect.

As regards the other four Ministers, I have nothing to add to my note of the 4th of January 1939.

H.D. CRAIK
Governor of the Punjab

3

CRAIK TO LINLITHGOW

Secret
D.-O. No. 206

Government House, Lahore,
January 8th, 1940

Dear Lord Linlithgow,

Sikander showed me this morning and asked my advice about a letter, of which I enclose a copy, which he received from the Jam Saheb[6] on his return to Lahore from Bombay about the end of December. He also told me he had heard from the Secretary of the European Association[7] about the lack of adequate publicity in the English press for the case of the minorities and the States. He did not show me this letter, but I gather that it too contained a suggestion that a personal visit to England by Sikander would be desirable, though the difficulties in the way were fully realised.

2. While in Bombay at X'mas Sikander had received an urgent invitation from the Nizam to go to Hyderabad for consultation and since his return to Lahore he has received a further telegram to the same effect. Sikander deliberately avoided going to Hyderabad from Bombay, as he thought his visit would give rise to much speculation and might be liable to misinterpretation but he imagines that the Nizam's object probably was to press him to go to England.

3. I should also mention that C.T. Allen, who is part proprietor of the *Civil & Military Gazette*, paid a visit to Lahore about the middle of December and stayed with me. He was concerned about the inadequacy of the arrangements for putting the case of the States and minorities before the British public and told me that he was in touch with certain of the

Princes, the European Association and Sikander with the object of organizing improved publicity and collecting funds for the purpose.

4. This pressure from so many quarters on Sikander puts him in a difficult position and he would be very grateful for your advice, particularly as he does not wish to mix himself up in any way in the affairs of the States without your knowledge and consent. The objections to his leaving India are obvious. His absence from the Punjab even for a short visit of a month or six weeks would cause serious dislocation and inconvenience. In any event it would be quite impossible for him to leave the Province till the conclusion of the Budget session, as from today the Assembly will be sitting almost continually till about the middle of April, and Sikander feels that a visit at that time might be too late. Further, if he is to do any good in England, he would have to have opportunities of access to the Cabinet and, in order to influence public opinion, would have to address the various Parliamentary groups and perhaps also make contact with the editors of leading newspapers. All this would mean that his visit would receive a great deal of publicity and it would be impossible to camouflage it as a holiday.

5. On the other hand, Sikander told me, somewhat to my surprise, that he had received reports from England which are disquieting to those who, like himself, are anxious to unite all the elements, i.e. the States, the Muslims and other minorities, the Europeans, &c., who are generally opposed to the Congress policy and particularly to the idea of a Constituent Assembly. According to information which has recently reached Sikander (I gather largely from Zafrullah), considerable pressure is being brought to bear on His Majesty's Government from the Dominions and from America to clarify their position and policy towards India; and he also added, what I find it difficult to believe, that both Churchill and Hoare are weakening on the question of a Constituent Assembly. You are, of course, in a far better position than myself to appraise the value of this information.

6. Sikander has so far not answered the Jam Saheb's letter. I advised him that if he felt he ought to send some reply at once, he might tell the Jam Saheb that he had discussed the matter with me and would certainly like to take Your Excellency's advice also; that he would do his best to come down to Delhi to meet the Standing Committee of the Chamber of Princes, but could only be absent from Lahore on Wednesday, the 24th of January (as our Assembly does not sit on Wednesdays), and it would suit him better if the Princes concerned would stay in Delhi over the week-end 27/28th of January. If he does go down to Delhi, he will doubtless ask for an interview with yourself.[8]

7. Sikander also gave me another interesting piece of information. I saw a report, either from our C.I.D. or from the Central Intelligence Officer,[9] that J.L. Nehru, when he visited Lahore on the 31st of December, made no attempt to see Sikander and rather pointedly avoided doing so. As a matter of fact he did dine with Sikander secretly on the night of the 31st and they had four hours' discussion together. Nehru gave Sikander the impression that he realised that the Congress had somewhat over-reached themselves in pitching their demands from yourself and His Majesty's Government too high, but he seemed to be genuinely anxious to secure rapprochement between the two great communities. Nehru is thoroughly "fed-up" with Jinnah's attitude, but Sikander warned him that he could not afford to ignore Jinnah, as if he did so, he would never succeed in getting unanimity among the Muslims. Sikander suggested to Nehru that he might let him know confidentially what Congress is prepared to concede to the minorities, and Nehru promised to consult Gandhi and the other members of the High Command on this point.[10] I did not have time to question Sikander in any detail on this last point, as he had to rush off for the Assembly sitting.

8. I should be very grateful if you would let me know as soon as possible what your reactions are to the suggestion that Sikander should visit England. My own view is that while there is no one better qualified than Sikander to put the case for the minorities in a moderate and convincing fashion, his absence even for a short period at this critical time would be a mistake, not only from the point of view of the Punjab but also from that of India generally.[11]

Yours sincerely,
H.D. CRAIK

ENCLOSURE TO NO. 3

NAWANAGAR TO SIKANDER HYAT KHAN

Jamnagar,
December, 1939

My dear Sir Sikander,

As you are aware, India is passing through a most acute phase of transition and next few months may decide its destinies for the coming generations. It is gratifying that at this juncture His Excellency the Viceroy has taken a correct and courageous line of action in his declaration[12] which is fair to all interests concerned and recognises the legitimate position of minorities including the Princes in this country. This declaration should particularly be welcome to those elements in the country who are inspired by the same patriotic ideals as ourselves for the successful prosecution of war.

I have, however, been receiving certain distressing news lately to the effect that attempts are being made by interested quarters to torpedo through political circles in England the position taken up by His Excellency in India.[13] It has been pointed out to me by friends who are in the know of things that our case is practically going by default in England. It is unfortunate that famine in the State makes it impossible for me personally to proceed to England and that certain forthcoming weddings in the family would make it impossible for His Highness of Bikaner also to leave his State for some time. Under the circumstances it has been suggested to me and I personally am of the same opinion that it is essential in the interests of us all as also for the legitimate protection of the minorities, the advancement of India and the best interests of the Commonwealth as well as for the successful prosecution of war, that you should take the trouble of flying to England for howsoever short a period as you could be spared to do the needful in England. I fully appreciate your pressing engagements in India, but I am convinced that there is no one in India today who can do such solid good and whose words would carry such weight in the circles that matter in England as yourself. Moreover, the vital importance of the issues involved prompt me to make this request to you. I would therefore request that you may discuss this matter with His Excellency the Governor of the Punjab and if need be with His Excellency the Viceroy, so that they may appreciate the importance of your mission and assist in securing your release from the Punjab for as short a period as you can be spared.

I am anxiously awaiting your reply to this letter and after you have settled the preliminaries, I would request your coming to Delhi for a day during the forthcoming meetings of the Standing Committee from the 23rd to the 26th January, when we could have a further talk with His Highness of Bikaner, His Highness of Patiala and Sir Akbar Hydari and settle further details.

I am sorry to learn from Maqbool[14] that you have not been keeping good health and that you have been forced to take some rest. This gives an additional reason why you should undertake this trip to Europe and I would personally request you to look after yourself.

Kindest regards.

Yours sincerely,
DIGVIJAYASINHJI

4

CRAIK TO LINLITHGOW

Private and Personal
D.-O. No. 207-F.L.

Government House, Lahore,
January 14th, 1940

Dear Lord Linlithgow,

I am sorry that the interval since my last fortnightly letter has slightly exceeded the prescribed fourteen days, but the Provincial report for the second half of December (which I now enclose) only reached me yesterday.

2. That report deals at some length with Jawaharlal Nehru's brief visit to Amritsar and Lahore on the 30th and 31st of December, but I can add a few details. The rally of the Hindustan Boy Scouts at Amritsar, which was the principal function of his visit to that place, was attended by 3,500 boys and 225 girls from all parts of India. This is a very poor total as compared with the size of our big rallies of the Baden-Powell Boy Scouts. There was a procession of Scouts armed with *lathis*, swords and imitation guns, which terminated at the Jallianwala Bagh, where Jawaharlal Nehru addressed a meeting estimated at 20,000 people. This is reported to have included no Muslims at all. The meeting was badly arranged and the Pandit was very annoyed at the intense confusion that prevailed. The meeting at Lahore attracted 30,000 people, but here again there were hardly any Muslims. Although Jawaharlal's public utterances were restrained, it is reported that his visit had considerable effect in dissipating the lethargy into which the Congress, the Left Wing generally and the nationalist Muslims in the Punjab, seem to have sunk. He made a strong bid for the support of the Ahrars in the preparations for Civil Disobedience.

I have already reported to you that Nehru dined with Sikander on the night of the 31st of December. The secret of this meeting has been very well kept and I have seen no reference to it in the press.

3. I am most grateful to you for passing on to Mudaliar the suggestion[15] that a conference on price control of the representatives of the wheat-growing Provinces should be held at Lahore this month, and I am glad to say that this has now been arranged for the 19th of January. Mudaliar is to stay with me for a couple of days. The last few days have seen a slight fall in the price of wheat and cotton, and although the subject of price control continues to occupy a lot of space in the columns of the press, I do not think that the discontent caused by the recent rapid rise has intensified during the last fortnight.

4. Our principal anxiety at the moment is about the famine in Hissar. I am afraid there is no doubt that the power of resistance of the people is rapidly weakening and that their health is beginning to deteriorate. There have been a good many cases of such diseases as dysentery, scurvy, cedama (weakening of the joints) and general debility. Our Director of Public Health,[16] who is an energetic and able officer, has paid more than one visit to Hissar recently and has made arrangements for the opening of a number of rural dispensaries. These have been arranged at the centre of circles with a 10-mile radius, so that in the worst affected tracts all villages are now within 5 miles of medical relief. The Deputy Commissioner[17] has also collected a number of the worst cases of debility in hospitals at the bigger centres. He has been given discretion to increase the number of relief works from 14 to 16 and arrangements have been made to meet, so far as possible, his urgent demand for warm clothing and nourishing food. There has been a good deal of criticism in the Congress press regarding the alleged inadequacy of the measures which Government is taking for relief, but I do not think that such criticism is really justified, as Government is doing everything possible. But there is still [a] wide field for the exercise of privately organized charity, and I have asked the Commissioner[18] to do everything he can to stimulate the response to his appeal for charitable contributions.

5. I presided during the fortnight at a series of Cabinet meetings at which the Budget for 1940-1 came under detailed review. In spite of every effort at economy we shall have to budget for a small deficit which will be somewhere in the neighbourhood of 25 lakhs. Regrettable as this is the situation is less serious than at one time seemed probable. Throughout the meetings there was complete harmony among the members of the Cabinet and I was impressed by the spirit in which they all approached the serious financial problems with which we are confronted.

6. You will have seen in the newspapers an account of a deplorable incident that took place at the Shahidganj Gurdwara yesterday when a young Muslim, who had secured admittance disguised as a Hindu, stabbed with a sword three of the Sikh Sevadars (guardians of the shrine) and inflicted very serious injuries on them. Fortunately the assailant was secured and handed over to the Police, but I am afraid the incident is likely to revive interest in the Shahidganj dispute,[19] which had receded into the background during the last 18 months.

My latest information as regards the appeal in the Privy Council is that it will come on for hearing during the course of the January sittings, which I believe commence about the middle of this month. Counsel for the appellants (i.e. the Muslims) is likely to ask for a postponement on account of the difficulty of the legal representatives from Lahore reaching London, but the respondents (the Sikhs) will oppose any postponement, and I understand that they have been informed by their Solicitors that the Court is unlikely to grant an adjournment on this ground.

You may remember that in his lengthy statement in the Assembly on the Shahidganj question on the 16th of March 1938 Sikander announced that his Government had under consideration "means to ensure the due protection of all places of worship so that a repetition of incidents like Shahidganj may be impossible in future" and that with this object in view it was intended to appoint a small informal committee of members of the Assembly to advise Government with regard to proposals for legislation. Such a committee, including representatives of all communities, was duly appointed and as the result of their deliberations a Bill has now been drafted which I discussed at length with Sikander yesterday. The Bill will require my previous sanction to its introduction under Section 299 of the Government of India Act, and I had to tell Sikander that I should find the greatest difficulty in giving my sanction to the Bill in its present form, as it appeared to me likely to have an effect precisely opposite to what was intended, i.e. it would open the door to a revival of the Shahidganj dispute itself. I need not at present trouble you with details, more particularly as I have not a copy of the Bill at hand, but Sikander appreciated my point and agreed that the Bill required substantial modification. He is to reconsider it in consultation with the draftsmen and will thereafter re-summon the committee of the Assembly and put the points that I raised before them. I hope the result will be a Bill in a more satisfactory form, whose introduction I shall be able to sanction, but the problem is a difficult and intricate one.

7. Your Bombay speech on the political situation[20] has had a good reception in the press here, particularly in the Muslim press. Several local Muslim newspapers take the line that India should now accept the promise of Dominion Status at the earliest possible moment and that agitation on the subject of further political advance should cease immediately, and I am told that the view of the general public is that the Congress ought to and probably will return to office very shortly.

8. I am glad to say that I have now practically completely recovered from the effects of my recent accident.

Yours sincerely,
H.D. CRAIK

5

CRAIK TO LINLITHGOW

Secret
D.-O. No. 208

Government House, Lahore,
January 16th, 1940

Dear Lord Linlithgow,

Many thanks for your secret letter of the 12th of January 1940 about the possibility of a visit by Sikander to England. I have told him that I have heard from you on the subject and that you are thinking over the suggestion. I ventured to add that I was sure you would be glad to see him when he goes to Delhi, which will probably be on the 25th or 26th of January, as our Assembly will be having a short holiday from the 20th to the 27th inclusive. Sikander has sent a reply to Jamnagar on the lines of the advice I gave him (see paragraph 6 of my letter to you of January the 8th).

I had today a further talk with Sikander about his discussion with Nehru on the 31st of December, and I am afraid that the first report of this discussion which Sikander conveyed to me somewhat misled me and that the account which I passed on to you was not altogether accurate. I now gather that the course of conversation between Sikander and Nehru was roughly as follows. Nehru took the line that it was very unfortunate that you had not seen your way to accede to the Congress demands. Sikander retorted that the Congress had pitched their demands far too high and that it was asking too much of the British Government that they should agree to "complete independence" or, in other words, should themselves sign the death warrant of the British connection with India. Sikander, I gather, formed the impression that Nehru was rather shaken by this but I was wrong in thinking that Nehru himself admitted that Congress had over-reached themselves. As regards communal differences, Nehru took the line that Jinnah's attitude was responsible for the complete failure of their talks and that he (Nehru) was prepared to go a long way to meet the demands of the Muslims and other minorities. On that Sikander suggested that Nehru should make it clear precisely what concessions he was prepared to make and Nehru promised to consult Gandhi and the High Command about this.

I am very sorry that I should have given you a misleading account of the conversation, but I was myself misled by Sikander. My talk with him on the day on which I wrote to you (January the 8th) was, as I mentioned in my letter, a somewhat hurried one, as he called in to see me on his way to the Assembly and had to rush off to be in time to answer questions.

Yours sincerely,
H.D. CRAIK

6

CRAIK TO LINLITHGOW

Confidential
D.-O. No. 209

Government House, Lahore,
January 19th, 1940

Dear Lord Linlithgow,

Many thanks for your confidential letter of the 13th of January about the orders which my Government proposes to issue prohibiting the carrying of arms in processions in certain districts and prohibiting drilling with or without arms throughout the Province. I will keep you informed of any developments that may follow the issue of these orders. I had a discussion with the Premier the other day about the date on which they are to be issued and it was decided that it would be courteous to consult the North-West Frontier Province Government, where the Khaksars are an important body, before we actually issue the orders. We are still awaiting a reply from that Province.

Yours sincerely,
H.D. CRAIK

7

CRAIK TO LINLITHGOW

Private and Personal
D.-O. No. 210-F.L.

Government House, Lahore,
January 28th, 1940

Dear Lord Linlithgow,

The principal event of the last fortnight has been the excellent fall of rain which we had on the 17th and 18th of January. Here in Lahore the fall was over two inches and I believe it has extended practically all over the Province. It has been of immense benefit to the standing *rabi* crops and my Finance Minister is going about pleased as a dog with two tails! Directly the rain began to fall the price of wheat dropped sharply in the Amritsar district and, as noted in a later paragraph, caused considerable panic among wheat speculators. This will have the effect of abating the clamour for the control of prices by Government.

2. Another event of the fortnight has been the very generous response made by practically all districts to the appeal for relief for the sufferers in the Turkish earthquake. I have not seen any figures of the total amounts collected, but they must come to a large sum.

I presided at a very successful meeting at Government House on the 18th instant in aid of the Red Cross and St. Dunstan's. It was addressed by the Premier, Sir Clutha Mackenzie and myself and a considerable sum was promised or given on the spot in aid of both these causes.

3. Mudaliar arrived here on the morning of the 19th of January and the conference of the wheat-producing provinces duly took place that afternoon. The Punjab was represented by the Premier and two other Ministers as well as by J.D. Anderson, who is our price controller, and other officials. The Premier of Sind[21] flew up from Karachi and the other three provinces, the United Provinces, North-West Frontier Province and Central Provinces, were represented by officials. Fortunately the excellent rain which fell on the 17th and 18th of January caused a sharp decline of about six annas per maund in the price of wheat and there was a considerable panic at Amritsar among the dealers who had been buying "futures" at foolishly high prices. These speculators are reported to be mainly Calcutta people who had been "playing up" the profits they had made in jute.

Mudaliar was, I am told, an admirable Chairman, and the conference was most useful. There was general agreement that at the moment there was no necessity for Government to control the price of wheat. It was also agreed that if and when that necessity may arise, it would be foolish for provinces to take separate and uncoordinated action. The question of the point at which control would become necessary was discussed, but no precise decision was taken. The Punjab proposal was that when the price at Lyallpur reaches Rs. 4 a maund, then it would be necessary to consider whether Government should fix the price, and our people pressed that if such fixation became necessary, Lyallpur prices should be taken as the basis. The Sind representatives suggested a somewhat higher figure, viz., Rs. 4/12/- at Karachi, which would represent about Rs. 4/8/- at Lyallpur. At the moment of writing (22nd January) the price is round about Rs. 3/2/- per maund.

4. I had an interesting talk on the 21st of January with Sardar Sant Singh, M.L.A. (Central), who is in pretty close touch with the Akali leaders. He is an old friend and talks freely to me; so I asked him to tell me what was the general attitude of the Akalis about the recruitment of Sikhs to the Army. He told me that with the exception of a few extremists the Akalis are solid in favour of maintaining and even strengthening the Sikh connection with the Army, as they recognise that the importance of the Sikh minority depends largely on this connection. As I think I have reported to you in a previous letter, the Akalis sent a deputation to Wardha about the end of November to interview the Congress High Command on this question. They received a disappointing and ambiguous reply and have since – according to Sant Singh – drafted a lengthy statement of their attitude, which they propose to forward for the consideration of the High Command. Sant Singh does not think this has actually been despatched yet. I asked him what would be the attitude of the Akalis if the High Command should decide that it would not be proper for them as supporters of the Congress to help in any way in the prosecution of the war. Sant Singh considered that in that event the Akalis, with the exception of a small extremist minority, would then break with the Congress.

I also asked him if he had any knowledge of the reported recent break between the Maharaja of Patiala and "Master" Tara Singh, the Akali leader. According to Sant Singh, the real cause of this quarrel is that Patiala had not paid up the two lakhs of rupees which he promised to give to the Sikh National College started a little over a year ago at Lahore. You may remember that I reported Patiala's visit to this College in paragraph 5 of my letter to you No. 123-F.L. of the 9th of February 1939. I doubt, however, if this is the real explanation of the disagreement. A more probable cause is that Patiala feels that Tara Singh's increasing political influence among the Sikhs threatens his own position as the traditional leading figure of the community.

5. The fortnightly report for the first half of January, which I enclose, refers to the trouble in Congress circles over the selection of a Congress candidate to stand at the bye-election of the Punjab Assembly in one of our western divisions. Since then there has been another incident of the same nature regarding the selection of a candidate to stand for the vacancy in the Central Assembly caused by the recent death of Lala Sham Lal of Rohtak. The Provincial Congress Committee nominated as their candidate another Sham Lal, who I believe is a Hissar pleader, but the newspapers report that Maulana Abul Kalam Azad has refused to sanction this selection. His decision has caused considerable resentment in local Congress circles

and has made the position of Dr. Gopi Chand, our Right-Wing Congress leader, even more difficult than before.

6. In spite of considerable tension between the communities, the Bakr Id passed off peacefully throughout the Province. Independence Day[22] was marked by considerably more enthusiasm and by larger processions and meetings than in the last few years, but I have not heard of any disturbance of any kind. In Lahore there were very large processions of students, both male and female, but there was no disorder. One small Muslim boy, who is described as a member of the Ahrar party, was arrested for singing an anti-recruitment song. The local police, who had a long day's work, were withdrawn about 8 p.m., by which time it was expected that all processions would have dispersed. Shortly after that hour, however, a small body of students marched up the Mall in a torch-light procession and made a somewhat fatuous demonstration opposite the Assembly Chamber, which was of course locked up for the night. This is unfortunate, as there is a strict rule in Lahore that no processions are to be allowed on the Mall or in the civil station. The procession, however, dispersed without disorder after they had made their demonstration.

7. I took part last night in a pleasant and rather exceptional function. This was a dinner given by the Punjab Club, membership of which is limited to Europeans belonging to the Services or engaged in commerce, in honour of the Ministry. There was a very large attendance of about 130 members and guests, some of the latter being Indians. The accommodation available was not nearly large enough for all who wanted to be present. The Chairman of the Club Committee asked me as the oldest member of the Club present to propose the toast of the Ministers, a toast which was received with great enthusiasm. My remarks were, as the journalistic phrase goes, "couched in lighter vein", but I emphasized the unique character of the gathering and interpreted it as evidence of the appreciation which the European community here feels for the sane and stable character of the Ministry's policy, and of the excellent relations prevailing between the Ministers and the Services. Sikander made a very happily phrased reply and he too stressed the happy relations of the Ministers with the Services and acknowledged in the most handsome way the great obligations which they owed to the Services. The general atmosphere was one of enthusiastic and cordial good fellowship. Unfortunately two of the Ministers, Manohar Lal and Abdul Haye, were unable to be present, the first owing to indisposition and the second because he was away attending some educational conference.

8. I have just had an interesting talk with Sikander about his visit to

Delhi. He goes down there again on the night of February the 1st, and stays till the evening of the 4th, to attend the Working Committee of the Muslim League.

I am off to Lucknow tonight and looking forward to a brief holiday. I expect to be returning via Delhi and halting there for a few hours on Sunday, the 4th of February, when I shall hope to have the opportunity of a short talk with you, if this could be arranged.

Yours sincerely,
H.D. CRAIK

8

CRAIK TO LINLITHGOW[23]
Telegram

Important
No. 3-G. *February 8th, 1940*

Your telegram, No. 190 of February 6th.[24] In Hindu circles in spite of failure of talks there is still a certain feeling of optimism. The *Tribune* believes that negotiations will be resumed and expresses the hope that present opportunity for a peaceful settlement will not be lost. Hindus in this Province are keenly aware of the danger of Muslims becoming more intransigent if Congress pitch their demands too high.

The Muslims are rather pleased at the breakdown of the conversations. They feel that there will be no settlement until Gandhi recognises that Congress does not speak for Muslims and that he must reach an agreement with the Muslims before further progress can be made.

9

CRAIK TO LINLITHGOW

Private and Personal
D.-O. No. 211-F.L.

Government House, Lahore,
February 19th, 1940

Dear Lord Linlithgow,

Having had a long talk with you so recently as the 4th of February I had practically nothing to report on February the 11th, when my fortnightly letter was due, and as I was leaving Lahore on tour on that date and was very rushed with work, I decided to leave this letter over till my return.

2. My tour was to two of the central districts, Gujranwala and Sialkot. At both these places I had an excellent reception and was presented with addresses of welcome by the local bodies and the Soldiers' Boards. I also had opportunities of renewing contacts with most of the leading men of both districts. At Gujranwala I was given a cheque for Rs. 30,000, to be spent at my discretion on objects connected with the war. I think I shall probably give about 10 per cent. of this amount to the Red Cross and St. Dunstan's Fund and send the balance eventually to your War Purposes Fund. In most districts of the Punjab similar collections are now being made, but I propose to wait till I can send you a really substantial amount from the Province as a whole.

Both in Gujranwala and in Sialkot there is a strong military tradition and the spirit of loyalty and the desire to help in the prosecution of the war were everywhere manifest. Sialkot is an industrial city of considerable importance, there being several large factories for the manufacture of sports goods and, in addition, there are at least two small metal factories, one of which manufactures surgical instruments and hospital appliances of excellent quality. I hope these will eventually obtain some orders from the Supply Department, to whom they might be of considerable use.

3. You will have read in the newspapers that as the result of Maulana Abul Kalam Azad's visit to the Punjab,[25] the differences between the two Wings of the local Congress have been settled, at any rate temporarily. Mian Iftikhar-ud-Din, M.L.A., a man of distinctly "Leftist" tendencies, has now been elected President of the Provincial Congress Committee in place of Dr. Gopi Chand Bhargava, apparently with the latter's consent. Dr. Gopi Chand has withdrawn his resignation of his seat in the Assembly, which he tendered a short time ago owing to differences with the Congress High Command. I doubt, however, whether this reconciliation will be permanent, as the differences in outlook between the Right and Left Wings are as deep-seated as ever.

4. An incident occurred recently, which has attracted considerable publicity and which illustrates the low tone of Punjab political morality. A notorious Ahrar agitator, Maulana Ataullah Shah Bokhari, is being prosecuted for delivering a seditious speech in the Gujrat district. One of the principal witnesses against him was a Police constable, who had made a shorthand note of his speech. Shortly before the trial came on this constable took leave and made a series of obviously flimsy excuses for not returning to duty. On the day fixed for the trial of the case in the Magistrate's Court the whereabouts of this constable were unknown to his

superior officers and they were on the point of applying to the Magistrate for an adjournment of the case till he could be produced in Court. At the last moment, however, he duly appeared, having apparently driven in a taxi from Lahore, accompanied by Diwan Chaman Lal, M.L.A., the Deputy Leader of the Congress party in the Assembly, who was appearing as Counsel for Ataullah Shah. The constable's deposition was to the effect that the original shorthand notes of Ataullah's speech, which he had recorded, had been taken from him and that he had been instructed by his superior officers to prepare another set of notes in which the tone of the speech was represented as far more reprehensible than that actually delivered. He further deposed that this false report of the speech was prepared on written instructions sent by the Premier's Personal Assistant. It was perfectly obvious that the constable had been suborned by the defence to give this entirely false evidence, and he was accordingly treated as a hostile witness. Since that hearing a very large number of pamphlets have been distributed all over the Province, giving the substance of his evidence, with the obvious intention of discrediting the Premier. The Government Advocate[26] was accordingly instructed to apply to the High Court that that Court should take the case against Ataullah Shah on to their own file and decide it themselves, and the High Court have agreed to do so. There seems to be little doubt that Diwan Chaman Lal is at the bottom of this disgraceful manoeuvre, and it may perhaps be found possible to produce sufficient evidence to convict him of grossly unprofessional conduct.

5. The state of communal feeling in the Province is, I regret to say, extremely acute. A day or two before the beginning of the Moharram celebrations an elderly and inoffensive Muslim shopkeeper was attacked and severely stabbed by some unknown assailants in Amritsar city. This incident, which gave rise to great excitement in the city, is thought to have been instigated by Hindus in order to induce the authorities either to prohibit the usual Moharram processions or to insist on their route being changed. The Deputy Commissioner[27] has taken strong measures and the Police force has been substantially reinforced. The procession taken out on the first day of the Moharram (Friday, the 16th) did result in a certain amount of disorder, but the Police were able to check this before it assumed serious proportions. I have not heard of any further incident in yesterday's processions, and I understand that security for good behaviour has been taken from a large number of the city bad characters who would be likely to provoke disorder.

6. I expect you will have read in the new papers of the attack made on

Isakhel town, the headquarters of the tahsil of the Mianwali district that lies west of the Indus, by the large Lashkar which had destroyed the Police post at Abbasa in the Bannu district of the North-West Frontier Province. The townspeople of Isakhel, who fortunately received warning of its approach, put up a stout defence and the Lashkar was driven off with a considerable number of casualties. It withdrew into the hills west of Isakhel and we subsequently heard that it had been reinforced by another strong body of raiders from the tribal area. The North-West Frontier Province Police were trying to cut off their retreat into their own territory and asked the Mianwali Police to prevent them escaping eastwards into the Punjab. The Mianwali Police force is not strong enough for such an operation against a body of 400 or 500 raiders, and the Commissioner of the Division[28] accordingly arranged for a battalion of Indian Infantry to be despatched from Rawalpindi for the purpose. I believe this battalion reached Kalabagh on the Indus on Saturday, the 17th, but I have not yet heard the result of the operations against the raiders.

7. The Commander-in-Chief has, I understand, kept you informed of the correspondence that has passed between him and myself and between Patiala and myself on the steel helmet question.[29] At the Akali conference held at Attari, midway between Lahore and Amritsar, on the 11th of February only a very brief and ambiguous reference was made to this controversy in the course of a long speech delivered by the President of the conference, one Teja Singh. According to my information the exact words used by the speaker were: "If the Sikhs were allowed to wear helmets during the war, they would also do so afterwards, and hence the ban on helmets would disappear and there would be a danger to the *Keshas*, and hence it was difficult to decide about the wearing of such helmets." No further reference was made to the subject at the conference, nor did it find a place in any of the sixteen resolutions passed.

On the 16th of February I received a curious letter from Patiala, in which he told me he had "heard from Master Tara Singh that some 'Police Commissioners' in India are asking the Sikh officials to wear the helmet on the ground that the Amritsar Sikhs have decided in its favour; and that this step on the part of the authorities concerned is greatly agitating the minds of the Sikhs." The Maharaja went on to say that "he was sure that my Government would not adopt such an inappropriate course at this delicate stage but if it is a fact that such instructions have been permitted to be issued in any other Province, he is afraid it will give rise to serious misgivings in the minds of a large section of the community and will seriously hamper his efforts to bring round the Sikhs to the acceptance of the use of the helmet." I have made enquiries and cannot find any confirmation of this extraordinary report. In the first place, we have no officials known as "Police Commissioners" in the Punjab; secondly, the steel helmet is purely an article of military equipment, with which neither the Police nor "Sikh officials" have anything to do; and thirdly, so far as I am aware, there are at present no steel helmets available in India. I imagine the story is a pure invention, which is being used by Tara Singh as justification for his unwillingness to make any pronouncement on the subject. I am about to reply to the Maharaja that, so far as I can ascertain, there is absolutely no truth in the report. I will send a copy of the correspondence on to the Commander-in-Chief.

8. You may remember that I mentioned to you a plan of Sikander's to send out parties of students to tour the Punjab to do propaganda work in connection with the war in rural areas. I think you will be interested in the enclosed note[30] by J.D. Anderson, describing the arrangements made for these parties. The idea is entirely Sikander's own.

9. I have just seen a reassuring note by our Director of Public Health on health conditions in the Hissar district, in which he has recently made a fairly extensive tour. He describes the arrangements under which the whole district has been covered by a network of Health Circles, each of which is in charge of a doctor. The medical staff has been greatly strengthened and every village is now within a five-mile radius from a central dispensary. The Director of Public Health reports:

> "The most alarming of the developments which in December last led to the above elaborate reorganization being carried out, was the sudden appearance of food deficiency disease in an acute form, in particular, scurvy. Some 89 acute cases of this disease alone were brought under treatment during the end of December 1939 and the beginning of January 1940, thousands of cases of night-blindness, and many hundreds of cases of lesser degrees of food deficiency disease, and of simple malnutrition due to lack of a sufficient quantity of food. Cases of absolute starvation were not difficult to find."
>
> "The contrast between conditions as I saw them two mouths ago, and as they are now, is remarkable. The vast majority of the scurvy cases are now well, the remainder are rapidly regaining their health, and very few new cases are being reported. Other less severe deficiency conditions, such as night-blindiness are greatly reduced in number, and no individual need suffer from sheer lack of food. These statements are based on what I have seen myself in villages, on the records kept at

dispensaries and treatment centres, and on the reports of the Nutrition Officer,[31] the three District Medical Officers of Health,[32] and the Assistant Director of Public Health, Eastern Range,[33] who between them have traversed the whole district within the last two or three weeks.

"One of the most striking changes is the altered outlook of the people. This is very noticeable. They feel now that something is really being done for them, and their former despairing attitude has gone. This dramatic change in health and outlook has led, in certain quarters, to statements to the effect that the alarm of December last could not have been wholly justified. Nothing could be farther from the truth. There was a crisis in December which would undoubtedly have ended in disaster had not appropriate measures been applied to prevent it. Food deficiency conditions are not only disease entities in themselves, but during the course of their development are accompanied by a rapid general lowering of resistance to disease of any kind. The increased death rate in Hissar prior to the appearance of acute deficiency conditions was undoubtedly due in large measure to this underlying specific cause.

"Fortunately, illness and lowered resistance due to food deficiency disappear quickly when the lacking food-factors are supplied. To make these factors available in concentrated form to the sick, and to bring them within the reach of every individual in the district as a prophylactic, was the most important single item in the public health programme of relief."

10. I enclose the provincial fortnightly report for the second half of January.

Yours sincerely,
H.D. CRAIK

10

CRAIK TO LINLITHGOW

Private and Personal — Government House, Lahore,
D.-O. No. 215-F.L. — *March 4th, 1940*

Dear Lord Linlithgow,

I have just returned from visits to the headquarters of four of our south-western districts – Montgomery, Multan, Muzaffargarh and Dera Ghazi Khan. In all four districts I received and replied to addresses from Local

Bodies and District Soldiers' Boards and in all I encountered the same unanimous conviction as to the righteousness of the cause for which the Empire is fighting and the same eagerness to give material help in the war. In Montgomery a parade of the retired military officers who have received grants of land on the Lower Bari Doab Canal, was held in my honour. About a thousand ex-officers took part and it was an inspiring sight to see these veterans march past. Both in that district and in Multan there was a general atmosphere of contentment and optimism due to the rising prices of cotton and wheat and a marked advance in the price of land. I heard of one case where a purchaser had recently given Rs. 12,000/- per square (a square is 25 acres) for 8 squares, and high prices are expected at forthcoming auctions of Government waste land and of house and shop sites in some of the new market towns. The prospects for the *rabi* harvest are excellent.

Muzaffargarh is one of the poorest and most backward districts in the Province with hardly any military tradition, but here too I found the same enthusiastic wish to help in the war. The Jagirdars and Zaildars of this district have offered to contribute the whole of their Jagirs and Inams amounting, I understand, to something like Rs. 44,000 annually for the duration of the war, and the employees of the District Board have offered to forego all interest on their Provident Fund investments for the same period. An offer was also made to contribute the whole of the village "Malba" fund (a fund subscribed by the village proprietors for the entertainment of guests and other common purposes) to the War Fund. Whether all these offers can be accepted is not quite certain. It will probably be necessary for each individual offer to be examined on its merits and there is a legal difficulty about accepting the offer of the "Malba" fund. The willingness of this very poor district to make sacrifices is, however, significant.

Dera Ghazi Khan district lies wholly beyond the Indus and is in many respects different from all other Punjab districts. The Tumandars and the tribal areas which they control are one of my special responsibilities as your Agent and you may perhaps be interested in that part of my speech delivered there which was specially addressed to the Tumandars. I enclose a report.[34] There has been a little quite unjustified resentment shown by some of them against the late Deputy Commissioner, Coates, who has now taken up an appointment under the Central Government, and it was necessary to give the Tumandars, some of whom are distinctly primitive and backward, a warning on this point. My speech was, however, well received and some of them thanked me for it afterwards. The Tumandars have promised to give Rs. 12,000 a year as a joint subscription to the War Fund "for the duration".

2. The orders banning drilling in military formation by "private armies" throughout the Province and also banning in three of our larger towns processions carrying arms or implements that can be used as weapons of offence issued on February the 29th. I have had previous correspondence with you – and my Government with your Government – about these orders. It is as yet too early to say what their effect is likely to be, as no pronouncement has so far been made by any of the bodies affected. The Khaksar leader, who rushed off to Delhi immediately after the issue of orders in an attempt to seek an interview with you, is reported to have asked important members of his movement to come to Lahore to consult him after his return from Delhi. I do not know whether this consultation has yet taken place. There has been a certain amount of criticism of the orders in the vernacular press: that in the Muslim newspapers is cautious in tone. The *Inqilab*, for example, which usually supports the Ministry, advises Muslim organizations "to furnish proof of their integrity and sagacity" by submitting to the restrictions. The Hindu press is naturally inclined to be more critical of the Ministry, but does not take the line that the orders are unjustified. Its criticism is to the effect that Government should have taken action against the Khaksars long ago, particularly when they were making a nuisance of themselves in the United Provinces, and has only acted when other communities formed organizations to counter the Khaksars. My impression was that the Opposition parties in the Assembly would generally welcome the issue of the orders, as they have been urging on the Ministry to take action against the Khaksars for some time; but today two notices have been given of adjournment motions on this subject, both by members of the Congress opposition.

My own feeling is that we shall be lucky if there is not a certain amount of active opposition, involving a good many arrests, to these orders on the part of the Khaksars and possibly also of the Akali volunteer organizations.

3. Moharram fortunately passed without any serious disturbance, though at several places there were incidents, such as bricks being thrown at *tazias*, which might have had disastrous consequences had it not been for speedy and effective intervention by the Police. The communal situation is, however, still acute. In paragraph 5 of my letter to you of February the 19th I referred to the special tension that existed at Amritsar at the start of the Moharram festival due to a murderous attack on a Muslim shopkeeper by some unknown assailants. This attack took place on the 14th of February and the victim died of his injuries on the 28th. It was feared that his funeral

might be made the occasion for a demonstration, but fortunately on the 26th of February the District Magistrate[35] had passed orders prohibiting 70 bad characters from leaving their houses between 6 p.m. and 8 a.m. for a period of two months, and the situation had eased in consequence of these orders.

4. There has been no further incident in the Isakhel tahsil of Mianwali, to which I referred in paragraph 6 of my letter of February the 19th. I gather that neither the Battalion of Indian Infantry despatched to Kalabagh nor the North-West Frontier Province police were able to establish contact with the raiders, who seem to have slipped away through the hilly tract to the west of Isakhel. A considerable number of the Hindu inhabitants of Isakhel have, however, moved to Rawalpindi with their families.

5. The provincial Budget was presented on March the 1st by Manohar Lal in a speech that was a very lucid and on the whole reassuring explanation of the financial position from the popular point of view. He was able to show that in spite of the enormous expenditure of 2¾ crores of rupees (including remissions of land revenue and canal charges) on famine during the last two years, he has by taking Extraordinary Receipts into the Revenue Account maintained equilibrium without the imposition of any substantial fresh taxation; and further that during the three years of their tenure of office, the present Ministry has remitted in land revenue and canal dues sums very greatly in excess of those remitted during the previous three years, while at the same time increasing substantially expenditure on the beneficent departments. The Budget is thus a "popular" budget and likely to raise the Ministry's stock. There is no doubt that Manohar Lal is an extremely able and sound guardian of our provincial finances.

6. It is somewhat early at present to estimate the reactions of public opinion to the Congress Working Committee's Patna resolution.[36] The only authoritative comment I have seen is a leading article in the *Tribune* of Sunday March the 3rd, which did not discuss the actual merits of the Congress decision, but spoke of it as disconcerting both to the High Command's open enemies and to their pretended friends, because it showed that there is no real difference in the view of the right and left wings. The article concluded by saying that conflict can only be avoided by His Majesty's Government conceding India's "right to shape her destiny and frame her own constitution". Nevertheless, I imagine that moderate Hindu opinion is seriously dismayed by the Congress High Command's decision and apprehensive of the struggle that now seems inevitable. Muslim opinion is probably pleased at the prospect of an early rupture between Government and the Congress and there is some ground for hoping that the attitude

taken up by the Congress may result in the Muslim League coming down openly, at its session at Lahore towards the end of this month, on the side of helping the Empire in the war.

7. I presided this morning at a brief meeting of the Cabinet, but had little opportunity for more than a few words with the Premier, as he had to be in his place at the commencement of the Assembly sitting. The session has already been a long one, but seems likely to be prolonged till at least the end of April, and the strain on the Ministers and especially the Premier is heavy. I have a large number of important and urgent matters to discuss with him, but find it difficult to get hold of him.

8. Here is a true story, taken from a recent Police report, which may make you smile. A Sikh saint of considerable local repute in Rawalpindi district announced publicly that he was going to die at 6 a.m. on February the 12th in fulfilment of a prophesy made some time ago. At about 5.30 a.m. on the fateful day his admirers placed him on the roof of a motor-bus in view of a crowd estimated at about 30,000 people who had come from far and near attracted by his announcement. It is said that there was heavy betting on the fulfilment of the prophesy. At 6.30 a.m. the saint had still failed to die and the crowd was becoming restive. At 6.45 a.m. they were in an ugly mood and tried to rush the lorry, but the Police with considerable difficulty managed to get the saint clear of the crowd and smuggled him to a Sikh shrine some six miles away from Rawalpindi. A crowd of disappointed backers wandered round the city for the rest of the day clamouring for the saint to die. So far as I am aware, he is still alive.

9. I enclose the provincial fortnightly report for the first half of February. That for the second half of February has not yet reached me.

Yours sincerely,
H.D. CRAIK

11

CRAIK TO LINLITHGOW

Secret and Personal
D.-O. No. 220

Government House, Lahore,
March 18th, 1940

Dear Lord Linlithgow,

Many thanks for your secret and personal letter of the 16th of March from Kapurthala, telling me of your recent talk with Jinnah. The friendliness which he exhibited seems to me to be somewhat significant in the case of a person of such a crabbed disposition.

2. Since the receipt of your letter I have had further talk with Sikander about the Khaksar problem and told him, of course without showing him your letter, that I understood Jinnah and conservative Muslims generally are very anxious that there should not be a serious clash between the Punjab Government and the Khaksars. Sikander is fully alive to the importance of avoiding such a clash and so far the Khaksars have shown no disposition to defy the ban on drilling. But a large number of them have arrived in Lahore and there is a strong rumour that they intend to insist on taking part in the procession which will mark the opening of the Muslim League conference here on March the 21st. I enclose a cutting[37] from today's *Tribune* on this subject. Sikander feels that if there is deliberate defiance of the ban, the orders of Government must be enforced even if it means the arrest of a large number of Khaksars. But he is doing what he can to avoid any such clash. He told me today that two Unionist M.L.As., who had belonged to the Khaksar organization, had just resigned from it and one of them has gone, I understand at Sikander's suggestion, to see Inayatullah, who has shifted his headquarters to Delhi. Sikander is not very hopeful that this emissary will be able to persuade Inayatullah to take a reasonable attitude, as Inayatullah is one of the most unreasonable of men and possibly not wholly sane. But Sikander says he is a coward and has not the slightest intention of risking imprisonment, and for this reason will probably not come to Lahore himself. Inayatullah is now publishing his newspaper at Delhi and one issue of it has just reached Lahore. It is published in vernacular and I have not seen a translation, but Sikander, who has read the vernacular version, tells me it is full of the most gross perversions of the truth and of what amounts to direct incitement to violence. My Government have asked, or are about to ask, the Chief Commissioner[38] to take action against this paper on the ground that it is a menace to the peace and tranquillity not only of the Punjab, but of India generally.

3. I have also to thank you very much for another private and personal letter of the 16th of March, which I have just received. Paragraph 3 of it is about the wearing of steel helmets by Sikhs and I think I ought to let you know that yesterday (Sunday) I received a message from the Maharaja of Patiala who was in Lahore for the Aitchison College Sports Day, that he wanted to see me, and I had a talk with him on this subject. The gist of what he had to tell me was that he found almost everywhere strong opposition on the part of the Sikhs to the wearing of the steel helmet and

I gather that he had been in touch both with political leaders, mainly of the Akali group, and some retired Indian Officers. I personally think that he has been misled by the Akali leaders into taking this opposition to be a good deal stronger than it really is. However that may be, Patiala is quite clearly not willing to come out with any statement to the effect that it is perfectly proper for Sikhs to wear the helmet, and I formed the opinion that he has not enough courage to face the unpopularity which such an announcement might bring to him. I was considerably disappointed by his general attitude, which, I gather, he had explained to you in a conversation with you on the night of your dinner party to the Princes.

On the 13th of this month the Adjutant-General[39] came to see me here, at the Chief's request, to ask my advice as to the treatment of this difficult problem and to explain the urgency of reaching an immediate decision. After we had discussed various suggestions, with which I need not trouble you, I advised the Chief to send for Patiala and to ask him definitely whether he was or was not prepared to come out with an immediate announcement in favour of the steel helmet, and not to take any further action till Patiala had given a reply one way or the other. As I was not aware whether the Chief intended to act on this suggestion, I got into touch with him on the telephone while Patiala was actually in my house and told him that if he wanted to see Patiala, the latter was prepared to come down to Delhi for the purpose tonight, although he had intended to visit Nowshera and Peshawar. Cassels replied that he had decided, I gather after consultation with yourself, that it was no use sending for Patiala again and that he had now practically decided on dealing with the matter by other means. I accordingly told Patiala, who had not of course heard this conversation on the telephone, that the Commander-in-Chief did not wish to trouble him to come to Delhi.

In this connection you will be interested to see the enclosed newspaper account of a speech[40] made by Sikander yesterday (Sunday) at the prize distribution at the Khalsa College, Amritsar. I have marked the passage in this speech in which Sikander discussed the steel helmet question. The newspaper report, however, does not mention one detail of which Sikander informed me this morning and which he considers significant. That was a speech by a Sikh named (I think) Dr. Sohan Singh entirely endorsing what Sikander had said.

4. I have just received a report of the proceedings of the University Syndicate on the 12th of March about Dr. Bhatnagar. The Syndicate unanimously decided to recommend to the Senate that his services should be lent to the Government of India as Director of the Board of Scientific

and Industrial Research for a period of two years in the first instance with effect from the 1st of April next. I do not think there is any reason to apprehend that the Senate will take a different view. Dr. Bhatnagar is coming to have a farewell talk with me shortly and has made all arrangements to leave Lahore at the end of this month.

Yours sincerely,
H.D. CRAIK

12

CRAIK TO LINLITHGOW

Secret and Personal
D.-O. No. 221

Government House, Lahore,
March 20th, 1940

Dear Lord Linlithgow,

It is indeed ironical that two days after my letter to you saying that we were doing our best to avoid any clash with the Khaksars, I should now have to report certain features of the lamentable incident that took place yesterday. So far I have been unable to obtain from any of the three principal officers who took part in it a first-hand account of the affair. Gainsford, the Senior Superintendent of Police, and Beaty, the Deputy Superintendent of Police, are, as you know, dangerously injured and both in hospital. Bourne, the District Magistrate, who was also slightly injured, is still on duty, but it would not be fair to ask him to come and see me, as he is fully engaged. I enclose, however, his report,[41] drawn up today, as to what took place. I also saw for a few minutes last night the City Magistrate,[42] who was present at the time, but escaped injury. He is a stout-hearted officer of Afghan descent and I do not think was exaggerating. He assured me that the attack by the Khaksars on the police was entirely unprovoked and carried out with savage fury. As he put it himself "they came on like wolves". They were all armed with formidable "Belchas" or spades, the edges of which had been specially sharpened, and the injuries they inflicted were most grave. One constable was killed on the spot and another has since died in hospital. Gainsford received a terrible wound on the face, but I am glad to say that the Surgeon who is attending him told me this morning that he was distinctly better and he was now hopeful that his life would be saved. Beaty also received a very severe injury on the face and it is practically certain that he will lose the sight of one eye, but I am told that his life is not in danger.

2. Of the officers concerned, Gainsford is one of our senior and best Superintendents of Police, specially selected for the important charge of Lahore, and a man of cool temper and resolute disposition. Bourne you probably know, as he was acting as Chief Secretary all last summer when my Government was in Simla. He is one of our most senior and most reliable District Officers, in whose character and capacity I have the highest confidence. He is the last man in the world to lose either his wits or his temper. (He must have learnt to control his temper early in life, as he was a boxing "Blue" at Oxford.) He received severe blows on the cheek and chin, but was saved by his helmet and his great height, and pluckily continued on duty throughout the day.

You will see from Bourne's report that the police officers had plenty of warning of the intended defiance of the ban and had made their dispositions in advance, though Bourne's report admits that the police forces as a whole were taken by surprise, by which I think he means that they had not expected such an unprovoked and ferocious attack. It would perhaps have been better if the police force which originally tried to oppose the march had been stronger and armed with rifles and bayonets. But it is easy to criticise after the event and as a matter of fact it is the usual police technique to try to check an unruly mob in the first instance with *Lathi* police and to keep the actual firing force out of sight, but "round the corner".

3. As regards the events immediately subsequent to the firing, you will see from Bourne's report that military assistance was immediately invoked and there is at the moment a Company of British Infantry in the Fort, which is very close to the scene of the firing, and a Company of Indian Infantry in Birdwood Barracks in the Lahore Civil Lines. These troops have not actually been employed. The District Magistrate immediately imposed a Curfew Order forbidding any persons residing within the walled city of Lahore being out of doors between 7 p.m. and 6 a.m. He also passed orders forbidding the carrying of arms or assemblies of five or more persons. Patrolling by police and magistrates was carried out throughout the night and there was no further disturbance. My information is that the city this morning is quiet and presents its usual aspect, shops being opened. The burials of the dead Khaksars were carried out early this morning under arrangements made by the Additional District Magistrate[43] and the police. The funeral processions left the city for the burial ground before 6 a.m., when the curfew was lifted and the whole thing was completed before most of the city was aware of it. I was able this morning to assure George Cunningham, who had rung up very late last night, that he need have no anxiety about the corpses of the Frontier

Khaksars (who I believe formed the majority of the mob) being brought back to their homes.

4. The decision to declare the Khaksars an unlawful association under the Criminal Law Amendment Act was taken by Sikander himself and I was not consulted, but I consider that the order was entirely correct and indeed inevitable. The raid on the Khaksar headquarters at Ichhra, a village in the suburbs of Lahore, which is described in paragraph 4 of Bourne's report, was carried out with admirable restraint and success, tear-gas being employed with excellent effect.

We received information this morning that three lorry loads of Khaksars from Ambala and Delhi passed through Jullundur at 11-30 a.m. Arrangements are being made to intercept these and any other such parties before they can reach Lahore. They will be stopped by a large body of police and the tear-gas squad will also probably be present. The Curfew Order will remain in force within the walled city of Lahore for a day or two longer.

5. I was very glad to hear on the telephone late last night that Inayatullah had been arrested at Delhi. The whole responsibility for this lamentable business rests on him. He is not only a most dangerous fanatic, but also a coward and a liar. He himself remained at a safe distance at Delhi and from there issued secret orders to his followers to defy the ban and published articles in his paper which, as I told you in my letter of the 18th, were the most open incitements to violence. He urged them, for example, to "surround the cot of Sikander with a bed of corpses". He should now be put out of the way of doing any mischief for a long time, and I am inclined to think that his movement must be now finally suppressed. Its claim that it is a non-communal organization for social service is the merest nonsense and it has now been proved twice, in Lucknow and here, that its methods are those of the Nazi storm-troopers on the model of which it is founded.

6. One of the most embarrassing complications of the whole business is that the Muslim League session is due to begin here tomorrow. A good many of the delegates have already arrived, including at any rate some Muslim League volunteers, and Jinnah is due from Delhi tomorrow morning. It is this aspect of the situation more than anything else which is worrying Sikander. He is doing what he can to influence the local organizers of the Conference here, the principal of whom is the Nawab of Mamdot, the Chairman of the Reception Committee and also Chairman of the now officially-recognised Punjab Branch of the Muslim League, to agree to a postponement. But he does not feel that his Government would be justified in all the circumstances in passing a definite order prohibiting its being

held. On this point I am in agreement with him. Should he pass such an order, it would give colour to the rumours that are already being spread by his local opponents in the League that Sikander deliberately provoked the clash with the Khaksars in order to bring about a failure of the League Conference (the actual truth, he strongly suspects, is that the rival branch of the Provincial League here, against whose affiliation to the Central League Jinnah has just decided, themselves encouraged the Khaksars to create a disturbance in order to discredit Sikander's Government and to make the Conference a failure). Moreover, if Sikander's Government were to prohibit the holding of the Conference, he thinks it might alienate the sympathy of the saner and more moderate elements of the Muslim public here who so far seem inclined to accept the view that the Khaksars were entirely in the wrong. At present it is only the lower classes in the city and particularly what is known as the *goonda* element who are taking the view that the Khaksars were the victims of brutal and unnecessary firing.

7. Sikander is thus in a peculiarly difficult position. He feels that Jinnah, as the President of the League, is the only person in a position to direct a postponement of its session. He feels further that, given Jinnah's peculiar idiosyncrasies, any direct appeal by Sikander to him might have precisely the opposite effect to what Sikander wishes. But he asked Khan Sahib Kuli Khan of the North-West Frontier Province, who was passing through Lahore yesterday on his way to Delhi, to see Jinnah and do his best to include [?induce] him to agree to a postponement without mentioning Sikander's name. He had, however, when I last saw him an hour or two ago, had no message from Kuli Khan.

8. These are the circumstances which induced Sikander to ask me to send you the message which I communicated by telephone to Laithwaite about 2-30 p.m. I need not repeat this message which doubtless was faithfully reported to you by Laithwaite.[44] You will, I am sure, realise that I was prompted to send it by my anxiety to help Sikander in a position of extreme difficulty. I have just now (5 p.m.) received Laithwaite's message in reply. I need hardly say that I fully appreciate the difficulty you felt in regard to any attempt to influence Jinnah yourself, and I am most grateful to you for asking Zafrullah to speak to him. I gather, however, that Jinnah is not responsive and that the session will now have to go forward. Tomorrow will be an anxious day, but you may rest assured that every possible precaution will be taken to prevent a further clash.

Yours sincerely,
H.D. CRAIK

13

CRAIK TO LINLITHGOW

Secret and Personal
D.-O. No. 222

Government House, Lahore,
March 21st, 1940

Dear Lord Linlithgow,

I am writing in continuation of letter of yesterday, as I think you would like me to keep you in close touch with day-to-day developments of the Khaksar trouble.

2. I held another conference this morning with Sikander, the Chief Secretary and the principal Police officers. The city is, I am glad to report, still quiet. The troops in or close to the city have been reinforced by another Company of British Infantry, which is now stationed at the Kotwali. A few more arrests of Khaksars have been made but I understand that there has been no further influx from outside Lahore. Khaksar headquarters in various other districts (Multan, Ambala and I think one or two others) have been raided and literature and arms taken over by the Police. In no case was any opposition offered.

3. The Police are somewhat disturbed by the fact that two of the Khaksars arrested since yesterday in Lahore were found to be in possession of revolvers. I have not yet been informed whether these were the revolvers that were stolen from Gainsford and Beaty when they were unconscious and, it is believed, were used against the Police in the mêlée of the 19th. But the Police are somewhat apprehensive lest other Khaksars should be so armed. Sikander has been given a strong guard at his residence and two gunmen, who are under orders to accompany him everywhere.

4. I am glad to be able to tell you that the report from the hospital about Gainsford this morning is much more reassuring. He is distinctly better. The report about Beaty is also encouraging.

5. Jinnah arrived in Lahore this morning and was met on the platform by a very large gathering, which included Sikander. I understand that there was no demonstration in favour of the Khaksars, but I am told that when Jinnah's train passed through Amritsar a very large crowd collected on the platform and did demonstrate their sympathy with the Khaksars by shouting such slogans as "Sikander *Murdabad*" etc. Jinnah addressed the crowd and told them that as he was not yet in possession of all the facts, he could not pronounce a judgement, which was in my view a somewhat unfortunate way of stating his position. He is putting up with the Nawab

of Mamdot, the Chairman of the Reception Committee, who is a member of the Legislative Assembly and a supporter of Sikander's.

6. Our chief anxiety at the moment is the course which discussions may take in the Muslim League session, which opens tomorrow. Sikander proposed to me this morning that in order that he should be able to cut short or forestall all discussion of Tuesday's incident, an announcement should be published immediately that Government have appointed a committee of enquiry into Tuesday's events consisting of two High Court Judges; and a telegram has been sent to the Chief Justice[45] (who is unfortunately not in Lahore), asking whether Mr. Justice Sale and Mr. Justice Din Muhammad can be made available for such an enquiry, which should not take more than three or four days.

I do not very much like the idea of any enquiry which might have the appearance of putting the Police on their trial, but at the same time I recognise the great tactical importance of an announcement that an enquiry is to be held. The scope of the enquiry will have to be strictly limited and the terms of reference most carefully framed. The terms I have proposed are: "To enquire into the circumstances in which certain officers were killed and injured and the Police opened fire on the morning of March 19th." I have no doubt whatever that the evidence of the officers who were present will convince the committee that the Khaksars made an unprovoked and savage attack on the Police and that the Police were compelled to resort to firing in self-defence. There is, of course, a risk that the committee may hold that the actual firing was not under proper control or that it was excessive; but there is a complete answer to this in the fact that all the superior Police officers had been rendered unconscious by their injuries and that the Police were naturally gravely incensed at seeing some of their comrades and all their officers (as they thought) murdered before their eyes. Moreover, Sikander cited the precedent of the enquiry held by an English Judge of the High Court at Bombay into the firing by the Police on a Muslim crowd on the first day when prohibition was enforced, and pointed out that pressure is certain to be put on him to appoint a similar committee. The intention is that the enquiry should be held *in camera*.

7. I asked Sikander what he proposed to do should a resolution be put forward at the session of the Muslim League condemning the action taken by him or his Government. His answer to this was that he was going to see Jinnah and the members of the Muslim League Executive this evening and was going to make it clear that should discussion of any such resolution condemning him or his Government be allowed, he and his followers would

leave the session and would immediately resign from the League. How Jinnah will take this I cannot of course say, but Sikander seemed to think that with these consequences clearly before him he would have to disallow any such discussion. He would of course be in a much stronger position in doing so if an announcement is made simultaneously or beforehand regarding the appointment of a committee of enquiry.

8. Another point which I put to Sikander was the risk that a crowd of the Lahore city sympathisers of the Khaksars might invade the League's *Pandal* and create disorder. He admitted that this is a possibility, but strong police precautions are to be taken to prevent anything of the kind happening, and I only hope that they will be successful. In addition to the troops we have over 500 extra Police in Lahore.

9. The three lorry loads of Khaksars reported to be arriving from Ambala and Delhi (see paragraph 4 of my letter to you of yesterday) did not arrive. It is possible that the lorries which the Jullundur Police thought were Khaksars actually contained people coming to Lahore for the Muslim League Conference.

10. A pre-censorship has been imposed on all newspaper articles regarding the firing on the 19th. In consequence of this the *Tribune*, which is the leading local newspaper, has refrained from making any editorial comment whatever: but I have seen articles in one or two of the moderate Muslim newspapers taking quite a sensible line, deploring the unprovoked violence of the Khaksars and referring in pointed terms to the absence of their leader in Delhi.

Yours sincerely,
H.D. CRAIK

14

CRAIK TO LINLITHGOW

Secret and Personal
D.-O. No. 223

Government House, Lahore,
March 22nd, 1940

Dear Lord Linlithgow,

You will have seen in the papers an account of the arrest yesterday in the Anarkali bazar, the Oxford Street of Lahore, of 8 armed and truculent Khaksars with the aid of tear-gas and without casualties. This was a most excellently managed affair and will, I think, create a good impression. I enclose a copy of a note[46] which I sent to the Premier this morning, suggesting the immediate formation of tear-gas squads in some of our large towns.

2. As regards the Muslim League, I gather that the present position is as follows. There was no open session of the League yesterday and the proceedings of the open session today were expected to be mainly of a formal character. When the Council of the League met last night, great excitement prevailed and a certain section led by Z.H. Lari, a U.P. M.L.A., was extremely bitter against Sikander. Jinnah preserved a neutral attitude and said they were all too excited at the moment to discuss the recent incidents in Lahore. He stated that these would be fully discussed at the meeting of the Subjects Committee this evening (March 22nd) and that after full discussion it would be decided what line of action should be taken, viz., whether a resolution condemning Sikander should be moved in the open session tomorrow morning. Sikander, I understand, was present at the Council meeting, but said little or nothing. I would not like to predict what attitude he will take at the Subjects Committee meeting this evening, but I hope he may have the courage to say that he is responsible to his own Legislature and not to the League and that he cannot allow the League any right of interference in regard to the way in which he and his Government are administering the affairs of the Punjab. I hope also that he will make it clear, as I imagine he has made it clear to Jinnah in private conversation, that if a resolution condemning him is allowed to be discussed, he and his supporters will resign from the League. I do not know whether I shall have an opportunity of seeing him this afternoon, but if I do, I shall urge this course on him.

3. I visited the hospital this morning and saw all the injured Police officers and men. Gainsford's facial injuries are pitiable and though he had dined with me the night before the disturbance, I could not recognise him. But fortunately he is in charge of an absolutely first-class surgeon, Col. Mirajkar, who thinks that in spite of both his upper and lower jaw on one side being fractured, he will not be permanently disfigured. But Mirajkar says he will lose the sight of his left eye, though Gainsford has not been told this yet. His general health is very much better and he is considered to be now out of danger. Beaty, who is a middle-aged man on the point of retirement, also suffered terrible injuries and his right eye had to be removed today. He is not yet out of danger. A European Inspector, named Disney, has a not very serious wound on his left thigh. There were also 10 Indian Police officers in the hospital, but two of these have now

been discharged. One was still too seriously injured for me to see him, but I saw the other seven who are all, I am glad to say, doing well. I subsequently went through one of the wards in which the injured Khaksars are accommodated. I was not feeling very sympathetic to them, but so far as I could judge, they are mostly the scum of the Peshawar bazars.

I also saw in hospital a young police officer, named Fryer, who was very severely injured in the head in a recent Frontier engagement and who has flown into Lahore for treatment. He still has a bullet or a fragment of it in his brain, and though he was reported to be a little better and was able to speak to me, he is still in very grave danger.

4. I have seen a large bound volume containing many hundred photographs of Khaksars on parade, which was recovered from the raid on their Ichhra headquarters on the 19th instant. There are also some photographs of sham fights in which cannon were employed, of "casualties" being treated in field hospitals, of sham forts and trenches, and indeed every kind of military operation. The pictures, all of which are apparently reproductions from Inayatullah's paper *Al-Islah*, represent scenes not only from various places in India but also from foreign countries including Persia, Turkey and Germany. The most significant photograph is a double-page illustration representing the march through Berlin of a part of Hitler's Labour Army, all armed with spades. A portrait of Hitler himself adorns the same page. I think this volume would be a valuable piece of evidence against the Khaksar leader. It certainly fully exposes the hollowness of his claim that the Khaksars are an organization devoted to social service and leaves not the slightest doubt that they are nothing but a "private army".

5. I was very glad to read Maxwell's reply of yesterday in the Central Assembly about Inayatullah's arrest. It is doubtful whether we shall be able to secure evidence sufficient to convict him of instigation of murder or rioting, but he must certainly be kept in restraint for a long time to come and indeed I doubt if it will ever be safe to allow him to return to the Punjab.

6. The attitude of the local Press is fairly satisfactory, but two Muslim papers controlled by Maulana Zafar Ali, M.L.A. (Central), today described the dead Khaksars as "shahids" (martyrs). Zafar Ali is also trying to exploit the fact that the wounded Khaksars in hospital are, in accordance with the usual custom, handcuffed to their beds. The Hindu Press are beginning to take the Muslim Press to task for encouragement of the Khaksars. They demand an enquiry, but the communiqué announcing the appointment of two High Court Judges has now been issued. The terms of reference are

practically identical with those suggested by me (see paragraph 6 of my letter to you of yesterday). The exact personnel of the committee is, however, not yet settled.

Yours sincerely,
H.D. CRAIK

15

CRAIK TO LINLITHGOW

Secret and Personal
D.-O. No. 224

Government House, Lahore,
March 23rd, 1940

Dear Lord Linlithgow,

Very many thanks for your secret and personal letter to me of the 21st, which I have just received. I am most grateful for your expression of sympathy with Sikander and myself in our difficulties. I have taken the liberty, which I hope you will forgive, of showing your letter to Sikander as I think it will greatly encourage him.

I am also most grateful to Zafrullah for handling his difficult interview with Jinnah with such tact. I realise now on looking back that it was almost impossible for Jinnah to postpone the conference at a moment when he must himself have been on the point of starting for Lahore. On the whole, his attitude here has been quite correct and impartial and he has not said a word, in public at any rate, to which my Ministers can take exception.

2. As regards the point raised in paragraph 2 of your letter of measures to save senior Police and I.C.S. officers from risks such as our officers here have had to undergo, I have already informed you of the advice I have given Sikander about the immediate formation of tear-gas squads in big towns. I will think over other aspects of the question you raise at leisure, but I am afraid that on occasions of serious disturbance it is absolutely essential that the District Magistrate and the Superintendent of Police should be present in person.

3. I fully appreciate the importance of our being in a position to refute by convincing evidence any suggestion that the Khaksars are a misunderstood body of men who have been harshly treated, and I hope to be able to send you on Monday the bound volume of photographs, which I described in paragraph 4 of my letter to you, No. 223 of March the 22nd. I am afraid it is not possible to allow this very valuable piece of evidence

to be sent out of the country, but perhaps you might be able to arrange through Puckle or Hennessy for a reproduction of it, or at any rate of the most telling pictures in it, to be made in Delhi for despatch to the Secretary of State. Other valuable pieces of evidence may have been found in some of our recent searches, but I have not yet heard of them. The issues of Inayatullah's own paper *Al-Islah* and more particularly the last issue, to which we drew Jenkins' attention, themselves provide useful evidence of the character you have in mind.

4. Since yesterday there has been no further disturbance of any kind in Lahore City. At the open session of the Muslim League held yesterday afternoon there was, I am informed, some interruption of the speech of the Nawab of Mamdot as President of the Reception Committee when he made a complimentary reference to the work done by the Unionist Government. A certain section of the audience started to shout "Sikander *Murdabad*" and similar slogans, but Sikander told me that they were shouted down by his supporters with slogans of "Sikander *Zindabad*". I am also informed that there was a hostile demonstration against two of my Muslim Ministers, Khizar Hayat Khan and Abdul Haye, when they left the *Pandal*, but Sikander did not seem to be aware of this till later. No direct reference was made in the open session yesterday to the Khaksar incident.

5. I saw Sikander for a few minutes about 8-15 p.m. last night, when he had just come from the open session and was going on to the meeting of the Council fixed for 8-30 p.m. He was then in good heart and told me there was nothing to worry about. He was confident that if the question of moving a resolution about the Khaksars came up in the course of the evening, he would be able to make out a convincing case in his defence and that Jinnah would not allow such a resolution to be moved, except possibly one merely expressing sympathy with the victims. According to this morning's *Tribune*, Z.H. Lahri, the U.P. M.L.A., tried to move at the Council meeting a resolution regarding the incident of the 19th, but Jinnah ruled it out of order on the ground that 15 days' previous notice had not been given, but agreed to the question whether such a resolution could be moved being discussed in the Subjects Committee tonight. The League is, I understand, discussing in its open session today the main political resolution, but the Subjects Committee is to meet about 8-30 p.m. tonight.

6. I had some discussion with the Chief Justice today about the personnel of the Committee of enquiry of two High Court Judges (see paragraph 6 of my letter to you, No. 222 of March the 21st). I explained to the Chief Justice that the intention was that the committee should not conduct a

judicial enquiry and that the terms of reference would be strictly limited. He would prefer that the committee should consist of himself and Mr. Justice Abdul Rashid. Sikander is quite agreeable to this and I expect that the above personnel will be announced tomorrow. I am not in any way apprehensive that the committee will come to a finding embarrassing to Government. It will probably be at least a few days before any of the injured officers are well enough to give evidence.

Yours sincerely,
H.D. CRAIK

16

CRAIK TO LINLITHGOW

Secret and Personal — Government House, Lahore,
D.-O. No. 225 — *March 24th, 1940*

Dear Lord Linlithgow,

Sikander came to see me today (Sunday) about 12-30 p.m. He was in good spirits and gave me the following account of what happened at the meeting of the Subjects Committee, which was held last night in the *Pandal* about 9 p.m. Between 300 and 400 delegates were present, but the proceedings were private, the Press being excluded.

Six differently-worded resolutions were moved about the Khaksar incident. Some were comparatively harmless, but others were mischievous. After these had been moved Jinnah called on Sikander, who made a speech for an hour and a quarter, explaining the facts and at the end inviting questions. This speech had, according to Sikander, an excellent reception: some of his audience were moved to tears when he described the brutal injuries inflicted on our officers and the savage and unprovoked nature of the Khaksar attack. Sikander made it clear in the course of his speech that there was every reason to believe that malign influences were at work behind the scenes with the deliberate object of causing an incident which would discredit him and his Government and cause disunity in the League session. He mentioned no names, but the reference was to a small group of Muslim members of the Punjab Assembly opposed to Sikander, viz., Barkat Ali, Mian Abdul Aziz and K.L. Gauba. When called upon to give names he said his audience might rely on his dealing severely with any people against whom he could secure proof.

This speech brought about such a change in atmosphere that Jinnah, who was in the Chair, announced that no further discussion would be necessary. It was then *unanimously* agreed to move a resolution in the open session today, which I understand will express regret at the incident as well as sympathy with *all* the injured persons and ask the Local Government to appoint an independent and impartial committee of enquiry which will command the confidence of the people. This latter point, as you know, is being met.

Sikander suggested to Jinnah that in the open session today the above resolution should be put from the Chair, which I gather under the rules of procedure would mean that the resolution is put and passed without discussion. Jinnah took the line that this would be difficult, as people might insist on speaking. I gather that the intention is that the resolution will be moved by Abdur Rahman Siddiqi of Bengal and supported by Khaliq-uz-Zaman of the United Provinces and possibly also by Sir Raza Ali, but the idea was that Jinnah should make it clear that the Subjects Committee were unanimous as regards the terms of the resolution.

Sikander added that he thought this morning the atmosphere was greatly improved. He told me that Bahadur Yar Jang, a delegate from Hyderabad, who, I understand, has taken a prominent part in the Khaksar movement there and had been active in their interest since his arrival in Lahore, came up and spoke to Sikander afterwards and said that every word he (Sikander) had said was true and that Sikander's account of the incident was corroborated by what a number of Khaksars in Lahore had told Yar Jang.

Sikander did not himself attend the open session today. He expected the proceedings would be completed by 1 p.m. He is giving a big garden party at his house this afternoon to prominent delegates, which I have promised to attend.

2. The only other points I have to report are:

(*a*) I heard this morning that small bodies of Khaksars had collected at various places in Lahore city with the object of defying arrest. One party was said to be assembled in a mosque known as the Golden Mosque. Endeavours are being made to persuade them not to do anything violent, but there is ample Police force to tackle them should they decide differently. The Police have strict orders to avoid the use of firearms, if possible. The tear-gas squads are available.

(*b*) A lorry load containing 15 Khaksars in uniform from Delhi was stopped and the passengers were arrested by the Ambala Police on the morning of the 20th. This party had booked their spades by rail to Lahore. I have heard of nò other considerable parties coming to Lahore.

(*c*) One Khaksar leader at Ferozepore, who is editor of an objectionable paper called *Waqt,* offered some slight resistance to arrest, but was duly arrested.

3. As I was writing this I received your secret and personal letter of the 23rd of March, for which I am most grateful. I am relieved to hear that I am not wasting your time with these daily letters. I will certainly let you have, when things have settled down, a comprehensive report on the use of tear-gas in these riots. Meanwhile, you will see from the enclosed cutting[47] from today's *Statesman* that my Government have accepted my suggestion and announced that they intend to set up tear-gas squads in some of our larger towns.

4. The main political resolution[48] adopted by the League of course enormously widens the gulf between the Muslims and Congress. I will let you have Sikander's views on the resolution in due course, but I am pretty sure that he does not approve of the scheme of having no Central Government at all.

Yours sincerely,
H.D. CRAIK

17

CRAIK TO LINLITHGOW

Secret and Personal — Government House, Lahore,
D.-O. No. 226 — *March 25th, 1940*

Dear Lord Linlithgow,

I hope this will be the last daily report about the Khaksar business which I shall have to inflict on you. The session of the Muslim League finished last night and I am glad to be able to report that my Ministers have emerged comparatively unscathed from a situation that at one time seemed extremely critical.

2. In case you may not have seen newspaper reports of yesterday's doings, I enclose two cuttings[49] from this morning's *Tribune* (there is no issue of the *Civil and Military Gazette* on Mondays). The first of these describes some further demonstrations made by the Khaksars in the City yesterday and Bourne tells me that it is an accurate account. The part played by Bahadur Yar Jang of Hyderabad, the man to whom I referred in paragraph 1 of my letter to you of yesterday, was distinctly useful and creditable to him.

3. The second cutting describes what happened in the final sitting of the open session on Sunday night. It gives the wording of the Khaksar resolution, to which on the whole little exception can be taken. You will observe that the resolution was in the end put from the Chair and that Jinnah was the only speaker on it.

I think it must be admitted that Jinnah handled a difficult situation with very great skill. His primary objective was, of course, to preserve unity in the League, and I do not suppose that he was actuated by any particular consideration for Sikander or his Ministry. But the general result has been better than at one time seemed likely.

4. I had an interesting talk this morning with Pir Akbar Ali, a Unionist member of our Assembly, who belongs to the Ahmadiyya community. He was not present at the Subjects Committee meeting on Saturday night when Sikander made his long speech, but had been told by some of those who had heard it that it was most impressive. He was present at the open session last night and told me that there was no hostile demonstration against Sikander. This is not altogether confirmed by Bourne's information; but it is certainly correct that the atmosphere last night was much better than on the previous day.

Pir Akbar Ali gave me two items of information which may interest you The Ahmadis, he said, have always considered the Khaksar movement a dangerous one and not a single Ahmadi has joined it. The second item was that Ahmadis as a body have not been allowed by the religious head of their movement to join the Muslim League. Akbar Ali himself has been allowed to join as a member of the Unionist Party for a term of six months only. The question whether his followers should be allowed to join the League is, I understand, shortly to be considered by the head of the community.

5. You will, I think, be interested to have an account of a conversation I had with Jinnah yesterday evening at the tea party which Sikander gave at his house to the leading delegates. The party took place in a very large Shamiana in which Jinnah was given a place of honour on the central sofa, the other seat on that sofa being reserved for me. All the leading delegates, including Fazlul Huq and Sir Nazimuddin of Bengal, almost all the Muslim members of the Council of State and Central Assembly, Chhatari and Sir Muhammad Ismail from the United Provinces, and many lady delegates were present. All treated Jinnah with the greatest respect and I formed the impression that their deferential attitude towards Jinnah, a completely self-made man of obscure origin, coupled with the striking personal ascendancy which he has established over the huge gathering of the League, has slightly

gone to his head. Nevertheless, his attitude to me was friendly and even cordial.

I began by expressing my regret that the success of the League's session should have been marred by the unfortunate clash of the 19th of March, but said I was morally convinced that this was no mere coincidence, but had been deliberately brought about by malign influences working in the background. He agreed that this was probably correct, but made a somewhat characteristic criticism that it was an error of judgement on the part of the Punjab Government to promulgate their order banning drilling two or three weeks before the League session began. To this I pointed out that the order applied not only to the Khaksars, but to a number of other communal organizations, which were in fact "private armies" and that repeated demonstrations by these bodies in our big towns had become an imminent menace to public order. Jinnah then went on to speak of his interviews with Inayatullah at Delhi and admitted that he was hardly sane, extremely difficult to reason with and dangerously fanatical. He spoke of the Khaksars as being an organization with "several lakhs" of members and when I told him I thought the numbers had been grossly exaggerated, he cited as evidence of his estimate that on the occasion of a recent visit to Aligarh he found that at least 500 students there had joined the Khaksars. He then went on to say that he hoped to be able to find sober and responsible men, of whom he said there were many among the members of the organization, to assume direction and control over it and to devote its energies into more useful channels, such as village uplift and what he vaguely referred to as "social service". He said the Congress had thousands of workers all over the country engaged on this kind of task and he saw no reason why the Muslims should not have at least an equal number. Actually I fancy he visualises the Khaksars as a potentially powerful propaganda agency on behalf of the Muslim League. He expressed the hope that if he was able to accomplish what he had in mind, my Ministry would agree to rescind their order declaring the Khaksars an unlawful association. At the same time he admitted that the military side of the Khaksars' activities, i.e. drilling, sham fights, &c., was a menace to the public peace and could not be permitted.

The next point he took was that the personnel of the committee of enquiry must be such as to inspire public confidence and expressed the view that if the committee were to consist of two Punjab High Court Judges, it would be considered to be too closely connected with the Punjab Government. Sikander had made exactly the same suggestion to me in the conversation which I had with him in the forenoon and had put forward the name of Niamatullah, a retired Judge of the Allahabad High Court, as a suitable colleague to sit with Douglas Young. After consulting Young, who told me he did not think there could possibly be a better choice and that he had the highest opinion of Niamatullah's straightness and impartiality, I wired to Hallett[50] yesterday asking if he could induce Niamatullah to accept the job. I have not yet had a reply. A possible alternative, whom both Douglas Young and Sikander think suitable, is Sir Abdur Rahman, a Delhi lawyer who is now a High Court Judge in Madras.

6. Jinnah had to leave the tea party about 5-45 p.m. to go back to the open session of the League which was still discussing the "political" resolution. When he said good-bye to me he was not certain whether the resolution on the Khaksars would be reached last night and thought it possible that the session would have to be resumed this morning. Fortunately this anticipation proved to be incorrect. Sikander told me he intended to go down to the open session about 8 p.m.

7. The delegates from other Provinces are all, I imagine, dispersing today and the state of affairs in the city has so much improved that the troops are being withdrawn. I think I can say we are now out of the wood, though it is possible that the question of the firing on the 19th March may be raised by means of an adjournment motion in the Punjab Assembly, which resumes its sittings after a break of about 10 days tomorrow; but I am doubtful if the adjournment motions which have been tabled will be moved, and in any case I think Sikander can rely on the support of the great majority of his party.

8. While I would not go so far as to say that the Ministry's prestige has not suffered, I am hopeful that such damage as it has sustained will not be permanent. The local press has been extremely well-handled by J.D. Anderson and Nur Ahmad, the Director of our Information Bureau, and I think it has now been clearly established that the Khaksars' attack on the Police was savage and entirely unprovoked. One other point has been established beyond all doubt and that is that Inayatullah Mashriqi has been completely discredited. All the comments I have seen in the Muslim newspapers are unanimous in holding that he behaved with cowardice in remaining at Delhi and from a safe distance exhorting his followers to violence in his published writings; and also that he had shown a complete disregard for the truth by publicly denying that he had so exhorted them. I do not think he will ever be in a position to resume the leadership of his organization, but for a long time to come he must not be allowed his liberty. A letter from an Indian which I received today recommended that he should be deported either to Mandalay or Sydney! I cannot understand why Sydney should be expected to receive such a visitor.

9. In conclusion, I should like to say again how very grateful both

Sikander and I are to you for your sympathy and support during these critical days and also for the prompt action taken by your Government to arrest Inayatullah. Sikander's own behaviour and bearing throughout have been admirable. Although he must have been overwhelmed with the business of the League and was, I believe, entertaining a house full of guests, he has found time to visit me daily, has taken me completely into his confidence and has been most ready to accept any suggestions or advice I have offered. At a time when the fate of his own Ministry was in the balance and his own political future at stake, only on one occasion (immediately after the firing) did I see him depressed. With this exception he has been his usual imperturbable and cheerful self and has constantly assured me that all will be well and that I need not be worried. Indeed, he showed an almost touching consideration for myself, as he has more than once sent me messages through my daughter or through members of my staff "to tell His Excellency not to worry". My already high opinion of his character and courage has been greatly enhanced by his behaviour.

Yours sincerely,
H.D. CRAIK

18

CRAIK TO LINLITHGOW

Secret and Personal
D.-O. No. 228

Government House, Lahore,
March 31st, 1940

Dear Lord Linlithgow,

Many thanks for your secret and personal letter of the 28th of March in reply to my letter No. 226 of the 25th. I have just had a talk with J.D. Anderson and was very glad to learn that you had after all had an opportunity of seeing him when he was in Delhi. I was most interested to hear from him about your conversation.

There is no doubt that the general view among Muslims is, as Chhatari indicated to you, that Jinnah's able handling of the difficult situation [over the Khaksar resolution] has placed Sikander and his Ministry under a considerable obligation to Jinnah. The latter, of course, was not actuated by any particular wish to help Sikander, but his real object was to preserve unanimity in the League and in that he has certainly succeeded. One result of this situation will, I am afraid, be that neither Sikander – nor for the matter of fact any other Muslim leader – will for a considerable time to come be in a position to criticise or oppose the League's attitude on the constitutional question. Although I have had little chance of any prolonged discussion with Sikander on the League's attitude, as he is so overworked and tired that I do not like to make too many demands on his time, I have little doubt that in his heart of hearts he realises the futility of the League's resolution.

I did have a few minutes' talk with Sikander yesterday. He is still carrying on conversations with Bahadur Yar Jang of Hyderabad, who is working to induce my Ministers to rescind the order declaring the Khaksars an unlawful association. I told Sikander that in my opinion the rescission of this order for some time to come would be a grave mistake and that if it is to be ultimately rescinded, it should be on clearly-defined conditions. These conditions should include the retention of the general ban on drilling and military operations; the complete abandonment of the practice of carrying any form of weapon, more particularly spades; the abandonment of the Khaksars' military activities and the direction of their energies into peaceful channels such as genuine social service; and a stipulation that the direction and control of the movement should be in the hands of responsible and sober-minded people.

Yours sincerely,
H.D. CRAIK

19

CRAIK TO LINLITHGOW

Private and Personal
D.-O. No. 229-F.L.

Government House, Lahore,
March 31st, 1940

Dear Lord Linlithgow,

My last fortnightly report was sent to you as long ago as March the 4th. I apologize for not having sent any routine report since that date, but the Khaksar incident and its consequences, about which I have kept you fully informed, have overshadowed everything else that has happened during the interval, and have incidentally made considerable demands on my own time.

2. The Legislative Assembly resumed its sittings the other day after a recess of about ten days for the Holi festival.[51] The demands for grants

have been passed in full without a single cut. It seems certain that the session will last till the end of April and the strain which this long session, following on recent anxieties, imposes on the Premier is a matter of some concern. He is looking seriously overstrained, but I am afraid there is no possibility of his getting a holiday before the end of the session. I shall try to persuade him to take a real holiday in May.

3. As regards the reactions to the Patna and Ramgarh resolutions of the Congress, I do not know that I can add anything of value to what I stated in paragraph 6 of my letter to you of March the 4th. A study of the local Hindu press has confirmed me in the view that moderate Hindu opinion, and even some Congress opinion, is seriously dismayed at the High Command's decision. Criticism in the Muslim press before the session of the Muslim League took its tone from Sir Abdul Halim Ghaznavi's published statement that the Congress attitude was "tantamount to suicide", and a leading article that appeared in the *Statesman* under the caption "The Suicide Club" was freely quoted.

4. As regards the results of the Muslim League session, I imagine you are in as good a position to appreciate these as I am. My own impression is that the session has greatly enhanced Jinnah's prestige and influence and that the unanimity and enthusiasm shown at the session have given the League a position of far greater authority than it previously enjoyed. I will not attempt to appreciate here the real significance of the League's solution of India's constitutional difficulties, as I am proposing to do this in reply to your recent telegram on the political situation generally.

5. Apart from the clash with the Khaksars on March the 19th, the last three weeks have been generally quiet and I do not think there has been any communal incident of importance. I have recently visited two districts, Lyallpur and Shahpur, and in both I found the same enthusiastic loyalty which I encountered on other tours undertaken this winter. At Lyallpur I was presented with addresses not only by the District Board, the headquarters' Municipal Committee and the District Soldiers' Board, but also by the "residents of the district". This address, which was read by one of the local M.L.As., a leader of the great Kharral clan, was of so remarkable a nature that I am sending you a copy of it, as I think it may have some publicity value in England. It was accompanied by a purse for war purposes of Rs. 1,08,000, which is more than double the amount I have received from any other district. Lyallpur is, of course, the richest agricultural tract in the Province. Sargodha (the headquarters of the Shahpur district), where I spent three days, is one of our two horse-breeding areas. I attended the Horse Show and the local races and talked with innumerable local people.

The enthusiasm for the war there is very high, as the district is one with a great martial tradition. There I received the usual addresses and was given a purse of R. 50,000 which, it was emphasised, was only a first instalment of the district war effort. In addition to this one of the big landlords gave me Rs. 1,500 and the boys of the local college a purse of Rs. 250.

6. The famine unfortunately still persists and the recent rain has done very little good in the famine area, as practically no crops have been sown except on irrigated lands. In Hissar alone we have no less than 2,82,000 people, receiving relief. A little under 2,00,000 of these, including dependants, are employed on relief camps and the remainder are receiving gratuitous relief in their homes. On this district alone our monthly expenditure is now in the neighbourhood of Rs. 5 lakhs and I fear may even become higher before the monsoon could be expected. There is also considerable expenditure in Rohtak.

7. I have referred in two of my previous letters to the incursion of a Lashkar from the tribal areas into the Isakhel Tahsil of Mianwali. The Commissioner[52] reported about the middle of March that there was still some nervousness in that area. The battalion which went from Rawalpindi to assist the civil authorities has now been moved to Bannu, presumably to take part in the operations in the Ahmadzai salient, but a detachment of about 40 men has been left behind at Isakhel to reassure the people. The inhabitants of that Tahsil have expressed their gratitude to Government for the assistance of the military, to which they attributed the dispersal of the Lashkar which had attacked Isakhel.

8. I do not think there is anything else of sufficient importance to call for special mention. I enclose the fortnightly report for the first half of March.

Yours sincerely,
H.D. CRAIK

20

MOON TO LAITHWAITE[53]

Secret
D.-O. No. G.S.-226 *April 1st, 1940*

My dear Laithwaite,

I enclose herewith a personal telegram from His Excellency the Governor to His Excellency the Governor-General in reply to the telegram[54] sent with your demi-official letter No. 1743-G.G. of the 29th of March 1940. I am sending this off by post tonight as agreed on the telephone yesterday.

Yours sincerely,
E.P. MOON

ENCLOSURE TO NO. 20

CRAIK TO LINLITHGOW
Telegram

Personal
[Unnumbered] *April 1st, 1940*

I agree generally with Your Excellency's appreciation of the existing situation as expressed in paragraphs 3-5 of your telegram of March 29th.

2. I have no comment to offer regarding the Princes. Your Excellency is in a far better position than I to estimate the implications of their attitude as disclosed in their Chamber's meeting in March.

3. Congress is of course a much less important factor in the Punjab than in other provinces. It is only a small minority in the Assembly and without Akali support, which may not always be accorded, would be almost insignificant; it is rent with internal dissensions; and it does not include a single outstanding personality. Moreover, Congressmen and Hindus generally are probably more alive here than elsewhere to the necessity of conciliating Muslim opinion and the danger to them of Muslim resurgence. So far as I can judge, the majority of moderate Hindus and even some sections of Congress think that the recent tactics of the Congress High Command have been unwise and that, as Your Excellency has put it, they have "overcalled their hand". This judgement is largely founded on articles in newspapers which are usually staunch supporters of Congress, but which have now condemned its refusal of the offer of Dominion Status.

4. As regards Muslims, three results have clearly emerged from the recent Muslim League Session: (*a*) the importance of the League as the representative Muslim organization has been immensely enhanced; (*b*) Jinnah's own personal prestige has greatly risen. His position as the one All-India Muslim leader is now unchallenged, and in practice he alone is in a position to dictate the League's policy; (*c*) Muslim opinion is now, outwardly at least, unanimous in favour of the partition of India. Only a very courageous Muslim leader would now come forward openly to oppose

or even criticise it. Such opposition on Sikander's part, for example, would inevitably mean a split with the League and possibly serious dissension among his own supporters in the Punjab. I do not think he will risk these consequences.

5. It is important to try to estimate the real significance of the partition resolution. As a hit back at Congress it is obviously very effective. It has completely torpedoed the Congress' claim to speak for India as a whole. This was clearly one of the objects with which it was put forward. Was it also meant as a serious solution of India's difficulties? The unthinking Muslim rank and file may so regard it. But I find difficulty in believing that the responsible Muslim leaders regard it – at present at any rate – as a genuine constructive proposal. Certainly Sikander has always both in public and in private utterances opposed any type of Pakistan Scheme, and I know that he tried, though unsuccessfully, to secure that the resolution should provide for at least some form of Central Government. In his heart, I believe, he still thinks partition impracticable, and I imagine many of his followers share his views.

On the whole it is, I think, reasonable at present to assume that Muslims would accept something less than partition, but the longer time that elapses without any concrete alternative being put forward, the more the support and favour partition proposals are likely to receive from the Muslim masses, who will now follow Jinnah's lead blindly.

6. The above comments on the general situation will give Your Excellency some idea of the present feeling in this Province on the broad constitutional issues. As regards the likelihood of civil disobedience (paragraph 7 of your wire), there is very little sign of preparation for it in this Province. Only spasmodic and ineffective efforts are being made to enrol volunteers, and it would be difficult at present to work up enthusiasm. Although civil disobedience does not appear probable in the near future, it will be attempted, though perhaps on a comparatively small scale, directly Gandhi gives the signal.

Muslims will, I think, oppose it and probably by force if it in any way threatens their economic interests. I agree with Your Excellency (paragraph 10 of your telegram) that its outbreak would almost certainly lead to communal disorder.

7. As regards the problem of tactics raised in paragraph 8 of your telegram, I am inclined to agree with Your Excellency's conclusions. Certainly as regards (*b*), I would say that a threat on the lines contemplated would detach from Congress no appreciable body of opinion, and would be likely to stiffen Congress leaders and rally thei supporters.

If any hint is required to be given to Congress that in time of war drastic measures would be taken against civil disobedience, this should certainly not be conveyed in a formal official communiqué: indeed I rather doubt the wisdom of conveying it to them in any *public* manner (e.g. by a speech in Parliament or elsewhere). It would be better to convey it through some private channel, if a suitable channel is available, and if you are convinced that the Congress leaders are in doubt as to the probable attitude of Government.

8. The appreciation of Congress' position contained in paragraph 9 of your wire seems to me to be unquestionably correct. Even if Congress choose outwardly to ignore the dangers which threaten India both from within and from without, there are other strata of opinion which are fully alive to them and more critical than usual of Congress tactics. It is therefore all the more important that we should avoid anything in the nature of a threat or challenge which might rally opinion to their support.

9. As regards the general line of policy to be followed in the existing circumstances, I venture to suggest that we should not remain entirely passive. If we simply allow the situation to develop, I fear that the result will be either the outbreak of civil disobedience or a steady widening of the breach between the two major communities, till all hope of bridging it vanishes. Left to their own devices they are unlikely to put forward any constructive suggestions for the solution of their differences. A positive and persistent effort on our part to bring them together and to suggest solutions for their consideration seems to be required.

10. The crux of the whole problem is the question of Hindu domination at the Centre. Muslims will not tolerate this, nor any method of framing a constitution (e.g. a Constituent Assembly whose decisions would be determined by a majority vote) which might produce this result. It is impossible for His Majesty's Government, especially when in close alliance with Islamic countries, to overlook the Muslim attitude on this matter. Apart from other considerations to do so would sooner or later involve the country in civil war.

It seems therefore that we should spare no effort (*a*) to persuade Congress that constitutional advance must be on lines acceptable to Muslims and that if they ignore this, they will be running their heads against a wall, and (*b*) to remove the suspicion that we hope to exploit this fact in order to retain our hold on this country.

11. Gandhi has recently written that if his projected Constituent Assembly failed to reach an agreement, it would automatically be dissolved. "An agreed solution would be its sole sanction." This suggests that he is open to argument and that (*a*) above is not an impossible task. While any

public pronouncement or overture might do more harm than good, persistent attempts at persuasion through private channels might usefully be made.

As regards (*b*) above, the best earnest of the sincerity of our intentions would be for ourselves to show that we are trying to assist India's constitutional advance by devising solutions for the communal problem at the Centre. What would seem to be required are various alternative constitutional expedients such as would ensure at the Centre something in the nature of a Coalition Government. Suggestions would have to be conveyed privately, at any rate to begin with.

12. Action on the above lines might prevent the situation from rapidly deteriorating. It might also be valuable later, if a break came, as evidence of the sincerity of our promise of Dominion Status.

13. I would also suggest that in any debate in Parliament, it should be made clear that His Majesty's Government's offer of Dominion Status still holds good; that we are ready to implement it as soon as the Princes and the peoples of India can agree as to the form of constitution; and that we are doing all that we can to promote agreement.

14. In paragraph 13 of your telegram Your Excellency mentions two arguments in favour of our taking a more positive line in opposition to Congress. The first argument has not, in my view, much force. The second is more weighty, but I do not think that the possibility of putting heart into our actual or potential supporters would justify our taking a course which would be represented by Congress as "banging and bolting the door".

15. I trust that Your Excellency will consider the importance of the issues involved a sufficient justification for the length of this reply.[55]

H.D. CRAIK
Governor of the Punjab

21

CRAIK TO LINLITHGOW

Secret and Personal — Camp, Rawalpindi,
D.-O. No. 230 — *April 3rd, 1940*

Dear Lord Linlithgow,

Many thanks for your secret and personal letter of March the 30th. We have duly received the book of Khaksar p ɔtographs, and I have now been informed that another copy has been found by the police in the course of their searches. I have asked our C.I.D. to make enquiries as to the scale on which this issue was printed off and have also enquired whether it would be possible to spare one of the copies available to send home.

2. I left Lahore on Monday night for a tour that had been arranged for some time to Rawalpindi (where I am at the moment) and Attock districts. Just before I left Sikander came round to see me and spoke to me about the possibility of rescinding the order declaring the Khaksars an unlawful association. He showed me a letter he had received from Jinnah urging this course and also made it clear that considerable pressure was being put on him by Nawab Bahadur Yar Jang, who is at the moment in Lahore, and by others. Sikander, who is clearly overstrained and overworked, seemed inclined to weaken on this point, but I repeated to him in the most forcible manner I could the advice I had previously given him, as explained in the last paragraph of my letter to you No. 228 of March the 31st.

3. He seemed to me to be nervous about the possibility of a further clash as there are still some considerable bodies of Khaksars collected in one or two of the Lahore mosques. Their aggregate number was about 80 yesterday. I offered to postpone my tour, but he would not hear of this, and I think it would have looked "panicky" to do so, but I told him that I would be ready to return from Rawalpindi at a moment's notice, should there be any further trouble in Lahore. Moon I left behind [in] Lahore with instructions to keep in touch with the Premier, the Chief Secretary, and Bourne, the District Magistrate, and he is sending me telephonic messages twice daily. So far he has had no actual trouble to report, but there is a good deal of nervousness in Lahore. I also managed to have a few minutes' talk with Bourne himself before leaving Lahore and told him that if the suggestion of rescinding the order declaring the Khaksars an unlawful association should come up in my absence, he should strongly oppose it. But I am quite sure that Sikander will not rescind the order without consulting me, as he must be aware that the question is one that attracts my special responsibility under Section 52 (1) (*a*).

Yesterday I reinforced my advice to Sikander on this matter by sending him the letter of which I enclose a copy.[56]

4. The tear-gas squad is still in Lahore, but I found that duHeaume, the expert, had returned to the Police Training School at Phillaur, of which he is Commandant. I told Bourne before leaving Lahore that in my opinion duHeaume should be recalled to Lahore and should stay there till the situation is clear, and I have no doubt that this has been arranged.

5. According to a Police report a "source", who was present at the meeting of Khaksar leaders at Meerut the other day, reported that there

was some talk there of individual Khaksars having recourse to acts of terrorism: in fact the assassination of Sikander was definitely put forward. I am told, however, that the reliability of this "source" is open to question; but the personal guard on Sikander and on his house has been strengthened.

6. One of the points I pressed on Sikander at our last conversation was that he should insist on Nawab Bahadur Yar Jang securing the departure of all the Khaksars at present assembled in Lahore as evidence of his power of control over them. According to a report which I have just received from Moon, there is little hope of Yar Jang being able to secure this. Yar Yang, who apparently met with little success at the Meerut meeting, is said to be regarded by the Khaksars in general as "Sikander's man", and the Khaksars are not inclined to acquiescese in his assuming control of the movement.

Another report I received from the Assistant Central Intelligence Officer, Delhi, speaks of attempts being made by Khaksars to bring out their newspaper *Al-Islah* from somewhere in Sind at an early date, publication having ceased in Delhi since the Chief Commissioner demanded security. This report also mentions that the headquarters of the movement have been transferred from Delhi to Aligarh and that batches of Khaksars continue to be sent from the United Provinces to the Punjab. If this report is correct, it may become necessary for me to ask you to press Hallett, and perhaps Graham too,[57] to declare the Khaksars to be an unlawful association in the United Provinces and Sind. The course of events in the next few days may perhaps make it clear that the Khaksars have become a menace to the peace and tranquillity not only of the Punjab but of India generally.

7. To turn to a different topic, you will probably have noticed the newspaper reports of speeches by Sir Chhotu Ram and Sir Sunder Singh Majithia on the subject of the Muslim League's recent "partition" resolution. I have some reason to think that these speeches were *not* made without Sikander's concurrence.

Yours sincerely,
H.D. CRAIK

PS. I hope you duly received the two Khaksar spades and daggers which I sent down with Her Excellency.

22

CRAIK TO LINLITHGOW

Secret and Personal
D.-O. No. 232

Government House, Lahore,
April 6th, 1940

Dear Lord Linlithgow,

I arrived back at Lahore early this morning from my tour to Rawalpindi and Attock and had a talk with Bourne at the Railway Station. It was generally expected that three or four parties of the Khaksars now putting up in various mosques in Lahore City would come out yesterday (Friday) and attempt to defy the ban on drilling by marching through the streets. On Thursday night Bourne issued a proclamation to the general public, warning them to keep well away from any such demonstrations in case the police should be compelled to open fire on the Khaksars. This, combined with bringing some troops back to their stations close to the city, had a discouraging effect on the Khaksars and the anticipated demonstration was not made.

2. Nawab Bahadur Yar Jang of Hyderabad, who has been in Lahore for some time in consultation with Sikander, left Lahore for Delhi on Tuesday or Wednesday last, and it is reported that he has gone to Delhi to consult Jinnah. Two important arrests were made on the evening of the 4th of April in Lahore. The persons arrested were: (1) Abdullah Shah Zinjani of Amritsar who is said to be an ardent adherent of Inayatullah and was present on guard duty at Inayatullah's residence at Delhi at the time of the latter's arrest. He has been staying in one of the Lahore mosques with other Khaksars. (2) Hamidullah, who comes from the North-West Frontier Province. Some documents were found in this man's possession. The police are searching for a man called Fazal Rahim Shah, who is said to be the commander in chief of the Khaksars at present in Lahore, and also for another leader known as the "Qazi Sahib".

3. I was disturbed to read in the *Civil & Military Gazette* of Friday the 5th, the article which I enclose,[58] indicating that the order declaring the Khaksars an unlawful association is likely to be withdrawn at an early date. This was obviously inspired from official sources and similar articles have appeared in most of the Lahore vernacular papers. I have not been able to see Sikander since my return but I have written to him today a letter, of which I enclose a copy, about these articles. I thought it best to put in writing my view, in which I feel confident you will agree, that the

situation is one that attracts my special responsibility under Section 52 (1) (*a*) for the prevention of any grave menace to the peace or tranquillity of the Province. I am pretty sure that Sikander already realises this, but it is desirable to put the point to him explicitly.

I also enclose the *Tribune* article[59] to which I have referred in my letter to Sikander.

4. The situation in Rawalpindi was in many respects similar to that in Lahore. There too a large number of Khaksars were gathered in various mosques, many of them people who had filtered through in twos and threes from the Frontier Province. I have asked Cunningham to try to stop further infiltration of this character and he has promised to do his best to do so. In Rawalpindi too a demonstration was thought possible yesterday (Friday), but none occurred.

5. About the book of Khaksar photographs, I enclose a copy of a letter dated the 4th of April which I received this morning from Bennett, the head of our C.I.D.[60] I have just heard that many copies of this album have been found at the printer's. Would you like me to send one copy direct to the India Office?

Yours sincerely,
H.D. CRAIK

ENCLOSURE TO NO. 22

CRAIK TO SIKANDER HYAT KHAN

Secret and Personal

Government House, Lahore,
April 6th, 1940

Dear Sikander,

I am most reluctant to add to your worries, but I feel that I must let you know that I was perturbed to read in the *Civil & Military Gazette* (dâk edition) of Friday the 5th, an obviously officially inspired note to the effect that negotiations with the Khaksars were making good progress and that an agreement was likely to be reached shortly. One or two of my visitors at Campbellpur, who had seen this note, commented on it with some surprise.

Since my return here I have received reports of articles in a similar tone having appeared in several of the vernacular papers, such as the *Shahbaz*, *Inqilab*, *Zamindar*, *Ahsan*, and *Milap*. All of these talk of the probability that Government might cancel at an early date the order declaring the Khaksars an unlawful association.

These announcements are in striking contrast to the proclamation issued by Bourne on Thursday night warning the public to keep away from any Khaksar demonstration in case the police might be compelled to open fire. The contrast is so apparent that I fear it may be interpreted as a sign of weakness and vacillation on the part of Government, see for example the articles in the "Notes and Comments" column of the *Tribune* of today.

I cannot find either in the numerous reports which I have read since my return to Lahore or in the state of affairs which I found at Rawalpindi (which is much the same as at Lahore, though perhaps not so menacing) the slightest sign of any change of heart on the part of the Khaksars. While it is true that they seem to be somewhat divided in their counsels, it is apparent that some of them are still as truculent as ever and that the danger of their offering violent opposition to the police is still imminent. It also seems clear that they are by no means prepared to accept Nawab Bahadur Yar Jang as their leader.

As I have told you at recent interviews, I do not think there can be any question of rescinding the order under the Criminal Law Amendment Act until we are satisfied that certain conditions have been fulfilled, these conditions being:

(*a*) We must have a guarantee that the direction and control of the movement has passed into the hands of reliable and responsible persons.
(*b*) As an earnest of the above the first step to be taken should be that all the bodies of Khaksars now assembled in Lahore and Rawalpindi (which are undoubtedly unlawful associations) must be cleared out.
(*c*) We must be satisfied of their intention to abandon the use of arms and uniforms and the practice of drilling, and I do not think we can be satisfied as to this until all *belchas* and uniforms have been given up.
(*d*) We must be satisfied that the organization intends to devote itself in future to lawful activities, such as social service.
(*e*) There can be no question of restoring Inayatullah to his position of leader of the organization.

Until the above conditions are satisfied, I do not see how I can possibly agree to the recision of the order under the Criminal Law Amendment Act. The situation is in my judgement clearly one that attracts my special responsibility under Section 52 (1) (*a*) of the Government of India Act for the prevention of any grave menace to the peace or tranquillity of the Province.

Yours sincerely,
H.D. CRAIK

23

CRAIK TO LINLITHGOW

Secret and Personal
D.-O. No. 233

Government House, Lahore,
April 8th, 1940

Dear Lord Linlithgow,

I am writing in continuation of my secret and personal letter to you, No. 232 of April the 6th, under cover of which I forwarded a copy of a letter of the same date which I had sent to Sikander. His reply to this letter, of which I enclose a copy, reached me at 11-45 p.m. last night (Sunday). Early this morning I sent him a line to say that there was of course no question of his no longer enjoying my confidence, which he had in the fullest measure, and I asked him to come round and see me as soon as he could. We have had a long talk this morning, which I think succeeded in completely clearing up the misunderstanding that had arisen.

2. With reference to the passage in Sikander's letter which I have marked "A",[61] I told him I quite accepted his statement of the position as correct, but that no question of my exercising any special powers had at the moment arisen. I had, however, a definite responsibility to the Secretary of State under Section 52 (1) (*a*), which I was under an obligation to discharge, and in order to enable me to do this it was clearly my duty to satisfy myself that appropriate steps were being taken to deal with the menace to the peace and tranquillity of the Province. I further assured him that I was completely satisfied as to the propriety of the steps taken by him on the 19th of March and immediately thereafter.

3. In regard to the sentence in his letter which I have marked "B",[62] I told him that I agreed that "the responsibility for clearing the aftermath resulting from the incident of the 19th of March" was primarily his and his colleagues'; but I pointed out that I too had a responsibility which I was equally with himself bound by the Act to discharge, viz., to satisfy myself that appropriate measures are in fact being taken. I explained that

my reason for sending him my letter of the 6th of April was that I inferred, from what I had read in the press regarding the alleged willingness of the Government to withdraw the order declaring the Khaksars an unlawful association, that the negotiations had reached a stage of which I was not aware; and that the articles had perplexed me and were also perplexing certain district officers.

I gave him again an assurance that he enjoyed my full confidence and that I was only too anxious to help him in a situation that I knew was a peculiarly difficult one for him.

4. Sikander denied that any of the articles I referred to had been, so far as he was aware, officially inspired. He said that the only incident which might be construed as any kind of official inspiration was that the Chief Secretary had rung him up either on the 3rd or 4th of April to say that a rumour was current that the negotiations between Sikander and Nawab Bahadur Yar Jang had broken down. The Premier authorised the contradiction of this rumour.

5. As regards the conditions on which the Government would be prepared to withdraw the order under the Criminal Law Amendment Act, you will see from paragraphs 2, 3 and 4 of Sikander's letter to me that he has in substance accepted all the conditions stated in my letter to him of the 6th of April, with the exception of that regarding the wearing of uniform. As to this latter point, which I regard as of minor importance, he is correct in pointing out that we did find that there was a real difficulty in banning the wearing of uniform for the reasons he mentions in paragraph 2 of his letter.

6. When asked about the progress of the negotiations, Sikander explained that after he had made the conditions clear to Nawab Bahadur Yar Jang, the latter left Lahore either on the 3rd or 4th of April, ostensibly to consult Jinnah. He has not since returned to Lahore, so far as Sikander is aware, nor has any communication been received from him or from Jinnah. Sikander agreed with me that one section at any rate of the Khaksars are not prepared to accept the control of Nawab Bahadur Yar Jang. There are still about a hundred Khaksars collected in the various mosques in Lahore city, and I think a slightly smaller number in Rawalpindi.

7. I am sorry to have to report that poor Beaty died last night. He had been completely paralysed on one side and unable to speak for some days, and although up till yesterday there was some hope of saving him, his death is perhaps a merciful release.

8. I believe that Young's enquiry starts the day after tomorrow. My

information is that there will be about 55 witnesses on behalf of the police, but we have at present no idea what witnesses will be produced on the other side. Government is to be represented by the Advocate-General[63] and his Assistant.[64]

9. Since writing the above I have received your secret and personal letter of the 6th of April, for which I am most grateful. It is, I am afraid, a fact that Sikander is suffering from a very severe strain at the moment. Not only has he had all the anxiety about this Khaksar business and the Muslim League session, but he is also extremely overworked with a seemingly interminable session of the Legislative Assembly, which is certain to go on till at least the end of this month. He has the added anxiety of the possible reactions likely to follow from the Privy Council's judgement in the Shahidganj case a week or two hence, and sooner or later he must clarify his position *vis-à-vis* the Muslim League partition resolution with his Hindu and Sikh colleagues. In conversation today with the most sensible of these latter (Mr. Manohar Lal) I expressed the hope that Sikander would be allowed plenty of time to think over this difficult problem before any pressure was brought to bear on him to make his position clear. Manohar Lal, who is a great admirer of Sikander's and I think genuinely attached to him, entirely agreed and promised to do what he could in the matter. As soon as the Assembly session concludes I shall do my best to persuade Sikander to take a real holiday.

11. [10.] There is one other matter which I ought to mention. In paragraph 3 of your letter to me of the 21st of March you stressed the importance of our being in a position to disprove without delay any suggestion that Inayatullah and the Khaksars are a harmless body of men who have been harshly treated. An interesting piece of evidence of this kind was brought to me yesterday by Raja Narendra Nath, one of the oldest and most respected Hindu citizens of Lahore. This was a compilation of extracts from Inayatullah's various writings, all tending to show that the whole basis of the Khaksar organization is the cult of violence and that its object is securing by force Muslim domination over the whole of India. Raja Narendra Nath told me in confidence that the person who had made this compilation was the editor of the Delhi newspaper *Tej*, whose name is, I think, Deshbandhu Gupta. The copy which he showed me I marked to the Premier and to the head of our C.I.D. with a suggestion that the extracts appearing in the compilation might be verified and might conceivably be a useful piece of evidence to be produced before Young's Committee. The document was reproduced on some kind of duplicating machine, not

on a typewriter, and I should think there ought to be no difficulty in securing from Deshbandhu Gupta another copy, if he is carefully approached. Perhaps Jenkins could manage to do this.

Yours sincerely,
H.D. CRAIK

ENCLOSURE TO NO. 23

SIKANDER HYAT KHAN TO CRAIK

Personal and Secret

Lahore,
April 7th, 1940

Dear Sir Henry,

Kindly refer to your secret and personal letter of 6th April. The note in the *Civil & Military Gazette* referred to by Your Excellency, so far as I am aware, is no more officially inspired or authentic than the article in which a statement attributed to Gainsford regarding inadequacy of precautions in spite of his repeated requests was published. On the other hand, the proclamation issued by Bourne was published in consultation with me and with my approval. The decision to issue this proclamation was taken in a conference held in my room on Thursday, April 4th, at which the Chief Secretary, D.I.G. (C.I.D.), D.C., Senior Superintendent of Police[65] and Superintendent of Police (C.I.D.)[66] were present.

2. I agree with Your Excellency that there can be no question of rescinding the order declaring the Khaksar organization unlawful unless the Government is satisfied that:

(*i*) they would nor defy law and order or the restrictions imposed on volunteer organizations in the Punjab Government notification of February 28th, 1940;

(*ii*) the organization will in future confine its activities to lawful pursuits and genuine social work;

(*iii*) the movement will be in the hands of law-abiding and responsible persons.

I am afraid it would be futile to impose restrictions on wearing of uniforms, as it would be almost impossible in practice to enforce them. You will recollect that we originally intended to ban the wearing of uniforms also, but had to drop the idea on account of legal and other difficulties in defining a uniform. For instance, grey shirts and trousers or white shirts and shorts would constitute a uniform just as khaki shirts or tunics and overalls would. If we ban dress of a particular type or colour, it would be easily evaded by changing into a different colour or pattern. What is needed is effective restrictions on drilling of a military character and marching in formation with or without arms or weapons. These evolutions are covered by the notification of 28th February.

3. I agree with Your Excellency that Inayatullah Khan Mashriqi should not in any case be allowed to reassume the leadership of the organization. Let us hope that the Government of India would also see eye to eye with us in this matter.

4. I might for your information state that I made it quite clear to Nawab Bahadur Yar Jang that it would not be possible for the Punjab Government to withdraw the order declaring the Khaksar organization unlawful unless and until we were satisfied that the conditions enumerated above were fulfilled and that, as an earnest of their *bona fides*, the Khaksars who came to the Punjab from other Provinces should return to their homes.

5. I must frankly confess that the penultimate paragraph of Your Excellency's letter has caused me no little pain. I must respectfully point out that the question of exercising your special powers under Section 52 (1) (*a*) of the Act could arise only if the Government failed to or refused to take precautions necessary for the prevention of any great menace to the peace and tranquillity of the Province. Your Excellency will, I trust, concede that the situation on the 19th of March (when senior police officers were seriously injured and over 100 persons were injured or killed including several policemen) was exceedingly grave and menacing and the question of attraction of Your Excellency's special responsibility would perhaps have been more germane on that occasion than now But, as you are aware, I unhesitatingly shouldered the responsibility for taking such steps (including the order declaring the Khaksar organization unlawful), as I deemed necessary for restoring peace and order regardless of the unpopularity and odium which is inevitably engendered by strong action. In spite of the extreme gravity of the situation, which was further complicated by the session of the Muslim League and the strong resentment and passions aroused amongst the populace on account of firing and the large number of casualties, I did not throughout that anxious period allow even for a moment the idea of requesting Your Excellency to share the responsibility with me of invoking your special powers. Apart from the constitutional impropriety of such a course, it would have been morally reprehensible on my part to try to drag you or your name in this affair and

thus expose Your Excellency also to unnecessary and undeserved criticism. I therefore venture to submit that, while I will continue to consult Your Excellency and to derive benefit from your mature experience and advice, the responsibility for clearing the aftermath resulting from the incident of the 19th March must continue to be mine and that of the Government. If, however, I no longer enjoy your confidence, I shall be glad to be apprised of it, as in that case it would be my clear duty to request Your Excellency to relieve me immediately of my office and responsibility as Premier of this Province.

6. I may add that I am treating, as desired, Your Excellency's letter as strictly confidential and have not shown it or my reply to my colleagues.

Yours sincerely,
S. HYAT KHAN

24

CRAIK TO LINLITHGOW

Private and Personal
D.-O. No. 236-F.L.

Government House, Lahore,
April 14th, 1940

Dear Lord Linlithgow,

The greater part of the fortnightly report for the second half of March 1940, which I enclose, is taken up with a detailed description of the clash with the Khaksars in Lahore city on the 19th March. I have kept you separately in touch with all important developments arising out of this incident, my latest letter to you on this subject being that of April the 13th,[67] with which I enclosed a copy of my letter of the same date to Cunningham regarding a report that a secret meeting of Khaksar officials at Peshawar had fixed April the 19th as "zero hour". I omitted to notice when I wrote to you yesterday that April the 19th has been announced by Jinnah as "Pakistan Day", a point which is perhaps of some significance.

The question whether we are to issue a press communiqué[68] (vide the last sentence of paragraph 2 of my letter of yesterday to Cunningham) is not yet finally settled. I told Sikander that I thought it should be discussed in Council and this is to be done tomorrow morning when a draft communiqué will be laid before us. Sikander is keen on putting out a communiqué, but I am not sure that all his colleagues will support him in this and I am personally somewhat doubtful as to its expediency. I have told Sikander that the whole question of these volunteer organizations and the policy to be adopted in relation to them is under your consideration.

2. My latest information is that there are now about 170 Khaksars collected in four mosques in Lahore city, but there is no sign of their making any attempt to defy the ban on drilling, and the city is quiet. Interest in the Khaksar affair has been overshadowed by the recent news of Germany's unprovoked aggression on Denmark and Norway. So far as I am aware, there are still rather less than 100 Khaksars in mosques at Rawalpindi, but there has been no further incident there. There was a little trouble in Rohtak caused by the incursion of a number of Khaksars from the United Provinces, but a few who were arrested were quickly convicted and given severe sentences and that ended the matter. I understand some Khaksars from the United Provinces have also been arrested at Ambala, but I am not yet in possession of details of what happened there. In no other district has there been any trouble. The Muslim Deputy Commissioner of Gujranwala,[69] who came to see me two or three days ago, told me that in his district the police had a complete list of 178 local adherents of the movement. There was a general round-up of these men immediately after the clash in Lahore on the 19th and 170 of them immediately resigned their membership and gave up such uniforms and spades as they had. The remaining 8 could not be traced and are believed to have left the district. The Deputy Commissioner told me that most of the men came from the menial classes, such as barbers, mochis, tailors, &c.

3. I do not think I have anything else to report in regard to the Khaksars, except that Young's committee began recording evidence on the 11th of April, when Bennett, the Deputy Inspector-General of the C.I.D., Wace, Deputy Inspector-General of the Central Range, and Bourne, District Magistrate, were examined. I am told that their evidence was most effective. A senior Muslim counsel, Khalifa Shuja-ud-Din, has been selected by Young to represent the Khaksar side of the case. I met Chaudhri Niamatullah, the retired Allahabad High Court Judge, who is Young's colleague on this enquiry at a social function the other day and was well-impressed. He is rather disturbed at the length of the time which the enquiry is likely to take, which he put at a month. I understand he has a considerable practice at the Lucknow Bar and is naturally anxious to get back to it as soon as possible.

4. An incident occurred the other day which may possibly be an outcome of the Khaksar clash. The police arrested one Muhammad Husain Shaifi, described as a Kashmiri, and searched his house. They found there a bomb, alleged to be intended to be thrown at the Ministerial benches in the

Assembly. This incident was reported in the press and caused considerable alarm. I understand that the detective staff in and around the Assembly Chamber has been substantially increased, but I am not aware whether any connection has been established between Muhammad Husain and the Khaksars.

5. A very disquieting murder took place in the Jullundur district a short time ago. It was committed by two Sikh soldiers who had deserted some weeks ago from their unit with at least one rifle and a large supply of ammunition. The victim was a Sikh, named Karam Singh, who some years ago had been rewarded with a grant of land for assistance given in rounding up one of the notorious Babbar Akali outlaws. It seems certain that this murder was committed at the instigation of some of the recently released Babbar Akali convicts. Unfortunately the murderers have not yet been apprehended.

6. The Muslim League scheme for the partition of India into independent sovereign states has been universally condemned by the Hindu and Sikh press and various Sikh associations have passed resolutions to the effect that they will resist the application of this principle in the Punjab "to the last ditch". There is much speculation in the press as regards Sikander's attitude to the Muslim League scheme which the Hindu press demands that he should clarify. I have not myself thought it fair to have any talk with him on this subject, as in my view he should have every opportunity of thinking out the matter at leisure when he is free from his present immediate preoccupations with the Khaksars and the Assembly session. I saw him yesterday on another matter and thought he was looking rather better and less strained.

7. The Assembly session has made rather better progress with its business during the last two or three days. The lengthy and contentious Relief of Indebtedness (Amendment) Bill has reached the third reading stage, and I do not think that the legislative measures that remain to be taken up this session are likely to take very long. At the moment it looks as if the session may end a little earlier than has hitherto been anticipated.

8. Since the beginning of this month I have visited two more districts, Rawalpindi and Attock, bringing the total number of districts which I have toured this cold weather up to fourteen. Both these districts have great military traditions and my visit to both was the occasion of the usual displays of enthusiastic loyalty and anxiety to help in the war. I received addresses from the District Soldiers' Boards and District Boards at both places and at Rawalpindi I was presented with a purse of Rs. 60,000, which I consider a very generous contribution from what is essentially a

poor district of small holdings with no canal irrigation whatever. The Attock Oil Company headed the list with a contribution of Rs. 10,000. In Attock collections for the War Purposes Fund are proceeding, but are not sufficiently advanced for a purse to be given me. I attended the District Sports at Attock, where there was an enormous crowd of, I should say, 20 or 30 thousand people, who seemed to be in the happiest of holiday moods.

9. I take this opportunity of thanking you very much for your secret and personal letter to me of the 6th of April, which I do not think I have yet acknowledged. Many thanks also for your letter of the 13th of April just received. I am most grateful to you for your clear exposition of the constitutional position in regard to matters attracting my special responsibility. I will take an early opportunity of pointing out to Sikander in conversation his misapprehension as to this position, but I do not think it would be wise at the moment to do so in a formal communication and I do not understand that it is your wish that I should take that course.

10. I am glad to hear that you have obtained a copy of the compilation of Inayatullah's writings, which Raja Narendra Nath showed me. I have given instructions for one copy of the book of Khaksar photographs to be sent to the India Office with a covering letter to Findlater Stewart and for another copy to be sent to Laithwaite. We now have plenty of copies available. I have also reminded Moon about sending you the specimens of Khaksar daggers.

Yours sincerely,
H.D. CRAIK

25

CRAIK TO LINLITHGOW

Secret and Personal — Government House, Lahore,
D.-O. No. 239 — *April 22nd, 1940*

Dear Lord Linlithgow,

My last letter to you about the Khaksar business was written on April 17th and enclosed a copy of a letter of the 15th which I had received from Cunningham.[70]

2. The press communiqué stating the terms on which the Punjab Government would be prepared to rescind the order under the Criminal Law Amendment Act, 1908, declaring the Khaksars an unlawful association

was published on April the 16th. The terms of this communiqué were discussed in Council on the 15th and the decision to publish it was unanimous. As I think I told you in one of my letters, I was at one time rather doubtful of the wisdom of making any such announcement, but after discussion I accepted the conclusion that an announcement was desirable (*a*) because it would dispel the rumours that were current, particularly in the Hindu newspapers, that Government were about to give in to the Khaksars and weakly rescind the order; (*b*) because the conditions laid down by Government were so eminently reasonable that the Khaksars would put themselves more than ever in the wrong if they refused them; and (*c*) because I had reason to know that some of our District Officers were in considerable doubt as to the attitude of Government.

3. The communiqué had a good press, except in some of the more extreme Muslim organs which have all along supported and justified the Khaksars. The latter were, however, not long in showing their reactions to the Punjab Government's conditions. On the afternoon of April the 17th, the day after the issue of the communiqué, a party of about 10 Khaksars emerged from one of the mosques in which they had been taking shelter and started to march up and down the Anarkali Bazar. They were not in uniform, but had badges on their arms and were carrying spades. They were tackled by the police and the Tear-smoke Squad, but there was a high wind and the use of tear-smoke was not very effective. The Khaksars charged the "Tear Squad" without provocation and several smoke bombs and grenades were thrown by the Squad in self-defence. One of the Squad constables was injured by a spade thrown by a Khaksar and the butt of a police musket was broken by a blow from a spade. Five of the ten Khaksars were arrested, but the others escaped in the confusion, leaving their spades behind. Most of these had been sharpened and pointed. The police do not seem to have managed this incident very successfully.

Later on the same evening five more Khaksars emerged from another mosque and immediately charged the police who had moved up to arrest them, inflicting injuries on a Head Constable. They were then overpowered and arrested. In this scuffle one of the Khaksars received a blow from a *lathi* on the head, which later proved fatal, and another was wounded by a police bayonet.

All the Khaksars concerned in these two incidents were men from outside the Punjab. They came from Bhopal, Hyderabad and the United Provinces.

4. On the following day, the 18th of April, two more small parties emerged from mosques and were successfully arrested. They did not put up any violent resistance.

On the same day 8 Khaksars, who emerged from mosques in Rawalpindi city, were arrested, apparently without resistance. They were armed with spades and two of them wore German helmets. They were all local men, including two bad characters. On the 19th a further batch of 6 Khaksars in Rawalpindi city surrendered peacefully.

Friday, the 19th, had been announced by Jinnah as "Pakistan Day" and there were expected to be further demonstrations in Lahore on that day, but none took place, nor were there any on the 20th. On the other hand, a body of about 13 Khaksars, who had been sheltering in one of the Lahore mosques, departed peacefully to their homes in the United Provinces, their railway fares being paid by the management of the mosque. The police allowed these men to proceed to the railway station without interference. I [am] told that a good many others are now tired of this business and would be glad to make a similar "get-away".

Yesterday, Sunday the 21st of April, a small body of the Khaksars emerged from one of the mosques at a time when the police pickets were not on duty. They marched up and down the street for some time, but on sighting a party of police making for them they ran back into the mosque. Another and more serious incident was a very inflammatory speech made by one of the Khaksars from the wall of the Sunehri Masjid, where the most truculent Khaksars, mainly from the North-West Frontier Province, are sheltering, to a large crowd assembled in the street below. I understand that the Premier is asking the Anjuman-i-Islamia, which manages this mosque, to warn the Khaksars stopping in it that the mosque is meant to be used for prayer and not as a place of residence, and they should therefore clear out. If they refuse, the Anjuman's warning will be published.

5. After the incidents of the 17th, which I have described above, I called a meeting of the principal police officers and emphasised that every possible precaution must be taken to prevent further casualties to our police officers or men. It seemed to me that the initiative had passed to the Khaksars, who were clearly out to harass the police in every possible way. They considered themselves immune from arrest so long as they remained in the mosques and their tactics were evidently designed to keep the police constantly on the alert and to take them by surprise. I pointed out the danger of letting it be thought that any one sheltering in a mosque or other sacred building was immune from arrest and asked whether it would not be possible to carry out arrests inside the mosques. There was, however, general agreement that this would not be politic, as such arrests were not likely to be effected without violence, and bloodshed inside a mosque would have deplorable effect on Muslim opinion. This view I felt bound

to accept. It was, however, decided that for the protection of the police themselves, buck-shot should be served out to them and should be employed against Khaksars who violently resist arrest. Buck-shot, if aimed at the legs, is less likely to cause fatal casualties than ball ammunition and also less likely to injure spectators. Bayonets are not really effective weapons against the Khaksar *belchas* and the police are not very well trained in bayonet drill. Tear-smoke is effective only if conditions are favourable and if those against whom it is directed are taken by surprise.

I enquired whether more pressure could not be brought to bear on the management of the mosques in which the Khaksars had taken shelter (it is estimated that there are still a hundred of them in the Lahore mosques). The District Magistrate will do what he can in this direction, but the mosque managers, though just as anxious as we are to get rid of these unwelcome visitors, are powerless in this matter. A suggestion which I put forward that electric light and water supplies might be cut off from these mosques was not considered advisable, as this would interfere with the use of the mosques by the regular congregation. The District Magistrate is, however, to warn the Mutwallis of the mosques that by harbouring these persons they are rendering themselves open to prosecution under the Penal Code.

6. I held a further discussion on April 20th with the Premier, the Chief Secretary, the Inspector-General of Police[71] and other police officers. On this occasion the Premier expressed strongly the view that it was unfair that the Punjab Government, the only government that has taken strong action against the Khaksars, should have to bear the whole brunt of their attack without any assistance from other Provinces. He referred to the prolonged strain imposed on our police force by the situation in Lahore, which has now lasted for more than a month, and particularly to the fact that owing to their preoccupation with this business our senior police officers are unable to devote sufficient attention to the steadily increasing threat of civil disobedience and to the possibility of a simultaneous revival of terrorism. He pointed out that the majority of the Khaksars now assembled in Lahore and nearly all those arrested after the 19th March are not Punjabis, but have come from other Provinces; that those still in Lahore are receiving continuous messages of encouragement from leaders in the United Provinces, the North-West Frontier Province and elsewhere; and that the Idara-i-Alia, or Khaksar headquarters, is still apparently functioning somewhere outside the Punjab. It was not fair, he said, that we in Lahore should have to deal with the violent rank and file while their leaders residing elsewhere enjoy complete immunity. The immediate problem is, in his opinion, to place these leaders, who are sending messages and instructions

to the Khaksars here, under restraint. But he further urged that the Governments of the North-West Frontier Province and the United Provinces should be pressed to follow our lead and to declare the Khaksars unlawful associations. He thinks that these Governments are most short-sighted if they expected that the Khaksars will ever be of any use to them, and that Jinnah is equally wrong if he thinks that the Khaksars will be useful to the Muslim League. In his (Sikander's) opinion they would always be a menace to law and order.

7. Sikander added that so far as the movement inside the Punjab is concerned, it had already almost collapsed. The majority of our Khaksars have dissociated themselves publicly from it and it is not [*sic*] being kept alive in Lahore only by the encouragement it receives from other parts of India. It is vital from the point of view of the Punjab that the situation in Lahore should be cleared up quickly, before the Privy Council judgement in the Shahidganj case is published. It is now known that the hearing of the appeal has been completed and it can only be a few days before the judgement is published. As soon as this is done, the interim order of the High Court prohibiting the Sikhs from erecting any building on the site of [the] so-called mosque must lapse, and the probability is that the Sikhs will at once start building. This may lead to a revival of the intense feeling caused by the Shahidganj controversy two years ago and the Khaksars may find in this tension an opportunity for making a bid for Muslim sympathy by leading attacks on the Sikhs. If civil disobedience is also started in the near future and terrorism revives, Sikander added, the Punjab might soon become an armed camp and he even hinted at the possibility of Martial Law.

8. While I admit that the strain which he has undergone for the last month may to some extent have coloured Sikander's views, I find myself in sympathy with his demand that more ought to be done in other Provinces to help us in "liquidating" the embarrassing situation which persists in Lahore, a situation which, as he has pointed out, may become much more serious if complicated by the Shahidganj and civil disobedience issues. I have read again the telegrams sent by the United Provinces and North-West Frontier Province Governments to the Home Department on the 21st of March last, in which both Governments stated their objections to declaring the Khaksars to be an unlawful association, and while I do not deny the force of the arguments put forward, I doubt if those two Governments realise the extent to which their policy of inactivity has added to our difficulties here. I enclose a summary of a note[72] prepared by our C.I.D. illustrating this point. I admit that the material contained in this

note is somewhat scanty, but the following considerations seem to me to be relevant to Sikander's suggestion that the time has now come for all-India action to be taken against the Khaksar association:

(1) The question of imposing a ban on private armies is really an all-India matter, especially in war time. It is true that we did not ask other Provinces to co-operate before issuing our notification of the 28th of February banning drilling and the carrying of arms in processions, but we did inform both the Central Government and the United Provinces and North-West Frontier Province Governments of our intention before the ban was actually issued. Moreover, one ground for our taking this action was the earlier display of violence by the Khaksars in the United Provinces.

(2) The Khaksars are an all-India association. The orders for the detention of its leader and the searching of its temporary headquarters were passed by the Central Government.

(3) Much of our trouble has been due to the intrigues occasioned or at any rate stimulated by the meeting at Lahore of the All-India Muslim League.

(4) There is undoubtedly some agency outside the Punjab that is responsible for staging the incidents that have taken place in Lahore since April 16th. In the rest of the Punjab, as I have already pointed out, the movement has practically collapsed and in the few places where there has been any tendency to defy the orders of the 28th of February that defiance has not taken the same violent form as in Lahore.

9. In the circumstances which I have described I venture to suggest that even though our information is admittedly meagre, the time has now come when it would be appropriate for you to press the Governments of the United Provinces and the North-West Frontier Province to take a more active share than they have done hitherto in helping to terminate our difficulties. If the leaders who are from outside the Province encouraging and directing the Khaksars here could be quickly located and arrested, the probability is that such action would suffice. But it must be taken speedily, as Sikander tells me that he has reason to believe that the efforts now being made to procure a much larger influx of Khaksars from other Provinces into Lahore may succeed. It is of course likely that the leaders may try to evade arrest. If so, it seems certain that it will be necessary sooner or later to declare the Khaksars an unlawful association in other Provinces, and on this ground alone it might perhaps be best to take that step at once.

10. Many thanks for your private and personal letter of the 18th of April, which I received yesterday. I have issued instructions regarding the use of the term "tear-smoke" and not "tear gas".

The Young enquiry is going on well. Young came to dine with me the other night and I had a long talk with him. He told me that the evidence put forward on behalf of the police had been admirable and had given him and his colleague a full and clear picture of what had occurred on the 19th of March. I gather that the cross-examination by the counsel representing the Khaksars had not been effective, and I understand that the evidence to be produced on behalf of Government will be concluded tomorrow.

11. In conclusion I must apologise for the length of this letter, but I know you like to be kept in close touch with what is going on and I have felt it right to give you a full statement of my Premier's difficulties and views.

Yours sincerely,
H.D. CRAIK

26

CRAIK TO LINLITHGOW

Secret and Personal
D.-O. No. 240

Government House, Lahore,
April 23rd, 1940

Dear Lord Linlithgow,

In continuation of paragraphs 8 and 9 of my letter to you No. 239 of yesterday, I now enclose a copy of a telegram intercepted yesterday, addressed to the *Tribune* newspaper of Lahore, from a man who is presumably its Peshawar correspondent. I have sent a copy of this telegram to Cunningham and also enclose a copy of my covering letter to him.[73]

This telegram seems to me to add considerable force to the suggestion put forward in my letter to you of yesterday that action should be taken against the Khaksars in other Provinces. It confirms Sikander's apprehension (see paragraph 9 of my letter of yesterday) that the efforts now being made to procure a much larger influx of Khaksars into Lahore may succeed.

2. There are two further pieces of material which add point to my plea for more vigorous action against the Khaksars outside the Punjab. The first is contained in the following extract from the "Survey of the activities of Foreigners in India" No. 14 for the week ending the 6th of April 1940:

"Pro-German activity amongst the students of the Aligarh Muslim University seems to have been revived. Professors Amir Hassan and Babar Mirza, who are both known for their German connections, and Rafiq and Durrani, who have hitherto not come to our notice, are said to have been organizing the students of the University to prepare for agitation against the Punjab Government's orders in connection with the Khaksar disturbances. It is reported that the means adopted to achieve this end will be violent or non-violent according to the dictates of the situation. Meanwhile, it is said that anti-British propaganda is openly done by Nazi propagandists inside the University."

The second piece of information was given me the other day by Malcolm Darling. He told me that during the course of his interrogation of enemy aliens at Ahmadnagar two or three enemy subjects, who would be likely to know, told him that they believed that the Khaksar association was financed by funds from Germany. This information, which must be on record in the Central Intelligence Bureau, has not, I believe, been fully verified, but is nevertheless significant.

Yours sincerely,
H.D. CRAIK

27

CRAIK TO LINLITHGOW[74]
Telegram

Personal and Most Secret
No. 7-G. *April 23rd, 1940*

Your telegram No. 182-S.C., April 17th.[75] The press reflects a growing expectation that civil disobedience will start very soon. Preparations in this Province have recently been intensified, e.g. enrolment of *Satyagrahis* has begun and a training camp for them is about to be opened in Lahore. Sikander in conversation with me on April 20th made it clear that he personally (*a*) apprehends an early outbreak, and (*b*) thinks that it may be accompanied by a revival of terrorism. As regards (*b*) I have myself seen little evidence suggestive of much activity by terrorist bodies apart from the recent murder in Jullundur of a Sikh who had been rewarded for assistance in rounding-up Babar Akali outlaws (vide paragraph 5 of my fortnightly letter, dated April 14th). But I consider that ordinary prudence now requires us to be prepared for a very early declaration of civil disobedience with all that it may entail and to formulate in detail the action which we propose to take.

2. I have more than once in conversation with Your Excellency expressed my agreement with you that we should do everything possible to paralyse the movement before it gains momentum. Presumably the Revolutionary Movement Act and supplementing Ordinance would be promulgated at once. Doubtless Your Excellency will send further instructions regarding the procedure to be followed for the enactment of the Act in Provinces where the ordinary constitution is still in operation.

3. As desired by you I have not yet consulted Sikander so am uncertain whether he would be willing to incur the odium of promptly arresting many of his political opponents who have hitherto been working as a constitutional opposition. It is possible that it might be necessary for Your Excellency to issue orders to me under Section 126 (5), Government of India Act. The question will also presumably form the subject of further correspondence.

4. I agree as to the desirability of the action proposed in (*b*), (*c*) and (*d*) of paragraph 3 of your telegram. I am doubtful about (*a*) which might tend to antagonise friendly sections of the press, viz., English and Muslim newspapers.

5. As regards the problem discussed in paragraph 4, there is little likelihood of a "no-rent" campaign in the Punjab. A "no-revenue campaign" is possible but is hardly likely to succeed on a large scale as civil disobedience will not be popular in rural areas.

One possible method of dealing with such a campaign would be to round up and sell off the cattle of those who refuse to pay. This might quickly bring people to their senses. But ordinarily sequestration of cattle and other movable property is a first resort in the event of non-payment. Recourse is only had to seizure of land in cases of determined obstinacy. If a no-revenue campaign received any considerable support there might be no alternative to seizing the land and farming it either directly or through lesees.

6. I agree as to the essential preparations which Your Excellency has suggested in paragraph 5. The necessary information regarding offices to be raided, persons to be interned, &c., could, I think, be secured without much publicity. We should also be ready with plans for (*a*) immediate strengthening of police forces, (*b*) provision of additional jail accommodation. (*b*) will almost certainly involve some publicity.

28

CRAIK TO LINLITHGOW

Private and Personal
D.-O. No. 243-F.L.

Government House, Lahore,
April 30th, 1940

Dear Lord Linlithgow,

Apart from the Khaksar business, I have not much to report since the date of my last fortnightly letter to you, No. 236 of 14th April. In paragraph 5 of that letter I mentioned a "political" murder in the Jullundur district, committed by two Sikh deserters. I am glad to say that one of the two murderers was arrested on the 21st of April in the Hoshiarpur district. He had with him a service rifle and over 200 rounds of ammunition. The other murderer is expected to be apprehended shortly.

2. "Pakistan Day" was fixed for the 19th of April. This was a very stormy day in Lahore and there was a heavy shower of rain in the evening when the meeting was held. Consequently the attendance was very small and the celebration was a failure. I had an interesting side-light on the significance of the Muslim League resolution from one of my visitors today, the proprietor of one of the Muslim newspapers here. His paper has consistently and strongly supported the Pakistan scheme. When I asked him what he really thought about it, he admitted with a smile that everybody knew that it was a perfectly impracticable scheme, but it had the merit of having exposed the Congress pretensions to represent the whole of India.

3. Preparations for civil disobedience have been intensified lately and have been given considerable space in the press. On the 19th of April the Working Committee of the Punjab Provincial Congress Committee passed a resolution under instructions from the High Command, constituting itself a *Satyagraha* Committee. There were 16 members of the Provincial Working Committee present and all but two of them signed the *Satyagraha* pledge. It was announced that a *Satyagraha* Training Camp is to be formed at Lahore on the 7th of May, where a week's training is to be given to the 234 delegates who represented the Punjab at the Ramgarh Congress session and to others who have signed the *Satyagraha* pledge. The instruction is to be in drill, first-aid, "constructive work" (whatever that may mean) and the exposition of Congress policy. The intention is that after this short course of training those who have undergone it are to start similar camps in their own districts. Gandhi's latest pronouncement in the *Harijan*

published yesterday[76] will, I imagine, have the effect of damping down preparations for civil disobedience considerably.

4. The Assembly session is now expected to finish in a day or two. Sikander and his colleagues will be greatly relieved when it does terminate, as it has been going on more or less continuously since October last. Sikander is still looking very strained and depressed. I have begged him to take a holiday as soon as he can get away from Lahore, but he does not seem very hopeful of being able to do so.

5. As regards the Khaksars, my letter to you of April the 22nd, No. 239, described the incidents that had taken place up to the previous day. Since then there have been almost daily demonstrations and a certain number of arrests have been made, but there have been no cases of violent resistance to arrest. The Khaksars' present tactics are to emerge in small bodies from the mosques and play a game of hide-and-seek with the police, dashing back into the shelter of the mosques, if possible, to avoid arrest. On the 23rd of April a small body of 8 or 9 women Khaksars wearing *burqas* and armed with *belchas* paraded the streets, but the police took no notice of them and this type of demonstration has not been repeated. On the 28th of April, 8 Khaksars from Lahore went over to Amritsar and took shelter in a mosque there. They were overawed by a very large number of police and surrendered peacefully to arrest. According to a newspaper report 7 of the 8 have new [now] tendered apologies, but have not yet been released. Their arrest inside a mosque created some excitement. There have also been a few arrests in Rawalpindi during the last week or so and 7 Khaksars from the United Provinces were arrested in Gurgaon on April the 20th.

According to my latest information there are still about 120 Khaksars left in three mosques in Lahore city. One of the mosques in which they were previously sheltering has now been evacuated, but it cannot be said that the situation in Lahore shows any improvement. Although most of the newspapers, and I think all sensible sections of public opinion, condemn the Khaksars' recent conduct, they still command the sympathy of the lower class Muslims, who doubtless enjoy seeing the police being chivied about in an undignified game of hide-and-seek and do all they can to help the Khaksars and to obstruct the police. I have again discussed the question of tactics with Sikander with special reference to the imminent announcement of the Shahidganj decision. He is still averse from attempting to make arrests inside the mosques, as these could not be effected without bloodshed. He has done what he can to bring pressure on the management of the various mosques to get rid of the Khaksars, but the reply invariably given is that much as they would like to do so, they are helpless in the matter. We are now considering the possibility of putting punitive police posts in the Mohallas in which the mosques are situated and recovering the cost of these posts from the inhabitants of the Mohallas concerned. Sikander seems to think that this might be a practical method of bringing pressure, and details are now being worked out. While I would not describe the situation at the moment as actually menacing, it is certainly embarrassing, and I have little doubt that the Khaksars would resort to violence again should a favourable opportunity present itself. Meanwhile of course the strain on the police is considerable.

6. Young's Enquiry Committee completed a day or two ago the examination of witnesses produced by Government and has adjourned till May the 6th, when it will commence examining witnesses on the other side. In the interval I imagine the concoction of false evidence is proceeding furiously!

7. I saw Gainsford the day before he left by air for England, where he is to be under the care of Gillies, the plastic surgeon. He was accompanied on his flight by his wife and one of our best I.M.S. doctors who was proceeding on short leave. Gainsford, though still terribly disfigured, was amazingly cheerful.

8. I enclose the fortnightly report for the first half of April.

Yours sincerely,
H.D. CRAIK

29

CRAIK TO LINLITHGOW

Secret and Personal
D.-O. No. 244

Government House, Lahore,
May 5th, 1940

Dear Lord Linlithgow,

I have to acknowledge the receipt of two letters from you about the Khaksars – one written on the 29th April and the other on the 1st of May.

2. As regards what you have referred to as the conflict of evidence regarding the happenings in Peshawar, you will by now have received Cunningham's telegram to me, No. 23-T. of April 29th,[77] which he repeated to you. His figures for North-West Frontier Province Khaksars arrested or sheltering here are slightly smaller than ours, but the difference is not serious.

But the point of my letter to Cunningham of April 23rd[78] was to let him know that we had reason to think that efforts were being made or likely to be made to encourage a large invasion of Khaksars from the North-West Frontier Province into Lahore. Although no such invasion on a large scale has yet taken place, further evidence of the intention has recently come to hand and I now enclose a copy of my letter of today's date to Cunningham (with its enclosures) explaining the nature of this evidence.[79]

3. The last account I gave you of Khaksar activities was contained in paragraph 5 of my fortnightly letter to you of the 30th April, No. 243-F.L. As the result of a further conference which I held on the 1st May, police measures in Lahore have been considerably tightened up. Strong police pickets have now been posted permanently outside the mosques in which the Khaksars are sheltering. People entering the mosques, who are suspected of carrying food to the Khaksars, are stopped and searched. A small force of female police have been engaged to search women so detained. I believe that barbed-wire obstacles have been placed round some of the mosques. The police pickets have orders to move on any crowd which stops to listen to Khaksars haranguing them from the walls of the mosques. The occupants of some of the neighbouring houses have been warned that their houses may be requisitioned for the accommodation of the police pickets, and press publicity has been given to the possibility that Government may decide to recover the cost of the additional police required from the people of the mohallas in which the Khaksars are sheltering. The effect of these measures is certainly to add to the difficulties of the Khaksars inside the mosques, and I hope that pressure may be brought upon them by the people of the mohallas concerned to clear out of Lahore. There are already indications that this is happening.

4. Nevertheless there is still much unrest in the city and continual demonstrations by crowds against Sikander, while the strain on the police force remains considerable. Moreover the Khaksars are extending their operations to other places, and there have been a considerable number of arrests in Amritsar, Jullundur, Rawalpindi, and Gujrat.

5. The announcement of the Privy Council decision in the Shahidganj case[80] has so far caused less excitement than I had anticipated. The real trouble will however commence if and when the Sikhs decide to build on the site of the old mosque. At the moment the Sikhs do not seem to be in any hurry to do so, and there is some reason to believe that they are not anxious at present to increase Muslim ill-feeling towards themselves.

6. My present intention is to leave Lahore on the night of Tuesday, the 7th May for Simla, staying for three days *en route* at Saharanpur and arriving at Simla on the morning of the 11th May. I shall of course defer

my departure should the situation here seriously deteriorate. But if things continue much as they are at present, I think it would be a mistake to alter my plans. Sikander will be remaining at Lahore till the 11th or 12th May, I think.

7. I have just received your letter of May 3rd, the first two paragraphs of which refer to the Khaksars. I am making enquiries as to the exact number of Khaksars from the North-West Frontier Province killed and arrested since the disturbances began, and will let you know the result as soon as possible.[81]

Yours sincerely,
H.D. CRAIK

30

CRAIK TO LINLITHGOW

Private and Personal
D.-O. No. 246-F.L.

Barnes Court, Simla,
May 15th, 1940

Dear Lord Linlithgow,

I will begin my fortnightly letter with an account of developments in the Khaksar affair since the date of my last letter to you on that subject, No. 245 of May the 6th. On May the 7th, the day on which I left Lahore, I held another Conference, which was attended by the Premier, the local officers and the Police chiefs, but this was devoted mostly to the discussion of some evidence about indiscriminate firing by the Police and their rough handling of wounded Khaksars that had been produced before the Committee of Enquiry on the previous day. There has been a considerable amount of evidence of this kind, much of it I am convinced being concocted, but I am not of course aware what effect it has produced on the members of the Committee. Late in the evening of the 7th of May Sikander came to see me and told me that he had been approached by a deputation of some 70 leading Muslims in Lahore with a request that he should order the withdrawal of the police pickets guarding the entrances to certain mosques, which were causing a lot of inconvenience and resentment to regular worshippers at the mosques. They promised that if he would agree to this suggestion, they would make every endeavour, with the help of the leading men of the *mohallas* concerned, to induce the Khaksars to leave the mosques and either disperse to their homes or surrender peacefully to the police. Sikander and I consulted Bourne, the District Magistrate, on this suggestion and found that he was in favour of it, and the pickets were accordingly withdrawn on the 8th of May, the understanding being that the leading Muslims would be given a reasonable period (I understand about a week was mentioned) within which they would bring their powers of persuasion to bear on the Khaksars. It was also understood that should they fail in their task, Government would be at liberty to use any means thought suitable to eject the Khaksars from the mosques.

This development was welcomed by the local Muslim press, which considered the Premier's action "both wise and diplomatic". It has, however, come in for considerable criticism by the Hindu press on the ground that it amounted to a practical admission of the immunity from arrest of persons taking refuge in sacred buildings. The Khaksars on their part made a responsive gesture by announcing that for some days they would refrain from any demonstrations outside the mosques, and for four or five days there were no demonstrations. But I see from this morning's telegrams that the usual type of "hide and seek" parade by small bodies recommenced yesterday (May 14th). The Khaksars in Lahore, who numbered 155 on May 13th, do not seem to be in any mood to yield to the persuasion of local Muslims and to disperse to their homes, and their attitude is that they cannot do so till Inayatullah Mashriqi is released and himself gives orders for their dispersal. You will have noticed in the press that Jinnah, in response to appeals made to him to come to Lahore in order to bring about a settlement between the Provincial Government and the Khaksars, has announced that he has no authority over the Khaksars and that there is no connection between them and the Muslim League.

Up to May the 2nd the total number of arrests were 387 in Lahore and 376 in other districts. The number of Khaksars who had publicly dissociated themselves from the movement was 2,126 up to that date.

2. Muslims have on the whole received the Privy Council judgement in the Shahidganj case with commendable restraint, and I have not noticed any objectionable articles in the press; but the excitement will begin, as I indicated in a previous letter, when the Sikhs start building on the site of the old mosque, and I received a report yesterday that plans for doing so are being considered.

3. The tension between the two rival groups in the Congress party remains as acute as ever. After Dr. Gopi Chand, the leader of the opposition in the Assembly, had resigned his seat one of the Akali members, Sampuran Singh, was elected to succeed him. His election is greatly resented by the minority group led by Dr. Satyapal and Diwan Chaman Lal, which broadly

speaking represents the Left Wing, on the ground that it will mean the control of Congress policy by the Akali group. Sampuran Singh, who was one of the Sikh representatives at the Round Table Conference, is a man of comparatively moderate views. I have known him for many years and have a low opinion of his intellectual capacity.

4. Developments in Norway during the first week in April caused great alarm and despondency and criticism of His Majesty's Government in the press was exceedingly outspoken, though not more so than that in some of the home newspapers. This set-back has unquestionably been a very severe blow to British prestige. The extremely grave situation caused by the invasion of Holland and Belgium is fully appreciated and the action of the Nazis universally and strongly condemned. There is general agreement that the danger to India itself is much more imminent and there is a demand for more vigorous steps to be taken to prepare India for her own defence. Gandhi's latest statement has been well received,[82] though he has been criticised by Muslim newspapers for his lack of courage in not advocating unconditional support for the Allies. Jawaharlal Nehru's statement,[83] on the other hand, has either been ignored or badly received by the press.

5. I have given my assent to 10 of the Bills passed during the last session of the Legislative Assembly. Three have been reserved for your consideration and to two of these your assent has been received. One Bill, the Punjab Relief of Indebtedness (Amendment) Bill, is still under my consideration. It will certainly have to be reserved, but I have not yet gone into the measure in detail or made up my mind whether it ought to receive assent in its present form. This Bill has been the subject of strong criticism from lawyers on the ground that it removes from the jurisdiction of the Civil Courts a very large class of cases which are now to be decided by Debt Conciliation Boards, before whom lawyers have no right to appear. A Bar Conference was held at Amritsar on the 27th and 28th of April which was attended by some 500 lawyers with the ex-Minister Sir Gokul Chand Narang in the chair. Among the resolutions passed at the Conference was one deciding that a deputation should wait on me, urging me to withhold my assent to this measure, and a few days ago I had a letter from Sir Gokul Chand asking me to receive such a deputation. I replied that I had not yet had time to study the Bill and that I was doubtful about the propriety of receiving a deputation, as the proper forum for the discussion of legislative measures is the Legislature itself. This reply was based on the view expressed in paragraph 8 of the Secretary of State's letter to you of September 30th, 1938, and paragraph 14 of your letter to me of April 29th, 1940. I have just received a further letter from Sir Gokul Chand

contesting the position taken in my letter to him, and I think I shall have eventually to give him an opportunity of stating his views to me, but I am not inclined to receive a formal deputation.

6. I have not seen any of my Ministers since I left Lahore a week ago and I do not think any of them have yet reached Simla. Sikander had intended to arrive here today or tomorrow but I hear he is down with an attack of diarrhoea and his doctors have advised him not to travel for the next two or three days.

7. I enclose the fortnightly report for the second half of April 1940.

Yours sincerely,
H.D. CRAIK

31

CRAIK TO LINLITHGOW[84]

Private and Personal
D.-O. No. 248-F.L.

Barnes Court, Simla,
May 29th, 1940

Dear Lord Linlithgow,

I have seen you so recently and talked to you so fully about Punjab affairs that I have little to report in this fortnightly letter.

2. The latest developments in France and Flanders have of course overshadowed everything else and have made Indians recognise the imminence of the menace to India herself. While there is considerable alarm and a very general demand for more active steps to be taken for the defence of India, I do not yet see any signs of panic, though a few districts report heavy withdrawals from the Savings Banks and in some places a tendency to demand rupees rather than currency notes. Enquiries are being made as to the extent of this movement, but I do not think it has yet reached anything like alarming proportions.

The tone of the press is as satisfactory as could be expected and in addition to the excellent public statements by the Premier many leading men have published statements exhorting all communities to sink their differences and to unite in the defence of their country and giving support to the Allies. Every post brings me numerous renewed offers of help and assurances of loyalty. Steps are being taken to increase the police forces.

3. I have kept you informed of recent developments as regards the Khaksars. There has recently been some det ioration, mainly owing to

infiltration into the Punjab of Khaksars from other provinces, who are pursuing the same tactics as their brethren in Lahore. A considerable number of Sindhis arrived in Multan, but were promptly dealt with by the local police, 16 being arrested inside a mosque and another party of 18 on their arrival in the town. At Rawalpindi there is a collection of some 50 or 60 from the North-West Frontier Province and in Hoshiarpur a number of Biharis have arrived and been giving trouble. There have also been some small demonstrations in the Gujrat and Sheikhupura districts.

In Lahore there are still about 200 Khaksars sheltering in various mosques and the last few days have seen some objectionable processions and demonstrations by students of the Islamia College and three or four local Muslim schools. All these institutions are under the management of the Anjuman-i-Himayat-i-Islam and that association has been called upon to show cause why the Government grant to the Islamia College should not be withheld. This will, I think, bring the management to their senses and the Deputy Commissioner[85] does not think that the student agitation will be maintained much longer. Nevertheless the situation in Lahore is still one of considerable embarrassment and the police are having a difficult time.

My latest figures for the total number of arrests are – in Lahore 509 and in other districts 439. The number of Khaksars who have forsworn the movement is now 2,431.

4. There have been no further developments about the Shahidganj judgement and allusions to this matter in the press are becoming less common. It is occasionally mentioned in the speeches delivered by Khaksars in the Lahore mosques.

5. I enclose the fortnightly report for the first half of May.

Yours sincerely,
H.D. CRAIK

32

CRAIK TO LINLITHGOW

Private and Personal
D.-O. No. 252-F.L.

Barnes Court, Simla,
June 14th, 1940

Dear Lord Linlithgow,

The principal local event since the date of my last fortnightly letter has been the very successful round-up of the Khaksars in the mosques at Lahore and Rawalpindi on the early morning of Tuesday last, the 11th of June. A full account of this has appeared in the newspapers and I have given you my own impressions orally. So I think it will suffice here to say that the operation was carried out with almost complete success in the sense that all the mosques in Lahore, with one small exception, were cleared of the Khaksars and that this object was attained with practically no bloodshed. Two hundred and seventy-six Khaksars were arrested in Lahore and of these only 14 were injured and are now in hospital. One Khaksar received fatal injuries, apparently in jumping out of a window to avoid arrest. I am glad to be able to report that the force of more than a thousand police who took part in the operation sustained only a few minor casualties. One officer, Morton, who was recently sent on a secret service mission to Egypt by the Defence Department, was savagely attacked by the Khaksars and received one or two minor injuries on his head and a compound fracture of the left elbow, but he is not in danger and is making good progress towards recovery. On the same night the Juma mosque at Rawalpindi was successfully raided and the majority of the Khaksars there, nearly all of whom came from the North-West Frontier Province, were arrested. A few who escaped were subsequently rounded up in the city. There were no casualties in Rawalpindi.

The success of these operations reflects the greatest credit on the police and, particularly on Orde, the Inspector-General, who personally worked out every detail of the plan of attack. It is most satisfactory that the arrests were carried out without causing bloodshed in the mosques, which was the one thing we were particularly anxious to avoid. This object was attained by the use of an overwhelming force of police and by the successful employment of tear-smoke.

The one mosque in Lahore that could not be cleared is surrounded by high houses and it was found that tear-smoke could not be effectively used till these houses had been evacuated. As the Tear Squad were urgently required for other mosques, the attempt to clear this mosque was abandoned for the moment, but I see from today's papers that it has now been evacuated by the Khaksars owing to pressure put on them by the local inhabitants. Some 30 or 40 local Khaksars have since the operations last Tuesday taken refuge in the Golden mosque, which has always been the principal scene of their activities, but I do not think they will remain there long, as popular sympathy with them seems to have declined, mainly owing to the success of the police action and partly also to the articles which have appeared in the press regarding the "Fifth Column" activities of the Khaksars generally.[86]

2. You will have seen the announcement in the press that Government have posted a force of 500 additional police at Lahore city for a period of one year. It has been announced that the cost of this force is to be recovered from all Muslim residents in the wallcd city, except those who have kept entirely aloof from the Khaksar agitation, and from those non-Muslims who have sympathised with the Khaksar movement or rendered assistance to it.

3. The firm action taken by Government has been generally welcomed and approved by the press. The commendation of the Hindu and Sikh press is unanimous, the only criticism being that the action should have been taken earlier. I have not yet myself seen the comments of the Muslim press, but I am told that these have been restrained in tone and have generally taken the line that the Khaksars have been "asking for it and have got it". The strong line taken by Government, together with the Premier's recent statement to the press, have tended to restore confidence in Lahore city and to allay the general feeling of communal unrest and panic. It is now generally recognised that Government is determined in these critical days to maintain internal peace and that they have the power to do so. In this connection I should mention that Government has decided to intern under the Defence of India Rules a considerable number of the more prominent communist and kisan agitators as well as a certain number of individuals with old terrorist connections. The majority of these are now, I believe, behind the bars.

4. In spite of the very grave news from the Western Front and Italy's entry into the war, I have the impression that the atmosphere of bewilderment and fear described in the first paragraph of the provincial report, which I enclose, has changed slightly for the better during the last few days. The run on banks has somewhat abated while the price of wheat has appreciated and that of gold has slightly fallen. These results are the effect, in my judgement, of the recent announcements about the formation of District War Committees and the Civic Guard, and about the contemplated increase in India's armed forces, though this increase has been generally criticized as inadequate. As you are aware, we have had District War Committees functioning in every district in the Punjab for some time, and I am going down to Lahore at the beginning of the next week to preside at the inaugural meeting of a Provincial War Board. I have invited about 150 leading men of the Province, representing all districts, interests and political parties, to serve on this Board, and practically all with the exception of a few Congressmen have accepted my

invitation. I do not think the Provincial War Board will really have much to do, as the District Committees will be the active war agency. But the Provincial Board will provide an opportunity for associating in our efforts some leading figures who might not take an active part in the more "official" local Committees.

5. I have had a preliminary discussion with my Ministers and certain senior officials regarding the formation of the Civic Guard and we were agreed in accepting practically all the proposals in this regard stated in the recent Home Department letter on the subject. I hope to have a further meeting while I am at Lahore with some senior district officers and high military officers, in which we shall discuss the matter in greater detail, and I hope that my Government will be in a position to make a public announcement regarding the scheme towards the end of next week. Sikander's general idea is to try and raise a force of about 30,000 strong, which would be roughly 1,000 for each district, with an additional force of 500 for each of our four or five principal cities. This is a somewhat ambitious scheme and the cost, even assuming the force is recruited on a purely voluntary and unpaid basis, will be considerable. But it will afford an admirable outlet for the energies of the very large number of persons who are genuinely anxious to assist in our war effort and should also have a valuable effect in the preservation of internal peace and especially in minimising the risk of communal disorder.

6. The *Satyagraha* Training Camp held at Lahore at the end of May is described in the provincial report. The attendance was very small and consisted almost entirely of office-bearers of the Congress. It included some 25 communists and many other people of communist sympathies paid visits to the camp. In spite of the publicity given to the camp by Jawaharlal Nehru's visit, the general public took practically no interest in it. I think it is safe to predict that the prospect of any effective civil disobedience movement in the Punjab is now remote.

7. I am leaving for Lahore, as already stated, on Monday next and shall stay there for four or five days. Apart from the inaugural meeting of the Provincial Board, I hope to have time to interview a number of leading men and I have no doubt that my Ministers, all of whom are coming down to Lahore, will do the same. The presence there of the whole Government should, I think, tend to restore public confidence and to discourage the forces which make for disunity.[87]

Yours sincerely,
H.D. CRAIK

33

CRAIK TO LINLITHGOW[88]

Secret
D.-O. No. 256

Government House, Lahore,
June 19th, 1940

Dear Lord Linlithgow,

I am writing in reply to your telegram of yesterday, No. 993-S, in which you asked to be kept in the closest possible touch with provincial reactions to the news of the French request for an armistice.[89] You will realise that my reply is largely based on my own personal impressions formed at Lahore. But I presided at a conference this morning, which was attended by the Deputy Commissioners of Amritsar[90] and Ferozepore[91] and the Commissioners of Multan,[92] Rawalpindi[93] and Jullundur,[94] besides the local Lahore officers. None of them had any particular reactions to report.

2. As regards the local press, the immediate impression in the Hindu papers, more particularly the *Milap* and the *Partap*, was one of despair. The Muslim papers take a stouter line and still believe in the ultimate success of Great Britain. The English press, i.e. the *Civil & Military Gazette* and the *Tribune*, are quite steady in tone. J.D. Anderson tells me that Churchill's speech[95] reported (in part) in this morning's papers is having a good effect even on the Hindus and he is trying to use it to keep them steady.

3. Apart from the press, the news that the French have asked for an armistice does not seem to have made any very marked difference in the internal situation, which was described in some detail in our last fortnightly report now being printed in Simla (if Laithwaite would ring up Wace,[96] D.I.G. of the Punjab C.I.D., he could secure an advance copy of this). The news that reached the Province on the night of the 17th took the form of a report that the French had actually surrendered, and I am informed that this caused great depression. Next morning, however, made it clear that the French had merely asked for a military armistice and that nothing had been settled, and this caused a swift reaction. Today again there is (I think) still greater confidence in Lahore as the result of our meeting last night at Government House for the inauguration of the Provincial War Board. This meeting was a really representative one and the proceedings were marked by enthusiasm and complete unanimity. The passages in my speech most loudly applauded were: (*a*) my assurance that the Provincial Government were fully determined and had the power to maintain internal order and

(*b*) my quotation of Churchill's announcement "we shall fight on unconquerably until the curse of Hitler is removed from the brows of men". I am doing my best by personal interviews and receiving deputations to reassure those who feel panicky.

4. As regards financial panic, the Manager of the Imperial Bank at Lahore reports today that there has been no important change in the last few days. Withdrawals of deposits continue but not on the same scale as previously. Changing of notes for silver also continues, but has been reduced by the fact that the price of silver has dropped.

5. You ask for daily reports covering the position in as much detail as possible for the next few days. These may be difficult to supply, as we depend for information mostly on weekly reports from district police; but I will undertake to keep you informed whenever there is any important change in the situation.

Yours sincerely,
H.D. CRAIK

34

CRAIK TO LINLITHGOW[97]

Government House, Lahore,
D.-O. No. 257 *June 20th, 1940*

Dear Lord Linlithgow,

I do not think I have anything material to report today about public reactions to the latest situation in Europe, but I have received from a good many people assurances that my speech and the Premier's on Tuesday night have had a good effect in allaying undue alarm. I took the opportunity, when addressing the meeting on Tuesday, of commending the Punjab press for its generally moderate and sensible attitude on the war, which, I said, had done much to steady public opinion. I think this expression of appreciation has had a good effect. This morning's *Tribune*, the paper with the largest circulation in Lahore, has a really admirable leading article on Churchill's House of Commons' speech.[98]

2. This morning I received a deputation of 7 or 8 of the great landholders of the western Punjab, Tiwanas and Noons of the Shahpur district and also Sir Muhammad Nawaz Khan of the Attock district. These gentlemen, whose loyalty is beyond all question, are very keen on being allowed to

raise at their own expense an irregular mobile force, as they did in the Mutiny, to repel possible invaders in the north-western Punjab, especially the three districts of Attock, Mianwali and Shahpur. In all these three districts there are innumerable places where troop-carrying aeroplanes could land and my friends undertake to raise a body of 2,000 men, about half of whom would be mounted, from their tenants and retainers to guard against such invaders. All the help they want from Government is arms, i.e. rifles and if possible a few light automatics. The force would not fit into our Civic Guard and would have to be under the command and at the disposal of the Army Commander.[99]

In my opinion we should gratefully accept this offer and I believe the Army Commander (with whom I had a long talk here) would agree. In these critical times we must put full confidence in our friends and I am absolutely convinced of the loyalty which has inspired this offer.

3. I also saw Nawab Sir Jamal Khan, the leading Tumandar in Dera Ghazi Khan. He too is very anxious to arm his tribesmen and asks for 2,000 rifles for the purpose. This is a more debatable proposal, on which I am not prepared to pronounce an opinion at the moment.

4. Today I gave a long interview to Raja Narendra Nath, who is perhaps the most respected Hindu citizen of Lahore. He and several other leading Hindus and Sikhs sent me a joint letter just before the War Board meeting, saying that they had certain "misgivings" which they would like to discuss with me, but which they did not intend to bring up at the meeting. His misgivings related mainly to communal questions and I think I was able to send him away reassured and happier.

5. I concluded a busy morning by receiving a deputation of five of the Lahore Muslim M.L.As. about the Khaksars. These gentlemen, who are all Sikander's political opponents, professed "to hold no brief for the Khaksars", but devoted more than an hour to attacking Government's policy towards them. They had some straight talking from Sikander, who was present, and also from Bourne, the Deputy Commissioner, and I wound up the proceedings by telling them quite plainly my own view of the Khaksar movement, its objects and methods, which seemed to startle them a good deal.

6. Many thanks for your private and personal letter of the 17th June, which I have just received. You mentioned in paragraph 3 of that letter the Muslim League's Bombay resolution[100] prohibiting Muslims from joining District War Committees, etc. This has been completely ignored by Punjab members of the Muslim League. Sikander is not only Chairman of our Provincial War Board (of which I am President), but is also Chairman of

two or three of its sub-committees. My other two Muslim Ministers are Vice-Chairmen and so is the Nawab of Mamdot, who is also Chairman of the Punjab Branch of the Muslim League. Many other members of the League have joined the Board and agreed to serve on sub-committees: so it is obvious that Jinnah's writ does not run in the Punjab and I fancy the final split between him and Sikander cannot be long delayed.

Yours sincerely,
H.D. CRAIK

NOTES

1. This letter is not included in R/3/1/61 (the volume of correspondence between Craik and Linlithgow for 1939).
2. See *P.P., 1936-1939*, No. 116.
3. Sir Bertrand Glancy was Political Adviser to the Crown Representative at this date.
4. See *P.P., 1936-1939*, Enclosure to No. 71.
5. Mr S.E. Abbott.
6. The Maharaja Jam Saheb of Nawanagar; Chancellor of the Chamber of Princes at this date.
7. Miss J.B. Allen.
8. A note of Lord Linlithgow's conversation with Sir Sikander on 25 January 1940 is printed in MSS. EUR. F 125/9, 2nd section, pp. 78-82. At the end of the conversation, Sir Sikander said that Sir Henry Craik was doing first-class work and he suggested that his term as Governor of the Punjab should be extended for a further year from the date of the conversation.
9. Mr W.D. Robinson.
10. Lord Linlithgow minuted: 'This is perhaps the most important bit of news that I have had since the leaders refused my offer.'
11. Lord Linlithgow minuted: 'P.S.V. – I had better wire to S./S. about this. I doubt if any one man can be both drummer for the minorities and Premier of the Punjab. But if the position at Home is at all wobbly at Home [*sic*] (which I doubt), I have no doubt that Sikander could do much to steady it.'
12. In his Statement 'India and the War' issued from New Delhi on 17 October 1939 (Cmd. 6121), Lord Linlithgow announced that he was authorised by the British Government to say that at the end of the war they would be very willing to enter into consultation with representatives of the several communities, parties and interests in India, and with the Indian Princes, with a view to securing their aid and co-operation in the framing of such constitutional modifications as might seem desirable. Lord Linlithgow also announced the immediate establishment of a consultative group, representative of all major political parties in British India, and of the Indian Princes, which would have as its object the association of public opinion in

India with the conduct of the war and questions relating to war activities.

13. Lord Linlithgow minuted: 'I suspect George Lloyd.'
14. Mir Maqbool Mahmud, Secretary to the Chancellor of the Chamber of Princes at this date.
15. See *P.P., 1936-1939*, No. 123, paragraph 4.
16. Lieutenant-Colonel C.M. Nicol.
17. Mr E.A.R. Eustace.
18. Mr J.W. Hearn, Commissioner of the Ambala Division.
19. The ownership of a ruined mosque within the confines of the Sikh gurdwara at Shahidganj in Lahore had been the subject of dispute (at times violent) between Muslims and Sikhs for many years. In January 1938 the Lahore High Court (in a majority verdict) ruled that the building was the absolute property of the Sikhs who were free to demolish it. The Muslims thereupon appealed to the Privy Council in London.
20. In his speech at Bombay on 10 January 1940, Lord Linlithgow repeated the offers already made for Indian constitutional advance including Dominion Status at the earliest possible date. The Viceroy reminded his listeners that the Indian States and minorities would not be ignored and that Government was determined to see justice done. Lord Linlithgow appealed again to the communities to reach an agreement.
21. Khan Bahadur Allah Bakhsh.
22. Since 1930 Congress had celebrated its aim of Purna Swaraj (complete independence) on 26 January.
23. The text of this document is taken from MSS. EUR. F 125/108.
24. This telegram asked for provincial and press reactions to the failure of Lord Linlithgow's discussions with Mahatma Gandhi on 5 February 1940. The Viceroy said that: 'Gandhi made it clear to me that Working Committee and Patel were strongly opposed to his renewing contact, and that Patel in particular had warned him immediately before the meeting to give nothing away.' Linlithgow added: 'It is in some ways more unfortunate that Congress should have been so unyielding in that this coincides with the public offers of Fazlul Huq and Sikander to consider coalition governments despite their objections to them as part of an all-India arrangement to ease the situation.' MSS.EUR.F 125/108.
25. As a result of voting which took place early in February 1940, Maulana Azad was elected President of the Indian National Congress. The election was to be effective from the date of the Ramgarh session on 20 March 1940.
26. Mr M. Sleem.
27. Mr A.A. Macdonald.
28. Mr P. Marsden.
29. In his letter D.-O. 211 of 28 January 1940, Sir Henry Craik forwarded to Lord Linlithgow a copy of a letter he had sent that day to Sir Robert Cassels. This followed a meeting between Craik and the Maharaja of Patiala on the

wearing of steel helmets by Sikh members of the Army. The Maharaja intended to persuade influential Sikhs to write to him supporting the wearing of such helmets by Sikhs. As soon as he had received a sufficient number of these letters, the Maharaja would be prepared to make a public statement saying that there could be no objection to Sikhs wearing steel helmets. In these circumstances, Craik felt the Commander-in-Chief should move slowly in this matter. R/3/1/62.

30. Not printed.
31. Dr Muhammad Musa Khan.
32. Dr Mathur Wazir Chand is listed as the District Medical Officer of Hissar at this time. It seems likely that two Additional District Medical Officers were appointed to deal with the famine emergency.
33. Dr Manjulal J.R. Thakor.
34. Not printed.
35. Mr A.A. Macdonald.
36. At its meeting held at Patna between 28 February and 1 March 1940, the Congress Working Committee passed a resolution declaring the determination of the Party to resort to civil disobedience unhesitatingly as soon as the organization was considered fit enough for it or 'in case circumstances so shaped themselves as to precipitate a crisis'. The resolution added that 'nothing short of complete independence can be accepted by the people of India.' The Patna resolution was reaffirmed by the All-Indian National Congress at its session at Ramgarh on 20 March 1940.
37. Not printed.
38. Mr E.M. Jenkins.
39. General Sir Roger Wilson.
40. Not printed.
41. Not printed.
42. Sardar Abdus Samad Khan.
43. Mr R.S. Lala Amar Nath.
44. The texts of Sir Henry Craik's telephone message to Mr. Laithwaite and of Laithwaite's reply have not been traced.
45. Sir Douglas Young.
46. Not printed. Sir Henry Craik suggested to Sir Sikander that it would have a most reassuring effect on public opinion if he could announce at once that it was the intention to set up complete, fully equipped and trained tear-smoke squads in several of the big cities. Craik felt there should be permanent squads in Lahore, Amritsar, Multan and possibly Rawalpindi. R/3/1/62.
47. Not printed.
48. The resolution passed by the All-India Muslim League on 24 March 1940, during its session at Lahore, became a milestone on the road to Pakistan. It read in part:

   'Resolved that it is the considered view of this Session of the All-India Muslim

League that no constitutional plan would be workable in this country or acceptable to the Muslims unless it is designed on the following basic principle, viz., that geographically contiguous units are demarcated into regions which should be so constituted with such territorial readjustments as may be necessary that the areas in which the Muslims are numerically in a majority, as in the north-western and eastern zones of India, should be grouped to constitute "independent States" in which the constituent units shall be autonomous and sovereign....'

In a later paragraph the resolution authorized the League Working Committee 'to frame a scheme of constitution in accordance with these basic principles, providing for the assumption finally by the respective regions of all powers such as defence, external affairs, communications, customs and such other measures as may be necessary.'

49. Not printed.
50. Sir Maurice Hallett was Governor of the United Provinces at this date.
51. In paragraph 4 of his letter 227 of 29 March 1940, Sir Henry Craik wrote: 'Sikander seemed fairly pleased with the result of the adjournment motion discussion in our Assembly [on the Khaksar episode] when the Ministry secured a majority of more than 2:1.' R/3/1/62.
52. Mr P. Marsden.
53. The text of this document is taken from MSS.EUR.F 125/108.
54. In his lengthy telegram 470-G of 29 March 1940, Lord Linlithgow asked for a general indication of Governors' views on the current situation in the light of recent political developments.

In paragraphs 3-5 of this telegram, Linlithgow said that he felt the general situation, in terms of a possible constitutional settlement, had definitely deteriorated since his interview with Mahatma Gandhi on 5 February. Linlithgow did not take too seriously Jinnah's claim for a partitioning of India though the rank and file members of the League were increasingly attracted by the partition proposals. It was clear that Government could not now accept the Congress claim to speak for India as a whole. As regards the Congress Patna/Ramgarh resolution on civil disobedience, Government must carefully consider the reaction of threats of this character on its relations with Congress. It must also consider whether it should continue to refrain from taking action against Congress.

In paragraph 8 of his telegram, Linlithgow asked for Governors' views on the wisdom of a clear indication then to Congress (*a*) that civil disobedience would not be permitted in war and/or (*b*) that if Congress continued active preparations for civil disobedience, appropriate action would be taken against them. Linlithgow was inclined to give a broad hint along the lines of (*a*) but was more doubtful about (*b*).

In paragraph 9 of his telegram, Linlithgow said he felt Congress were not really too happy. Their claim to speak for India as a whole grew more insubstantial every day and the unreality of the demand for complete independence was becoming more patent. However any direct challenge from Government would give Congress something to rally round. It was important for overseas reasons to make it clear that it was not the British Government, but intrinsically Indian considerations and elements, that stood in the way of constitutional advance.

In paragraph 13 of the telegram, Linlithgow said he knew there was a view in many quarters that if the British Government came out against the Congress, there might be some hope of more effective opposition to Congress claims consolidating in the ex-Congress provinces. There was a further argument that if the British did nothing, persons well-disposed to them in the minorities or even in Congress might misunderstand their position. The Viceroy was not convinced by the first argument and did not attach undue weight to the second. MSS. EUR. F 125/108.

55. It is clear from papers in the Moon Collection at the British Library (IOR: MSS. EUR. F 230/39 and 46) that this Enclosure was drafted by Mr Moon and was sent substantially in the form in which it was drafted.
56. Not printed.
57. Sir Maurice Hallett was Governor of the United Provinces and Sir Lancelot Graham was Governor of Sind at this date.
58. Not printed.
59. Not printed.
60. Not printed.
61. This relates to the first two sentences of paragraph 5 of Sir Sikander's letter reproduced as the Enclosure to the present document.
62. This relates to the penultimate sentence of paragraph 5 of Sir Sikander's letter.
63. Mr M. Sleem.
64. Mr Monir Mohammad.
65. Mr J.A. Scroggie.
66. Syed Sayad Ahmed Shah.
67. Not printed.
68. See No. 25, paragraph 2.
69. Malik Noon Sahib Khan.
70. On 13 April 1940, Sir Henry Craik had written to Sir George Cunningham asking him to take all possible steps to prevent any influx of Khaksars into the Punjab even if this necessitated using the Defence of India Rules.

    In his reply of 15 April Cunningham said that he was proposing to arrest immediately Arbab Sher Akbar Khan the real leader of the Khaksars in the N.-W.F.P. He would detain three further leaders if there was any sign that they, or a sizeable number of Khaksars, were about to go into the Punjab. R/3/1/62.
71. Mr P.L. Orde.

72. Not printed.
73. The telegram enclosed, dated 22 April 1940, was from Atul Singh. It gave details of a secret meeting believed to have been held the previous night in Peshawar. Six hundred Khaksars were reported to be ready to make their way into the Punjab on various routes.

    In his letter of 23 April Sir Henry Craik hoped that Sir George Cunningham would do his best to paralyse, as far as possible, the Khaksar organization in the N.-W.F.P. R/3/1/62.
74. The text of this document is taken from MSS. EUR. F 125/108.
75. In this telegram Lord Linlithgow informed Governors, in a preliminary and personal way, how he viewed the position regarding a Congress campaign of civil disobedience.

    Paragraph 3 of the telegram read: 'I have in this connection asked my Advisers to consider the desirability of: (*a*) (this has been urged on me from certain press quarters) declaring as an offence against the law any reference in a newspaper or in press telegrams to civil disobedience as such; (*b*) active steps to intercept or delay or suppress communications in connection with a civil disobedience campaign passing between persons engaged in civil disobedience, whether by post or by telegram; (*c*) strict censorship both internal and external; (*d*) further and more stringent use of what I may call standstill orders, i.e. orders for local internment or of confinement to a particular village or area irrespective of the standing of the person concerned.'

    In paragraph 5, Linlithgow said it was essential they should be prepared well ahead with lists of offices to be raided, of persons to be locally interned or arrested, of the whereabouts of bank deposits, and the like. MSS.EUR.F 125/108.
76. Writing in the *Harijan* for 27 April 1940 under the caption 'Civil Disobedience', Mahatma Gandhi declared that as far as he could see at present, mass civil disobedience was most unlikely because in the face of the lawlessness that prevailed in the country, civil disobedience would easily pass for lawlessness.
77. This telegram is not included in R/3/1/62.
78. See No. 26, note 73.
79. With his letter of 5 May 1940 to Sir George Cunningham; Sir Henry Craik enclosed a translation of a letter from Dr Kazami to Arbab Sher Akbar Khan of Tekhal sent on 2 May. In his letter Dr Kazami envisaged an influx of Khaksars into Lahore from the N.-W.F.P. and their despatch from Lahore to other places in the Punjab. R/3/1/62.
80. Early in May 1940, the Judicial Committee of the Privy Council had confirmed the Sikhs' ownership of the site containing the Shahidganj mosque. India Office papers on this subject are on L/P&J/7/886.
81. Sir Henry Craik provided Lord Linlithgow with the promised statistics on the Khaksars in his letter 245 of 6 May 1940. Of the 32 Khaksars killed on

19 March, 4 were from the N.-W.F.P. but many of the dead were not identified. On the same day, 109 arrested Khaksars were from the N.-W.F.P. out of a total number of arrests given in the press as 217. Between 20 March and 5 May, 71 of the arrested Khaksars were from the N.-W.F.P. out of a total number of arrests estimated at 736. R/3/1/62.

82. See No. 28, note 76. In the same issue of *Harijan* (27 April 1940), Mahatma Gandhi reproduced an interview he had granted the *New York Times*. In this he said: 'The legal status of India, whether it is Dominion Status or some thing else, can only come after the war.... The only question is what is the British policy? Does Great Britain still hold the view that it is her sole right to determine the status of India or whether it is the sole right of India to make that determination.'
83. Pandit Nehru in a speech in Poona on 6 May 1940 said that neither the Muslim League nor the Hindu Mahasabha had a positive programme. Nehru characterised the Pakistan scheme as foolish, declaring that it would not last 24 hours. Besides it was highly anti-national and pro-imperialist which no freedom-loving man would accept.
84. This Report is not included in R/3/1/62 and the text has been taken from L/P&J/5/243: ff 175-7.
85. Mr F.C. Bourne.
86. On 15 June 1940, Sir Henry Craik sent Lord Linlithgow a telegraphic report received from Mr J.T.M. Bennett [Deputy Inspector-General of Police (C.I.D.)]. This report began: 'The situation in the Lahore city was very satisfactory and in fact was considerably better than it had been for weeks. The police are now definitely on top....' R/3/1/62.
87. No fortnightly letter was sent at the end of June 1940 as Sir Henry Craik was confined to bed with lumbago. Moon to Laithwaite, 1 July 1940. L/P&J/5/243: f 148.
88. This letter is not included in R/3/1/62 and the text has been taken from L/P&J/5/243: ff 169-70.
89. This letter, and the following letter, appear to have been the only situation reports sent in response to Lord Linlithgow's request.
90. Mr A.A. Macdonald.
91. Mr M.R. Sachdev.
92. Mr C.V. Salusbury.
93. Mr P. Marsden.
94. Mr E. Sheepshanks.
95. This was the famous Parliamentary statement which Mr Churchill concluded with the words: '... the "Battle of France" is over. I expect the battle of Britain is about to begin.... Let us therefore brace ourselves to our duty and so bear ourselves that if the British Commonwealth and Empire lasts for a thousand years men will still say, "This was their finest hour."' *Parl. Debs.*, 5th ser., H. of C. (18 June 1940), Vol. 362, cols. 51-61.

96. The Civil Lists throughout 1940 show that Mr Wace was in fact Deputy Inspector-General of Police for the Central Range of the Punjab.
97. This letter is not included in R/3/1/62 and the text has been taken from L/P&J/5/243: ff 171-2.
98. See No. 33, note 95.
99. General Sir John Coleridge, General Officer Commanding-in-Chief, Northern Command.
100. Passed by the Muslim League Working Committee at its meeting at Bombay on 17 June 1940. At the same meeting the Committee recommended that every Provincial Muslim League should organize regular bands of volunteers to be known as Muslim League National Guards. Sir Sikander Hyat Khan was present at the meeting.

CHAPTER 2

Documents for July-December 1940

35

CRAIK TO LINLITHGOW[1]
Express Letter

Immediate
No. 10-G

Barnes Court, Simla,
July 4th, 1940

As I told Your Excellency orally, my first reaction to news contained in your telegram No. 1185-S., dated the 1st July 1940,[2] was that we should leave Congress out of account and go ahead on the lines of Jinnah's offer; but Jinnah's letter, the substance of which you communicated in your subsequent telegram of July 2nd,[3] entirely alters the situation. His demands, especially (*b*) and (*c*) are altogether extravagant and "usurious". Demand (*c*) is contrary to all democratic cannons and would, if conceded, put Jinnah more or less in a position of a "dictator". For Muslim League executive is, I believe, nominated by him and most of them are men with little stake in country coming from Provinces where Muslims are in a minority. They really represent very little. Several of the nominees from the Punjab are mere men of straw and political opponents of Sikander. If, as seems probable, Jinnah's real object is to secure a monopoly of power for himself and his caucus both at the Centre and in the Section 93 Provinces, a bargain with him on these lines might actually have the effect of weakening and discouraging those elements in the country which really desire to sink political issues and stand together with us in the face of the present dangers.

In the circumstances I agree with Your Excellency that you should come back at Jinnah at once and point out to him that his new proposals are in certain respects quite unacceptable.

2. It looks as though the attempt to secure the co-operation of the

Congress or the Muslim League will have to be regarded as a failure. At the same time there is an obvious and pressing need for some action which will hearten the very considerable number of people in this country to help, and will give them a real share in the shaping of war policy.

3. The Governments of two major Provinces (Bengal and Punjab) and two minor Provinces (Assam and Sind) are already co-operating. Perhaps therefore a possible course would be to give representatives of these Governments places on Your Excellency's Council. Seeing that they would be the nominees of popularly elected Governments, this would be a means of giving popular representatives some voice in the general conduct of the war. It might be possible to add representatives of special communities, e.g. orthodox Hindus, Sikhs, or Depressed Classes, who would be willing to co-operate.

4. It is also for consideration whether some further declaration should not be made on behalf of His Majesty's Government on the lines sketched by Your Excellency in your talks with Gandhi. Presumably some statement will have to be published by Your Excellency regarding these talks, and I venture to think (despite Gandhi's opposition to such a course) that this statement should explain the nature of the offer made and include a pronouncement regarding His Majesty's Government's attitude towards India's political future. I believe Sikander is in favour of a pronouncement such as you outlined to Gandhi, and it might possibly be encouraging to those moderate elements who feel that India's fate is bound up with Britain's, but who are still doubtful about Britain's political intentions.

H.D. CRAIK
Governor of the Punjab

36

MOON TO LAITHWAITE

Secret
[Unnumbered] *July 6th, 1940*

My dear Laithwaite,

His Excellency had some talk with Sikander this morning regarding Fazl-ul-Huq's visit to Simla, and he has asked me to convey to you the gist of it.

Fazl-ul-Huq, it seems, had hurried up to Simla, as he was alarmed at the possible turn that Jinnah's conversations with the Viceroy might have taken, especially as Jinnah himself had remained absolutely silent.

Fazl-ul-Huq and Sikander have now sent a joint letter to Jinnah, reminding him that at the recent meeting of the Muslim League he had simply been authorised to discuss matters of principle with the Viceroy and not to enter into details. The two points which he was to make to the Viceroy were: (1) that Muslims should be given an assurance that they would not be let down in regard to any future constitution for India; (2) that whatever Congress might decide, Muslims should be given an opportunity of co-operating with Government in the prosecution of the war.

They went on to say that they were disturbed at his silence and that unless he came out pretty soon with a clear statement that the Muslim League were ready to offer their co-operation, the position of Muslims in Bengal and the Punjab would become very difficult. In other words, they seem to have hinted fairly clearly that they might break with him. They also indicated that he ought not, by entering into matters of detail, e.g. the persons to be taken on the Viceroy's Council, bring about a breakdown in the discussions with the Viceroy.

2. Though this is a somewhat different matter, His Excellency thinks it worth mentioning that Sikander expressed considerable doubt whether Jinnah was right in suggesting that the Akalis would break with the Congress and co-operate. If the Akalis were really ready to do this, Sikander said that he would be prepared to take an Akali leader (Sardar Sampuran Singh) into his Cabinet and release Sir Sundar Singh Majithia to be the Sikh representative on the Viceroy's Council.

Yours sincerely,
E.P. MOON

37

CRAIK TO LINLITHGOW

Private and Personal
D.-O. No. 278-F.L.

Barnes Court, Simla,
July 16th, 1940

Dear Lord Linlithgow,

With this letter I enclose the Provincial fortnightly report for the second half of June, the first paragraph of which paints a somewhat gloomy picture of the reactions in the Province to the War situation. I have, however, within the last day or two seen later reports from all districts, nearly all to the effect that the panic caused by our reverses in Europe has distinctly abated and that signs of defeatism are less apparent. This improvement is attributed to the following causes:

(*a*) the stern action taken to prevent the French Fleet from falling into the hands of our enemies, which has been received everywhere with warm commendation and hailed as our first substantial success since the War started;
(*b*) Churchill's recent reassuring and courageous announcements;
(*c*) the arrival of the monsoon, which means that in rural areas people are now busy ploughing and have something to occupy them other than speculation as to the War;
(*d*) the firm action taken by the Provincial Government to check internal disorder and more particularly the very successful round-up of the Khaksars in the middle of June and the recent arrests of 84 dangerous communist and kisan agitators;
(*e*) the establishment of the Provincial War Board and intensification of the efforts of District War Committees in regard to propaganda and countering false rumours;
(*f*) the announcement regarding the establishment of the Civic Guard;
(*g*) the measures announced for the expansion of the fighting forces and the provision of munitions.

2. Gandhi's recent pronouncements, and more particularly his advice that both Great Britain and India should rely solely on non-violence in meeting the attacks of our enemies, have provoked a great deal of unfavourable comment and a certain amount of ridicule even in the Hindu nationalist press which, as a rule, never dares to indulge in any kind of criticism of the Mahatma. There is very little sympathy too with his demand for a declaration of complete independence as the price of Congress co-operation, and I am convinced that the great mass of thinking opinion in the country is eager to help in all War measures. Indeed, I think I am right in saying that Gandhi's stock is at the present moment lower than it has been for years.

3. All my Ministers are at the moment in Lahore for a special session of the Legislative Assembly. The Opposition asked the Premier to have the Assembly summoned in order that the recent arrests of communists, who include five Sikh members of that Assembly, might be discussed. The

Premier in agreeing to hold a session for this purpose stipulated (at my suggestion) that it would have to be a secret session, as it was not possible for him to make public the details or sources of the information on which it was decided to make these arrests. He also out-manoeuvred the Opposition by getting his own party to table a motion approving the action of Government in making these arrests and expressing confidence in Government, and it was this motion that was debated yesterday. I have not at the moment heard whether the debate was concluded yesterday or whether it was adjourned to today, but I think there is no doubt that the Ministerial motion will be carried by a large majority.

4. Sikander has taken the opportunity of this brief visit to the plains to hold several public meetings in the Jullundur and Jhelum districts. These were, I understand, attended by very large audiences and marked by great enthusiasm to co-operate in all War efforts. The Premier has made some stirring speeches and has expressed his determination to deal sternly with any kind of internal disorder. He also announced his intention of himself joining the Civic Guard. Sir Chhotu Ram also recently had one or two successful meetings in other districts.

5. Although, as I have stated above, what one may describe as "war panic" has considerably subsided, the situation as regards communal unrest has, I regret to say, deteriorated. The feeling between Sikhs and Muhammadans is at the moment very intense and there have been two incidents lately, which might, if they had not been carefully handled, have led to communal rioting on a disastrous scale. The first of these took place at Sargodha, the headquarters of the Shahpur district, on the 7th of July. Moon has sent Laithwaite a copy of the communiqué issued by the Commissioner[4] describing this incident. It is somewhat unfortunate that both the Deputy Commissioner[5] and the Superintendent of Police[6] in this district are Muhammadans, a combination which we always do our best to avoid but which was forced on us in the present case owing to the paucity of British officers. I am afraid there is still a good deal of uneasiness among the Hindus and Sikhs of Sargodha.

The second incident took place at Gujranwala on the 13th of July. It appears that a Muhammadan fanatic attacked with a knife a prominent local Sikh, who was a member of the Punjab Provincial Congress Committee, and inflicted injuries on him which eventually proved fatal. After making this attack the Muhammadan attacked a group of Sikhs outside a shop, but was himself killed by them. In this district too the Deputy Commissioner[7] is a Muslim: he seems to have handled the situation promptly and efficiently and my information is that it is now well in hand.

6. The Khaksars have now faded almost entirely out of the picture. It was reported in the press the other day that Dr. Muhammad Ismail Nami, one of the two men who have been organizing the agitation from behind the scenes and whom we have been trying to arrest for some time, had appealed to Jinnah to "open negotiations for a settlement" with the Punjab Government. Jinnah agreed to do this and Nami (whose whereabouts are still unknown) thereupon announced in the press that the Khaksars were to suspend all demonstrations till July the 27th. When I saw this announcement about Jinnah opening negotiations, I wrote to Sikander (who was then away from Simla) and expressed the hope that he would not agree to any relaxation of the conditions on which he announced some months ago that he would be prepared to withdraw the order declaring the Khaksars an unlawful association. Sikander replied to me in a letter of the 13th of July stating that he had not yet had any approach from Jinnah. He added "his (Jinnah's) two statements issued from Simla and Bombay during the last week were most inopportune and, I suspect, were deliberately made to create mischief in order to give a fillip to the movement, which had practically died out. There is of course no intention of making a departure from the conditions already laid down for rescinding the order of the 19th of March."

I rather doubt whether Jinnah has any serious intention of taking up the cudgels on behalf of the Khaksars.

7. The position as regards the Muslim League's ban on any of its members joining the War Committees is still obscure. I have not yet heard that any Muslim Leaguers, who had joined the Provincial or District Committees, have sent in their resignations. Today it is reported in the press that the Working Committee of the Punjab Provincial League met yesterday at the residence of the Nawab of Mamdot, who is its President, and decided by a majority to send a deputation of three of its members, including the Nawab himself, to wait on Jinnah "to explain to him the peculiar position in the Punjab and to request him to reconsider the resolution banning members of the Muslim League from joining the War Board or its Committees". The Deputy Commissioner of Amritsar[8] reported that a meeting of the City Muslim League of that city held recently with Shaikh Sadiq Hasan, one of the local M.L.As., in the chair unanimously passed a resolution supporting the decision of the All-India Muslim League that members of the League should not join the War Committees. In spite of this Shaikh Sadiq Hasan, who is a member of the District War Committee, is continuing his work on that Committee! I have myself little doubt that very few of our Muslims who have joined the War

Committees will resign from those bodies even if Jinnah refuses to modify his attitude. I fancy that a final rupture between Jinnah and Sikander cannot now be long delayed, and it is possible that this question may be made the occasion for it.

Yours sincerely,
H.D. CRAIK

38

CRAIK TO LINLITHGOW

Private and Personal
D.-O. No. 283-F.L.

Barnes Court, Simla,
July 31st, 1940

Dear Lord Linlithgow,

Reports from districts regarding the restoration of confidence as to the issue of the war continue to be reassuring. I have recently read interesting reports from Deputy Commissioners of all districts regarding the work of their War Committees, which I think is of real value particularly in allaying panic and contradicting false rumours. The Sub-Committees of the Provincial War Board are also showing commendable activity and the response to the appeal for the War Purposes Fund is distinctly satisfactory. Subscriptions to the Defence Loans are, however, considerably less than I would have liked, and although an excellent example has been shown by Government servants of all classes in this respect and also by leading landowners, the moneyed and commercial classes are still holding aloof from the loan, partly I think owing to lack of confidence in the future and partly perhaps owing to general trade depression. But more strenuous efforts are now being made to encourage subscriptions to the loan.

The Deputy Commissioner of Lahore mentions a curious incident. The landowners of a certain village declined to pay their land revenue demand, saying that they would pay it in due course to the Germans. Lahore is, however, a district which has always been notorious for difficulties in collecting this demand and the Deputy Commissioner says that the attitude of these villagers was in no way typical of public opinion. This is corroborated by the fact that in the Kasur Sub-Division of that district a sum of Rs. 80,000 has already been collected for the War Purposes Fund, as much as Rs. 3,000 being subscribed at each of several village meetings.

2. Although there has been no further serious communal incident since

the date of my last letter (July the 16th), tension between Muslims and Sikhs is still extreme and the resentment caused by the recent incidents at Sargodha and Gujranwala is only slowly subsiding. My Ministers have taken various steps recently with the object of preventing communal clashes. Some time ago they passed an order under the Defence of India Rules, prohibiting the carrying of arms or articles capable of being used as arms in processions. Within the last day or two they have passed a further order under Rule 56 of the same Rules prohibiting all processions other than funeral or marriage processions, the customary periodical religious processions and processions duly licensed under the Police Act. The object of this order is to stop processions of a political or communal character, which so often lead to communal clashes. District Magistrates have also been instructed to raid and search any place in which they have good reason to believe that illicit arms are stored and to seize any arms so found. The District Magistrates of Lahore and Amritsar, where drilling by communal volunteer corps is most common, have been instructed to warn the organizers of those bodies that any such drill of a military character, even if it takes place in private premises, is a violation of the recent general prohibition on drilling; and that if such drilling continues, the Deputy Commissioners will have no option but to take action against the organizers. A warning on these lines conveyed by the District Magistrate of Lahore to the Congress volunteer[s] has led to the suspension of drilling for the present. I have not yet heard of the reactions in Amritsar.

3. It is reported that the Punjab Provincial Congress Committee has after prolonged deliberation informed the All-India Congress Committee that the next session of the Congress cannot be held in the Punjab unless sufficient funds are provided from the Centre. The usual practice is that the Province in which the session is held has to meet all the expenses, whereas any profits from tickets of admission, &c., go to the Central Committee.

4. The Khaksars have been completely quiet during the last fortnight, but some of the convicted prisoners in the Multan District Jail have recently given a good deal of trouble and were inclined to be violent. They were, however, firmly dealt with and the incident has not been reported in the papers. Jinnah has not, so far as I am aware, yet made any approach to Sikander regarding a settlement of the Khaksar issue.

The Khaksar newspaper *Al-Islah*, continues to be published from Calcutta, edited (and apparently mainly written) by the notorious Dr. Muhammad Ismail Nami, the man whom we have been trying to arrest for the last few months and who approached Jinnah to open negotiations. A recent issue which I saw contained much vilification of Sikander and innumerable references to "the sacred blood of the Khaksar martyrs", &c. My Government addressed the Bengal Government some time ago regarding the desirability of taking security from this paper, but have hitherto had no reply.

5. I am glad to say that we have had excellent rain practically all over the Province. The greater part of the Hissar district had a particularly good and timely fall a few days ago and with ordinary luck this should mean the end of the famine, which has put such a tremendous strain on our finances during the last two years.

6. I enclose the fortnightly report for the first half of July.

Yours sincerely,
H.D. CRAIK

39

CRAIK TO LINLITHGOW

Secret

Barnes Court, Simla,
July 31st, 1940

Dear Lord Linlithgow,

Two days ago three of my officers – Penny (Chief Secretary), Anderson (Joint Chief Secretary) and Bennett (Head of the C.I.D.) – attended by invitation a conference at A.H.Q. about the recent Central India Horse incident. The Adjutant-General[9] presided and I understand several other Staff Officers were present. Yesterday afternoon Sikander and I discussed with these three officers the proceedings of the Conference and I enclose a note written by Anderson of those proceedings.

2. It seems that very little is known of the causes which led to this deplorable incident but we have sent a Sikh Deputy Superintendent of Police to Bolarum at the request of A.H.Q. to help in the interrogation of the mutineers, and I expect that the background of the affair will eventually be cleared up.

3. Meanwhile I consider that for the reasons set forth in paragraph (2) of Anderson's note it is essential that no general orders, e.g. for the stoppage or drastic curtailment of Sikh recruitment, should be passed without consultation with the Punjab Government or without your approval. I say this because my officers present at the Conference received the

impression that it was possible that A.H.Q. might pass such orders and merely send them to us for information. Any precipitate action of this kind might have disastrous consequences.

4. Sikander made a suggestion that a meeting of Sikh leaders should be summoned, either by you or by myself, and the whole position as regards these recent incidents put before them, together with a clear explanation of the reactions which these incidents must have on the recruitment of Sikhs and therefore on the economic interests and position of the whole Sikh community. I would be prepared, subject of course to your approval, to act on this suggestion but obviously I cannot do so at [the] moment:

(*a*) because both the recent C.I.H. incident and previous similar incidents have hitherto been kept completely secret; and
(*b*) because the causes leading up to the C.I.H. mutiny have not yet been ascertained.

Yours sincerely,
H.D. CRAIK

P.S. – You will appreciate my reasons for writing this in my own hand, and for sending on Anderson's note in original. I am keeping no copy of this letter or the note.

ENCLOSURE TO NO. 39

NOTE BY ANDERSON

July 30th, 1940

The conference held on 29th July 1940 at A.H.Q. to discuss the situation arising out of the recent desertions by Sikhs.

(1) A. G.'s points were:

(*i*) it is no longer possible to be certain that any Sikhs ordered overseas will not on arrival at the port refuse to embark;
(*ii*) the trouble is mainly due to bad influences in their homes. (But the feeling among the soldiers at the meeting seemed to be that on account of the notorious badness of the B.Os. in the C.I.H., it would be difficult to shoot any of the mutineers);
(*iii*) the position in the Punjab is such – private armies, Khaksars, universal armament and politics in general that Sikh soldiers take

the line: "We are not going overseas to a war which is not our own, but shall stay in India to fight our own war with the Muslims." Muslim soldiers are beginning to say: "Why should we go overseas, and weaken our strength in comparison with the Sikhs who refuse to go."

(*iv*) therefore it is useless to recruit men who are not trustworthy. Recruitment of Sikhs for M.T. and similar corps should stop at once, and though Sikh recruitment in the old regiments will continue, there will be none in the new battalions. The responsibility for recruiting is A.G.'s alone and he cannot divest himself of it.

(2) My objection to the conclusion is that assuming (1) (*iii*) to be true, the action proposed to be taken in (1) (*iv*) may have very much greater results than a change in the composition of the Indian Army. If the opinion of the serving soldiers of both communities has been rightly described, the step proposed might lead to communal disturbance on the scale of civil war. The matter cannot be decided by A.G.'s fiat, and in particular there must be preliminary discussion with the Punjab Government – not only with officers of it summoned by telephone – and no orders can be passed without the concurrence of the Punjab Government. Serious as the state of the Sikh soldiers is, armed rebellion – whether communal or not – in the Punjab would be far more serious for the Empire.

(3) We do not yet know the full facts of the C.I.H. mutiny, or of the desertions from other units which have followed it. A preliminary report about the mutiny was read at the meeting, but some of the conclusions set forth in it were rejected by all present as patently impossible.

J.D. ANDERSON
30.7.[19]40

40

CRAIK TO LINLITHGOW

Secret and Personal
D.-O. No. 284

Barnes Court, Simla,
August 6th, 1940

Dear Lord Linlithgow,

Will you please refer to Moon's letter to Laithwaite of July the 6th, which gave an account of a joint letter sent about that date by Fazlul Huq and

Sikander to Jinnah regarding the course of negotiations between Jinnah and yourself.

2. Sikander came to see me this morning, after he had seen the announcement made by the A.P.I., that you are to give Jinnah an interview on the 12th of August at Bombay, and asked me to convey to you the message contained in the following paragraphs.

3. Sikander had a telephone message yesterday from Bombay from Syed Abdul Aziz, who was recently a Minister in Bihar and is now a Minister in Hyderabad State. Abdul Aziz saw Jinnah a day or two ago in Bombay and told him that there was much uneasiness in League circles in the United Provinces and Bihar, because it is believed that the negotiations between yourself and Jinnah are being unnecessarily prolonged on the question of personalities, i.e. on the question of individuals to be invited to join the Central and Provincial administrations. Abdul Aziz told Jinnah that the general feeling among Muslims was that Jinnah was only to discuss questions of principle during these negotiations and not matters of detail.

4. At this point I asked Sikander what exactly was meant by "questions of principle" and he replied that the two important points of principle were as, stated in Moon's letter to Laithwaite of July the 6th:

(1) that Muslims should be given an assurance that they would not be let down in regard to any future Constitution for India

(2) that even if the Congress finally decides not to co-operate, Muslims should be given an opportunity of co-operating with Government in the prosecution of the War and should be invited to join the Central and Provincial administrations.

According to Sikander the mandate given to Jinnah by the Working Committee's meeting at Bombay about the middle of June was that he should negotiate with you on these two points of principle, and it was understood that if satisfactory assurances were received by him on these two points, he was then to issue a further statement asking Muslims to give Government their wholehearted support in the prosecution of the War. No such statement has yet been issued by Jinnah and according to Sikander "the Muslim world is now being misled by Jinnah's henchmen into thinking that satisfactory assurances on these two points of principle have not in fact been forthcoming."

5. The telephone message from Syed Abdul Aziz to Sikander went on to state that Jinnah assured Abdul Aziz that he (Jinnah) would not press in his negotiations with you his proposal that the Muslim League should be

allowed to nominate the individuals to serve on the Central or Provincial Governments and would only ask for assurances in regard to the two points of principle stated above.

6. Sikander is evidently doubtful whether Jinnah will at his forthcoming interview with you take the line which he promised Abdul Aziz that he would take, i.e., whether he will confine his demands to the two points of principle. If in the event you find yourself in a position to concede these two points and if Jinnah in spite of this is still obdurate and shows an inclination to prolong negotiations on matters of detail or in regard to personalities, then Sikander suggested that you should authorize him (Sikander) to announce to Muslims that the two main points of principle had been conceded; and in that event Sikander would be prepared immediately to call on Muslims to co-operate actively in the War.

I pointed out to Sikander that his suggestion in effect amounted to this that in case Jinnah's attitude at your forthcoming interview turns out to be unsatisfactory, you should break off negotiations with him and substitute Sikander for Jinnah as the representative of Muslim opinion generally. I feel that Sikander realises that this course may be difficult, but he thinks that Muslims are becoming extremely restive about the prolongation of the negotiations and Jinnah's failure to give them a lead regarding co-operation in the War.

Sikander is leaving Simla this afternoon and will attend the funeral at Luddan in the Multan district tomorrow of one of his principal supporters, Khan Bahadur Mian Ahmad Yar Khan, who has just died at Karachi. After this ceremony he returns for a few days to Lahore, where his address is "98, The Mall". He will be away from Simla for about a week.

Yours sincerely,
H.D. CRAIK

41

CRAIK TO LINLITHGOW[10]
Telegram

Personal and Secret
No. 12-G *August 9th, 1940*

Your telegram No. 482.[11] The best Indian I can suggest from the Punjab for War Advisory Council is Dewan Bahadur S.P. Singha who holds one of Indian Christian seats in Provincial Assembly. By profession he is

Controller of Examinations in the Punjab University and is reliable, intelligent and respected. Representative of Indian Christian community in the Punjab is not of great importance.

As representative of soldiers I cannot suggest better name than Sir Muhammad Nawaz Khan of Kot. He is well educated, intelligent, moderate landlord and commands great local respect and influence. Possible alternative would be General Sir Umar Hiyat Khan Tiwana, but he is elderly and generally regarded as somewhat reactionary. There is moreover some jealousy of Tiwana influence.

As regards a Sikh if you take Sir Sundar Singh on Your Executive Council probability is that Sikander will invite Sampuran Singh, leader of Akali Party in the Punjab Assembly, to join his cabinet with the object of detaching them from Congress. I suggest with the same object which I regard as of great importance in its bearing on Sikh recruitment invitation to join War Advisory Council be extended to Master Tara Singh. I cannot of course guarantee that invitation would be accepted but I am inclined to think acceptance probable. Ujjal Singh though intelligent and loyal would be regarded as merely Sir Sundar Singh's understudy and would have no influence with Akalis.[12]

42

CRAIK TO LINLITHGOW
Telegram

Immediate
Personal and Secret
No. 13-G *August 12th, 1940*

Sikander told me today that he will attend meeting of Muslim League Working Committee at Bombay on August 17th. He also contemplates making an announcement near that (?date) since the object with which he and his Party joined League, viz., to safeguard the rights of Muslims in the future constitution has been fully secured by the terms of your statement of August 8th. He and his Party will now withdraw from League. As their Member, it has proved in many ways embarrassing to his Government in dealing with local administrative questions. He is confident that he will carry with him practically all Muslim Members of the Unionist Party but before making announcement he will consult Bengal Muslim Minister [*sic* ?Fazl-ul Huq]. His opinion at present is that he should withdraw from the League whatever may be Jinnah's reaction to your recent announcement.

He considers it almost certain that Jinnah will offer you full co-operation and would accept a seat on Executive Council if invited assuming that Congress refuses to co-operate.

43

CRAIK TO LINLITHGOW
Telegram

Important
No. G-15-C *August 17th, 1940*

I have just seen Sikander and conveyed to him gist of your telegram to me of 15th August.[13] He has promised to do what he can to expedite meeting of Muslim League Working Committee but thinks Jinnah is probably awaiting decision of Congress Committee which meets tomorrow. In the event of Congress deciding on attitude of uncompromising opposition Sikander thinks Jinnah will probably attempt to make his own terms stiffer but is unlikely himself to refuse to co-operate.

44

CRAIK TO LINLITHGOW

Secret and Personal Camp, Ambala,
D.-O. No. 286-Camp *August 17th, 1940*

Dear Lord Linlithgow,

I arrived here early this morning and was met by Sikander, who had come down from Simla last night in response to a telegram from me. I conveyed to him the gist of your private and personal telegram to me of the 15th of August[14] and telegraphed to you[15] after our conversation was concluded (I enclose a copy of my telegram).

2. I told Sikander I could not understand Jinnah's motive in issuing his announcement of August the 12th after his first interview with you, postponing the meeting of the Working Committee of the Muslim League from August the 17th "till further intimation"; nor could I understand why even after his second interview with you on August the 13th, at which all doubtful points must have been cleared up, he had still not announced any

date for the meeting of the Working Committee. Sikander considers from his knowledge of the working of Jinnah's mind that he (Jinnah) is purposely postponing a decision by the Muslim League till the Congress have announced their own conclusion, as Jinnah probably thinks that he would be in a stronger position *vis-à-vis* yourself should the Congress decide on an attitude of flat non-co-operation (as now seems probable).

3. Sikander also told me that he himself had been in correspondence with Abul Kalam Azad. I gather the latter had written to Sikander deprecating Sikander's first published statement[16] about your announcement of August the 8th, and Abul Kalam Azad is the "esteemed correspondent" to whom Sikander referred at the beginning of his second published statement[17] which appeared in newspapers of Friday, the 16th. Sikander had replied to Abul Kalam Azad, urging him to see you in order to elucidate any matters in regard to which he felt doubt and begging him not to refuse any invitation you might send him for an interview.

4. Sikander also showed me a telegram which had been despatched to him from Simla last night by Shiva Rao, the Simla correspondent of the *Hindu*. It ran as follows:–

"Rajagopalachariar earnestly requests you to reach Wardha convince Gandhiji. Your presence likely prove fruitful. (Sd.) SHIVA RAO."

Sikander for obvious reasons could not accept this invitation and in any case he could not have reached Wardha in time for the meeting of the Congress Committee, which is fixed for tomorrow, the 18th. But the telegram is interesting as indicating that Rajagopalachariar is endeavouring to persuade Gandhi to be reasonable.

Many thanks for your secret and personal letter of 11th of August in answer to mine of the 6th. Your letter only reached me this morning.

Yours sincerely,
H.D. CRAIK

45

CRAIK TO LINLITHGOW
Telegram

Immediate
Secret and Personal
No. 16-G *August 18th, 1940*

I saw Sikander immediately on my return to Simla this morning and gave him the message contained in your telegram, No. 621-S.C.,[18] regarding the possibility of defiance of ban on drilling. There is no organized body of Muslim League volunteers in the Punjab and Sikander is not aware how far they are organized in the United Provinces. There is no sign that they have any intention of defying ban though it is just possible that if Congress volunteers decide on defiance contagion might spread. Sikander is however sceptical of defiance by Congress volunteers even though Nehru may advocate it. At present he thinks it would be tactical mistake for him to take any action that might suggest that defiance by the Muslim volunteers is apprehended, but should he see any tendency on the part of Muslim volunteers to defy the ban, he will do all he can to discourage it.

[2.] Reference paragraph No. 4 of my letter, dated 17th August, No. 286. Sikander saw Shiva Rao last night and subsequently despatched lengthy identical telegram to Gandhi and Kalam Azad as well as briefer telegram to Rajagopalachari and Nehru. These messages urged Congress leaders not to refuse co-operation and pressed them to interview you in Delhi if possible. Sikander also assured Shiva Rao he would be ready to meet Congress leaders in Delhi should they decide to go there. Sikander still has hopes that Congress may co-operate.

3. Reference my telegram No. 15. On Sikander's suggestion Maqbool Mahmud telephoned Jinnah last night to expedite meeting of the League Working Committee but received the reply that Jinnah not yet in a position to fix date. Sikander is asking other members of the Working Committee to wire Jinnah to expedite meeting.

4. Reference my telegram No. 13. Sikander repeated his intention of early withdrawal from League but not of course until after conclusion of your negotiations with Jinnah. He said if Jinnah refuses to co-operate break with League is obviously inevitable.

46

CRAIK TO LINLITHGOW

Secret and Personal
D.-O. No. 287

Barnes Court, Simla,
August 19th, 1940

Dear Lord Linlithgow,

In paragraph 2 of my secret and personal telegram to you, No. 16-G. of yesterday, I mentioned that Sikander had been in telegraphic correspondence with the Congress leaders, urging them to seek an interview with you. Sikander this morning received the following telegram from

Abul Kalam Azad. This was despatched from Wardhaganj this morning, presumably after consultation with Gandhi and other leaders:

"Thanks your wire. Optimism after Amery's speech[19] surprising. Door seems to be closed to Congress. Apart from other questions of fundamental nature Amery's conception National Government and its powers widely different even from our Delhi picture. Given fruitful possibility of discussion suggested by you I would not hesitate, but will you kindly communicate if you have any solid grounds of hope."

2. To the above telegram Sikander is despatching today the following reply:

> "Your telegram of date. Thanks. I strongly feel you should see Viceroy and ask for elucidation regarding complexion and functions proposed Central Government. If representative Government can be constituted on the lines of Delhi talk, I consider that it should be accepted. Would strongly urge your meeting Viceroy and deferring final decision till after interview."

3. I asked Sikander what the expression "our Delhi picture" in Azad's telegram to him meant. He explained that it referred to the conversations which he (Sikander) had at Delhi in June last with Gandhi, Azad and Rajagopalachariar. Sikander then understood that Congress did not intend to press for a Government at the Centre responsible to the Legislature, but for a representative Government, i.e. an Executive Council shorn of the present official element. But Sikander thought then, and still thinks, that they might agree to the retention of part of the official element, provided that the new Members selected are not allotted portfolios of minor importance; and that if you were to point out to the Congress leaders that an Act of Parliament would be necessary before the official Membership can be reduced below the minimum of three laid down in the Statute, they might agree to the retention of three officials.

4. Sikander asked me to add that he is prepared to come down to Delhi immediately if you think a personal discussion with him would be useful. He fully recognises the objections to an interview being reported in the Court Circular, but he thinks he could arrange to see Laithwaite without the fact becoming public property. I imagine, however, that if you do receive a request from Azad for an interview, the interview would now have to take place in Simla.

5. It was announced on the radio last night that a meeting of the Muslim League Working Committee has been called for the 31st of August at Bombay.

6. As you are to be in the train today and there is some risk that a telegram might miss you, I am sending this letter by a special messenger, who has been instructed to go direct to Boyd's house in New Delhi, where I see you are to have breakfast tomorrow morning. I am telephoning to Boyd to see that the messenger is allowed access to his house.[20]

Yours sincerely,
H.D. CRAIK

47

CRAIK TO LINLITHGOW

Personal and Most Secret
D.-O. No. 289

Barnes Court, Simla,
August 22nd, 1940

Dear Lord Linlithgow,

In Your Excellency's telegram No. 677-S.C. of the 20th August[21] you asked for my advice as to the reply which you should send to certain commentaries received from the Secretary of State regarding the recent Sikh difficulty and situation discussed in the Commander-in-Chief's letter to myself of August the 1st.[22] I enclose my reply, which I have put in the form of an Express Letter. The first two paragraphs are perhaps not strictly relevant to the Secretary of State's enquiries, but are necessary in order to make a complete picture of the cause contributing to the misconduct of Sikh troops in the Army.

Yours sincerely,
H.D. CRAIK

ENCLOSURE TO NO. 47

CRAIK TO LINLITHGOW
Express Letter

Personal and Most Secret

Simla,
August 22nd, 1940

Your cypher telegram No. 677-S.C., dated August 20th, regarding disaffection amongst Sikh troops. The Sikh community as a whole is more politically minded than any other in the Punjab. Large numbers have gone abroad and are well acquainted with political, social and economic conditions in other countries. There is regular intercourse between Sikhs abroad and their relations at home, and many emigrants have returned and settled down in the Punjab. Some Army officers believe that the main seditious infection comes from the men's homes before enlistment. But the fact that the Police draw their recruits from the same source as the Army and yet have never had such trouble as the Army is now experiencing shows that infection at home before enlistment is not the only factor.

2. In most recent desertions there have been two constant factors. One of these has been faulty recruitment. Many of the persons who have given trouble should never have been in the Army at all. They were allowed to get in owing to faulty verification of their characters and antecedents. For instance, the ringleader in the Central India Horse mutiny was the nephew of a well-known political agitator, who was recently externed from Bihar for instigating labour unrest in Jamshedpur. Since the outbreak of the war the Punjab Government have endeavoured to minimize the risk of undesirable elements entering the Army by arranging for the Police to verify the character and antecedents of all recruits, although this imposes a heavy burden on them.

The second factor has been failure to eject promptly from the Army subversive or potentially subversive elements when once they have been detected. A notorious instance is that of Sadhu Singh, a Naik Reservist of the M.T. at Meerut, whose brother Vasdev Singh is a State prisoner in the Lahore Central Jail. The Punjab Government warned Sadhu Singh's Commanding Officer that he had dangerous connections; but no action was taken. Subsequently Sadhu Singh was largely responsible for the trouble in the M.T. in Egypt and his name figures prominently in the investigation made into the mutiny in the Central India Horse.

3 The total removal of subversive influences in the soldiers' homes is impossible without widespread repressive measures. The Punjab Government have, however, consistently taken action both under the ordinary law and under the Defence of India Act against persons openly preaching sedition and spreading disaffection. They have also, since the Defence of India Act and Rules made this possible, taken vigorous action against those carrying on subversive activities underground. Since the outbreak of the war they have agreed to detention under the Defence of India Rules of 103 communist workers, of whom 77 have already been traced and arrested. They are also now preparing to take action against persons mentioned as instigators in the statements of the Central India Horse mutineers, copies of which have only just been received. But such

action is likely to prove ineffective unless the main communist workers in other Provinces are also hunted down and locked up.

4. Recent investigations into disaffection amongst troops in Egypt and elsewhere have shown that much of the infection has come from a Sikh communist centre at Meerut. This group was originally established at Amritsar, where it published the *Kirti* newspaper; but owing to the action taken by the Punjab Government under the Press Laws the group left the Punjab and established itself in Meerut under the more accommodating Congress Government of the United Provinces. The Punjab Government warned both the United Provinces Government and the Government of India of the danger of permitting this communist cell to carry on its activities, but no action was taken.

5. It is believed that there is no communist centre at work in the Punjab comparable to the Meerut cell; but communist influences are at work in the countryside from which recruits are drawn. Although few regular meetings are held, individual communists travel from village to village and engage villagers in talk.

6. A number of the disaffected troops who disobeyed orders in Egypt have been mustered out and returned to their homes. They are now centres of discontent. The leniency shown to these men by the Army was, in my opinion and in the opinion of my Government, a grave mistake, and has had a bad effect in the districts from which they were drawn.

H.D. CRAIK
Governor, Punjab

48

CRAIK TO LINLITHGOW

Private and Personal
D.-O. No. 290-F.L.

Barnes Court, Simla,
August 27th, 1940

Dear Lord Linlithgow,

I owe Your Excellency an apology for not having sent a fortnightly report since July the 31st, but we have been in constant correspondence since that date and there has been little to report in the provincial sphere, the principal events of August having been of an all-India character.

2. I enclose herewith the provincial reports for the second half of July and the first half of August. The whole period has in the Punjab been a

quiet one and there has been no serious communal incident. Indeed I would say that relations between the Muslims and the Sikhs have somewhat improved. The two districts where feeling was most intense were Shahpur and Gujranwala. In the former conditions are now reported to be practically normal, thanks largely to the efforts of a "Unity Committee" composed of some 40 or 50 of the leading local personalities. In Gujranwala the position has sufficiently improved to permit of the release of the six leaders whose arrest under the Defence of India Rules was reported in paragraph 7 of the provincial report for the second half of July. The abundant rains which have fallen throughout the greater part of the province during the mouth have contributed towards allaying communal excitement, as in all rural areas people are now busily occupied in ploughing and sowing.

3. The spirit of panic and defeatism that was so apparent in June has now almost completely subsided, though there was a slight recurrence in certain places about the first week in August owing to rumours of an imminent attack by the Italians on Egypt. The evacuation of British Somaliland has caused less depression than might have been expected. Recruits are forthcoming in ample quantities, the War Committees continue to do good work, and contributions are flowing in on a fairly generous scale to the War Purposes Fund. I shall be sending you shortly a substantial remittance (probably about Rs. 5 lakhs) as the second instalment from the Punjab to your War Purposes Fund. But the commercial and industrial classes are still hanging back and are not supporting either the War Purposes Fund or the Defence Loans as generously as one could wish. At my suggestion Sikander wrote a few days ago to Sir William Lamond, the Governor of the Imperial Bank, suggesting that the Lahore branch of that Bank should set an example by giving a substantial donation to the Lahore War Planes Fund (a branch of my War Purposes Fund) and should encourage the other leading banks of the city to do the same. Unfortunately the reply was that the Imperial Bank is prohibited by the terms of its Charter from giving subscriptions of this nature, but as soon as my government gets down to Lahore a more systematic effort will be made to enlist the sympathy of the bigger commercial firms.

4. The reactions to Your Excellency's statement of August the 8th[23] are described in the provincial report for the first half of August. I do not think I can usefully add anything to that appreciation, except to say that I do not think it sufficiently emphasizes Muslim satisfaction at the declaration that His Majesty's Government fully recognises its obligations to the minorities and will not acquiesce in their coercion to a form of constitution which they do not approve.

5. There has been no tendency to disobey the recent notifications issued by the Government of India banning drilling and the wearing of uniforms, but it must be remembered that similar orders have been in force in the Punjab for some months. Such parades by volunteer bodies as are still held are now mainly confined to physical exercises, which do not of course come within the terms of the ban. Mr. R.S. Pandit visited Lahore about the middle of August, apparently with the object of encouraging the Congress volunteers to defy the ban by telling them of the successful defiance that seems to have taken place at Cawnpore on August the 11th. In spite of the recent resolution of the All-India Congress Committee on this point[24] I doubt whether Congress volunteers in the Punjab, who are not a formidable body, will make any organized attempt to defy the ban.

6. There has been no renewal of activity on the part of the Khaksars. I received a telegram from Hallett the other day telling me of an interview between his Chief Secretary[25] and Mian Ahmad Shah, just before the announcement published in the Press of the Khaksars' decision not to defy the all-India ban. The telegram stated that Mian Ahmad Shah was anxious to come to Simla to see Sikander. After consulting the latter I sent a reply that he would be prepared to see Mian Ahmad Shah, but his readiness to do so was not to be construed as in any way an invitation to an interview. So far as I know, Ahmad Shah has not yet come to Simla.

7. In paragraph 3 of my letter to you of July the 31st, I mentioned a report that the Punjab Provincial Congress Committee had decided that the next session of the Congress could not be held in the Punjab unless sufficient funds were provided from the Centre. It now appears that the necessary funds can be found by the Centre and, as reported in paragraph 4 of the provincial report for the first half of August, it has been decided to hold the next session in the Punjab. The precise venue has not been settled, but Rawalpindi is mentioned as a likely place. The last session held in the Punjab was in 1929, when the notorious independence resolution was passed, with Jawaharlal Nehru as President.[26]

8. We have discussed recent developments in Sikh politics so recently and so fully that I do not think I need refer to these in this report, except to say that I have had innumerable applications, both written and oral, within the last few weeks from Sikhs of all parties who are anxious to be appointed to the expanded Executive Council or to the War Advisory Board. Many of these have been received from members of the Akali party, although that party is still nominally allied to the Congress. I expect you have by now seen the very outspoken reply[27] which Gandhi sent about the middle of August to "Master" Tara Singh, the Akali leader. It is difficult to see

how the Akalis, whose declared policy is now to maintain and strengthen the Sikh connection with the Army, can remain within the Congress fold.

9. About a fortnight ago I presided at an informal meeting of my Ministers at which they put forward a suggestion for a 10 per cent. cut in the pay of the services. They agreed, however, that it would be unfair to impose such a cut on the services under the control of the Local Government unless a similar cut is imposed on the Secretary of State's services. I was asked to approach you informally in regard to this matter, but when we got down to details I found that the Ministers' ideas were somewhat indefinite. Some of them were in favour of a uniform 10 per cent. cut on all Government servants in receipt of a salary exceeding Rs. 40 p.m. on the lines of the cut enforced during the financial depression of 1931-4. Others wished the minimum limit of salary to be raised to Rs. 50 p.m., a modification which would make a very considerable difference in the total amount of saving effected. Further, they were by no means unanimous whether the cut should be a uniform one of 10 per cent. or a graduated cut of 10 per cent. and 7½ per cent and 5½ per cent according to the amount of salary drawn. Rough calculations made showed that a 10 per cent cut on all gazetted officers, both of the Secretary of State's services and Provincial services, would mean a saving of about 17½ lakhs; and if the cut were to be applied to clerical and subordinate establishments with a minimum limit of Rs. 40 p.m. salary, the saving would be roughly about Rs. 40 lakhs. The additional police made necessary by the war are calculated to cost about Rs. 9½ lakhs per annum and the Civic Guards Rs. 10 lakhs per annum, but these are only very rough estimates, and it would be difficult to justify the proposed cut as essential from the point of view of provincial finances. Indeed, the proposal was definitely put forward as a war emergency measure.

I have told the Ministers that they must be more precise in their proposals before I could be in a position to address you on the subject. I also pointed out that there was good reason to believe that the rates of income-tax would shortly be substantially enhanced and further that to the best of my belief Government servants generally had set a good example in contributing to the War Purposes Fund and the Defence Loans. The view of the Ministers is, however, that while some Government servants have shown a good example in this respect, there is considerable popular feeling that in war time substantial reductions should be made in all public expenditure other than that directly connected with the war and that there has been much criticism of Government servants continuing to enjoy what is generally felt to be an unduly high rate of emoluments.

I am at the moment awaiting a more precise formulation of their proposals from my Ministers. Meanwhile, all the I.C.S. officers of my Government serving in Simla have resolved to contribute one day's pay each month to the War Purposes Fund and to invest at least an equivalent amount in War Savings Certificates or Defence Loans. I enclose a copy of a letter[28] of August 8th in which this decision was communicated to I.C.S. officers serving elsewhere, and I anticipate that this example will be generally followed by I.C.S. officers all over the Province. I invite attention to the last sentence of the printed letter.

Yours sincerely,
H.D. CRAIK

49

CRAIK TO LINLITHGOW

Confidential
D.-O. No. 291

Barnes Court, Simla,
August 28th, 1940

Dear Lord Linlithgow,

In paragraph 6 of my letter to you of yesterday I mentioned the approach made to Sikander by Mian Ahmad Shah on behalf of the Khaksars, but added that so far as I was aware, Ahmad Shah had not yet come to Simla.

I have just heard that he did arrive here yesterday and had an interview of two hours with Sikander, at which Penny, the Chief Secretary, and Bennett, the head of the C.I.D., were also present. After the interview Mian Ahmad Shah wrote to Sikander the letter a copy of which I enclose. I also send a copy of Sikander's reply[29] and of a draft press note[30] which Sikander intends to have released in the newspapers of Sunday next, the 1st of September.

Sikander left Simla last night for Hissar *en route* to Bombay for the Muslim League Working Committee meeting, but Penny has given me an account of the interview with Mian Ahmad Shah. He tells me that Sikander was quite firm in refusing to consider the release of Inayatullah Mashriqi, which, he pointed out, was entirely a matter for the Government of India. He also refused altogether to consider the claim put forward by Mian Ahmad Shah "for compensation to survivors of the deceased". He only agreed to release those prisoners who had been convicted of offences not involving violence. None of those arrested during the original clash with the police on the 19th of March last or during the final round-up of the

Lahore mosques of the 11th of June will be included among those to be released. But there are a good many convicts in jail who were merely convicted of being members of an unlawful association and who did not violently resist arrest. Many of them must have served the greater part of their sentences by now and it is just as well to get rid of them from the jails. Penny is taking steps to prepare a list of those who will be entitled to release under Sikander's assurance.

I understand that Sikander has not come to any conclusion as regards the banking accounts of Mashriqi, which have been attached. He has two accounts – one at a Lahore bank and the other at a Delhi bank, both being personal accounts. We are of course only concerned with the Lahore account.

Penny told me Sikander was evidently anxious to be in a position to announce at the Muslim League meeting at Bombay that he had agreed to withdraw the notification declaring the Khaksars an unlawful association.[31]

Yours sincerely,
H.D. CRAIK

ENCLOSURE TO NO. 49

SHAH TO SIKANDER HYAT KHAN

Muslim Hotel, Simla,
August 27th, 1940

Dear Sir Sikander Hyat Khan,

As the Punjab ban, dated 28th February 1940, is now covered by the all-India ban, dated 6th August 1940, and as we have decided not to defy the all-India ban, the Punjab ban will also be observed by the Khaksars as they are a body devoted to social work. I therefore now hope that the release of all convicts and under-trials and the restoration of property confiscated by Government as also the question of compensation to survivors of the deceased will be favourably considered by the Punjab Government. The release of Allama Sahib and the restoration of his personal property confiscated by Government will also, I hope, receive due consideration.

This letter may be treated as confidential and should not be published.

Yours sincerely,
M.A. SHAH

50

CRAIK TO LAITHWAITE

Barnes Court, Simla,
September 11th, 1940

Dear Laithwaite,

I enclose a copy of the letter I spoke to you about on the telephone this morning.

Yours sincerely,
H.D. CRAIK

ENCLOSURE 1 TO NO. 50

SETHI TO CRAIK

Amritsar,
September 10th, 1940

May it please Your Excellency,

Your Excellency may be interested to know that Master Tara Singh, the well-known Akali leader, has resigned the membership of the All-India and the Provincial Congress Committees. He has been in correspondence with Maulana Abul Kalam Azad and Mahatma Gandhi, and he intends to publish the correspondence shortly.

I have with me the copies of the letter[s] exchanged between Master Tara Singh and Mahatma Gandhi,[32] as he has received no reply to [from] Maulana Abul Kalam Azad. I send you herewith copy of a prefatory note written by Master Tara Singh and another of his resignation addressed to the President of the Punjab Provincial Congress Committee. I hope you will enjoy reading these. I shall endeavour to send you copies of the other letters tomorrow.

If Your Excellency may not mind it, this letter and its enclosures may be shown to the Hon'ble Sir Sikander Hyat Khan, who will be interested in this matter.

I am trying to exercise my influence with Tara Singh in this connection, and have had a talk with him about the damage to the cause of the Sikhs in the Army through the unreasonable attitude of the Akalis.

I have, &c.,
G.R. SETHI

ENCLOSURE 2 TO NO. 50

PREFATORY NOTE BY TARA SINGH

I wrote a letter to Maulana Abul Kalam Azad regarding my attitude towards the Army. I sent copies of this letter to Mahatma Gandhi, Babu Rajendra Prasad and Mr Rajagopalachariar. I feared my attitude may not be quite consistent with the policy of the Congress, so I wrote that I shall not give public expression to these views of mine, if they advise me against publication of these views. I received no reply from anybody except from Mahatma Gandhi. Mahatmaji's letter says nothing about the advice I sought, but it gives astounding advice. The purport of this letter leaked out and got publicity in the press in a form far worse than its real one. So I wrote to Mahatmaji to permit me to publish his letter. I got his permission and I am now releasing his letter along with those of mine for publication.

ENCLOSURE 3 TO NO. 50

TARA SINGH TO PRESIDENT, PUNJAB PROVINCIAL CONGRESS COMMITTEE, LAHORE[33]

Amritsar,
September 10th, 1940

Sir,

I beg to tender my resignation from the membership of Punjab Provincial Congress Committee; (which of course includes my resignation from the All-India Congress Committee) for I feel I am insulted by Maulana Abul Kalam Azad Sahib and I do not wish to remain in a position in which he may be able to insult me again. There was an incorrect news published in the press which I immediately corrected, though my contradiction was published only in the Punjab Press. On the basis of this press canard Maulana Abul Kalam Azad Sahib wrote to the President of the Punjab Provincial Congress Committee to make inquiries from me. The President of the Punjab Provincial Congress Committee met me and satisfied himself with regard to the falsity of the said piece of news on or before 1st September. But I was astonished to find that Maulana Sahib had given it to the press before he had received any intimation from the President,

Punjab Provincial Congress Committee, that he had asked certain explanation from me. It is hard for me to put up with such a treatment. I am not accustomed to it. I, therefore, resign from all the positions where Maulana Sahib can have any control.

I have some differences with some of the Congress leaders which came to light during the last few days. But those differences are not the cause of my resignation. In fact, I thought of resigning on that very date when I saw the statement of Maulana Sahib in the press; but to avoid misunderstandings I refrain from doing so, as the above referred to differences [?which] also had come to light during those very days. I now resign purely upon personal grounds. Though my differences with the Congress I [?are] being brought to the forefront on account of my circumstances; but they are not the cause of my resignation just now. I advise my friends to carry on with their duties and responsibilities which they have in the Congress, and not to too much emphasise the insult which has been offered to me. My own resignation is a sufficient protest.

51

CRAIK TO LINLITHGOW

Private and Personal
D.-O. No. 297-F.L.

Barnes Court, Simla,
September 24th, 1940

Dear Lord Linlithgow,

I am afraid I have again allowed nearly a month to elapse since the date of my last report to you, but the month has been, from the provincial point of view, a quiet one and events on the all-India stage have overshadowed provincial affairs. I now enclose my Government's fortnightly reports for the second half of August and the first half of September.

2. Paragraph 4 of the later report refers to the almost unanimous opposition of the press to the idea of launching civil disobedience. I have studied the press carefully and have been much struck by this unanimity, especially among the Hindu papers which usually support Congress blindly. There has been considerable criticism in the columns of these papers of the recent inconsistencies and changing front of the Congress High Command, while the Muslim press takes the line that Congress prestige has never stood lower than it is at the moment. Although occasional references are made at Congress meetings to the necessity of preparing

for sacrifice, &c., I think it would be proper to say that Congressmen on the whole are unenthusiastic, listless and perplexed by the attitude of their leaders.

3. Paragraph 3 of the same report gives an account of the events leading up to Master Tara Singh's resignation from the Punjab Provincial Congress Committee and the All-India Working Committee. It is doubtful whether the other Akali leaders will follow his example. There is still considerable division of opinion among them, but I think they are all agreed that everything possible must be done to maintain and encourage Sikh recruitment, and in these circumstances I do not see how a final rupture with the Congress can be long delayed. There have been no bad reactions among the Sikhs to the Central India Horse incident. Although the punishments awarded to the mutineers have not been publicly announced, I fancy it is pretty generally known that the four death sentences have been carried out, and I have information that some of the Akali leaders have in private conversation admitted that these sentences were deserved.

4. Our communist security prisoners are giving a good deal of trouble. Nine out of ten who are confined in the Montgomery Central Jail have been hunger-striking and two of these (one Sikh and one Hindu), both of whom are described as dangerous terrorists, were a few days ago reported to be sinking. They were accordingly, under the orders of Government, sent to the Mayo Hospital at Lahore for treatment. They are still of course in custody there.

5. Subscriptions to the War Purposes Fund are flowing in steadily. The total amount hitherto received by my Secretary exceeds Rs. 14 lakhs, exclusive of the Lahore District War Planes Fund which now stands at between 2 and 3 lakhs. Besides these amounts there must be 2 or 3 lakhs in the hands of Deputy Commissioners, which have not yet been paid into the central account.

I telegraphed the other day a lakh of rupees to the Lord Mayor of London for his fund for the relief of sufferers in London's air raids, and I have received two substantial cheques from Indian gentlemen for the same purpose. I have also received numerous messages of sympathy and congratulation about Their Majesties' recent escape when Buckingham Palace was bombed.

6. Paragraph 6 of the provincial report for the second half of August gives an account of the events leading up to the cancellation of my Government's order of March last declaring the Khaksars an unlawful association. As there explained, the question of the release of Khaksars serving sentences for offences not involving violence is now being examined, but the actual orders for release have been held up, as the attitude

of the Khaksars is still somewhat ambiguous, and it is doubtful whether they are prepared to implement the undertaking given to the Premier by Mian Ahmad Shah to behave lawfully in future. It is also doubtful whether Ahmad Shah himself is really in a position to guarantee their future good conduct. Another Khaksar leader, Dr. Muhammad Ismail Nami, who is believed to be in Calcutta but whose arrest we have never been able to effect, recently announced in the press that the Khaksars' activities were only suspended up till the 30th of September, and demands for the release of Inayatullah Mashriqi and all the Khaksar prisoners and also for compensation to the dependants of those killed in the original clash are still being made. Moreover, we have some information that preparations are being made to recruit more Khaksars in Lahore and elsewhere. In these circumstances I advised the Premier to go slow over ordering the actual release of any Khaksar convicts, and he has accepted this advice.

7. The Bombay decision of the Muslim League Council to lift the ban on its members serving on the War Committees has been received with general relief by Muslims in the Punjab, and the three or four members of the Provincial War Board, who had sent in formal notice of their resignation, have now asked to be allowed to rejoin. Of the 37 or 38 Muslim M.L.As. who are members of the Provincial Board, the only one who resigned in obedience to the League's resolution was Nawab Sir Shah Nawaz Khan of Mamdot, who is President of the Punjab Provincial Muslim League. After the Bombay meeting of the League Council he wrote to Sikander asking to be allowed to rejoin the Board, and at Sikander's suggestion, I then sent for him and explained to him in plain terms that I took a serious view of his conduct in placing his obligation to a political caucus above his loyalty to the King-Emperor and the Government of India. I pointed out to him that not only had he been allowed by Government to succeed to the largest landed estate in the Punjab (from which his grandfather and his father had been expelled in the early eighties for gross misrule and oppression) but also had been granted by Government a Jagir worth Rs. 80,000 per annum and the hereditary title of "Nawab". In the Sanads both of the Jagir and the title there was an explicit condition of loyalty and good conduct and Government is the sole authority to determine whether this condition has been observed. I told him that "loyalty" meant active loyalty and not merely abstention from disloyal acts, and it seemed to me questionable whether his conduct in resigning from the War Board at a time of great crisis was consistent with that condition. My talk evidently "shook him up" considerably, and in today's papers it is announced that he has sent a contribution of Rs. 50,000 to the Lahore War Planes Fund, evidently a gesture intended to prove his active loyalty.

8. I know that you are closely interested in the problem of the traffic in illicit arms. I saw two days ago a report that five arrests had been made in the Lyallpur district of persons suspected to be concerned in the smuggling of "Pass-made" rifles from the Frontier into the Punjab. I have not so far received any details, but the arrests go to show that the staff which we have placed on special duty to check this traffic are being active.

9. Two of my Ministers, the Premier and Malik Khizar Hayat Khan, intend to be present at the meeting of the Muslim League Council which Jinnah has called at Delhi on the 28th and 29th of September. Thereafter these two, as well as Mian Abdul Haye and Sir Chhotu Ram, propose to do an extensive tour in the eastern Punjab to stimulate war efforts. They expect to address a large number of big meetings during the course of this tour. All the Ministers will reassemble at Lahore about the 12th of October.

10. In paragraph 9 of my letter to you No. 290-F.L. of the 27th of August I referred to a suggestion put forward by my Ministers for a 10 per cent. cut in the pay of the services and explained that I was still awaiting a more precise formulation of their exact proposals. I have not yet received this and shall not of course move further in the matter unless I do so.

Yours sincerely,
H.D. CRAIK

52

CRAIK TO LINLITHGOW

Government House, Lahore,
D.-O. No. 301 *October 16th, 1940*

Dear Lord Linlithgow,

On my way to Lahore I had a conversation at Amritsar with Mir Maqbool Mahmood, whom you have probably met. He is a close connection of Sikander's by marriage and, besides being Secretary to the Chancellor of the Chamber of Princes, is a member of the Punjab Assembly, a Parliamentary Secretary and much in Sikander's confidence. I told Maqbool that I was greatly surprised at the Muslim League's refusal to accept your offer of representation on the enlarged Executive Council[34] and at the part which Sikander had played in this refusal. Maqbool's explanation of Sikander's attitude was that, having secured from Jinnah an undertaking that the members of the Muslim League would be free to co-operate wholeheartedly in the prosecution of the war, he did not feel that such co-operation would be made more effective by the presence in your Council of two nominees of Jinnah's, who, Sikander was convinced, would be secretly pledged to resign whenever Jinnah gave them the order to do so. This explanation of Sikander's attitude struck me at the time as somewhat surprising and not very convincing.

2. A day or two later I had a talk with Sikander himself on the same subject. He took more or less the same line as Maqbool, but he mentioned also certain other considerations which had influenced his attitude. He thought Muslims might find themselves in a very difficult position if after sending their representatives to the Executive Council and thus assuming their share in the responsibility for a policy of repression towards Congress, should that become necessary, the Congress should at some subsequent date reconsider their attitude and themselves decide to accept your offer. He further expressed the view that if the Muslims accepted your offer and both the Congress and the Hindu Mahasabha held aloof, communal relations would become steadily more and more bitter. There is possibly some force in this latter argument, but I am still considerably puzzled at Sikander's attitude.

3. One thing, however, is certain and that is that he and Jinnah are now on much better terms than they have been for some time past. Sikander told me that Jinnah made a very good speech at the meeting of the Muslim League Council at Delhi on September 28th, but the newspaper report did not do justice to it. According to Sikander, Jinnah strongly emphasized the obligation on all Muslims to give full co-operation in the war, more especially in view of recent developments such as the menace to Egypt, and went so far as to say that all Muslims should spend "the last drop of their blood and their last rupee" for the protection of Islamic countries. If this account is correct, it seems curious that the newspaper reports of Jinnah's speech should not have contained any reference to this passage. But it is certainly significant that immediately after the League meeting at Delhi Sikander made a series of public speeches in the Gurgaon, Rohtak and Ludhiana districts, advocating in the strongest possible terms full co-operation in Government's war effort and castigating people who had not subscribed to the War Purposes Fund or Defence Loans in proportion to their means. Sikander told me that all three of the meetings had had large and enthusiastic audiences.

4. In the course of our conversation I asked Sikander what he now felt about withdrawing from the League. I think I informed you that some two

months ago he told me that the time had now come for him and his party to withdraw from the League, as the object with which they joined it, viz., the consolidation of Muslim opinion vis-à-vis the Congress and the Hindu Mahasabha and the securing of a pledge that Muslim claims would not be ignored in framing the new constitution, had been secured. He told me he still had this idea in his mind and had mentioned it to Jinnah at the Delhi meeting. Jinnah pointed out that withdrawal at the moment, immediately after the termination of negotiations between yourself and Jinnah, might be misinterpreted as indicating disagreement between Sikander and Jinnah regarding the latter's attitude during those negotiations. Nevertheless, Sikander still thinks that the time will soon come – though he did not give any indication exactly when – for him and his followers in the Punjab to withdraw from the League.

5. I noticed today a press report to the effect that Sikander is to preside on the 15th of November over a Conference of the Sind Provincial Muslim League at Larkana. I am not aware whether this report is true, but I propose to tell him that in my opinion he will find this a distinctly embarrassing engagement in view of the state of communal feeling in Sind at the moment, and also to point out the constitutional impropriety of the Premier of one province presiding over such a gathering in another province.[35]

Yours sincerely,
H.D. CRAIK

53

CRAIK TO LINLITHGOW

Private and Personal
D.-O. No. 302-F.L.

Government House, Lahore,
October 16th, 1940

Dear Lord Linlithgow,

The move down from Simla delayed the printing of the provincial report for the second half of September, which I now enclose, and it only reached me today. I have not very much to add to it.

2. Gandhi had an extremely poor press after the publication of the correspondence between yourself and him at the end of September.[36] I do not think I have seen a single article expressing unqualified approval. Even the Hindu newspapers have quite definitely condemned his attitude. For instance, the *Daily Herald* of the 1st of October wrote as follows:

"It is clear that Mahatma Gandhi in his mission to the Viceroy acted not as the spokesman of a political organization, as the Congress really is, but as the leader of a pacifist organization which the Congress is certainly not. The freedom of speech granted to conscientious objectors in the United Kingdom is the farthest limit to which any Government can go. And by precipitating a crisis or a conflict on the issue raised by Mahatma Gandhi the Congress would be fighting for something which the Congress Working Committee, not long ago, ruled out as unwise and impracticable."

The following day's leading article contained the following sentence:

> "It is very tragic to see the apostle of fearlessness trembling before the consequences of the present war and pleading for an ignoble peace and surrender to Hitlerism at the present juncture.... Now when the Mahatma thinks Hitlerism to be in the wrong and Britain in the right it is difficult to understand his advocacy of an attitude of non-participation in the war."

The *Tribune* of the 3rd of October referred to Gandhi as making (in his published letter to yourself) "that confusion between himself as the supreme apostle of non-violence and the Congress, which is a purely political body charged with a specific political mission, that has vitiated all his recent utterances".

One or two of the Lahore Muslim papers have openly referred to Gandhi as "senile".

3. The decision that civil disobedience is to be only by individuals and not general will, I am confident, be received with general relief by all classes. Sikander told me the other day that his information was that Gandhi had nominated about 40 individuals to take part in civil disobedience, of whom presumably Vinoba will be the first to start the campaign. Sikander is not aware whether any of the 40 persons belong to the Punjab, but I imagine not.

I am informed that Gandhi sent for Mian Iftikhar-ud-Din, M.L.A., who is President of the Punjab Provincial Congress Committee, to Simla and told him to suspend all preparations for the next session of the Congress, which was to have been held in the Rawalpindi district.

4. I halted for a day at Amritsar on my way down from Simla and besides other functions presided at an informal Durbar, at which I was handed a purse of Rs. 1,76,000 as the contribution up to date of the district and city to the War Purposes Fund. I talked with a large number of the leading people of the district that day and found them completely unanimous in

the view that public opinion on the war is sound. Not only is there a general desire to help, but there is also complete absence of the panic that prevailed in June last and a general confidence in Britain's ultimate victory. I was, however, told by two Sikhs, who are employed as Assistant Recruiting Officers, that the number of Jat Sikhs presenting themselves for enlistment is short of the demand. One of these gentlemen told me that the influence of the communists is now distinctly on the wane. This was indeed only to be expected, since about a hundred of the leading communists have been arrested under the Defence of India Rules, but a certain amount of secret propaganda is still going on. In this the various Kisan Committees are taking a part, but they have always been practically indistinguishable from the communists.

5. A few weeks ago Khan Bahadur Mian Ahmad Yar Khan Daultana, M.L.A., Chief Secretary (a post which corresponds to Chief Whip) of the Unionist Party organization, died. The Party has now suffered another loss by the death yesterday of Syed Afzal Ali Hasnie, M.L.A., who was the Resident Secretary of the Party. Both these gentlemen were popular personalities, and I am afraid the Party will find considerable difficulty in replacing them. Their death after the Party has been in office for 3½ years and at a time when it ought to be making active preparations for the next general election is particularly unfortunate.

6. In paragraph 6 of my letter to you of the 24th of September I mentioned that Sikander had accepted my suggestion to go slow over ordering the actual release of any of the Khaksar prisoners, mainly owing to the wild statements made in the Khaksar newspaper *Al-Islah* (which is now published in Calcutta) by Dr. Muhammad Ismail Nami. In today's papers, however, it has been announced that the releases are now to proceed, Dr. Nami having given an assurance that he has no intention of defying the law himself or asking others to do so.

7. There have been no further developments as regards the suggestion for a cut in the pay of the services, which I mentioned in paragraph 9 of my letter to you of August the 27th, but the fact that such a proposal is under consideration has now become public property and has been discussed in one or two newspapers. I enclose a cutting[37] from today's *Civil and Military Gazette* on this subject. In one or two vernacular papers a suggestion has been made that I turned down the Ministers' proposal for a cut. This is of course untrue, as I expressed no opinion in the discussions that took place on the subject, but merely made it clear that precise proposals must be formulated before I could approach you as to the possibility of a cut being imposed on the All-India Services.

8. As you are aware, we had an excellent monsoon rainfall up to the end of August and had hoped that this would see the end of the famine. Unfortunately there were only a few scattered showers during September in the greater part of the Hissar district and a hot west-wind blew throughout the month, doing considerable damage to the crop sown in July and August, most of which will be a failure. It may become necessary to reopen relief works on a reduced scale somewhere about the end of this month, but my Ministers have not come to a decision on the point. They are waiting to see whether emigration in search of labour takes place. In any event it is anticipated that there should be plenty of fodder for the cattle.

9. In paragraph 8 of my letter to you of the 24th of September I mentioned that certain arrests had been made in the Lyallpur district of persons suspected of being concerned in the smuggling of arms from the Frontier into the Punjab. I have since seen a detailed report regarding these arrests, which makes it clear that there is a considerable traffic of this kind. The Police have collected a good deal of information about the methods of the smugglers, and I now enclose a copy of a note[38] written on the 2nd of September by the Deputy Inspector-General in charge of the C.I.D., which shows that active steps are being taken to check this dangerous traffic and to recover as many of the illicit arms as possible. My Ministers are fully alive to the importance of doing so.

10. I hope you are enjoying your holiday in Kashmir and having good sport.

Yours sincerely,
H.D. CRAIK

54

CRAIK TO LINLITHGOW

Confidential
D.-O. No. 304

Government House, Lahore,
October 28th, 1940

Dear Lord Linlithgow,

I feel I owe you an explanation regarding the point about preparations for the Punjab session of the Congress, mentioned in paragraph 3 of your most interesting letter to me of the 24th October. You point out that the report (made in my letter to you of the 16th of October) that Gandhi had sent for the President of the Punjab Provincial Congress Committee to Simla and told him to suspend all preparations for the next session of the Congress, did not agree with the C.I.O's. report[39] for the first half of October, which was to the effect that the Punjab Congress President had been instructed by Kalam Azad to proceed with arrangements for the annual session.

I did not see this report of the C.I.O's. till the 17th of October, i.e. the day after I had written to you, but I think the explanation is that Gandhi's instructions given at Simla to Iftikharuddin were to suspend preparations pending the decision of the Congress Working Committee, which took place at place at Wardha on (I think) the 13th of October. Presumably Gandhi felt that if he did not get his way at the Working Committee and if it was decided to proceed immediately with mass civil disobedience, in that event there could be no question of having the usual annual session. As soon as his plan for individual *Satyagraha* had been accepted, he felt that preparations for the annual session might as well go forward and Kalam Azad instructed the Punjab President accordingly.

Such preparations as are in train are, however, according to my information, of a very indefinite and hesitating character. Our Provincial Congress committee is extremely short of funds and no decision has yet been taken as to the venue of the annual session. Various people have promised substantial contributions towards the expenses, but only on condition that the session is held at the place of their choice. So until a decision is arrived at on this important point it is unlikely that the Provincial Committee will be in a position to incur any expenditure on the erection of the Pandal and the provision of accommodation for visitors, &c.

Yours sincerely,
H.D. CRAIK

55

CRAIK TO LINLITHGOW

Private and Personal
D.-O. No. 305-F.L.

Government House, Lahore,
November 1st, 1940

Dear Lord Linlithgow,

The month of October has been a very quiet one throughout the Province. All my visitors – and I have seen a very large number during the last few weeks – assure me that public opinion on the war throughout the rural areas is absolutely sound. Confidence in our ultimate victory has been in no way shaken by recent events, and the vast majority of people are eager to help in every way possible. In urban areas the readiness to co-operate is less apparent, e.g. in the matter of subscriptions to the war loans or funds, but even in these areas there is no evidence of panic. Muslim opinion has been deeply stirred by the growing menace to Islamic countries, particularly by the bombing of Bahrain and the invasion of Greece, and I have noticed in the Muslim press a tendency to criticise the unresponsive attitude of the Muslim League in face of the imminent menace to Islam. The same papers have given a stern warning to Gandhi and Abul Kalam Azad not to attempt to make Muslims join in the civil disobedience movement, as they are preoccupied with the problem of helping the Islamic countries threatened by the Dictators.

2. I had an interesting guest at my dinner table the other day in the person of Tahsin Rustu Bey, Counsellor of the Turkish Embassy at Kabul, who is spending a few weeks on holiday in India. I had a telegram from Cunningham suggesting that it was desirable to show him informal courtesy; so I asked him to dinner where he met the Premier, who gave a party in his honour the next day, the Chief Justice,[40] and the Air Marshal, who happened to be staying with me. Tahsin Rustu Bey unfortunately only speaks French and Persian, but I did my best in the former language. He is clearly very pro-British and was greatly excited about the news which had been received that day of the Italian invasion of Greece. He expressed his firm conviction that his own country would honour its obligations and resist to the utmost if invaded; but he displayed some apprehension lest Russia should take this opportunity of settling old scores with Turkey. He spoke highly of the Turkish President[41] and their Chief of the General Staff,[42] describing the latter as a man of strong character and great military experience.

3. Singularly little interest seems to be taken in the Punjab in Gandhi's campaign, the people being preoccupied with the graver issues arising out of recent war developments. This lack of interest is no doubt partly due to the absence of news since the recent prohibition by your Government of the publication of news or comments on the campaign. The local press, to whom the scope and purpose of this prohibition were explained at a meeting by J.D. Anderson, have taken it on the whole fairly well and there has been no attempt to defy it; but there is of course much criticism on the general lines that any restriction on the freedom of the press is an invasion of fundamental democratic principles.

Before the prohibition was promulgated the press comment on the campaign was surprisingly critical and outspoken. For example, the *Milap*, a Hindu paper usually of a strong pro-Congress complexion, stated in its issue of the 19th of October that "it is clear that the country and even the Congress are not united on the issue". The *Tribune* of the 18th of October said that the issue on which Gandhi had chosen to fight was "not only incredibly narrow and confused, but obviously irrelevant". The tone of the Muslim press has been one of bitter and contemptuous derision. For instance, the *Inqilab* of the 18th of October wrote "Does this silly old man imagine that a man in a loin-cloth talking nonsense will secure freedom from a nation unmoved by Hitler's bombs?" Elsewhere in the same issue it spoke of Gandhi's campaign as "a painful and regrettable joke" and Gandhi himself as "a clever agent of aggressors". In an article two days later the Congress was described as having "made a fool of itself by placing itself in the hands of such a person at such a critical juncture", and in the issue of the 25th of October this sentence occurred in a leader: "Gandhi in the name of freedom is helping Fascism: no well-wisher of the country can ever agree with him."

I do not remember any newspaper previously writing in such derisory terms of the Mahatma.

4. The General Secretary of the Punjab Provincial Congress Committee issued a circular, dated the 23rd of October, to all primary Congress Committees in the Province. This enclosed a cyclostyled copy of a summary of Vinoba Bhave's stock speech. It also contained a number of directions from the President of the Punjab Provincial Congress Committee to local Committees and a list of the names of Congressmen appointed to look into alleged cases of extortion for the war funds and loans.

Up to the 26th of October the Police had succeeded in seizing 2,980 copies of this circular letter out of 3,300 prepared and more are expected to be seized; but some copies may filter through and it is just possible that the summary of Bhave's speech may be reproduced in local papers. But, as explained above, the Press has been warned about this.

5. I paid a visit the other day to Sheikhupura, a district adjoining Lahore on the west, where I was presented with addresses and a purse for the war funds. The main theme of my speech on this occasion was an appeal to the urban classes for contributions to the defence loans and the War Purposes Fund. You may care to read the comment in today's *Tribune* on this speech, of which I enclose a cutting.[43]

6. As I explained to you in my letter No. 304 of the 28th of October, preparations for the Punjab session of the Congress are still proceeding, or at any rate being discussed. At a recent meeting of the Provincial

Congress Committee Mian Iftikharuddin M.L.A., its President, said that the Punjab had been chosen for the next session, because it is "the centre of reactionary and recruiting activity". It is reported that he has promised to give Rs. 5,000 from his own pocket for the expenses of the session, but only on condition that he is chosen as Chairman of the Reception Committee. No progress has been made with the selection of a venue for the session. The places being canvassed include Taxila in the Rawalpindi district and Kurukshetra, an important place of pilgrimage in the Karnal district.

7. The position of Sikhs *vis-à-vis* the Congress is still very obscure. Several fairly prominent with [Sikh] leaders have announced in the press that they have no intention of seceding, and even Tara Singh is obviously hedging. At a public meeting the other day he stressed the point that his quarrel with the Congress was a purely personal one, an attitude hardly consistent with his earlier announcement quoted at the end of paragraph 3 of the provincial report[44] (enclosed herewith) for the first half of October.

8. We have recently held two long Cabinet meetings to discuss certain measures of taxation which my Ministers propose to introduce at the forthcoming session of the Legislative Assembly. The first of these is a Bill imposing a tax on sales of goods, to which all dealers with a turn-over of over Rs. 5,000 per annum are to be liable. This Bill is modelled on the Madras Act passed by Rajagopalachariar's Ministry. The second Bill imposes taxation on "urban lands and buildings", the tax being calculated on a percentage of the capital value, which will in most localities be 25 times the annual rental, but may be a smaller multiple in places where rents are particularly high. The difficulty about this latter Bill will be the task of assessing the annual rental. At the moment this is only ascertainable in a very few towns (Lahore and one or two hill stations) where a municipal house-tax is in force. Both Bills will, I fear, require the provision of a large staff for purposes of assessment and collection, and it may also be necessary to provide a special staff for the disposal of appeals. With the prospect of Central taxation being increased in the near future these Bills will be far from popular, but my Ministers seem determined to proceed with them. They will of course mainly affect the urban population.

9. I noticed the other day a report giving details of the recovery of illicit arms in the Shahpur district. This district adjoins Mianwali, the Pathans of which are the chief smugglers of illicit firearms from the Frontier. The number of firearms recovered in Shahpur was 190, including 48 rifles (presumably pass-made), 5 carbines, 66 guns and 76 pistols and revolvers.

10. Nehru's arrest was published in this morning's papers, simul-

taneously with the announcement of your own extension of office. I congratulate India on both events, but I am not sure whether I ought to congratulate you personally on the latter!

Yours sincerely,
H.D. CRAIK

56

CRAIK TO LINLITHGOW

Private and Personal
D.-O. No. 309-F.L.

Government House, Lahore,
November 15th, 1940

Dear Lord Linlithgow,

The fortnight since I last wrote to you on the 1st of November has again been a very quiet one. The Provincial fortnightly report, which I enclose herewith, deals with the second half of October, but I have seen most of the District Officers' reports for the first half of November and a large number of them are positively dull reading.

2. For the first week in November I was away on tour in the north-western Punjab and visited Gujrat, Kalabagh on the Indus, Mianwali and Jhelum. All these are places with a fine military tradition and the warm welcome which I received and the general spirit of confidence and cordial co-operation were most heartening. At Kalabagh, for example, where most of the people are Pathans of the Niazi and Bangi Khel tribes, the impression I received was that practically the entire male population either had been or is now in the Army. One old retired officer told me that he had no less than 21 sons and nephews now actually in service. In all these areas subscriptions to the War Fund are, considering the comparative poverty of that part of the Province, amazingly good and I am convinced that they are completely voluntary. In such an atmosphere Gandhi's civil disobedience campaign and the attitude which it represents seem extraordinarily remote and unreal. I am confident that the great mass of the people in the rural Punjab, and especially the Muslims, are heart and soul with us in this war.

3. The only disquieting feature that came to my notice was that in several of the recruiting areas the supply of Jat Sikhs is not yet equal to the demand. The campaign of anti-Government propaganda carried on for so many

years by the Akalis on the one side and the communists on the other is, in my judgement, largely accountable for this. But a very reliable retired Indian officer, whom I have known for many years and who is employed as Assistant Recruiting Officer, told me that he did not think there was any bad political influence at present at work among the Sikhs. He considers that their failure to come forward in sufficient numbers is partly due to the fact that the new canal schemes have brought them such prosperity that the economic argument for enlistment has no longer much force and partly because illicit distillation has increased to such an extent that a great many Sikhs have now lost their martial spirit owing to the drink habit.

4. Sikh affairs are described at considerable length in paragraph 3 of the enclosed report, to which I have little to add. In his report for the first half of November the Deputy Commissioner of Amritsar,[45] who is very closely in touch with Sikh affairs, has expressed the opinion that Master Tara Singh is making very little headway in his policy of detaching the Akalis from the Congress and encouraging Sikh recruitment. Possibly, however, Gandhi's recent decision that all prominent Congressmen are to offer themselves for arrest will lead to the resignation of certain of the Akali leaders. Some of them will certainly dislike exceedingly the prospect of going to jail as Congressmen.

5. Nehru's arrest and conviction aroused singularly little interest in the Punjab and even in Congress circles there was no marked reaction. In some of the bigger towns there were *hartals* after his arrest, but of a very partial character. In Lahore, for example, only a few shops in the biggest bazar were closed, but according to Sikander most of these were only closed as the result of extreme pressure, with in some cases threats of physical violence, from local Congress leaders. In Amritsar an attempted *hartal* was an ignominious failure and the same was the case in Rawalpindi and Sialkot. At Montgomery the local Congressmen proposed to hold a *hartal*, but the Congress President, on the Deputy Commissioner[46] pointing out to him that the date fixed coincided with the festival of the Id, immediately agreed to call the *hartal* off. A few meetings were held, but these were sparsely attended.

6. The suggestion that Gandhi might shortly embark on a fast caused some consternation in Hindu circles, but the comment in the Muslim press continued to be bitter and contemptuous. The *Inqilab* referred to the proposed fast as "utterly futile and baneful for the high ideals of India", and the *Ihsan* referred to it as "throwing a light on Gandhi's lowness of character".

His decision to extend in the immediate future the scope of *Satyagraha* so as to include all prominent Congressmen is not yet generally known. According to our calculations, between now and the end of the year we shall have about 90 Congressmen in jail, i.e. the Punjab members of the All-India Congress Committee, members of the Working Committee of the Punjab Provincial Congress Committee and Congress members of the local and Central Legislatures. The rank and file of the Punjab Provincial Congress Committee, who number about 230, are not to offer themselves for arrest till after January the 1st, and some of the weaker vessels may wriggle out of the obligation. So far as I can judge from the present temper of the Province, I do not think it is likely that these arrests will cause any great excitement or any really serious hindrance to our war efforts. But if a large proportion of these prisoners take to hunger-striking and Gandhi thereafter himself starts a fast, the position will become considerably more difficult.

7. Our police have had some success in dealing with communist underground organizations. Some important arrests were mentioned in the latest report of the Central I.B., which you have doubtless seen. An organization that has been distributing communist leaflets at the important Dhariwal Woollen Mills in the Gurdaspur district was recently detected and a certain quantity of its literature was seized. Three arrests have been made and clues that may lead to other arrests are being followed up. A Sikh ex-employee of the same Mills was also arrested the other day by the Hoshiarpur police with a number of communist leaflets in his possession. This man, after leaving the service of the Mills, had enlisted in the Motor Transport Training Battalion, apparently with the express intention of corrupting the men of the Battalion, from which he was on leave when arrested.

Yours sincerely,
H.D. CRAIK

P.S. – Your family arrived here this morning, all in good heart. It is delightful to have them here again. I was very glad indeed to hear from Her Excellency the reassuring news about Sikander's son.[47] He is on tour at the moment and I have sent him a telegram of congratulation from us both. I have just taken his second boy, who is still too young to get into the regular Army, on my staff as A.D.C.[48]

57

MOON TO LAITHWAITE[49]

Confidential

Government House, Lahore,
November 24th, 1940

Dear Laithwaite

With reference to your cypher telegram No. 2412-S of the 20th of November, His Excellency desires me to say that there has really been no important reaction in this Province to His Excellency the Viceroy's speech to the Central Legislature.[50] It had everywhere been foreseen that the proposal for the expansion of the Executive Council and for the constitution of a War Advisory Committee would be held in abeyance. A number of papers have expressed disappointment that there is no indication of a fresh move to resolve the present political deadlock, but some of them have also commented that the door is not closed.

Yours sincerely,
E.P. MOON

58

CRAIK TO LINLITHGOW

Private and Personal
D.-O. No. 311-F.L.

Government House, Lahore,
November 30th, 1940

Dear Lord Linlithgow,

The last fortnight has again been a quiet one in this Province in spite of the starting elsewhere of the *Satyagraha* campaign on a large scale. The Lahore Hindu newspapers have for the last week been "splashing" the arrests of leaders in other parts of India and are trying to create the impression that the whole country is watching the campaign with absorbed and exclusive interest. Actually, however, I see very little sign of enthusiasm or indeed of any great popular interest in the new movement outside Lahore and Amritsar. In these two cities the audiences at political meetings show a tendency to increase in size and students and extremists generally are becoming somewhat restive. Their view, however, is that "individual *Satyagraha*" is an ineffective gesture and they are impatient for some more vigorous line of action. On the other hand, the view taken by more moderate Hindu opinion was reflected in a recent leading article in the *Tribune*, which pleaded with some effect that the Punjab should be exempted, as Sind has been, from the present campaign, partly because there are very few really prominent Congress leaders in the Province and partly because the withdrawal of most of the Opposition Members of the Assembly just at a moment when two important taxation Bills are to be discussed would amount to a deplorable neglect of the interests of their constituents. Another significant incident is that the Piecegoods Association of Amritsar, the biggest piecegoods market in the north of India, has decided to have no more *hartals* on the occasion of the arrests of leaders, as they lose too much business by closing their shops.

2. The local Muslim press continues to denounce the whole movement in scathing terms. The *Inqilab* in a recent issue described Gandhi as "the greatest cheat and hypocrite and not truthful at all". Another issue of the same paper alleged that the underlying motive of *Satyagraha* was not only hostility to Government but also hostility to the Muslim community. It characterised the movement as "a shameful one" and demanded Gandhi's immediate arrest. Another Muslim paper has recently published an effective article on what it calls "the fifth column activities of the Congress". Gandhi's description of Punjab soldiers as "mercenaries" has provoked great resentment in the Muslim press and Sikander in recent speeches has made considerable capital out of this indiscreet utterance. I feel certain that if Gandhi's close control over the movement is relaxed and discipline breaks down, communal trouble is certain to follow. If, for example, any attempt is made to make Muslim shops close during a *hartal*, I have little doubt that this would lead to retaliation by physical forces.

3. As regards the actual campaign in the Punjab, my information is that most of the prospective *Satyagrahis* are in reality extremely lukewarm. There is said to be a list of some 2,000 such *Satyagrahis*, but of these only about 700 at an outside estimate are dependable. Among the 40 odd Congress M.L.As. only 8 are genuine volunteers for the sacrifice: 10 others have been coerced into offering themselves, but it is doubtful whether they will honour their pledge. The Akalis and Dr. Satyapal's group are so far holding aloof from the movement with a few exceptions. The Ahrars are ready to join the movement, but only on condition that the necessary funds will be provided by the Congress. This is generally considered to be merely a device for filling the empty coffers of the Ahrar organization. Some of the small group of the Muslim M.L.As. who oppose the Ministry

have been sounded, but I do not think that anyone of them have agreed to go to jail.

It was originally announced that the campaign in the Punjab would be initiated by Mian Iftikharuddin, M.L.A., President of the Provincial Congress Committee, on the 26th of November, but a day or two before that date "a message" was sent by the local Congress Executive to Abul Kalam Azad (who was then in Sind) and it was announced that no action would be taken pending his arrival in Lahore. I suspect that this message was a plea that the Punjab should share the exemption from the campaign which Abul Kalam Azad had agreed to in the case of Sind. However, Azad when he reached Lahore would not consent to this or even to the exemption of the Congress members of the Assembly in order that they might be available to oppose the taxation Bills. His decision on this last point has been freely criticised by the Hindu press. After this preliminary fumbling Iftikharuddin made his "demonstration" at 8 p.m. last night at Baghbanpura, a suburb of Lahore where he resides, and was duly arrested. Handbills had been distributed announcing the event and I am told that there was a crowd of about 10,000, mostly students and city riff-raff. Thus Gandhi's instructions prohibiting the assembly of crowds were altogether ignored. There was no difficulty about sending Iftikharuddin away in the prison van, but after his departure there was a certain amount of jeering and the Superintendent of Police[51] was hit by a brick, but not seriously hurt. The Police thereupon made what is known as a "light *lathi* charge" upon the crowd, which very quickly dispersed. Iftikharuddin is a man of strong communist tendencies and exercises some influence owing to his wealth, which is considerable. I understand that in all probability the sentence that will be imposed will be one of a month's imprisonment and a fine of Rs. 5,000, which there should be no difficulty in recovering by distress. The second *Satyagrahi* was to have been Dr. Gopi Chand Bhargava, who is almost the only genuine and whole-hearted supporter of Gandhi in the Punjab. He informed the District Magistrate,[52] that he would make an anti-war demonstration in the Anarkali Bazar (the Oxford Street of Lahore) this afternoon. But as such demonstration might have led to considerable excitement and possibly to counter-demonstration on the part of Muslims, my Ministers wisely decided to arrest him beforehand under the Defence of India Rules. This was duly done in the early hours of this morning.

4. It has now been announced that the venue of the next annual session of the Congress will be some place between Amritsar and Lahore, either Baghbanpura or the large village of Attari, but it is of course generally

recognised that there is very little chance of the session being held at all.

5. I have alluded above to the increasing restiveness of students. Their annual conference, which was held at Lahore on the 23rd of November, was attended by about 4,000 students, including 300 girls. The President was Dr. Ashraf, a communist from (I think) the United Provinces. He was served with an externment order to leave the Punjab within 12 hours of his arrival at Lahore, but managed to deliver his presidential address before obeying the order. A bad speech was made at this conference by a communist known as Comrade T.D. Bedi, who is to be arrested and detained under the Defence of India Rules. This man has a brother[53] who is a member of the I.C.S. and a District and Sessions Judge in the Punjab.

6. The Assembly session opened on the 18th of November and is causing the usual delay in the disposal of administrative business, as the Ministers have little time to devote to the daily routine business. Unfortunately Sir Sundar Singh Majithia, the Revenue Minister, has been seriously ill from about the middle of this month, the trouble being, I believe, dropsy. The doctors have ordered him to take complete rest and recommended that he should be given four months' leave; but there is of course no provision in the Government of India Act for the grant of leave to Ministers. At the moment his work is being distributed among his colleagues, the great bulk of it falling on the Premier, but this is obviously an arrangement that cannot continue much longer, especially as the Premier will probably be going to Egypt for a brief visit soon after the middle of December.

Sir Sundar Singh is himself too ill to receive visitors, but I had a talk the other day with his eldest son Sardar Kirpal Singh. The latter is a sensible man aged between 40 and 50, who ordinarily resides in the Gorakhpur district where he manages a large sugar factory owned by the family. I told him that I was greatly distressed at his father's illness, as we have been friends for over 30 years, and I was afraid that even when he is restored to normal health, he would still at his age (he is in his 69th year) find the burden of his work as Minister too heavy for his physical powers; and that greatly as I should regret his having to leave the Ministry, I hoped that his family would do their best to persuade him to do so purely in the interests of his own health. Kirpal Singh expressed his personal full agreement and promised to do what he could, but said that at the moment he did not wish to worry his father with any matters of a serious nature, as he is only allowed to see him for a few minutes daily. I cannot say whether the outcome of this conversation will be that Sir Sundar Singh will tender his resignation, but that would be by far the best solution of the present situation. Sikander agrees with this and indeed it was at his suggestion that I saw Kirpal Singh. But Sikander himself is evidently too soft-hearted to ask for the Sardar's resignation, though he would be glad to see him replaced by a younger and more active man.

7. The Assembly has so far only passed a single-clause Bill extending the life of the Punjab Criminal Law (Amendment) Act of 1935, which was due to expire this month, by another term of five years. I have given my assent to this measure. As regards the two taxation Bills mentioned in paragraph 8 of my letter to you of the 1st of November, a motion for a Select Committee on one of them was made yesterday. No progress has been made with the other. Since Congress Members of the Assembly are not to attend any further sittings, the Bills will presumably have a fairly easy passage.

8. Confidence in the ultimate issue of the war has been strengthened by the recent news from Greece and Albania, and all war efforts are being pushed on vigorously. Contributions to the war funds continue to come in satisfactorily and in one or two districts new funds have been started for the purchase of war planes. Lahore last week-end had a series of entertainments in aid of various war charities, which, I am informed by the organizers, will bring in the most creditable total of over Rs. 20,000. Some two months ago I sent a contribution of a lakh of rupees from my War Purposes Fund to the Lord Mayor of London for his fund for air-raid sufferers, and I have been advised by the War Funds Sub-Committee of the Provincial War Board to remit a further sum of half a lakh for this purpose, which I will do. My Ministers have also decided, subject of course to the approval of the Assembly, to give a donation of Rs. 50,000 from Provincial Revenues to this fund. I have also sent a sum of half a lakh, with my Ministers' approval, to the Hellenic War Fund opened by the Consul-General for Greece in India,[54] as an earnest of the sympathy and admiration felt by the people of the Punjab for the gallant resistance of the Greek nation. I have received a most grateful reply from the Consul-General.

9. The police campaign against the possession of illicit arms has had good results. In the four months from June to September inclusive the total number of such arms recovered was 291 rifles, 250 pistols, 44 revolvers, 46 guns and nearly 800 rounds of rifle ammunition and nearly 600 rounds of pistol and revolver ammunition. These recoveries were made mainly in the Lahore and Rawalpindi Police Ranges.

10. I enclose the fortnightly report for the first half of November.

Yours sincerely,
H.D. CRAIK

59

CRAIK TO LINLITHGOW[55]

Telegram

No. 19-G *December 11th, 1940*

Your telegram No. 2654 of December 10th.[56] No ex-Ministers have been arrested in the Punjab and I think my Government would object having to find accommodation in the Punjab jails for ex-Ministers from other provinces. On general merits of suggestion I agree with the views expressed in the second paragraph of your telegram.

60

CRAIK TO LINLITHGOW

Private and Personal Government House, Lahore,
D.-O. No. 317-F.L. *December 29th, 1940*

Dear Lord Linlithgow,

I am afraid a whole month has elapsed since the date of my last fortnightly letter (30th of November 1940), but we had so full a discussion of local affairs during my visit to Calcutta that I did not think it necessary to trouble you with a letter in the interval.

2. Sikander left for Egypt on the evening before my return to Lahore, but was unfortunately held up for three days at Karachi as the Imperial Airways plane was delayed by engine trouble at Singapore. I received an Air Mail letter from him yesterday from Lake Habbaniyeh, where he had again been held up by a storm. So I am afraid his absence from India will be somewhat longer than we had anticipated. Before leaving Sikander handed over the temporary charge of the Law and Order portfolio to Malik Khizar Hayat Khan. He also told me that I could assume his consent to any decision I thought proper; but I am of course consulting Khizar on important matters.

3. Sir Sundar Singh Majithia is still on the sick list and has now left Lahore for his Gorakhpur Estate, where he expects to stay till at least the end of January. I went to see him just before he left and found him looking somewhat better than I had expected. He carried on a fairly long con-

versation without visible fatigue, but I doubt very much whether he will be fit to resume the burden of office. He did not make any direct reference to the possibility of resigning, but hinted that he would like his eldest son, who now manages the Gorakhpur Estate, to return to the Punjab and seek election to the Legislative Assembly, the implication apparently being that his son might succeed him as the Sikh member of the Cabinet! To this somewhat surprising suggestion I pointed out that the selection of a Minister was primarily a matter for the Premier and expressed the hope that Sir Sundar Singh would concentrate on recovering his physical health and would not worry about the future.

4. I have little to add to what has appeared in the Press about the *Satyagraha* campaign in the Punjab. Such popular excitement as was caused by the first two arrests (Mian Iftikharuddin and Sampuran Singh) has almost completely died down. Nothing has done more to pour ridicule on the movement than Henderson's excellent judgement in Sampuran Singh's case, which aroused Homeric laughter and practically no criticism. Any sympathy which I might have felt for Sampuran Singh (who is more fool than knave) is discounted by two points about this incident which have not been reported in the Press. The first is that before making his "demonstration" Sampuran Singh sent a message to J.D. Anderson, our Joint Chief Secretary, stating that he would be glad if during the course of his trial questions could be put to him that would give him an opportunity of explaining that he was in favour of Sikh recruitment to the Army and was performing *Satyagraha* merely out of a sense of discipline. The second point is that he is a Director of a flourishing steel business at Tatanagar, which has extensive contracts from the Defence Department, and is presumably making large profits out of them.

The sentence imposed on Iftikharuddin, who is a wealthy man, was one of a year's imprisonment plus a fine of Rs. 6,000, and three of his cars were immediately seized to meet the fine. This sentence has, I think, had a valuable deterrent effect.

As you are aware, Gandhi suspended *Satyagraha* in the Punjab immediately he learnt of the Sampuran Singh incident, but allowed its resumption a few days later: then came his order for a general suspension of *Satyagraha* throughout India till after the Xmas holidays. Presumably demonstrations and arrests will begin again after the 5th January, but I have a feeling that much of "the kick" will have gone out of the movement in the Punjab. There is, however, still a list of between 1,100 and 1,200 prospective *Satyagrahis* which has been sent to Gandhi, and the Provincial Congress Committee has taken steps to remove its records to some secret depositary. The other day the Lahore City Congress Committee received notice from the landlord of its office to vacate his premises within a fortnight, obviously because he fears that the premises may be attached by Government.

Abul Kalam Azad is now in Lahore concerting plans with the local Congress leaders. It is reported that Sampuran Singh has succeeded in making his peace with the Maulana[57] and the latter has publicly expressed his conviction that Sampuran Singh was quite wrong when he told Gandhi that no one in the Punjab believed in "non-violence".

The Ahrars have started *Satyagraha* on a small scale, but quite independently of the Congress. Their plan is that one Ahrar leader should shout slogans in a mosque every Friday. So far I believe only two arrests have been made and there is clearly little enthusiasm behind this "stunt".

5. In paragraph 5 of my letter to you of the 30th of November I mentioned the increasing restiveness among students at Lahore.[58] This was intensified during the month by the arrest of two brothers, Mahmud Ali and Mazhar Ali, who are the sons of Nawab Muzaffar Khan, a cousin of the Premier. These two youths are ardent communists and have given a good deal of trouble lately both to their parents and to the authorities. They both announced that they intended to commit *Satyagraha* and an order was served on them under the Defence of India Rules restricting them to the Premier's tea estate at Palampur in the Kangra district. They disobeyed this order and were immediately arrested and sent to jail. As they are both prominent figures in student circles, their arrests caused considerable excitement and I received definite information from the C.I.D. that a demonstration was likely to be staged at the University Convocation, which was held on the 21st of December. The information was precise and included the names of the organizers and the various alternative forms of demonstration contemplated. This put me in a somewhat awkward position, as I ordinarily preside as Chancellor at the Convocation and on this occasion I was to have received an Honorary Degree. Moreover, Sargent,[59] who had accepted my invitation to deliver the Convocation address, was staying with me at the time. I decided, on the unanimous advice of the Ministers present in Lahore and of the Police chiefs, not to attend the Convocation. I was doubtful whether Sargent should deliver his address in person, but he was very keen on doing so and I eventually consented to this. In the event the Convocation passed off without any incident whatever and Sargent described his audience as one of the most attentive he had ever addressed. But the C.I.D. have told me that if I had attended, there would in their opinion have been some form of

demonstration. The Press were anxious to obtain the reason for my absence, but were merely informed that I had been unable to attend for private reasons, and there has been no comment on this in the newspapers.

6. Before dispersing about the middle of December for the Xmas recess, which will last about a month, the Assembly passed the Bill for the taxation of urban immovable property and also the Primary Education Bill, which has now been before it for nearly three years and has twice been considered by a Select Committee. Neither of these measures has yet been submitted for my assent, but the Taxation Bill has aroused great opposition, and I have received many protests both from commercial bodies and from private individuals. There was a fairly complete *hartal* at Amritsar the other day as a protest against this measure which, I am afraid, will be the subject of bitter controversy for a long time to come and may have the effect of alienating some of the Ministers' supporters. There has also been a good deal of ill-feeling about the Education Bill, which prescribes Urdu as the medium of instruction in primary schools, a provision which is resented by the Hindus and Sikhs. I have been informed that there was a stormy meeting of the Unionist Party just before the adjournment, at which heated speeches were delivered, partly about the Education Bill and partly about certain alleged acts of discourtesy by Sir Chhotu Ram and Mian Abdul Haye to some of their supporters. One of Sikander's first tasks on his return to India will be to compose these differences among his followers, but he will doubtless succeed in doing so.

7. The striking successes of the British forces in Libya have been hailed with great enthusiasm and there is a general feeling that the tide has now turned and that eventual victory is certain. These successes have acted as a stimulus to the Punjab's war effort. Figures are now available of the amounts collected in the Punjab up to the 30th of November for the War Purposes Fund and other charities and for the Defence Loans, and these may interest you. The total amount contributed to my branch of the War Purposes Fund is in round figures 34¾ lakhs; other war charities (mainly the Punjab branch of the Red Cross) Rs. 1,04,000; investments in 3 per cent Defence Bonds, 223 lakhs, in the interest-free loan 5 lakhs, and in Post Office Savings Certificates just under 22 lakhs, a total of 2½ crores. The actual investments in the war loan are probably a good deal higher than this, as a large sum has been subscribed through banks or brokers in Calcutta. This would be counted as an investment from Bengal.

The total number of civic guards enrolled up to the same date was just under 9,000. This latter figure is somewhat disappointing, as our original estimate was 30,000 for the Province, but in some districts enrolment is not being made till arrangements can be completed for training recruits. This force has not, however, attracted many recruits from rural areas, which is not altogether surprising.

I would emphasise that these figures represent the effort up to the end of November. The final figures will of course be considerably higher.

8. I had a talk two days ago with Major Taylor of the I.M.S., the doctor who accompanied Gainsford, the Superintendent of Police who was so terribly injured in the Khaksar clash last March, home in April last. He told me that Gainsford is still under treatment at Sir Harold Gillies' Hospital and the treatment has had a considerable measure of success, though Gainsford has completely lost the sight of one eye. Taylor described Gainsford as extraordinarily brave and cheerful and he hopes to return to India before many months have elapsed. Taylor himself was torpedoed two days after leaving England in (I think) the *City of Simla*, which also had among its passengers three of our new I.C.S. recruits. They have all now arrived safely, though they had to wait for over a month before securing passages in another ship.

9. I received a telegram two days ago from George Cunningham, telling me he had just granted an interview to Mian Ahmad Shah, the Khaksar leader, and that Ahmad Shah was anxious to see me about the course of the negotiations between the Khaksars and Sikander. I felt that such an interview would be embarrassing as I have no precise information of the stage which these negotiations had reached before Sikander's departure, and I am doubtful about Ahmad Shah's credentials as a leader. I accordingly replied that I did not think it would be suitable for me to receive Ahmad Shah in the absence of the Premier.

10. The Turkish Military Mission arrived here from Peshawar on the morning of December the 24th and left the same evening for Karachi en route to Ankara. They were entertained to breakfast by Malik Khizar Hayat Khan and spent the forenoon visiting the Fort, the Badshahi mosque and Shahdara. I then gave a luncheon party in their honour and later in the afternoon Mian Abdul Haye entertained them to a tea party, which I attended. They all seemed very pleased at the cordiality of their reception. Unfortunately none of them spoke any English and only one or two of them French.

11. I enclose the provincial fortnightly reports for the second half of November and the first half of December.

Yours sincerely,
H.D. CRAIK

NOTES

1. This document is taken from MSS. EUR. F 125/108.
2. In this telegram, sent to all Governors, Lord Linlithgow reported that he had now seen Mahatma Gandhi and Mr Jinnah. Jinnah was perfectly prepared to co-operate but only from within Government. He felt that a substantial number of political groups would agree to co-operate. If Congress refused to participate in a renewal of Linlithgow's earlier offer, H.M.G. should go ahead at the Centre without them. As regards the provinces, Jinnah urged that the Governors should take in non-official advisers from parties represented at Centre. In this way it might be possible to put an end to Section 93 administrations.

   Gandhi was friendly but uncompromising. Nothing less than the full Congress demand for complete freedom would meet their case. Gandhi begged the Viceroy that he should not make any declaration which stated that Indians would be responsible for certain areas of Government. Gandhi was also very averse to any preliminary exploratory processes. He thought these might provoke a clash of interests and retard rather than advance progress.

   Linlithgow asked for Governors' comments on these developments, particularly Jinnah's suggestion of non-official advisers in the provinces. The Viceroy was conscious of the possible effects on Congress of any move but he felt it would be difficult to resist for very much longer, certainly in respect of the Centre, pressure for some broadening of the basis of government. MSS. EUR. F 125/108.
3. In this telegram (No. 1198-S) Lord Linlithgow informed Governors of a letter he had received from Mahatma Gandhi which remained uncompromising. The Viceroy had also received a supplementary letter from Mr Jinnah. This asked that no pronouncement should be made which would prejudice the 'two nations' position; that there should be a definite and categorical assurance that no interim or final scheme of constitution would be adopted by His Majesty's Government without the previous approval and consent of Muslim India; and that Muslim India leadership must be fully treated as equals. In accordance with this: (*a*) the Viceroy's Council should be expanded by such numbers 'as may be settled by further discussion', but on the basis that the Muslim League should have the majority of the additional members if the Congress did not come in, and equality with the Hindus if they did; (*b*) in all Section 93 Provinces non-official advisers were to be appointed, the Muslims to be in a majority; (*c*) additional Muslim members of the Viceroy's Council and non-official advisers to be chosen by the Muslim League; (*d*) a War Council of not less than 15 members to be appointed. 'The representation of Muslim India must be equal to that of the Hindus if the Congress come in, otherwise they should have the majority.' Ibid.
4. Mr P. Marsden, Commissioner of the Rawalpindi Division.

5. Mr Amin-ud-Din.
6. Sardar Abdul Ghafur Khan.
7. Malik Sahib Khan Noon.
8. Mr A.A. Macdonald.
9. General Sir Roger Wilson.
10. The text of this document has been taken from MSS. EUR. F 125/108.
11. On 8 August 1940, Lord Linlithgow issued a statement with the authority of His Majesty's Government which became known as the 'August Offer' (Cmd. 6219). The Statement began by reviewing the political and constitutional developments which had taken place since the start of the war. Despite differences which had prevented the achievement of national unity, H.M.G. did not feel they should postpone the expansion of the Governor-General's Executive Council nor the creation of a War Advisory Council. Lord Linlithgow was accordingly authorized to invite a certain number of representative Indians to join the Executive Council and to establish a War Advisory Council which would contain representatives of the Indian States and other interests in India's national life.

    In the developments which had taken place since the war had begun, two points of doubt had emerged as to H.M.G's. intentions. These related to the minorities and the constitutional future of India. With regard to the minorities, H.M.G. reiterated that any future constitutional scheme did not exclude examination of the Act of 1935 or the policy on which it was based. 'It goes without saying that they [H.M.G.] could not contemplate transfer of their present responsibilities for the peace and welfare of India to any system of government whose authority is directly denied by large and powerful elements in India's national life.' Nor could H.M.G. 'be parties to the coercion of such elements into the submission of such a Government'. With regard to the constitutional future the Statement contemplated 'the setting up after the conclusion of the war with the least possible delay of a body representative of the principal elements in India's national life in order to devise the framework of the new Constitution'. The Statement emphasised that the 'attainment by India of that free and equal partnership in the British Commonwealth ... remains the proclaimed and accepted goal of the Imperial Crown and of the British Parliament.'

    The telegram under reference informed Governors that, in accordance with the terms of the 'August Offer', Lord Linlithgow was intending to establish a War Advisory Council of about 20 members. He asked Sir Henry Craik if Sir Muhammad Nawaz Khan of Kot would be a good representative of the Army interest. He would also act as a representative of Muslim landowners. The Viceroy was disposed to take a Sikh onto his Executive Council and asked whether Sir Sundar Singh was not the best man available. MSS. EUR F 125/108.
12. On 22 August 1940 Sir Henry Craik wrote to Lord Linlithgow (Letter No. 288) asking if he might have the opportunity of again discussing the

personnel of the War Advisory Council as there had been rather significant developments in the Akali attitude since the present telegram had been sent. Ibid.

13. This appears to be a reference to Lord Linlithgow's telegram 593-S.C. of 14 August 1940. In this he told Sir Henry Craik that he had had two interviews with Mr Jinnah who 'has been very sticky and continues to press for more precise information. He makes great play with the extreme difficulty which he says he anticipates from his organization....' The Viceroy had told Jinnah that he could not give him any guarantee as to who would or would not be in the new Council. Linlithgow explained to Craik: 'I suspect that he [Jinnah] is a little anxious to manoeuvre himself in the probable absence of Congress into the post of Prime Minister, which is not of course a position I would be prepared to contemplate for him for the moment.'

    Linlithgow then gave the text of a letter he had sent Jinnah that day. This made the following points: (1) the 'August Offer' had clearly safeguarded the Muslim position and provided a basis on which Muslims could co-operate at the Centre; (2) The Viceroy did not contemplate introducing non-official Advisers in the provinces at that stage; (3) the expanded Executive Council would be in the neighbourhood of 11 members of which two would be from the League. (Sir Zafrullah Khan would not count against the League's figure.) The Viceroy asked Jinnah for a panel of four names so that he (Linlithgow) could select two; (4) The Viceroy also asked for a panel of names for the War Advisory Council on the assumption that there would probably be about five League representatives out of a total in the neighbourhood of twenty.

    Linlithgow asked Craik to tell Sir Sikander in confidence the terms of what he had said to Jinnah. The Viceroy welcomed anything Sikander could do properly and discretely to expedite the meeting of the League Working Committee. R/3/1/62.

14. See No. 43, note 13. The date should be 14 August 1940.
15. No. 43.
16. In a statement, reported in the Indian press on 9 August 1940, Sir Sikander said it appeared that 'shorn of superfluous diplomatic verbiage, the declaration contains a substantial concession to Indian opinion.' He hoped the Congress and League would concentrate their attention on points of substance which provided ample scope for a realistic approach.
17. In his second statement Sir Sikander said that 'an esteemed friend, who holds an eminent position in the political life of India, has expressed his disappointment over my [earlier] statement'. Sikander went on to amplify his views. He felt that the 'August Offer', taken with Mr Amery's speech (see note 19 below), conceded the Indian demand for freedom and for representative government at the Centre. At the same time they met the demands of Muslims, Indian Princes and others. Sikander concluded: 'The Viceroy and the British government have done their duty. It now remains for the Indian leaders of the political parties in this country to do theirs.'

18. This telegram has not been traced.
19. Mr Amery's speech was made at the start of a House of Commons' debate on the 'August Offer' which took place on 14 August 1940. Referring to Congress demands, Amery, among other things, made it clear that the enlarged Executive Council would still be responsible to the Governor-General and could not be responsible to the Legislature in the strict constitutional sense. See *Parl. Debs.*, 5th ser., H. of C., Vol. 364, cols. 870-80.
20. Lord Linlithgow replied to Sir Henry Craik in a letter dated 22 August 1940. He said he hoped that Sir Sikander had not misunderstood his position. There was no question of going beyond the terms of the 'August Offer' and Mr Amery's speech. 'Thus it would be quite impossible for me to consider eliminating officials from my Council or accepting any obligation of any sort in regard to being bound by the views of the majority or the like.' Linlithgow added:

> 'I feel myself that there may be some risk of Sikander, to put it perfectly frankly and for your own eye only, burning his fingers if he tries to bring about a reconciliation between Congress and the League through intermediaries such as Shiva Rao, and I think we ought to be very careful about this. I should be most uneasy if I thought that there was the least risk of his getting into discussion up to a point at which either side might find themselves able to suggest, with however little foundation, that he had encouraged them in hopes for which there could be no basis whatever. Where he can be of real value, as I see it, is in connection with the Muslim League, and I venture to think that it is there his assistance could most usefully be lent.' R/3/1/62.

On 21 August 1940 the Congress Working Committee, meeting at Wardha, passed a resolution in which it stated that it could not be a party to accepting the proposals in the 'August Offer' nor could it advise India to accept them.

On 2 September 1940 the League Working Committee, meeting at Bombay, welcomed the 'August Offer' but complained that neither Mr Jinnah nor the Committee had been consulted on the proposed expansion of the Executive Council and had not been informed which portfolios would be allotted to the League. They had also not been told which parties they would be called upon to work with. The Committee also considered the panel system of appointment to be unsatisfactory. It called upon Mr Jinnah to clarify these points before accepting the Viceroy's invitation.

At the same meeting the League Working Committee passed a resolution giving full individual freedom to all members of the League to join War Committees and other war efforts.

21. In this telegram Lord Linlithgow passed on Mr Amery's observation that as Sikh reservists and recruits had also shown signs of trouble, it appeared that contamination must have come mainly from the men's homes in towns and villages. Amery was anxious to know whether the Punjab Government had

considered the possibility of taking steps against instigators outside the Army. R/3/1/62.

22. This letter has not been traced.
23. See note 11 above.
24. The Congress Working Committee, meeting at Wardha between 18 and 22 August 1940, passed a resolution directing that the normal activities of the Congress Seva Dal and other Congress volunteers should continue to be carried on.
25. Sir Francis Mudie.
26. On 31 December 1929, the Indian National Congress, meeting at Lahore, passed a resolution which had been drafted by Mahatma Gandhi. This stated that *swaraj* in the Congress creed should mean complete independence. In accordance with this creed the resolution called for a complete boycott by Congress of the Central and Provincial legislatures and authorised the All-India Committee to launch a programme of civil disobedience 'whenever it deemed fit'.
27. Mahatma Gandhi wrote to Master Tara Singh on 16 August 1940 in reply to a letter in which Tara Singh had argued that Congress should not prevent recruitment to the Army. Gandhi wrote: 'I have told you, in my opinion, you have nothing in common with the Congress nor the Congress with you.... With your mentality, you have to offer your services to the British Government unconditionally and look to it for the protection of the rights of "your community".... You have to be either fully nationalist or frankly communal and therefore dependent upon the British or other foreign power.' See Government of India, Publications Division, *The Collected Works of Mahatma Gandhi*, Vol. lxxii (New Delhi: The Division, 1978), pp. 395-6.
28. Not included in R/3/1/62.
29. Not printed. In his letter of 27 August 1940, Sir Sikander wrote that, in view of Mian Ahmad Shah's assurance, he was prepared to rescind the notification declaring the Khaksar organization unlawful. Sir Sikander was not in a position to concede the other suggestions in Mian Shah's letter but he would consider sympathetically the cases of prisoners not convicted of any offence involving violence with a view to their release within the following few days. R/3/1/62.
30. Not printed.
31. Lord Linlithgow minuted: 'This seems all right.'
32. This correspondence, of which Mr Sethi promised Sir Henry Craik copies, is not printed in R/3/1/62. See, however, note 27 above.
33. Mian Iftikhar-ud-Din.
34. The League Working Committee, meeting at Delhi on 28 and 29 September 1940, had decided that it was unable to accept the 'August Offer'. The League's decision followed a further meeting between Lord Linlithgow and Mr Jinnah.
35. In his letter No. 303 of 18 October 1940, Sir Henry Craik informed Lord

Linlithgow of a talk he had had the previous day with Sir Sikander on the Sind League Conference. Sikander explained that he had not definitely accepted the invitation to preside and in any case had made it clear that his acceptance would need the approval of the Governor of Sind. In view of the communal situation in Sind, Sikander would neither preside at, nor attend, the Conference. R/3/1/62.

36. See *Collected Works of Mahatma Gandhi*, Vol. lxxiii (New Delhi, 1978), pp. 71-3, 450-1.
37. Not included in R/3/1/62.
38. Not printed.
39. This report is not included in R/3/1/62. The Central Intelligence Officer was Mr W.D. Robinson.
40. Sir Douglas Young.
41. President Ismet Inönü.
42. Marshal Fevzi Cakinak.
43. Not printed.
44. In paragraph 3 of this report it was stated that Master Tara Singh had said the only fundamental difference he had with Congress was that he believed a strong army was necessary. Tara Singh was also reported to have remarked at a recent meeting: 'My fundamental difference with Mr Gandhi is that he wants Swaraj without military power whereas I hold that there can be no Swaraj without an Army. If I were asked to choose between Swaraj and the Army, I must choose the latter.' L/P&J/5/243: f 58v.
45. Mr A.A. Macdonald.
46. Mr N.M. Buch.
47. Major Shaukat Hayat Khan.
48. Lord Linlithgow minuted: 'Is this a "regular" A.D.C. If so, it represented, I think, an innovation. Is that correct?'
49. The text of this letter has been taken from MSS. EUR. F 125/108.
50. In this speech (of 20 November 1940) Lord Linlithgow announced that, although it did not intend to withdraw the proposals in the 'August Offer', His Majesty's Government had decided it would not be justified in proceeding at that time with the expansion of the Executive Council or the establishment of the War Advisory Council.
51. Mr J.A. Scroggie.
52. Mr K.H. Henderson.
53. Mr Tarlochan Das Bedi.
54. Dr M. Presvelos.
55. The text of this document has been taken from MSS. EUR. F 125/108.
56. In this telegram, Lord Linlithgow told Governors that Mr Amery thought there was a good deal in the suggestion that it was very undesirable ex-Ministers should be confined to jail in their own provinces. This was because there was a danger that police and prison services might be tempted to curry future favours from the prisoners. Alternatively these officers might be in

danger of future victimisation. In paragraph 2 of his telegram Linlithgow said he considered that the ideas behind this proposal would: '(*a*) be seen through and interpreted as an indication that Government knew the convicted persons were bound to return to power in due course and (*b*) be ineffective'. MSS. EUR. F 125/108.

57. On 18 December 1940, Sardar Sampuran Singh had been expelled from the Congress Party by Maulana Azad. Azad wrote: 'Your replies in the court clearly demonstrate that you do not agree with the decision of the Congress about war. In spite of this, you offered yourself as a *Satyagrahi* and made both yourself and the party … ludicrous.'
58. Lord Linlithgow minuted: 'I feel sure that we shall have in increasing degree to depend upon Police and C.I.D. action inside the Universities. It is the only line of policy that may sting the University authorities into doing something approaching their duty.'
59. Mr John Sargent, Education Commissioner with the Government of India.

CHAPTER 3

Documents for 1941

61

CRAIK TO LINLITHGOW

Private and Personal
D.-O. No. 319-F.L.

Government House, Lahore,
January 13th, 1941

Dear Lord Linlithgow,

Sikander arrived back from his trip to Egypt on the evening of the 11th of January and within an hour of his arrival came round to see me, after he had made a brief visit to his house and given an interview to a number of pressmen. He looked very well and was in the highest spirits. His experiences in Egypt were full of interest and incident. He was shown all round Sidi Barrani and flown over Bardia. He also visited Khartoum and made a fairly extensive tour in the southern Sudan, in the course of which he interviewed a Daffadar who had been wounded in the incident in which Sikander's son was taken prisoner. He also saw a Sudanese who managed to escape from the Italians and who had seen Shaukat Hyat and was able to tell the Premier that his wounds, which were slight, had healed. Altogether Sikander was delighted with his experiences and tells me he was received with the utmost kindness by everyone concerned, including General Wavell. He emphasised that the Indian troops did splendidly at Sidi Barrani, a fact recognised by everybody concerned and particularly by the Australians. Their morale is very high and they are all determined to see the business through. Many of the wounded whom Sikander interviewed in hospital (including the Daffadar mentioned above) begged that they should not be sent back to India, but allowed to rejoin their units in the Field. Altogether Sikander's trip seems to have been an outstanding success, and should have valuable results both in Egypt and in India.

He is to speak tonight to a large gathering of journalists in one of the Lahore hotels, which I shall attend. Tomorrow night he goes down Delhi to see the Commander-in-Chief about the provision of certain urgently required amenities for the Indian troops. I think he would like to give you personally an account of his visit on your return to Delhi.[1]

2. I had another long talk with Sikander today on various matters of business, decisions on which were awaiting his return. On the conclusion of this he asked me when I was handing over to Glancy and then took me considerably aback by hinting that he thinks the time has now come when he should himself be relieved of his office. I gather that the reasons underlying this suggestion are partly his anxiety to devote himself to work directly connected with the war and partly financial. His private means are limited and he has a very large family. He must have spent in the four years of his Premiership a great deal more than his official salary, and he hinted that he would like to be able to give more time to the business in which his family has a large interest – the Wah Cement Works. He feels that he has had enough of the constant strain of political life and also that he has completed his task of starting the machinery of the new constitution on smooth and stable lines. He would like to talk this matter over with you when an opportunity presents itself.

I told him that he would be extremely difficult to replace and stressed the point that it would be only fair to Glancy that he should continue in office for at least some months after Glancy becomes Governor. He realized the force of this suggestion.

3. Our very striking victories in Libya have been received with immense enthusiasm throughout the Province and have thrown the *Satyagraha* movement completely into the shade. *Satyagraha* was revived on the 5th of January after the "Christmas recess", but only four or five M.L.As. have since offered themselves for arrest. There has been no popular excitement, any kind, and interest in the movement seems to be rapidly waning. In the Rawalpindi Commissioner's Division there has been no *Satyagraha* at all, as not a single candidate for arrest has come forward.

One section of the Ahrars has now identified itself completely with the Congress campaign, I suspect as the result of a financial transaction between the leader of this section, Maulvi Daud Ghaznavi, and Abul Kalam Azad. Daud Ghaznavi and his supporters published a statement in which they announced that they intended to "completely identify their political activities and programme with those of the Congress", and in accordance with this announcement three or four Ahrars have courted arrest. Another section of the Ahrars, however, is wholly opposed to this change of policy and has issued a counter-statement denying altogether Daud Ghaznavi's authority as an Ahrar leader.

4. Sikh recruitment is still very unsatisfactory. I had a talk the other day with Short, one of the Liaison Officers working under General Haughton. Short is in close touch with several of the Akali leaders and particularly Master Tara Singh. According to Short, Tara Singh and his party are genuinely anxious to stimulate recruitment, but are afraid to come out in the open themselves, as they fear that by doing so they would be attacked as reactionaries and supporters of Government. They are, however, willing to supply agents and propaganda for a recruiting effort. Short impressed on them that the maintenance of the Sikh connection with the Army must depend on the efforts of Sikhs themselves and that no movement based on the support of Government and its officers would be likely to have much effect.

Sikander means to suggest to the Chief that a certain number of soldiers, who have been through the recent fighting in Egypt, should be brought back to India to form the nucleus of new units and generally to encourage recruitment. One or two of our District Officers have expressed the view that more war propaganda is wanted for recruiting purposes, i.e. that more publicity should be given to the doing of Indian troops overseas and to the part played in our recent victories. I think there is some force in this view and the other day when the news of the fall of Bardia was received I arranged that flags should be flown on all public buildings in Lahore and that a holiday should be given to the pupils of all Government schools. I also took the opportunity offered by a recent Rotarian dinner to emphasize publicly the tremendous significance of our recent victories, and the bravery and high morale of the Indian troops who contributed to them.

5. The Assembly is to resume its sittings on the 20th of this month. I have given my assent to the Urban Immovable Property Tax Bill, but the Bill imposing a tax on sales of goods has not yet been passed. The Primary Education Bill I am referring back to the Assembly on the advice of the Minister concerned for a small amendment on a purely technical point. I find that I was mistaken in telling you, in paragraph 6 of my letter of the 29th of December last, that this Bill prescribed Urdu as the medium of instruction in primary schools. As a matter of fact the Bill contains no such provision and does not in any way alter the existing position as to the language to be used as the medium of instruction. What happened was that the Education Minister opposed and the House rejected an amendment moved by a Hindu member that would have placed local bodies under an

obligation to provide instruction in Hindi and Gurmukhi, whenever required to do so. In resisting the amendment the Minister said something to the effect that it was his policy that the principal medium of instruction should continue to be Urdu, but there is no statutory provision to this effect in the Bill. Nevertheless the agitation against the Bill, although groundless, persists and I see from the newspapers that a deputation of Hindus and Sikhs intends to approach me with a request that in the exercise of my responsibility for the interests of minorities I should refuse assent.

6. I enclose the provincial fortnightly report for the second half of December 1940.

Yours sincerely,
H.D. CRAIK

62

CRAIK TO LINLITHGOW

Personal and Secret
D.-O. No. 320

Government House, Lahore,
January 21st, 1941

Dear Lord Linlithgow,

My Government has just sent an official reply to the Home Department's secret letter No. 3/25/40-Political (I) of the 20th of December 1940, in which its views were invited regarding the probable development of the civil disobedience movement. But Sikander has asked me to put forward in this connection a suggestion of his own, which we did not think could suitably be included in our official reply. It is as follows:

> "The best way of preventing the *Satyagraha* movement from gaining more popular support would be, in Sikander's opinion, to set up some machinery for working out the general scheme of the future constitution. For instance, action might be taken on the lines of the suggestion which emanated recently from Congress sources that the Premiers or ex-Premiers of all the Provinces should meet and discuss this all-important question. Other leaders of important sections of public opinion might also be included in these conversations. There should be no question of reaching conclusions by the counting of votes. The proceedings should be purely exploratory, but even so useful preliminary work might be done. If the Congress ex-Premiers dec' ned to co-operate, they would

be putting themselves more than ever in the wrong. Possibly Your Excellency might yourself preside at or at any rate inaugurate such a conference."

I am giving this suggestion more or less in Sikander's own words. I do not myself feel that his scheme has much chance of success, as it seems almost certain that the Congress ex-Premiers would decline any such invitation, even if the complication caused by their being at present in jail could be got round. A conference without any representation of Congress would of course have little or no effect in diminishing such popular interest as is at present attached to the *Satyagraha* movement.[2]

Yours sincerely,
H.D. CRAIK

63

CRAIK TO LINLITHGOW

Private and Personal
D.-O. No. 321-F.L.

Government House, Lahore,
February 10th, 1941

Dear Lord Linlithgow,

I did not trouble you with a fortnightly letter at the end of January, as I knew we were to meet within a day or two, and I had very little to report.

2. After leaving Delhi I paid brief visits to Rohtak and Hissar. The war effort of both these districts has been and is most striking. There is a steady flow of recruits of all classes and in spite of adverse famine conditions of the last three years the two districts between them have contributed nearly Rs. 5 lakhs by way of gifts to war charities and invested about Rs. 18 lakhs in the war loans. In Rohtak the district quota of civic guards is now complete, and I inspected a parade at which nearly 1,000 attended, including a large proportion of ex-soldiers, and was impressed by their smart and serviceable appearance in their grey uniforms.

3. There has been excellent rain throughout practically the whole Province during January, particularly in the eastern districts. In Rohtak and Hissar I found that the people had been able to sow some catch crops of barley and *tara-mira* and the prospects for the *rabi* harvest are distinctly improved. The peasantry are generally in better heart than they have been for 2½ years, but relief measures on a small scale must continue at least till the harvest is actually reaped. Some 25,000 people in Hissar are still

receiving gratuitous relief and we are maintaining a strong District Health Staff, one of whose main duties is the distribution of germinated grain to counteract deficiency diseases.

4. The attitude of the general public towards the war remains all that could be desired. Our recent successes in Africa have received excellent publicity through Sikander's public accounts of what he himself saw during his recent visit to the Middle East. We are celebrating the surrender of Benghazi by a public holiday today. Money is coming in freely to a special fund which Sikander has started to provide amenities for the Indian troops in the Middle East.

The only disquieting feature is the continued deficiency in Jat Sikh recruitment. The newly-formed "Khalsa Defence of India League" has hitherto done little or nothing to justify its existence. One of the resolutions passed at the meeting on January the 19th, at which this League was constituted, was that a deputation of leading Sikhs should wait on the Commander-in-Chief, but when I was in Delhi Auchinleck told me that he had not till then been asked to receive a deputation. I am impressing on all my Sikh visitors the vital necessity of immediate action by the Sikhs themselves to stimulate recruitment. But so long as the Akalis refuse to associate themselves with it, it seems unlikely that the new League will have any great measure of success.

5. In paragraph 7 of my letter to you of the 29th of December, I gave some figures of the Punjab's war effort up to the end of November. I am now in a position to give corresponding figures up to the 15th of January 1941. The total amount received in donations for the War Purposes Fund and other war charities (mainly the Red Cross) was in round figures Rs. 41,40,000 including a sum of nearly Rs. 18,000 subscribed by the newly started I.C.S. Officers' War Fund. The total amount invested in the various branches of the War Loan was Rs. 2,76,47,000, so far as can be ascertained. I do not think this includes a sum of Rs. 50 lakhs invested by the Lahore branch of the Imperial Bank.

It is interesting to compare these figures with the corresponding figures for the last war. During the four years 1914-18 the amount contributed as "gifts" was 55 lakhs, while the amount invested in loans was 870 lakhs, the proportion of gifts to loans being 1 to 16. In the present war the proportion is at the present moment about 1 to 6. We are now telling our District Officers to do all they can to encourage investments in the war loans, and I fully expect this will have a good response in due course. Indeed I have heard of several biggish investments during the last few days.

As an instance of Punjabi war enthusiasm I may cite what a recent visitor, Khan Bahadur Saadat Ali Khan, M.L.A., of the Montgomery district, said to me. This gentleman is the leader of the Kharral clan, one of the tribes which has benefited greatly by the extension of canal irrigation to that part of the Province. Besides donating some Rs. 1,200 to the War Purposes Fund he and his sons have invested Rs. 12,000 in war loans. He also made an offer to the district authorities to surrender for the duration of the war the income of 16 villages, which he estimates at between 15 and 20 thousand rupees a year, and to sell by public auction seven squares (175 acres) of fertile land for the benefit of the War Purposes Fund. The district authorities did not see their way to accept these very generous offers, but the Khan Bahadur at his interview with me expressed what seemed to be genuine disappointment at their refusal and pressed that the offer to sell the seven squares of land at any rate should be accepted. He has also succeeded in enlisting a fair number of his own tribesmen in the Army, though they are not a class who had ever previously been recruited.

6. *Satyagraha* excites very little interest and it is significant that reports of arrests, &c., have now been relegated to a back page of the *Tribune*. I have never known a time when the Congress credit stood at a lower ebb and there is a general reluctance on the part of Congressmen themselves to court arrest. The cash assets of the Provincial Congress Committee are reported to be only about Rs. 600, of which Rs. 200 are owed as salaries to paid employees. There were I think only five arrests during the first half of January, and though Gandhi is reported to have approved a list of 650 *Satyagrahis*, who were to seek arrest between the 27th of January, when the second phase was supposed to commence, and the 28th of February, there were only three more arrests up to the 1st of February. The infliction of fines in suitable cases has been a valuable deterrent.

There have been two or three more arrests of important communist workers and the Punjab Communist Party has now been practically completely disorganized.

7. The Assembly adjourned a few days ago for a ten-day recess on the occasion of the Muharram festival, which has passed off throughout the Province without incident. Before adjourning the Sales Tax Bill was passed, but has not yet been submitted for my assent. The agitation against this Bill continues, though with somewhat abated vigour. I am personally very doubtful as to the wisdom of this measure and as to the amount of revenue that it will produce.

8. I have referred above to the attitude of the Akalis towards Sikh recruitment. It is generally known that Master Tara Singh and Giani Kartar

Singh encouraged the formation of the Khalsa Defence of India League, though I believe neither was present at the meeting on the 19th of January. But on the 20th of January, the President of the Akali Dal published a statement that the Dal had taken no part in the meeting and "is not participating in the newly formed League". In these circumstances it seems certain that Tara Singh and his party will not have the courage openly to support the League, though they have promised to supply Parcharaks (preachers) to do propaganda in villages in favour of recruitment. The Akali Dal is to hold a conference at a village in the Jullundur district on the 15th and 16th of February, at which the various alleged grievances of the Sikhs against the Unionist Ministry will be discussed. These "grievances" include:

(*a*) the Primary Education Bill, the agitation against which is, as explained in paragraph 5 of my letter to you of the 13th of January, entirely unfounded; and

(*b*) a private member's Bill to amend the Sikh Gurdwaras Act by constituting a Board of seven members to audit the expenditure of the income from Sikh shrines. At present this expenditure is entirely controlled by the Shiromani Gurdwara Parbandhak Committee and a large part of it is believed to be used for political purposes, e.g. the election expenses of Akali candidates. Here again the grievance is not a genuine one, for the Bill is not a Government measure and Government, although not opposing its introduction, have in no way committed themselves to supporting it and have done nothing to expedite its passage through the Assembly. Sikander assures me that his intention is, should further progress be made with this Bill, to leave it to be decided by the votes of the Sikh members.

9. You may have noticed in the newspapers a report that the All-India Muslim League had expelled from membership three prominent Punjabis who disobeyed the resolution of the League directing all its members to resign from provincial and district war committees. The three gentlemen in question are:– (1) Nawabzada Khurshid Ali Khan, a nominated member of the Council of State, who is closely associated with the Unionist Party machine; (2) Nawab Muzaffar Khan, M.L.A., a retired officer of the Political Department who is Sikander's first cousin; and (3) Major Sir Muhammad Nawaz Khan, M.L.A., of Kot, who is, I think, at present serving with a Territorial Unit. The expulsion of three such prominent personalities has been much criticised by local Muslims as displaying ignorance on the

part of the All-India League of Punjab conditions, and is not calculated to increase Jinnah's popularity in the Unionist Party.

Sikander has said nothing more to me about his contemplated resignation – see paragraph 2 of my letter to you of the 13th of January.

10. There have been some slight, and hitherto not very successful, attempts to revive Khaksar excitement in Lahore, and I have received a large number of telegrams, mainly from obscure individuals in the Rawalpindi district, demanding the release of Allama Mashriqi. The situation is being closely watched. The trial has recently concluded of about 185 Khaksars arrested in the round-up in the Lahore mosques about the middle of June last, practically all of them being convicted and sentenced to substantial terms of imprisonment.

11. I enclose the provincial fortnightly reports for the first and second halves of January.

Yours sincerely,
H.D. CRAIK

64

CRAIK TO LINLITHGOW

Private and Personal
D.-O. No. 323-F.L.

Government House, Lahore,
February 28th, 1941

Dear Lord Linlithgow,

The number of arrests in connection with the *Satyagraha* movement has increased considerably, as pointed out in paragraph 2 of the fortnightly report for the first half of February (enclosed herewith). Up to the middle of this month the total number of arrests since the movement started was 72, but another 74 arrests were made during the week ending the 22nd of February. But none of the persons arrested were of any importance and there has been no increase of popular excitement other than the disorderly incident at Rawalpindi mentioned in the provincial report. The "third phase" of the movement is advertized to start on the 1st of March and it has been announced that a list of between 700 to 1,000 *Satyagrahis* is ready. I doubt very much whether so many will actually offer themselves for arrest. It is significant that the total primary membership of the Congress in the Punjab has fallen since last year from 191 thousand to 110 thousand.

2. The big Akali conference at Rurka Kalan in the Jullundur district on

the 15th and 16th of February passed off without any special incident. The numbers attending on the second day are said to have reached 35,000. The speeches made by the leaders gave no clear indication of any constructive policy on the part of the Akali Dal, though a number of resolutions were passed condemning various alleged misdeeds of the policy of the Unionist Ministry. The Shromani Gurdwara Parbandhak Committee, which is the statutory body appointed under the Sikh Gurdwaras Act for the management of Sikh shrines, subsequently endorsed the resolutions passed and presented a kind of ultimatum to the Unionist Ministry, calling upon it to "change its communal policy" and to give proof of doing so by taking certain specified action within a period of one month. Failing compliance with this demand the Sikhs would have "to make sacrifices again for the preservation of Sikh culture and religious integrity, and all Sikhs prepared to make such sacrifices to fill in a pledge." This ultimatum has been reported in the Press, but I do not think it has actually reached Government yet. It is an ambiguous document and I doubt whether it need be taken very seriously. It is reported that at the Rurka Kalan conference very little enthusiasm for a *morcha* (direct action of any kind) was exhibited.

On the other hand, the Rurka Kalan gathering was certainly symptomatic of the deterioration in the relations between Sikhs and Muslims and of the increased apprehension which the Pakistan scheme is causing among the Sikhs. It is unfortunate that at this juncture Jinnah should have decided to visit Lahore. He is due here tomorrow to inaugurate a "Students' Pakistan Conference".

3. At the Rurka Kalan conference not a word was said on the subject of Jat-Sikh recruitment to the Army, and it seems clear that the Akali leaders either do not appreciate or are deliberately ignoring the vital importance of this question in relation to the future economic and political importance of their community. I have, however, been informed by several recent visitors, which are in a position to know, that the Khalsa Defence of India League is really beginning to have some effect on Jat-Sikh recruitment, in which there has been some improvement within the last week or two notably in the Amritsar district. Some six or seven Parcharaks (or paid propagandists) have been supplied by Master Tara Singh and his friends to preach recruitment in villages, and one or two people who have heard these men speaking report that their speeches are having a good effect. One of them certainly spoke effectively at a recruiting meeting at Kasur in the Lahore district, where the General Commanding the District and the Commissioner of the Division[3] were present.

4. There has been no further development in regard to the Khaksars

since the arrests mentioned in paragraph 2 (*c*) of the provincial report, except that the Khaksar newspaper is now being published at irregular intervals in Lahore. Some of its articles are distinctly truculent in tone, but the last issue which I saw was comparatively moderate.

5. I have just given my assent to the Punjab General Sales Tax Bill, which imposes a tax on the sale of goods (with certain exceptions) in the province. A point of some interest was raised by my Legal Advisers in connection with this Act. The definition of "sale" is framed so as to include "a transfer of goods on the hire-purchase or other instalment system of payment", and my Legal Advisers have expressed the view that this section is *ultra vires* on the ground that a hire-purchase transaction has been held by rulings of the Courts, both in India and in England, to be not a sale, but a contract of hire coupled with an option to purchase, and that a tax on such contract cannot be held to fall within Item 48 of the Provincial Legislative List.

I am not altogether satisfied as to the correctness of this advice, for the intention of the Act is only to tax hire-purchase transactions after the option to purchase has been exercised and when the purchase has in fact been actually completed: but whether I am right or wrong on this point, it is clearly laid down in the instructions I have received from you on this subject (vide particularly paragraphs 13 and 18 of your letter to me of June the 14th, 1938, and paragraphs 12 and 13 of your letter of April the 29th, 1940) that a doubt as to the *vires* of any particular piece of legislation is not a ground for reservation.

6. In your secret letter to me of the 15th of February 1941 you referred to the traffic in illicit arms in the Punjab and asked whether I was satisfied that the Police were exercising sufficient vigilance in this matter and whether I had any specific suggestions for reducing still further the inflow of prohibited arms or controlling the sources from which they are drawn.

I have just received a fairly comprehensive review of this question from the C.I.D., but before sending this on to you I wish to consult as regards specific suggestions the Inspector-General of Police[4] and also Sikander, who takes a considerable personal interest in this matter.[5] Meanwhile I suggest that if you have not already seen it, you should ask the Central Intelligence Bureau to show you a recent report which our C.I.D. sent up to the Bureau under cover of a letter[6] of the 4th of December last. This report gave a comprehensive picture of the extent of the traffic in illicit arms between the North-West Frontier Province and the Punjab and also gave statistics of such arms seized in the Punjab since June last.

You may be assured that neither I nor my Police Advisers are disposed to underrate the gravity of this question.

7. Manohar Lal presented his Budget to the Assembly yesterday and I understand that he received an ovation when he had completed his speech. It was certainly an admirably lucid and heartening performance. I need not trouble you with details, which you will have seen in the newspapers, but I am glad to be handing over the Province to my successor in a fairly stable financial position in spite of the fact that during my three years of office the famine has cost us in round figures some 2¾ crores of rupees.

Yours sincerely,
H.D. CRAIK

65

CRAIK TO LINLITHGOW

Personal and Secret
D.-O. No. 324

Camp, Rawalpindi,
March 3rd, 1941

Dear Lord Linlithgow,

In my last fortnightly letter to you of the 28th of February I mentioned an "ultimatum" presented, or about to be presented, to my Ministers by the Shiromani Gurdwara Parbandhak Committee. Since writing that letter I have received a letter, of which I now enclose a copy, from Master Tara Singh. You will observe that he refers to my special responsibility to protect the interests of minorities and offers to discuss the Sikh demands if I so desire. He also encloses a copy of the so-called ultimatum.

2. The letter is typically disingenuous, and while professing not to wish to create difficulties for the Government, Tara Singh has, I suspect, chosen this moment to deliver an ultimatum because he realises that owing to an imminent change of Governors it would be particularly inconvenient. The specific demands put forward are described as urgent on the ground of the "immediate need of easing the present communal tension": but with the exception of the first demand, none of them in fact refer to questions that are in any way urgent. The first demand relates to a recent incident at Sargodha; where a number of the local Sikhs deliberately defied the orders of the District Magistrate[7] (a Muslim member of the I.C.S.) about the route of a Sikh procession and made a somewhat serious assault on certain

Police officers who tried to restrain them. Some of the Sikhs involved in this incident are awaiting trial.

3. So far there is little sign of any great popular enthusiasm for the proposed *morcha*, i.e. for whatever form of direct action may be signified by the phrase "entering upon the path of sacrifice once again". But it would be unwise on this account to belittle the dangers underlying the threat. A number of Akali leaders, though unwilling to court imprisonment in pursuance of Gandhi's non-violence campaign, would be only too ready to demonstrate by courting imprisonment their willingness to make sacrifices for their own community. The Sikh community is easily led into foolish and mischievous action and it might well be that the Akali leaders would be able to organize, in defiance of existing prohibitions, processions and demonstrations which might gravely embarrass Government and possibly lead to communal disorder.

4. There is thus a risk that a somewhat grave situation might arise for my Ministers vis-à-vis the Sikhs and, subject to any advice which Sikander may give me, I propose to ask Tara Singh to come and discuss the situation with me (possibly in Sikander's presence). I would point out to him the unreality of most of his demands and try to convince him that he is wrong in thinking that the Ministers' policy is directed against Sikh interests. I would also stress the fact that the really urgent matter for the Sikhs at the moment is the maintenance of their connection with the Army. I may of course be unable to convince him, but I feel it would be a mistake to dismiss his representation summarily and that it is advisable to give the Sikhs a relatively soft answer, or at any rate to expose the hollowness of the case on which they propose to attack Government.[8]

All this of course has a considerable bearing on the Pakistan issue, regarding which I have just received your personal and most secret telegram of the 1st of March,[9] as I believe this issue is the real cause of the present unrest among the Sikhs. Sikander is, I hope, meeting me here tomorrow and I will sound him on the question discussed in your telegram. The discussion will, however, require careful handling, as on previous occasions when we have discussed the advisability of his taking the action which he outlined to you, my advice has been rather in favour of such action on the ground that it would tend to ease communal tension in the Punjab. To be quite frank, I do not altogether see eye to eye with you in regard to this matter, as Sikander's present equivocal attitude towards Pakistan has put him in a difficult position vis-à-vis his non-Muslim colleagues and supporters, whom he cannot afford to ignore, and might even, if persisted in, mean the eventual break-up of the Unionist Party. I will, however, sound him as discreetly as possible and will put before him the considerations mentioned in paragraph 2 of your telegram, of course without bringing your name into the discussion at all. I will write to you fully after I have had my talk with Sikander.[10]

Yours sincerely,
H.D. CRAIK

ENCLOSURE 1 TO NO. 65

TARA SINGH TO CRAIK

Teja Singh Hall, Amritsar,
February 28th, 1941

Your Excellency,

Most respectfully I beg to forward herewith a copy of a resolution passed at the All-India Akali Conference, Roorka, held on 15th and 16th February 1941; and a copy of another resolution passed in the General Meeting of the Shiromani Gurdwara Parbandhak Committee held on 22nd February 1941. Both the resolutions are identical in their purpose and represent the feelings of the Sikh community.[11] I am fully aware of the present difficulties and pre-occupations of the Government; and I assure you that the demands of the Sikhs as adumbrated in the enclosed resolution of the S.G.P.C. are only those which could not be further postponed. The Sikhs wish to avoid all complications and do not wish to create difficulties for the Government at the present critical juncture, but they expect the present Government of the Province also to desist from taking steps to weaken the position of the Sikhs and specially from attacking their religion, culture and honour.

The present Punjab Government has persistently followed a communal and narrow-minded policy during the past four years. The communal policy, the speeches and the private talks of some of the Ministers of the Punjab Government have created a highly arrogant attitude in many of the Muslim officials and other Government employees. The result is that Hindu and the Sikh employees in the services are being made to feel their subservient position, and the Sikhs and the Hindus everywhere are being harassed and coerced. It is not possible to give details in this short letter and it may not be possible or advisable for Your Excellency to hold an enquiry under the present circumstances. Hence only such demands are being submitted to

Your Excellency as are evidently reasonable and just, and the fulfilment of which will create a sense of security amongst the Sikhs for their religious and cultural rights at least. Under the Government of India Act of 1935, Your Excellency is empowered to protect the minority communities and specially their religion and culture. I, therefore, appeal to Your Excellency on behalf of the Sikh community to take steps and see that these perfectly reasonable and moderate demands of the Sikhs may be met till [*sic*] first of April 1941. The fulfilment of these demands will create a certain amount of sense of security amongst the Sikhs and the present communal tense atmosphere will be a good deal eased. There is certainly immediate need of easing the present communal tension. I hope Your Excellency will respond to this humble appeal of mine. I may add here that I am prepared to discuss these demands if Your Excellency so desires. My aim is to create better atmosphere and better understanding which can easily be done if the Sikhs get some practical proof that their religion, culture and honour will not be allowed to be assailed.

I have the honour to be, Your Excellency,
Your Excellency's most obedient servant,
TARA SINGH
President,
Shiromani Gurdwara Parbandhak Committee

ENCLOSURE 2 TO NO. 65

RESOLUTION OF S.G.P.C.

After going through the resolution passed by the All-India Akali Conference at Roorka concerning the religious freedom of Sikhs (which also includes the cultural freedom) and after fully considering over all the points raised therein the S.G.P.C. feels that the continuance for some time more of the present unbearable attitude of the Unionist Government towards the religious and cultural matters of the Sikhs will deal a heavy blow to the religious existence of the Sikhs and will stop their religious evolution. This General Meeting of the S.G.P.C. therefore fully supports the demands contained in the above said resolution of the Akali conference and urges upon the Unionist Government to change its discriminatory communal policy within one month from the date and to give practical proof of this change by conceding the following demands:

(1) Unconditional withdrawal of the cases against the Sikhs arrested at Sargodha.
(2) Declaration establishing a convention that as long as communal representation forms the basis of the country's constitution, legislation affecting the religious matters of any community would be enacted by an absolute majority of the Assembly Members of that community alone; and the Government should afford facilities for such legislation. The concurrence of the S.G.P.C. should be deemed essential for any legislation affecting the management of the Gurdwaras.
(3) Special facilities including budget provision should be afforded for popularising and teaching the Punjabi Language.
(4) Amendment of the compulsory Primary Education Bill so as to provide for the teaching of Gurmukhi in all public schools where at least seven students desire it. Hindi should also be placed on the same footing.
(5) Removal of restrictions on the use of *Jhatka* meat within the precincts of public institutions by affording the same facilities to *Jhatka* as are given to *Kutha* (meat prepared according to Muslim rites).
(6) Property belonging to religious, educational and charitable institutions to be exempted from taxation under the Urban Immovable Property Tax Act.

The S.G.P.C. feels that in case the above demands are not conceded within the specified period, then in order to preserve the religious and cultural freedom of the Sikhs, the Sikh community will have to enter upon the path of sacrifice once again. And keeping in view this contingency the S.G.P.C. appeals that all those who wish to make sacrifices should fill up the pledges published by the Shiromani Akali Dal for this purpose.

This General meeting of the S.G.P.C. authorises Master Tara Singh, its President, to do all that is needed for the fulfilment of the object of this resolution in consultation with the executive members of the S.G.P.C. and to form a Council of Action if need be.

This meeting requests the Hindu and Muslim brethren and the Punjab press to support the Sikhs in their struggle for truth, justice and religious freedom.

TARA SINGH

66

CRAIK TO LINLITHGOW

Personal and Secret
D.-O. No. 325

Camp, Rawalpindi,
March 4th, 1941

Dear Lord Linlithgow,

I am writing in continuation of my personal and secret letter to you of yesterday, No. 324.

2. Sikander arrived here this morning and I have just concluded a long talk with him. I began by discussing the ultimatum received from the Shiromani Gurdwara Parbandhak Committee, regarding which he agreed that I should ask Tara Singh to come and see me. I am writing today to Tara Singh in this sense.

3. I then introduced the Pakistan issue by saying that I thought this was at the bottom of the present unrest among the Sikhs. Sikander does not altogether share this view, as he tells me that Tara Singh and his friends are well aware as a result of more than one discussion with the Premier that the latter and his party do not see eye to eye with Jinnah on this issue. He thinks Tara Singh's present attitude has been induced by a feeling that his influence is on the wane owing to a split among the Akalis. Some of the Akalis have actually committed, or are contemplating committing, themselves to supporting the Congress *Satyagraha* campaign and Tara Singh, as you know, has broken away from the Congress. He is therefore trying to work up enthusiasm for some form of direct action by the Sikhs against the Unionist Ministry, which will appeal to that considerable section of the Sikhs which does not believe in Gandhi's creed of non-violence. Tara Singh also feels that the support he is known to be giving to the Khalsa Defence of India League may have led to his being classed as a supporter of Government by some of his own followers, and he therefore desires to make some gesture which will show that he is "agin to the Government".

4. However this may be, my mention of Pakistan led us on to a discussion of Sikander's position at the moment vis-à-vis Jinnah, and I gained the impression that Sikander has already committed himself pretty deeply to a rupture with Jinnah. When Sikander attended the meeting of the Muslim League Executive at Delhi about ten days ago he pressed Jinnah to abandon the catch-word of "Pakistan" which he considers provocative, but when he found himself in a minority of one on this occasion, I gather that he

said something to the effect that it was no use his remaining a member of the League Working Committee. During Jinnah's visit to Lahore on the 1st and 2nd of March he and Sikander did not meet at all and neither made any effort to do so. At Jinnah's public meeting last Sunday none of the Muslim Ministers or Parliamentary Secretaries and very few of the leading members of the Unionist Party were present, a fact which has of course been the subject of Press comment. Sikander thinks that Jinnah is now perfectly well aware of his intention to resign from the Working Committee, but not from membership of the League. Sikander has only withheld publication of his resignation till after Jinnah's visit to Lahore and because he has to prepare a carefully worded statement of the reasons for his resignation to be published simultaneously with the resignation itself.

5. I formed the impression that Sikander had carefully thought out the implications and consequences of the action he contemplates and that he is convinced that the indefinite retention of his present equivocal position as regards Pakistan must eventually lead to a split between himself and his non-Muslim supporters, i.e. the Khalsa National Party and the important rural Hindu group led by Sir Chhotu Ram. Without their support his party could not command a majority in the Assembly or hope to secure a majority at the next general election.

6. I asked Sikander whether if he splits with Jinnah, the latter could not secure the return at the next general election of a number of Muslim Leaguers in seats now held by Unionists. Sikander thinks that apart from the six or seven urban seats Jinnah would not be able to secure the return of more than one or two Muslim Leaguers in rural constituencies. At the last general election Jinnah did put up a number of Muslim League candidates, but only one was returned. In spite of the greatly increased prestige of the League and of Jinnah personally since 1937, Sikander is confident that the result of the next general election would not be substantially different; so that with the support of the rural Hindus and the Khalsa National Sikhs the Unionist Party would still have a substantial majority.

7. At this stage of the discussion I put to Sikander specifically the suggestion that a split in the Muslim League at the present moment might act as a great encouragement to the Congress and the anti-war party. He did not seem to think that there was any great danger of this, but he admitted that the statement he contemplates publishing would have to be carefully worded so as to avoid giving any handle to the Congress of the kind suggested.

On the other hand, Sikander seems quite convinced that with a general election now fairly imminent he cannot much longer maintain his present equivocal ("neutral" is the word he himself used) attitude towards Pakistan without running a grave risk of the breaking up of his party and the loss of his own political influence and position, and I think he suspects Jinnah of deliberately pressing the Pakistan issue at the moment in order to embarrass him.

8. I could not conscientiously advise him to reconsider the action which he contemplates, because I feel that he is in the main right in his estimate of its consequences. If there is a split and if the elections are to be postponed till the conclusion of the war, Sikander should be able to carry on with his majority till then. Although he might lose the support of a few extremist Muslims and miscellaneous malcontents the mass of the rural Muslim members would stand by him. The effect of the loss of a few Muslim votes on the stability of Government would be more than offset by the reassuring effect which a clear declaration of his views about Pakistan would have on the non-Muslim communities. On the other hand, if the elections are not postponed and take place some time towards the end of the present year, Sikander could appeal to the electorate on the platform of a "united war effort and no interference from outsiders". I do not believe that Jinnah could make much headway against such a platform.

9. Finally, I do not myself consider that there is much ground for apprehending that a split in the Muslim League at the present moment would have the effect of encouraging the anti-war party. It might even tend to increase the enthusiasm of moderate elements, who genuinely desire to clear the communal atmosphere so that they can get on with their war effort.[12]

Yours sincerely,
H.D. CRAIK

67

CRAIK TO LINLITHGOW

Secret
D.-O. No. 329

Government House, Lahore,
March 13th, 1941

Dear Lord Linlithgow,

The enclosed cutting[13] refers to what seems to have been a plot to murder Sikander.

According to the account given me by the Inspector-General[14] the police received information of the existence of this plot from a "source" who was well-known to our C.I.D. He had been employed as a police informer on previous occasions, but had been discarded (I believe some years ago), because he was detected acting as an *agent provocateur*. In spite of this man's bad record the police attached importance to the story told by him of this plot and decided to follow it up, partly because the story was obviously one that could not be ignored and partly because the informer was brought to the police by Pir Mohayuddin Lal Badshah of Makhad, an M.L.A., whom I have mentioned in previous letters to you.

The informer's story was that two men would make an attempt on the Premier's life when he visited the Regal Cinema here on the evening of Friday, March the 7th (as a matter of fact Sikander had no intention of visiting the Cinema that night). The police watched the Cinema and saw two men behaving in a suspicious way. Khan Bahadur Said Ahmad Shah with another police officer and his chauffeur followed these two men when they left the Cinema and saw them turn into the compound of the Roman Catholic Cathedral. Here the officers challenged and arrested them. One of the two men, Mushtaq Ahmed, bade no resistance, but the other Abdul Aziz, resisted desparately, but was overpowered. A fully loaded six-chambered revolver was found on him.

Khan Bahadur Said Ahmed Shah, the Deputy Superintendent who effected the arrests, displayed courage of a very high order. He was himself unarmed and is over 55 years' old, his service having been extended. Nevertheless he tackled a man whom he had every reason to suspect was armed. He is already a holder of the King's Police Medal for gallantry and I shall probably recommend him for a Bar to that Medal.

Of the two men arrested, Abdul Aziz is reported to be an M.A. and to be employed as a teacher in the Jinnah Girls School at Lahore, an institution of which I had never previously heard. I have not heard what Mushtaq Ahmed's antecedents or profession are, but I believe both men came to notice during the Khaksar troubles in Lahore last summer. They are both in police custody and are being interrogated. Mushtaq Ahmed has, I understand, made certain disclosures, but Abdul Aziz has so far refused to say anything.

The special precautions that are always taken for the Premier's personal safety, viz., an armed guard on his house and gunmen to accompany him everywhere, have been reinforced.

Although we are not yet in possession of the full facts of the conspiracy, it is obviously significant as showing the fanatical character of the Khaksar movement.

Yours sincerely,
H.D. CRAIK

68

CRAIK TO LINLITHGOW

Private and Personal
D.-O. No. 330-F.L.

Government House, Lahore,
March 17th, 1941

Dear Lord Linlithgow,

Opinion as to the war throughout the province remains optimistic, possibly unduly so. Apprehension as to developments in the Balkans is doubtless causing a good deal of uneasiness among people who read and understand newspapers, but I doubt whether this apprehension has penetrated into our more remote districts, where the general attitude is one of complete confidence in our ultimate victory. On the whole it is well that this atmosphere of somewhat unreasoning confidence should prevail, for so long as it lasts there will be plenty of recruits forthcoming and a better chance of attracting further investments in the Defence Loans. It is panic that militates against recruitment and prevents people coming forward to invest their savings.

Up to the end of February donations for the War Purposes Fund, the Red Cross, &c., exceeded 51 lakhs and the total amount invested in War Loans was about 3¼ crores. As I have informed you in a separate letter, we are now starting a drive to encourage investments.

2. Up to the end of February the total number of *Satyagrahis* arrested was 227 and there were about 81 arrests in the first week of the present month. Since then, however, the pace has slackened considerably. There has been no general increase of public interest in the movement, though there have been minor disorderly incidents at Multan, where the police making an arrest were stoned, and at Hoshiarpur.

3. The state of communal feeling in the province continues to give ground for uneasiness. Tension was aggravated at the beginning of the month by Jinnah's visit to Lahore and by the Hindu conference over which Dr. Syama Prasad Mookerjee of Bengal presided. It was further aggravated by the Census, at which all communities did everything possible to swell their population figures. There have been general complaints of intentional omissions and artificial inflations, and I am afraid that in certain of the towns very little reliance can be placed on the returns actually made. Hindus, Muslims and Sikhs are equally to blame. In Lahore the Deputy Commissioner[15] estimates that no less than three lakhs of bogus names were recorded in the municipal area. This may be an exaggeration, but

there have been so many complaints of this kind of thing from all communities that I think there must be a good deal of truth in it. In part ignorance and lack of patience on the part of enumerators are to blame. The Deputy Commissioner of Montgomery,[16] for instance (an Indian officer), reported that among his own servants a mistake of 30 years was made in his Ayah's age; his chauffeur, a Pashtu speaking Pathan from Kohat, was recorded as speaking Urdu and born in Quetta; his bearer, who can speak nothing but Punjabi, was recorded as Urdu speaking; and his Bengali cook was omitted altogether!

There was a small communal riot at Amritsar on the afternoon of the 14th of March arising out of the Holi festival. One Hindu was stabbed and some 16 other persons were injured. The local police took very prompt action and the disorder was quickly suppressed.

4. In my secret and personal letter to you of the 4th of March I wrote to you about the "ultimatum" presented to Government by the Shiromani Gurdwara Parbandhak Committee and mentioned my intention of asking Master Tara Singh to come and see me about this. He came yesterday and had a long conversation with Sikander and myself. We went through the ultimatum point by point and were, I think, able to reassure him on several of the points taken in the ultimatum. Sikander's attitude was most reasonable and he announced his readiness to consider any representation that Tara Singh would care to present him personally about most of the questions at issue. As regards the first demand in the ultimatum, however, he adopted a firm attitude. This was a demand for the withdrawal of the prosecution of some 20 odd Sikhs who had defied an order issued by the Muslim District Magistrate[17] about the route of a Sikh procession at Sargodha and who had committed fairly serious assaults on the police who tried to restrain them. Sikander made it clear that he was prepared to withdraw the prosecution only if the Sikhs concerned submitted a suitable apology. As a matter of fact the attitude of Government on this point is well known to the local Sikhs, who are quite prepared to make the men at fault apologize, if only outsiders such as Tara Singh himself would refrain from interference, and who according to my information would be glad to see the whole incident liquidated.

The general impression I received from the interview was that Tara Singh is not really keen on starting any campaign of direct action, for which there is actually little enthusiasm on the part of his followers. On the other hand, he seemed rather anxious to prolong negotiations indefinitely. After we had finished discussing the "ultimatum" I told him that I intended to give him some advice and proceeded to impress on him as forcibly as I could the extreme importance from the point of view of Sikhs themselves of concentrating all their efforts at the present moment on maintaining and strengthening their connection with the Army. I repeated fairly closely what I had said in my speech at the Khalsa College, Amritsar, on March the 6th (which I think Auchinleck passed on to you) on this point, and what I said seemed to make some impression on Tara Singh. He admitted that the problem of recruitment was urgent and that both the economic and political importance of the Sikhs as a minority community depended almost entirely on their connection with the Army.

Tara Singh cut a poor figure in argument with Sikander. He was shaky as to his facts and has no gift for expressing himself lucidly, but like most Sikhs he is extraordinarily tenacious of his own point of view and incapable of seeing that there can be any other.

5. My Sikh visitors tell me that there has been a slight improvement in Sikh recruitment, notably in Ludhiana and to a less extent in the Amritsar district, but the supplies still fall very far short of the demand. Sardar Bahadur Sardar Ujjal Singh, one of our Parliamentary Secretaries, gave me today the following figures for the Lahore recruiting area, which he told me had been supplied to him by the Recruiting Officer. The total demand for March, including the shortage in February, was 484 Jat Sikhs and 656 other Sikhs. The actual recruitment up to the 10th of March was only 62 of each class or 124 in all. I asked Ujjal Singh whether the Khalsa Defence of India League was doing any effective work and he told me that moderate Sikhs (by which he meant Sikhs of the Khalsa National Party) distrusted this League, because they consider that it is too much in the hands of the Akalis, who supply the paid propagandists and control the disbursement of the funds supplied by Patiala. Although there are a certain number of moderate Sikhs on the League's Executive, including the President, these are mere figureheads. Ujjal Singh told me that he had suggested to Patiala that all Sikh M.L.As., both Central and Provincial, should be invited to join the Executive, but Patiala after consideration turned this suggestion down on the ground that it might mean the creation of "a party within the party". I am afraid the fact is that Patiala is now very much in the hands of the Akali leaders and on their advice is studiously refraining from having anything to do with the Khalsa National Party, whom he distrusts because they support the Unionist Ministry.

6. The five Khaksar leaders who were arrested recently for organizing some unlawful drilling at Rawalpindi have given written apologies and a complete undertaking to refrain in future from all activities which they

might be warned were illegal. The prosecution has accordingly been withdrawn. There has been no further Khaksar incident of any kind.

7. I enclose the fortnightly report for the second half of February.

Yours sincerely,
H.D. CRAIK

69

CRAIK TO LINLITHGOW

Private and Personal
D.-O. No. 333-F.L.

Government House, Lahore,
April 2nd, 1941

Dear Lord Linlithgow,

Confidence in victory continues to grow stronger as the result of our recent successes in the various theatres of war. News of the capture of Keren and Harar was received with great enthusiasm, which was intensified by the astonishing *coup d'état* in Yugoslavia and by yesterday's news of the great naval victory in the eastern Mediterranean. As one of my visitors this morning remarked with a delighted smile, *fateh par fateh ho gai.*[18]

Various districts in the Punjab have now had an opportunity of hearing Indian soldiers who have returned from the Middle East on leave or escorting Italian prisoners of war. Several public receptions have been arranged for these men and the accounts they have given of the fighting in Libya and Eritrea have had an excellent effect. Donations to the War Purposes and other charitable funds up to the 15th of March exceeded 55½ lakhs, i.e. they have topped the total of donations made during the four years of the last war. Investments in the War Loans up to the same date were over 3½ crores of rupees. Recruitment figures are not of course published, but I believe they are satisfactory in all recruiting areas, and even among Jat Sikhs there has been some improvement during the last month.

2. The third phase of *Satyagraha* was supposed to begin on the 15th of March, but only 25 arrests were made during the week ending the 22nd. I have not yet seen the figures for the last week of March, but there has certainly been no increase in popular excitement and the quality of *Satyagrahis* now coming forward is very poor.

3. I am glad to be able to report that the threatened Sikh "Morcha" will not now take place. Shortly after his interview with Sikander and myself

on the 16th of March "Master" Tara Singh published a misleading and inaccurate account of it, adding that he was not satisfied with the replies made to his various demands. On the 24th of March the Akali leaders met at Amritsar and decided to resort to direct action unless the Punjab Government (*a*) unconditionally released the Sikhs arrested in Sargodha in connection with the incident of January the 4th; and (*b*) established a convention that any legislation affecting the religious affairs of the Members of the Assembly representing that particular community.[19] It was announced in the newspapers that unless Government gave satisfactory assurances on these two points by the 29th of March, direct action would be initiated by the despatch of *jathas* from Amritsar to Sargodha on the 4th of April. Tara Singh further announced that he was sending me a letter on the subject, but actually I have received no communication from him.

On the 27th of March Sikander made an important statement in reply to a short notice question in the Assembly on the whole subject of the Sikh demands. This statement, regarding the wording of which he consulted me and which was in part drafted by myself, you no doubt saw in the newspapers. It reiterated his previously announced readiness to promote the establishment of a convention regarding "religious" legislation on the lines demanded by the Sikhs, should this be the general wish of the Assembly. As regards the case of the Sargodha Sikhs, Sikander repeated what he had already told Tara Singh at the interview of March the 16th, viz., that Government were prepared to withdraw the prosecution provided the local Sikhs expressed regret and gave assurances that they would endeavour to prevent a recurrence of such incidents in future. As a matter of fact, a deputation of the local Sikhs, who had always been anxious to have this incident "liquidated", waited on the District Magistrate at Sargodha on the 27th and to him expressed their regret and gave the required assurances. The District Magistrate after referring to Government then gave orders for the withdrawal of the prosecution and the accused persons, who had been in jail for nearly three months, were released on (I think) the 29th of March.

Sikander's statement had on the whole a very good press, though there was some criticism of it in one or two of the Muslim papers. The subsequent release of the Sargodha Sikhs completely took the wind out of Tara Singh's sails and he really had no option left but to call off the threat of direct action, though he has published a typically Sikh statement claiming the release as a victory for himself and his party. I do not think that his claim will cut much ice, as it was quite obvious that he had put forward in his final ultimatum only two demands in regard to which he knew perfectly well that Government were prepared to meet him; and that he did so because he realised that there was no enthusiasm for a "morcha". There is unquestionably general relief that the threat of direct action, which would have seriously hampered our war effort, has been averted.

On the whole I think Sikander has managed this business with considerable skill and has avoided the appearance of giving in to threats of direct action. I would myself have preferred to insist on an expression of regret from the Sikhs accused in the Sargodha incident themselves, instead of one from the local Sikh leaders; but it must be remembered that the accused have been in jail for nearly three months and that the original incident arose out of a somewhat hasty and indiscreet order regarding the route of a procession passed by the Muslim District Magistrate. In any case, the difference is not one of any substantial importance, and I agreed to the action that was eventually taken mainly in order that Glancy should not be faced immediately after assuming office with an embarrassing communal crisis. As things are I think the communal atmosphere is now distinctly better than it was ten days ago.

4. The Khaksars announced that they would celebrate a "martyrs day" on the 19th of March, the anniversary of the original clash between the Khaksars and the Police in Lahore. The celebrations in Lahore and Amritsar were on a very restrained scale and were not accompanied by any contravention of the restrictions on drilling. Apparently nothing much happened except that black paper flags were distributed to Muslim shopkeepers.

5. Poor old Sir Sundar Singh died here early this morning, within a few hours of his return to Lahore from his Gorakhpur Estate. I am afraid he undertook the journey when he was not fit for it, in order to bid me good-bye, and it killed him.[20] This sad event has cast a shadow over my last few days of office, and I have had to postpone till tomorrow the farewell garden party I had arranged for this afternoon. Sikander will not have an easy task in selecting his successor, but I do not imagine he will put forward any name for approval before I leave.

6. Glancy arrives here on the morning of April the 7th and I leave the same evening. I am glad that I am handing over to him at a moment when the Province is in a strong financial position and its war effort is at the apex of enthusiasm and confidence; and particularly when the communal outlook – always our main anxiety here – is not darkened by any imminent cloud. This will be the last of my fortnightly reports to you, and I should like to take this opportunity of telling you how interesting, and from my point of view instructive, this correspondence has been and how greatly I

have appreciated your comments on the reports which I have sent you.

7. I enclose the provincial fortnightly report for the first half of March 1941.

Yours sincerely,
H.D. CRAIK

70

GLANCY TO LINLITHGOW

Private and Personal
D.-O. No. 336-F.L.

Government House, Lahore,
April 11th, 1941

Dear Lord Linlithgow,

Though I fear I have very little information to give you, I do not think that I should delay sending you a copy of the Punjab fortnightly report for the second half of March, which I now forward with its enclosures.

Since I took over charge a few days ago the only provincial event of any great importance has been the appointment of a Minister to take the place of the late Sir Sundar Singh Majithia. The Premier, as I think Craik has told you personally, came to the conclusion that delay in choosing a successor to Sir Sundar Singh would lead to further complications, also that a selection should be made from the Sikh party which has supported the Punjab Government. There was no candidate of outstanding merit, and out of about a dozen possible competitors Sir Sikander's choice eventually fell on Sardar Dasaundha Singh, lately Deputy Speaker of the Punjab Assembly: Craik concurred in this conclusion, and, as far as I have been able to judge, no better selection could in the circumstances have been made. Sardar Dasaundha Singh can certainly not be described as an impressive personality, but he is loyal to the Punjab Government, he is a pleasant-spoken gentleman and is quite well educated: he is a Jat Sikh of the land-owning class and has been for many years one of the leading pleaders in Ludhiana. On the whole his appointment appears to have been reasonably well received, though it has not given rise to any tidal wave of enthusiasm.

Yours sincerely,
B.J. GLANCY

71

GLANCY TO LINLITHGOW[21]

Government House, Lahore,

D.-O. No. 341 *April 18th, 1941*

Dear Lord Linlithgow,

I write in reply to Your Excellency's letter to Craik, dated April the 1st, regarding the holding of the Provincial Assembly elections.

2. In my opinion there should be an enabling amendment of the Government of India Act empowering a suitable authority to prolong the life of a Provincial Assembly. I agree that a suitable authority would be the Governor in his discretion rather than the Secretary of State or the Governor-General. I am not in favour of any rigid provision barring general elections for the duration of the war, as in Provinces where Provincial Autonomy is still functioning it might be awkward if the Prime Minister wished to have the Assembly dissolved and fresh elections held, and this was not possible.

3. Though of course uniformity is desirable, and should not be difficult to secure in the Section 93 Provinces, the decision whether to postpone elections or not will have to be taken separately for each Province according to the circumstances prevailing there. It appears probable that postponement will everywhere be found to be desirable unless there can be shown to be overwhelming reasons in favour of a contrary conclusion.

4. Grounds for postponement, if publicly acknowledged, should in my opinion be stated as concisely as practicable. The following appear to me to be the grounds which could be publicly acknowledged:

(1) Elections at the best of times are liable to give rise to excitement and dissensions, which are undesirable in time of war.

(2) They are bound to lead to dislocation of ordinary administration, to the dissipation of the energies of both officials and non-officials which would be better devoted to the successful prosecution of the war, and to considerable expenditure both on the part of Government and of the candidates at a time when money might be better employed.

Yours sincerely,
B.J. GLANCY

72

GLANCY TO LINLITHGOW

Private and Personal Government House, Lahore,
D.-O. No. 343-F.L. *April 28th, 1941*

Dear Lord Linlithgow,

The outstanding item of local interest during the last few weeks has been the organization by the trading classes of a widespread movement designed to defeat certain economic enactments passed, but not yet brought into effect, by the Punjab Government – in particular the Agricultural Produce Markets Act and the General Sales Tax Act. The Punjab Government have, as you are well aware, lost few opportunities of late to proclaim and give practical illustration to their policy of improving the lot of agricultural classes and distributing the burden of taxation more evenly between the rural and urban communities. A series of legislative reforms intended to secure these purposes has led the trading classes to express belief that their interests were being consistently sacrificed and that the time had come for them to mobilise their forces. They proceeded accordingly to advertise and prepare for a general cessation of business designed to coincide with the time when the producer must bring his harvest to the market. The announcement by Government that the enforcement of the Markets Act was to be postponed until next September did not suffice to allay the traders' agitation. To what extent they could be successful in organizing a general business *hartal* of any duration throughout the Province may be open to doubt: still it was obvious that a grave situation was threatened, since even a partial and temporary closing down of grain markets would have been a calamitous affair, leading almost inevitably to extensive outbreaks of disorder. Suggestions have been made that Government should themselves or through their agents arrange to purchase the bulk of the harvest, but the practical value of this idea appears to be very doubtful, since there is no adequate machinery available for so adventurous a programme.

Realising the danger of the position, the Premier and his colleagues have very wisely decided to adopt a conciliatory attitude. They have agreed to modify in various respects the Markets Act as originally passed and the rules framed thereunder, and they have given out both in the Assembly and elsewhere that all interests concerned will be given a fair hearing and fair treatment. The amendments to be made in regard to the Markets Act go a very long way to meet reasonable objections. In the matter of the

General Sales Tax Act also action has been taken to reassure the commercial community. The tension has now to some extent declined, though it cannot be said as yet that the forces arrayed for battle have been demobilised; there are, however, grounds for hoping that wiser counsels will prevail.

Many responsible people express the view that the Punjab Government have been showing a tendency to rush their fences in the matter of agrarian and economic legislation. However laudable their intentions, they would have been well advised to space out their programme of reforms instead of delivering a series of blows at short intervals to the trading classes, the cumulative effect of which has brought the victims to the verge of revolt. Also they would have done well to have made a more thorough preliminary examination of the measures on which they felt it necessary to embark. There can be no denying that the Markets Act and Rules as originally framed contained a number of serious defects, at least one of which would have reacted very unfavourably on the producers, whom the enactment was designed to protect. Considerable difficulty may be anticipated in bringing the General Sales Tax Act into practical operation.

Recent events in the Balkans and Libya have given rise to no little despondency in certain quarters, and there is a general realisation that the war is drifting nearer and nearer to India. Recruiting in Sikh areas is still much below par, but this may be partially explained by the fact that harvesting operations have been in full swing. His Highness of Patiala came to see me the other day and expressed his intention of doing all that he possibly could to help in the matter of recruitment. He said that he was rigidly abstaining from taking part in Punjab politics and that he felt sadly hurt by allegations that he was intriguing against the Unionist Party. I suggested that the best way in which he could counter these stories would be by keeping in as close personal touch as possible with the Premier and the Punjab Ministers. I have no reason to doubt his genuineness in regard to the recruiting campaign, but I fear that his advisers are sometimes inclined to lead him out of his depth, and I doubt whether he will ever succeed in harnessing the wild forces of the Akalis. The Khalsa Defence of India League, of which Patiala is the central figure, might well have been more representative of stable Sikh interests; so far it has achieved no very striking results.

I am very much interested in the account which Your Excellency has been good enough to give me of your talks with Sapru; I fully appreciate the difficulties in the way of turning his advances to practical account.

I enclose the Provincial Fortnightly Report for the first half of April.

Yours sincerely,
B.J. GLANCY

73

GLANCY TO LINLITHGOW

Private and Personal
D.-O. No. 344-F.L.

Barnes Court, Simla,
May 17th, 1941

Dear Lord Linlithgow,

The general *hartal* of shops as a protest against the *General Sales Tax Act* has now been brought to an end and business has been resumed. So far as the *hartal* in the grain mandis is concerned, the impasse still continues: various amendments in the *Marketing Act* have been made by the Punjab Government, but this action has not yet had the effect of inducing grain dealers to open up business. It has seemed on more than one occasion that a solution was imminent: attempts are still being made in this direction and it is to be hoped that they will be successful before long. Up to the present no very serious results have arisen from the deadlock, but its general effect is distinctly unsettling, and producers who have in some places had to sell their grain by secret transactions instead of in the open market have suffered financially.

News from Iraq has given rise to a good deal of depression. The Premier lost no time in holding a conference with Press representatives, and on the whole the tone of newspapers in the Province has been commendable. Though the threat to India is generally recognized, there is little indication of any popular movement to sink domestic quarrels and concentrate on the war. The communal situation cannot be said to have improved. One very serious danger to the peace of the Province consists, as Your Excellency well knows, in the large number of unlicensed arms to be found throughout the Province. Certain measures to deal with this menace have already been taken and have been attended by a considerable degree of success: the question continues to engage the active attention of Government.

A minor communal clash occurred at Bhiwani in the Hissar district not long ago. The situation was dealt with promptly and effectively by the local authorities and so far there have been no untoward developments. There have been indications of a revival of Khaksar activity in various places.

Rulings have recently been given by two separate single benches of the

High Court to the effect that the mere tendering of notice to the authorities of the intention to deliver anti-war speeches, &c., does not constitute an offence. The question of releasing prisoners now under detention on this count is being considered.

I enclose the provincial fortnightly report for the second half of April.

Yours sincerely,
B.J. GLANCY

74

GLANCY TO LINLITHGOW[22]

Telegram

Immediate
Personal and Most Secret
No. 4-G *May 23rd, 1941*

Your telegram No. 1060-S., May 22nd.[23] I would be personally disposed to favour for the time being restriction of changes at the Centre to the creation of an Advisory War Council. As to the addition of non-official Members to Your Excellency's Council, I am doubtful whether individuals of the required calibre and commanding sufficient respect will be available – especially from Muslims if as I understand members of the Muslim League are to be excluded.

75

GLANCY TO LINLITHGOW

Private and Personal Barnes Court, Simla,
D.-O. No. 346-F.L. *May 30th, 1941*

Dear Lord Linlithgow,

The chief recent event of provincial importance, as I told Your Excellency the other day, has been the calling off of the *hartal* in the grain markets.

Business is now being transacted as usual in the Mandis and this is a great relief to almost everyone concerned. The traders are still not wholly satisfied with the position and it is possible that trouble may recur later on. I hope that this will not be the case, but if so, we should at least be in a somewhat better position to deal with the difficulty.

The attitude of the public towards the war continues to be much the same. There has been a good deal of general depression as the result of unfavourable war news, but press publications in regard to Iraq have on the whole been satisfactory. Nor has there been any material change in the communal situation. The riot which broke out in Bhiwani has not been followed by any serious repercussions. A meeting has recently been staged by Mian Iftikharuddin at Lahore with the object of encouraging a better feeling amongst the main communities; the results of this are yet to be seen. One disquieting feature has been an attempt on the part of the Akalis to launch a scheme whereby the Sikhs will provide armed support for Hindus in the event of serious danger arising, the cost involved being met by the Hindus. This movement appears to have been supported by several influential Hindus, and steps have been taken to discourage the project.

I enclose the provincial fortnightly report for the first half of May.

Yours sincerely,
B.J. GLANCY

76

GLANCY TO LINLITHGOW[24]

Barnes Court, Simla,
D.-O. No. 347 *June 10th, 1941*

Dear Lord Linlithgow,

Would you kindly refer to your letter of June 4th regarding the postponement of general elections to the Provincial Legislative Assemblies?

2. I have consulted the Premier. He fully agrees that provision should be made for the postponement of elections, and he sees no objection to the amendment of Section 61 (2) of the Government of India Act on the lines suggested by the Secretary of State.

3. We are both agreed that it will be preferable to provide for post-

ponement till 12 months rather than 6 months after the conclusion of the present war. It is, in our opinion, unlikely that criticism will be appreciably less violent if the postponement is only for the shorter period and owing to climate and other conditions it may well prove difficult, if not impossible, to arrange for general elections within 6 months of the end of the war.

Yours sincerely,
B.J. GLANCY

77

GLANCY TO LINLITHGOW

Private and Personal
D.-O. No. 349-F.L.

Barnes Court, Simla,
June 23rd, 1941

Dear Lord Linlithgow,

The firm action taken by the Central Government in causing the Khaksars to be declared an unlawful association throughout India has successfully averted a serious menace to the peace of the country in general and the Punjab in particular: it would certainly not have been practicable for the Punjab to deal effectively with the activities of the Khaksars as long as their organization was free to conduct the campaign from bases situated beyond our borders. Since the blow was delivered there has so far been no serious difficulty in the way of rounding up Khaksars inside the Province. Measures were taken in advance to prevent their establishing themselves in mosques and arrests have been peaceably effected in fairly large numbers. There is very little feeling of sympathy for the Khaksars among the general Muslim public: the misuse of mosques as an ambuscade is naturally distasteful to Imams and all genuine worshippers, though they have been as a rule too cautious to protest of their own motion: in Lahore city distrust of the Khaksars has been reinforced by a desire to avoid a reimposition of the punitive police set up as the result of last year's disorders. Some of the Muslim papers have complained that Government's action in regard to the Khaksars has been unduly severe as compared with the toleration shown to provocative elements belonging to other communities. There is some truth in this criticism. Apprehension has been caused in several places by a noticeable increase in the number of "Nihangs", a variety of Sikh devotees, who are in the habit of arming themselves with spears of menacing proportions. It seems likely that steps will have to be taken before long to curb these activities.

A deputation of the Khalsa Defence League came to see me the other day; this, as you know, is the organization sponsored by the Maharaja of Patiala and designed to promote the enrolment of Sikhs in the Army. A fairly large number of more or less influential Sikhs of varying shades of opinion have also been calling on me independently of late. So far, as regards recruitment, I think that the Defence League are genuine enough in their professions. Akali influences are stronger in the League than they should be, but even the Akalis have come to realise that a decline in the Sikh military quota must result in a serious setback to the community and it is obvious that any Sikh aspiring to the position of a leader may land himself in difficulties if he preaches non-co-operation with Government in the war. I have done what I can to encourage the League's war activities; so far they have achieved no striking results, but they have now drawn up a plan of campaign allotting to various Punjab districts and Indian States a specified number of recruits, and with some degree of official assistance it is to be hoped that they will be more successful in the near future. I have suggested that the basis of the League should be broadened in order to make it more representative and that it should contain a larger proportion of the Khalsa Nationalist Party, the supporters of the Unionist Government. This suggestion was not received with any enthusiasm by the Akali section of the League, who aspire to the sole right of controlling the policy of the Sikh community: it appears, however, that Patiala is moving in the desired direction. Patiala is, I think, not free from misgivings as to the Akalis and their intentions, but he is not altogether fortunate in his advisers. He has made some attempts of late to establish contact with Sikander, a course of action which I commended to him in Lahore some two mouths ago.

Sikh visitors who have been to see me have made a point of professing their loyalty to the British Government and complaining that they are now under the heel of a hostile Muslim "Raj". I have done my best to impress on them that Sikhs have their due share in the Government of the Punjab, that they should strive to live in amity with other communities and that they should give a fair trial to the new Sikh member of the Cabinet, in whose capacity many of them, especially his rivals, express, I am sorry to say, a distressing lack of confidence. I am afraid that few of the Sikh "leaders" can be expected to co-operate either with the Unionist Government or with any other form of administration; they are for the most part interested mainly in maintaining their own individual prominence and they conceive that the easiest and most successful way of appealing to their followers lies in continual opposition to whatever Government is in power.

Mian Iftikharuddin, whose professed attempts to promote communal unity I mentioned in my letter of the 20th of May, still continues his activities. Suspicion is growing in certain quarters that his campaign is little more than an endeavour to restore the influence and prestige of the Congress party, which have suffered severely in consequence of the *Satyagraha* fiasco.

Since the battle of Crete the preoccupation of Germany on the Russian front and the comparative lull in the storm against Great Britain and her allies have led to a temporary decline in public interest in the war I think that it would be well to wake people up and to take the public as far as possible into confidence in regard not only to A.R.P. but also to tentative plans for evacuation, &c. If discreet action is now taken in this direction, it seems to me that there will be less likelihood of panic than if an undue measure of secrecy is maintained.

I enclose the Provincial fortnightly reports for the second half of May and the first half of June.[25]

Yours sincerely,
B.J. GLANCY

78

GLANCY TO LINLITHGOW

Secret and Personal
D.-O. No. 350

Barnes Court, Simla,
June 26th, 1941

Dear Lord Linlithgow,

I write in reply to your secret and personal letter of the 20th of June. I am very glad to hear that the Cabinet have given their general approval to the scheme put forward by Your Excellency for the greater association of non-official opinion with the prosecution of the war.

You have asked for my views on certain matters connected with the composition and working of the proposed National Defence Council.

I am definitely in favour of the suggestion that Sikander should be invited to become a member of this Council, and though I have not of course sounded him, I think he would be willing to serve. Although, as you say, Jinnah's actions are not predictable, it does not seem likely that he would be able to raise any serious trouble about this. Sikander as Premier is already patently assisting in the war effort and the same can be said in varying degrees about the other Muslim Prime Ministers[26] who are to be invited to join the Council. If Jinnah attempted to prevent them joining, he would be seriously straining the cohesion of the Muslim League and might even cause its disruption, as influential sections of Muslim opinion are strongly in favour of co-operating in the war effort.

2. I understand that in addition to Sikander you contemplate that the Punjab should have two other representatives on the Defence Council. It is difficult for me to suggest any names except very tentatively without taking Sikander into confidence. As Premier of the Punjab and as head of the prospective Punjab team on the Defence Council, he should certainly in my opinion be consulted before a final choice is made.

3. There is, I think, much to be said for a Punjab team which would be representative of Hindus and Sikhs as well as of Muslims. If this is accepted, one solution that deserves consideration is that not only the Muslim representative, viz., Sikander, but the Sikh and Hindu representatives also should be drawn from the Provincial Cabinet. In this case the Hindu and Sikh representatives would be Sir Chhotu Ram and Sardar Dasaundha Singh. Sir Chhotu Ram is a man of marked ability, application and energy. His defects, which have lately come into increasing prominence, are that he is strongly biased against the urban classes and that he is apt to be intemperate in his words and actions. If he were selected to serve on the Defence Council, I would warn him of these defects. Sardar Dasaundha Singh is certainly not a man of outstanding capacity, but he has the reputation of being honest, loyal and well-meaning.

This suggested solution does not appear open to any serious objection and it has some definite advantages. All three representatives would be persons who have won popular approval in the elections and who have proved that they can work together amicably and effectively. There is clearly little or no possibility of the Punjab Government being represented on the expanded Executive Council and there is therefore much to be said for their being strongly represented on the Defence Council. Furthermore, if this plan were adopted, it would make the task of selection less invidious and it might even have a steadying effect on Jinnah, who might possibly feel less objection to Muslim Premiers serving on the Defence Council if non-Muslim Ministers were included on the same principle.

4. If this idea is not favoured, I would suggest for consideration (subject to what is said in paragraph 2) the following names:

(*a*) *Muslims.* – Sir Muhammad Nawaz Khan of Kot, already suggested by Craik would, I think, be as good as any, but he represents much the same interests as Sikander and also belongs to the same district. As already suggested, it may be desirable not to have a second Muslim from the Punjab in addition to Sikander.

(*b*) *Hindus.* – Rai Bahadur Lala Ram Saran Das M.C.S., or his son Rai Bahadur Lala Gopal Das, M.L.A., Rai Bahadur Lala Sohan Lal, M.L.A. (Chairman of the Lahore Electric Supply Co.).

(*c*) *Sikhs.* – S.B. Ujjal Singh, M.L.A., and Sardar Naunihal Singh, M.L.A. – Supporters of the Unionist Government and disappointed candidates for the post of Sikh Member of the Cabinet. Of the two Ujjal Singh has made himself more prominent politically, but Naunihal Singh is, I should say, distinctly more attractive. Baldev Singh – Akali sympathiser. A wealthy industrialist (Tatanagar): if he should be selected, it would be explained for the benefit of the Khalsa Nationalist Party that he has been prominently connected with Munitions work. S.B. Mohan Singh – Lately Adviser at the India Office.

5. I am strongly in favour of the suggestions contained in paragraph 8 of Your Excellency's letter, viz., that the provincial representatives on the Defence Council should have discussions with the Cabinet[27] (or with the rest of the Cabinet) before and after Defence Council meetings and that they should co-operate fully with the Provincial War Board or other organization set up to further the Defence and War effort of the Punjab.

Yours sincerely,
B.J. GLANCY

79

GLANCY TO LINLITHGOW

Secret and Personal — Barnes Court, Simla,
D.-O. No. 352 — *July 1st, 1941*

Dear Lord Linlithgow,

Will Your Excellency please refer to our correspondence about the proposed Defence Council and our conversation of last Friday? I sounded Sikander on Saturday last in accordance with your instructions and had a fairly long conversation with him yesterday after he had had time to think things over. He left Simla last night and I have only just received a written note from him about possible candidates for the Council.

Sikander, I am glad to say, is quite willing to serve on the Council himself, if Your Excellency thinks that this will be of general assistance. He thinks it possible that this may lead to a clash with Jinnah, but considers that no open rift is probable if the Premiers of other Provinces are also brought in; he would prefer that he himself and the other Premiers should be invited to serve *qua* Premiers.

His suggestions in regard to candidates from the various communities are as follows:

(*a*) *Muslims–*

(1) Major-General Nawab Malik Sir Umar Hayat Khan Tiwana, of Kalra, district Shahpur.

(2) Honorary Lieut.-Colonel Sardar Sir Muhammad Nawaz Khan, M.L.A., of Kot Fateh Khan, Attock district.

(3) Nawab Sir Muhammad Shah Nawaz Khan, Nawab of Mamdot, M.L.A.

(4) Khan Bahadur Nawab Fazl Ali, M.L.A., of Gujrat.

(5) Nawab Sir Muhammad Jamal Khan Leghari, M.L.A., of Choti Zerin, district Dera Ghazi Khan.

Of these Sir Umar Hayat Khan is, Sikander thinks, not altogether suitable, as he is getting on in years and has practically withdrawn from public life since the appointment of his son, Major Malik Khizar Hayat Khan, as Minister.

No. (3) would not be a wise choice, as he is President of the Provincial Muslim League and might find it embarrassing to serve on the Council if Jinnah, as is to be expected, declines to co-operate. If the Nawab of Mamdot resigned from the Muslim League, Jinnah might well make trouble; moreover the Nawab's position as President of the local League would probably be taken up by someone less amenable to reason and control and this would cause embarrassment locally.

No. (5) is a man of limited interests and influence and is not very well known outside the Multan Division.

The choice therefore, in Sikander's opinion, lies between No. (2) and No. (4). Both of these are gentlemen of standing and influence and command esteem and respect in their own districts and outside. They are men of character, straightforward, loyal and are giving their full support to the war effort of the Province. Though it is difficult to choose between them, Sikander considers on the whole that No. (2), Sardar Sir Muhammad Nawaz Khan, would be the more suitable, as he is better educated and has also some experience of the Army. He was educated at the Chiefs' College and subsequently went to Sandhurst, where he is said to have done quite well, and on his return was posted to a British Cavalry Regiment, with which he remained until he resigned his Commission. He is an Honorary Lieutenant-Colonel in the Indian Territorial Force and since the outbreak of the War has made several attempts to go abroad on active service. He is one of the few large landholders of the Province and owns a big estate in the Attock district as well as a large area in the Lyallpur Colony.

I agree with Sikander that Sir Muhammad Nawaz Khan would be the most appropriate choice.

(*b*) *Hindus–*
(1) Diwan Bahadur Raja Narendra Nath, Lahore.
(2) Rao Bahadur Captain Chaudhri Lal Chand, of Rohtak.
(3) Dr. Sir Gokal Chand Narang, Lahore.
(4) Rai Bahadur Lala Ram Saran Das, Lahore.
(5) Diwan Bahadur Diwan Krishna Kishore, Lahore.

None of the last three names would, in Sikander's opinion, be suitable. He considers that even among Hindus the appointment of either Sir Gokal Chand Narang or Rai Bahadur Ram Saran Das would be unpopular; moreover they are both businessmen on a fairly large scale and are said to be making considerable sums out of military contracts. Neither of them appears to have contributed anything but paltry subscriptions towards the War Funds.

Diwan Bahadur Diwan Krishna Kishore belongs to a well-known aristocratic Hindu family of Lahore and is a gentleman of the old school, but he takes little interest in politics and is not in close touch with the Hindu intelligentsia or the public outside Lahore.

If a Hindu representative of the martial classes is to be selected, Sikander would recommend No. (2), Rao Bahadur Captain Lal Chand. He did very good work during the last war and commands considerable influence in the south-west Punjab. His appointment would be quite popular with Hindus of the agriculturist class and also with Hindu martial classes throughout the Province. He is at present serving as a member of the Punjab Public Services Commission.

If an urban Hindu is to be chosen, Sikander thinks that the most suitable selection would be No. (1), D. B. Raja Narendra Nath. He is well advanced in years, but he is mentally quite alert and commands respect and influence amongst all sections of non-agriculturist Hindus. He is the ex-President of the All-India Hindu Mahasabha and his sphere of influence extends beyond the Punjab.

My own view is that Raja Narendra Nath would be the best choice. I think that it would be well to nominate a Hindu, if one is to be chosen at all, who is associated with the urban community, though I understand now that it is doubtful whether any Hindu at all can be taken from the Punjab. I would certainly not recommend Sir Gokal Chand Narang, as he is a consistent and rather bitter opponent and critic of the Punjab Government. I should not have thought that R.B. Ram Saran Das would be a bad choice, but perhaps his work as a contractor makes him scarcely suitable, and I agree with Sikander that Raja Narendra Nath would be a better selection.

(*c*) *Sikhs*–
(1) Sardar Sir Jogendra Singh, Simla.
(2) Sardar Baldev Singh, M.L.A., Contractor, Tatanagar (Ambala district).
(3) Master Tara Singh, President, S.G.P.C.
(4) Lieut. Sardar Naunihal Singh Man, M.L.A., of Sheikhupura district.

Sikander is not in favour of Sir Jogendra Singh, whom he regards as an unpractical and superficial idealist; he thinks that Sir Jogendra Singh would be more of a nuisance than a help in the Council, and I certainly doubt whether he would be of any practical assistance. Though he is pleasant enough socially, Sikander does not think that he commands any influence worth the name among the Sikhs.

Sikander is very definitely opposed to the selection of Master Tara Singh and I agree with his opinion. Master Tara Singh is, as you know, the leader of the Akalis. He is an Arora Khatri Sikh from the Rawalpindi district. His father is a Hindu and one of his brothers is understood to be still a Hindu. Though he commands considerable influence with many people among the Sikh masses, he is not a *persona grata* with the Sikh gentry, who almost exclusively belong to the agricultural classes. His appointment would in fact create resentment amongst these classes. Also the appointment of an Arora Sikh is not likely to promote recruitment among Jat Sikhs. From the political point of view his appointment would be open to very serious objection.

Sikander considers that No. (4), Sardar Naunihal Singh Man, would be the best choice. He is a Jat Sikh, the head of the well-known Man family of Sheikhupura and commands considerable influence in his district. His family has a very creditable record of services to the administration and his father rendered valuable assistance during the last war.[28] He is a member of the Legislative Assembly and is popular with all sections of the Sikhs. His appointment would be welcomed by the Khalsa National Party and the Sikh gentry, and Sikander has reason to believe that it would not be unpalatable to the Akalis. He is thoroughly loyal and reliable and is at present serving as Assistant Recruiting Officer in the Lahore recruiting area. I agree with Sikander that Naunihal Singh would on the whole be the best choice; he is in my opinion an intelligent and attractive personality.

Sikander's second choice, and here again I agree with him, is Sardar Baldev Singh. He has pleasant manners and considerable force of character. He is a big contractor at Tatanagar, where his father set up a lucrative business, which is now said to be earning very large profits as a result of the war. He is closely associated with the Akalis, who depend to a considerable extent on him for financial support. He is said to have paid them large sums during the last general election and was returned from the Ambala Sikh Rural constituency with their support. But he lives ordinarily at Tatanagar and has no regular direct contact with the Sikhs of the Punjab. It appears doubtful whether being a contractor on a fairly large scale his appointment to the Defence Council would be appropriate.

Sikander strongly urges that there should be at least four representatives from the Punjab. This would allow of one Muslim apart from Sikander himself, one Hindu and one Sikh. The Premier considers that in view of the Punjab's war effort and the fact that the Punjab is the main recruiting ground for the Indian Army this would be fully justified; a larger representation from the Punjab would assist the Defence Council in the work of harnessing the man-power of the country for the combatant and technical services. The Premier has also suggested that, as the Sikh member will represent the Sikh Community not only in the Punjab but throughout India, it would not be unreasonable to regard this member as falling outside the allotment of the Punjab proper. I have told Sikander that I fear that there is very little chance of the Punjab representatives numbering more than three including himself. At the same time I think that there is much in what the Premier says on this point, and should it be possible to inflate the Punjab numbers to four, I would certainly welcome this as a better equation of the communal balance.

Sikander in the course of his conversation with me made one or two more suggestions about the proposed Defence Council, which he said he would like me to pass on. He thinks that it would be well for ex-Premiers who have now resigned their appointments in other Provinces to be sounded informally as to their willingness to serve; I do not imagine that anything tangible would result from this action. He also suggested that leaders of the various parties in the Assembly should be invited to serve and that they should be given a hint that the Defence Council would not only be of value for war work but would also help to bring together the divergent elements of various communities. He further suggested that, if serious difficulties arose in deciding between the various claims of different candidates, especially in Section 93 Provinces, individuals might be asked to serve by rotation.[29]

Finally, Sikander suggested, with reference to a possible expansion of the *Executive* Council, though I did not tell him that any such expansion was likely to occur, that the position should be kept fluid, that is to say, that expansion should take place gradually, so that candidates who might otherwise feel disappointment and resentment might still have reason to hope that they might personally be selected later on as necessity for a further increase might occur.

Yours sincerely,
B.J. GLANCY

80

GLANCY TO LINLITHGOW

Secret and Personal
D.-O. No. 354

Barnes Court, Simla,
July 6th, 1941

Dear Lord Linlithgow,

Will Your Excellency kindly refer to your secret and personal letter of the 3rd of July about the proposed Defence Council?[30]

Sikander left Simla on tour Monday last and is not due back here until Tuesday next. I sent him by special messenger a letter conveying your thanks to him and telling him that there were likely to be only two Punjab representatives on the Council – himself and Sardar Baldev Singh. I have just received a telegram asking me to request you to defer the final decision until his return, as he considers the proposed allotment unfair to the Punjab both as regards numbers and personnel. I shall be very grateful if you can see your way to accede to Sikander's request, so that he may be given his say: for what it is worth my own opinion is still that Sardar Naunihal Singh would be definitely a better choice than Sardar Baldev Singh: possibly, though he has not said so, Sikander may have thought of another Sikh candidate.[31]

Yours sincerely,
B.J. GLANCY

81

MOON TO LAITHWAITE

Confidential

Barnes Court, Simla,
July 8th, 1941

My dear Laithwaite,

As desired in your confidential demi-official letter No. 2448-G.G. of the 17th of June 1938, I forward a note recorded by His Excellency the Governor on the various Punjab Ministers.

Yours sincerely,
PENDEREL MOON

ENCLOSURE TO NO. 81

NOTE BY GLANCY

July 8th, 1941

Sir Sikander Hyat Khan has continued to hold his party and his Cabinet together with remarkable success. What with his difficulties created by the War, the increasing communal tension in the Province and the roarings of Jinnah outside the gates, this has been no easy task, and Sikander deserves all credit for what he has achieved. He is a very attractive personality, resourceful and diplomatic, loyal to Government and to his friends, and he still enjoys, and rightly so, a reputation for conspicuous freedom from communal bias in the ordinary sense of that expression. Of late, thanks to the somewhat precipitate legislation in which the Punjab Government have been indulging, the cleavage between the rural and urban classes has been steadily growing, and this has not been without its effect on Sikander's good name for impartiality. But even his enemies are for the most part prepared to admit that he is personally fair-minded, and, so far as his own followers are concerned, he retains with few exceptions their confidence and their admiration. He is very hardworking, and would be all the better for a brief rest from his heavy labours and responsibilities.

Sir Chhotu Ram is by nature a crusader and supplies the most dynamic element in the Cabinet. Brought up in the south-east Punjab he has chafed from his earliest days at the power and influence wielded by the Bania community, and his consistent aim has been to free the agriculturist from what he sincerely regards as the tyranny of the trader. He has pursued this object with relentless energy, and he is the main driving force behind the various measures for agrarian relief that have passed in quick succession through the Punjab Legislature. He is quite unbridled in his denunciations of the urban classes, and he has made many enemies not only for himself, but for the Government as a whole. There is of course a very great deal to be said in favour of Sir Chhotu's policy if advanced with moderation, and he is certainly a man of marked ability and great devotion to duty. A knight-errant can scarcely be expected to shine in the matter of discretion, but if Sir Chhotu could combine a modicum of this virtue with his other talents, he would be an altogether outstanding character.

Khizar Hayat Khan Tiwana has considerable capacity and much determination and forcefulness. He takes a keen and effective interest in the Departments entrusted to his charge. Coming as he does from a great land-holding family he has little sympathy for townsmen and traders. His outlook on life is largely baronial, and he is apt to be intolerant and to indulge at times in sabre-rattling. Still he pulls his weight in the team and is a distinctly valuable member of the Cabinet. His value should increase with age and experience.

Sir Manohar Lal is a courteous and cultured gentleman. He is not in the least in sympathy with legislative measures directed against the urban classes, to which community he belongs himself: he perceives clearly enough the dangers to which hasty action of this nature may lead, but he does little to apply the brake. He is an academician rather than a warrior, and is content to seek relief from practical politics in the study of pure economics. As Minister in charge of Finance he may be said to have been eminently successful: he has been fortunate in his subordinates.

Mian Abdul Haye is shrewd enough, gets through his business more or less adequately and is amenable to reason. But he is certainly not one of the Cabinet stars, and is inclined to swim peacefully with the tide.

Sardar Dasaundha Singh is a recent acquisition, having now been three months a member of the Cabinet. He is pleasant and well-spoken, but has not yet succeeded in finding his feet: it seems that he will take no little time in doing so. He does not appear to command any great respect among the Sikhs, many of whom are disinclined to accept his valuation of his own capacity. His intentions are good, but up to the present he has found considerable difficulty in disposing of his work.

B.J. GLANCY
Governor, Punjab

82

GLANCY TO LAITHWAITE

July 13th, 1941

Dear Gilbert,

Sikander has just this moment left me after handing over the enclosed two documents, which as you will see are of a most disturbing nature. I have done my best to steady him, as I have told you on the telephone, and there seems to me to be a possible way out. If it can be arranged, I should like to come and discuss things with His Excellency tomorrow. Would you kindly let me know if this is possible? I apologise for this nuisance, but it has only just been sprung on me.[32]

Yours ever,
B.J. GLANCY

ENCLOSURE 1 TO NO. 82

SIKANDER HYAT KHAN TO GLANCY

Secret

Simla,
July 13th, 1941

Dear Sir Bertrand,

There are persistent rumours that it has been finally decided to expand the Executive Council of the Governor-General and that an announcement regarding the personnel of the reconstituted Council is imminent. I gather that the representatives of the press are being invited to receive the announcement within the next day or two. I further understand that, while it is proposed to expand the Council to no less than nine Members – including a non-official Indian as Defence Member – it is not likely to include a single Punjabi or any representative from the four Provinces which have been and are still working the constitution. And what is even more disquieting from our point of view, I gather that it has been decided to entrust the Defence portfolio to a non-Punjabi.

I do not know whether there is any basis for these rumours. I earnestly hope that they are not true. The Punjab under normal conditions even in an unexpanded Council has, except for one break, always been accorded a place in the Executive Council from 1919 onwards. To deprive it at this juncture of representation in the Central Government, if I may say so, would constitute a gross injustice and would imply an undeserved slur on the Province which not only gave a lead to the rest of India but has done more than any other Province to stimulate war effort in this country. Moreover, in the reported exclusion from the expanded Executive Council of the major Provinces of Bengal and the Punjab (as also of Sind and Assam) would not unnaturally be construed as an indication of the policy of the British Government to discountenance deliberately the claims of these Provinces which – unlike the other non-co-operating Provinces – have been and are still working the constitution. The rumoured complexion of the reconstituted Central Executive, if correct, would confirm the impression and not without justification that the policy of letting down "friends" still holds the field. This impression if it becomes widespread, as I am afraid it will, would seriously hamper our war effort – a development which would be most unfortunate at this crucial juncture. Further, it would, I must frankly state, go a long way to justify the accusation that it is the nuisance-value which counts with Government and those who are helping or have proffered their full co-operation to further intensify war effort provided they are given their due share in the Executive Council are being deliberately ignored.

I recognise that it is entirely within His Excellency the Viceroy's discretion to appoint whomsoever he likes to his Council; but, in view of the fact that when the proposal for the expansion of the Executive Council was first mooted His Excellency was pleased to consult the leaders of the various political parties and other prominent non-officials with regard to the strength and even the personnel of the Council, I feel that the Punjab was entitled at least to the courtesy of being apprised of the impending changes – particularly with regard to the defence in which it is so intimately concerned. Indeed my previous conversations with His Excellency the Viceroy on this subject led me to the belief – which I now find was an erroneous belief – that if and when it was decided to transfer the Defence portfolio I would be afforded an opportunity to put forward the point of view of the Punjab before a final decision was taken. Lest I may be misunderstood, let me make it clear once again that in view of my obligations to my Province and the Party I have never been an aspirant, in the circumstances, to a post in the Central Executive. My repeated expression of concern to His Excellency the Viceroy regarding the Defence portfolio was meant, as I always emphasised, to ensure that the peculiar interests of the Punjab – which is and has been providing the bulk of the combatants for the Indian Army – are duly protected consistently with the war efforts and the needs of the country as a whole. In this connection, I deemed it my duty, even before the outbreak of the war and ever since, to impress on various occasions on His Excellency the Viceroy and the successive Commanders-in-Chief that in the best interests of India and the Empire the pace of India's preparedness for defence as a strong unit of the British Commonwealth should be accelerated, and that with this purpose the Princes and the leaders concerned of the Indian public opinion should be taken in the fullest confidence in order to enable them to lend their wholehearted support in our war effort.

I must gratefully acknowledge that His Excellency the Viceroy – obviously in view of the importance of the Punjab in any scheme relating to defence – has hitherto invariably extended to me the privilege and courtesy of discussing the important question of the transfer of Defence portfolio in order to explore the possibility of a change-over without impairing the efficiency of our fighting services and the war effort of the country. It is, therefore, all the more surprising that the Punjab should not have been taken into confidence – as I claim it is entitled to on account of its peculiar position, great military traditions and its unstinted and generous contribution in men and material – particularly at this juncture, when we are in the throes of a life and death struggle and are engaged in raising an adequate, efficient and well-equipped force to avert the danger which threatens the very existence of the British Commonwealth. In the circumstances, I consider it my duty to point out that the rumoured decision, if correct, would come as a most disagreeable surprise to the Province, as apart from other considerations it would indicate that the sacrifices made by the Punjab and its fighting classes, who have been and are still coming forward in their thousands to fight for the safety of their country and the integrity of the British Commonwealth, do not count for anything, and that the representatives of the Punjab no longer have the same confidence of His Excellency the Viceroy which they enjoyed till the beginning of the present year when this subject was last broached by His Excellency the Viceroy during the course of our conversation in Delhi.

I need hardly mention that, notwithstanding the various political and other difficulties which created formidable obstacles in our way, we in the Punjab, even at the risk of being misunderstood, have not only been successful in surmounting those obstacles but have set a standard of war effort which if emulated by other Provinces would place India in the front rank among the components of the British Commonwealth in the matter of war contribution. But, if unfortunately the rumours to which I have referred prove to be correct, the result will be that, instead of being in a position to focus our energies and efforts on further intensifying the war effort of the Province, we will have to contend with ridicule and taunts of those who are opposed to any form of co-operation with Government in its war activities on the one hand, and the commiseration and contempt of our friends on the other. I venture to suggest that it would be unwise and inexpedient to take a step which obviously cannot conciliate the two major political organizations (the Congress and the Muslim League), or prove attractive even to the moderate element, but which must, inevitably alienate the sympathies of those Provinces which are working the constitution and have managed to create public opinion and secure popular support in favour of their war activities. Moreover, I doubt if the proposed expansion will create any enthusiasm among important minorities such as Scheduled Castes; and it is bound to create justifiable disappointment among the Hindu, Muslim and Sikh martial classes. It may be that individuals in the co-operating Provinces and elsewhere will continue to render such assistance as they can; but I am afraid the ardour, zeal and enthusiasm, which distinguish spontaneous and genuine popular effort from laboured co-operation and assistance under official influence of pressure, must inevitably suffer. In the circumstances, I consider that open or even tacit acquiescence of the plan which might conceivably result in retarding the war effort in this country, at the present crucial juncture, will be against the best interests of the Punjab, India and the British Commonwealth.

Having regard to all these considerations, it is the clear though unpleasant duty of my colleagues and myself to request Your Excellency to relieve us of our present office. I am sending this letter with the concurrence of my colleagues, who share my regret that our association so happily begun shall come to a close so abruptly through circumstances beyond our control.

I should, however, like to take this opportunity to express the grateful thanks of my colleagues and myself to Your Excellency for the courtesy and kindness which you have invariably extended to us, and which made it possible for us to continue the highest traditions of Ministerial responsibility possible under the present scheme of Provincial Autonomy. I enclose herewith the resignations of my colleagues and myself for favour of necessary action when the reported impending announcement is made. At the same time, I would request Your Excellency to summon a special session of the Assembly immediately to enable the Ministry to make a formal statement regarding the step which we have been constrained to take.

Yours sincerely,
S. HYAT KHAN

ENCLOSURE 2 TO NO. 82

SIKANDER HYAT KHAN TO GLANCY

Simla,
July 13th, 1941

Dear Sir Bertrand,

For reasons embodied in my letter of today's date to Your Excellency I hereby beg to tender my resignation from the office of Premier.

Yours ever,
S. HYAT KHAN

ENCLOSURE 3 TO NO. 82

CHHOTU RAM AND OTHER MINISTERS TO SIKANDER HYAT KHAN

Simla,
July 13th, 1941

Dear Sir Sikander,

In view of the circumstances explained to us by you and for reasons embodied in your letter of today's date to His Excellency the Governor, we beg to place our resignation of our office as Ministers in your hands.

We are, Yours sincerely,
CHHOTU RAM
MANOHAR LAL
KHIZAR HAYAT
ABDUL HAYE
DASAUNDHA SINGH

83

GLANCY TO LINLITHGOW[33]

Telegram

No. 6-G *July 23rd, 1941*

Apart from Sikhs no very notable reactions have as yet resulted from statement about expansion of Your Excellency's Council, &c.[34] In official circles satisfaction felt is tampered [?tempered] to some extent by apprehensions as to antics in which Jinnah may indulge. Expounders of nationalist views make their usual complaint that changes do not go far enough and are in effect illusory. Sikhs are clamouring that they have been slighted by absence of Sikh representation on expanded Council and some supposedly responsible individuals like Jogendra Singh, Datar Singh and Buta Singh are fanning this alleged grievance. It is doubtful whether this outcry will have any practical effect, but it may possibly result in some setback to Sikh recruitment: this would of course be in worst interests of Sikh community, as we will point out to sponsors of movement.

84

GLANCY TO LINLITHGOW

Private and Personal
D.-O. No. 359-F.L.

Barnes Court, Simla,
August 2nd, 1941

Dear Lord Linlithgow,

I am afraid I have been rather remiss in my reports of late, but I have had several opportunities of discussing matters personally with Your Excellency; and I have not thought it necessary to trouble you with a fortnightly letter.

The Punjab has been peaceful on the whole during the past four weeks. A couple of stabbing cases occurred in Amritsar and there was a good deal of local excitement in consequence. But the District authorities took prompt action, bad characters likely to give trouble were effectively rounded up and there have been no untoward developments. The Khaksar trouble has subsided. The "Nihang" nuisance, which I have mentioned to you, looks as if it should admit of solution without any great difficulty: we are trying to make an arrangement with those who have for a long time past been enlisting genuine Nihangs whereby they will confine their recruits to reasonable numbers, supply us with periodical lists of their followers and provide such Nihangs with badges or certificates establishing their identity. We propose to refrain from prosecuting genuine certified Nihangs so long as they behave themselves. Spurious Nihangs will be dealt with as they deserve and this process has already begun to have a marked effect in bringing about the desertion of undesirable characters.

Russia's entry into the war continues to be almost universally welcomed, not that it has resulted in detaching communists from their opposition to Government. Japan's aggressiveness is condemned on all sides, and there seems to be a feeling that there is no very great menace threatening from this quarter. The Press is on the whole considerably more optimistic than was the case a month or two ago, and there is a tendency again towards complacent apathy in regard to the outcome of the war. We are proceeding vigorously with A.R.P. measures and other precautions, and are just embarking on another substantial increase in the Police Force. Recruiting for the Army has, generally speaking, been encouraging and there has been some improvement as far as Sikhs are concerned. But the Akalis, in spite of their association with the Khalsa Defence League, have not got their heart in the business, and the League's efforts have so far been disappointing. Tara Singh and those of his kidney prefer to direct the attention of their followers to the shortcomings of the Unionist Government rather than to the successful prosecution of the war.

The announcement about the expansion of the Executive Council and the creation of the Defence Council has come in for much criticism, in most cases more factious than genuine. Sikhs have been complaining loudly that their just rights have been ignored, and certain more or less influential members of the community headed by Sir Jogendra Singh have broadcast a statement, as you are aware, to the effect that Sikhs have been deliberately insulted and should now devote themselves to dealing with the tyranny for which the Punjab Government are responsible in the Province. I have spoken to two of the signatories and pointed out to them that the result of their declaration may well be a fall in Sikh recruitment, which would clearly be in the worst interests of the community. Their ultimate excuse has been that they were misled into signing the statement and were uncertain of its contents. No Sikh who has been to see me has been able to suggest the name of any member of his community who could aspire on his merits to a post on the Executive Council.

In Ministerial circles there is a certain amount of uneasiness in regard to the course of action which Jinnah may pursue. His *amour propre* appears to have been grievously wounded, and he is busily engaged in rocking the boat to the best of his ability. Whether he will go to the length of expelling the offending Muslim Premiers from the League remains to be seen: I am told that the Working Committee of the League is not empowered to deal with the case of Sikander in this way, since Sikander, like Fazl-ul-Huq, is not the Provincial head of the Muslim League, but I have not been able to verify whether this is correct. Anyhow, if one or more of those concerned are driven from the League, it looks as if the others will follow suit. Jinnah has received telegrams assuring him of support from certain of Sikander's personal opponents, and he has very likely exaggerated the importance of this backing.

The *Satyagraha* campaign is languishing. The desertion of Dr. Satyapal and quarrels between Iftikhar-ud-Din and Gopi Chand have further weakened the Congress position. Attempts to reason with the Mahatma and induce him to suspend his crusade have not succeeded in extracting any further inspiration from the oracle.

Rain is very badly needed in the south-east of the Punjab and if the break in the monsoon is protracted much longer, we shall be faced with another year of famine.

I enclose the fortnightly report for the first half of July.

Yours sincerely,
B.J. GLANCY

85

MOON TO LAITHWAITE

Telegram

No. 7-G *August 7th, 1941*

His Excellency has asked me to let you know for His Excellency the Viceroy's information that Sikander is holding a party meeting in Lahore on 9th and 10th with a view to rallying his supporters and preparing them for a special session of the Assembly to be held from 17th to 24th. At this session a resolution would be moved expressing confidence in the Ministry and urging them to redouble their efforts for the successful prosecution of the war. This is of course with a view to strengthening Sikander's position against any possible move by Jinnah.

86

GLANCY TO LINLITHGOW

Telegram

No. 9-G *August 16th, 1941*

Thank you for your two telegrams[35] about reactions to Muslim League criticisms.

Sikander had a most successful meeting at Lahore of Muslim Members of Unionist Party. Over 60, including Nawab of Mamdot, President of Provincial Muslim League, have handed him their resignations from Muslim League to use if necessary. Remaining members (about 12) who were absent from Lahore have been asked by letter whether they wish to follow this lead and a favourable response is expected. Sikander's present intention is to attend in person the meeting of Working Committee at Bombay, 24th.

In view of success of Lahore meeting idea of holding a special session of Assembly has been abandoned.

87

MOON TO LAITHWAITE

Barnes Court, Simla
August 26th, 1941

Dear Gilbert,

I enclose herewith a copy of Sikander's letter of the 24th of August to His Excellency Sir Bertrand Glancy.

Yours,
PA.,DY [PENDY] (E.P. MOON)

ENCLOSURE TO NO. 87

SIKANDER HYAT KHAN TO GLANCY

Taj Mahal Hotel, Camp, Bombay,
August 24th, 1941

My dear Sir Bertrand,

The Working Committee of the All-India Muslim League met today and considered the question of the association of the Muslim Premiers, who are Members of the Muslim League, with the National Defence Council. I took a firm stand on the fact that as we had been invited to represent our respective Provinces on this Council by virtue of our office, we agreed to serve on it and that if I had been appointed as a Member of this Council to represent the Muslim community only, I would, in fairness to my Province and my community, [?not] accept to be associated with it. I was, however, put in an embarrassing position when Mr. Jinnah apprised the meeting of a letter, dated the 20th July 1941, from the Governor of Bombay,[36] communicating to him a message from His Excellency the Viceroy, in which it was *inter alia* stated that "The Viceroy regards it as essential that the great Muslim community should be represented on that Council by persons of the highest prominence and capacity. He has accordingly invited the Premiers of Assam, Bengal, the Punjab, and Sind to serve as members of it, and he has extended invitations also to certain other prominent Muslims." This gave entirely a different complexion to the basis of our appointment on the National Defence Council and made it impossible for me, in fairness to my Province as well as to the Muslim League, to continue to serve on it on this basis. Accordingly, I felt that in these unexpected circumstances I could not allow the cause of the war effort to suffer, particularly in view of the delicate situation in Iran, the solidarity of the Muslim League to be ruptured at this critical juncture and myself as Premier of the Punjab to be placed in an embarrassing position of representing only one community on the National Defence Council. I have accordingly decided to sever my connection on this basis from the National Defence Council and am writing to request Your Excellency kindly to convey my resignation to His Excellency the Viceroy. I have informed the Working Committee of the Muslim League of my decision in the aforesaid circumstances. I shall apprise you of further details when I return to Simla.

Yours sincerely,
S. HYAT KHAN

88

GLANCY TO LINLITHGOW

Telegram

No. 363 *September 8th, 1941*

Your telegram No. 2187, dated the 6th September.[37] National Defence Council. I have not again asked the Premier whether he would now be willing to serve and I think it would be preferable to avoid doing this and to give his place to someone else. The most appropriate substitute would, I think, be Sir Chhotu Ram, who is the next senior Punjab Minister, and I understand that this is also the view of Sir Sikander.

2. I understand that Begum Shah Nawaz will probably refuse to resign. If she does resign, I can suggest no woman from here to take her place, and if no other suitable women, Muslim or other, can be found from elsewhere in India, the place might be left vacant.

3. In general I think that some at least of vacant places should be filled. If suitable Muslims are not available, then members of other communities might take their place.

89

GLANCY TO LINLITHGOW

Private and Personal
D.-O. No. 364-F.L.

Barnes Court, Simla,
September 10th, 1941

Dear Lord Linlithgow,

The main events that have of late commanded political interest have been the Premier's visit to Bombay to defend his acceptance of a place on the National Defence Council, his unexpected surrender to the dictation of Jinnah and his attempts to justify his action on his return to the Punjab. Sikander left for Bombay entirely confident of his ability to maintain his position, and he certainly had the dice heavily loaded in his favour. He proceeded, however, to strike his flag without a struggle on being confronted at the League meeting with the message sent to Jinnah by the Governor of Bombay, which Jinnah professed to interpret as meaning that the Muslim Premiers had been invited to serve on the Council merely as

Muslims and not in their official capacity. As you are aware, Sikander had been shown this letter at Bombay well in advance of the actual meeting, and he should have had sufficient time to collect his thoughts and to realise that Jinnah's interpretation was manifestly dubious: in any case, as he has repeatedly stated, he was well aware that he had himself been asked to join the Council in his capacity of Premier and that he had accepted the invitation on that basis.

In the circumstances it was natural enough that Sikander's defeat at the hands of Jinnah should have given rise to feelings of astonishment and in some quarters consternation. The Premier returned home in an uneasy frame of mind with his personal dislike and distrust of Jinnah strongly intensified. Since then he has been at pains to explain his surrender and, though his arguments may have carried little conviction to critical minds, he has exhibited a considerable degree of political agility. He has prudently placed the war in the forefront and stressed the paramount necessity of maintaining at full pressure the War efforts of the Province. His Muhammadan followers he has reminded of the importance of ensuring Muslim solidarity: the non-Muslims of the Unionist Party have been invited to accept the proposition that the Premier's continuance on the National Defence Council as a purely Muhammadan representative would have been unfair to all other communities. Many among the audience are still bewildered by the turn that events have taken; they are inclined to feel as if they had been called upon to witness a not very edifying contortionist entertainment, but they are for the most part genuinely relieved to think that the principal performer has survived his series of convolutions without finally losing his equilibrium. The Premier's Party retains to all outward appearances its unity and cohesion. The main consolation is that the War programme of the Province seems unlikely to suffer.

The Sikh community in general continues to express its resentment at the failure to appoint a Sikh representative on the Viceroy's Executive Council. This calamity is attributed to the manoeuvres of the Premier and the Unionist Government and there is an outcry led by the Akalis that such oppression can no longer be tolerated. An election is about to take place in the Batala Sikh constituency of the Gurdaspur district to fill the seat in the Punjab Legislative Assembly left vacant by the death of the late Sir Sundar Singh Majithia: Sardar Kirpal Singh, Sir Sundar Singh's son, is opposing a candidate put forward by the Akalis, who are straining every nerve to win the contest: a considerable volume of party feeling has been worked up over the event and some heads are likely to be broken. Sikh recruitment has shown a marked improvement of late; it is manifestly in the interests of the community that this should continue, and it is scarcely probable that Akali leaders will think it worth their while to try and interfere. Danger from "Nihangs" has largely subsided, and as the result of action taken against bogus "Nihangs" in various places many recent disciples have disappeared from the ranks. Communal tension shows little sign of improving, but such incidents as have occurred have been dealt with promptly and effectively. The Congress *Satyagraha* campaign appears to be on its last legs so far as the Punjab is concerned.

The Muslim Press has not on the whole been commendable for its comments on the Iran situation, and there has been strong tendency to ignore the danger with which India and Iran itself were threatened as the result of Nazi infiltration. Many sections of the Hindu Press have been responsible for mischievous articles calculated to stir Muslim papers to further indiscretions. The swift success of the operations in Iran will, it is to be hoped, exercise a restraining influence. Japanese aggression does not seem to be regarded with any very serious apprehension.

There has been a fair amount of rain in the south-east of the Punjab, where it was badly needed, and the agricultural outlook is better than it was, though parts of Hissar are still in a poor enough condition. The price of wheat and various other commodities has risen and demands have been voiced that control should be introduced; it seems very doubtful whether in the long run this remedy would prove effective. The growing shortage of textile materials caused by the economic measures taken against Japan is seriously affecting mill centres, such as Amritsar, and some increase in unemployment is to be expected.

I enclose the provincial fortnightly reports for the first and second halves of August.

Yours sincerely,
B.J. GLANCY

90

GLANCY TO LINLITHGOW[38]

Barnes Court, Simla,
D.-O. No. 365 *September 20th, 1941*

Dear Lord Linlithgow,

I write in reply to Your Excellency's letter of August 4th, regarding judicial decisions invalidating important Provincial Acts.

2. Two important Punjab Acts have been challenged in the Courts, viz.:

(1) The Punjab Restitution of Mortgaged Lands Act, 1938, and
(2) The Punjab Alienation of Land (Second Amendment) Act, 1938.

Both these were highly contentious measures and it was expected that considerable efforts would be made to impugn their validity.

3. I enclose herewith brief notes[39] on the litigation concerning these two Acts. The Restitution of Mortgaged Lands Act has been challenged mainly on the ground of "repugnancy". A Full Bench of the Lahore High Court have upheld the Act; but I understand that the plaintiffs are likely to appeal to the Federal Court.

When this Act came to my predecessor for assent, the question whether it might not be held to be in certain respects "repugnant" and whether therefore it ought not to be reserved *ex-majore cautela* was considered; but there was such a consensus of opinion that there was really no repugnancy – a view which has so far been confirmed – that ultimately my predecessor decided to give assent to the Bill and not to reserve it. It has, however, generally been the practice here to reserve *ex-majore cautela* in the case of any doubt.

4. The Punjab Alienation of Land (Second Amendment) Act has been held by the Lahore High Court to offend against the provisions of Section 298 (1) of the Government of India Act. This decision is partly the inevitable result of a defect in the drafting of Section 298 (2) of the Government of India Act. This sub-section purported to save from the provisions of Section 298 (1) all measures such as the original Punjab Alienation of Land Act, but it failed to do so because it only mentioned sales and mortgages of agricultural land and omitted to mention exchanges, gifts, wills, &c. The defect in this sub-section was well known here; but short of amending the Government of India Act there appeared to be no remedy.

But in the litigation regarding this Act there is also involved a really difficult point of interpretation. The Lahore High Court have held that even sales and mortgages effected before the commencement of the Act of 1938 are not protected by the provisions of Section 298 (2) (*a*), and that therefore the Act of 1938, in so far as it seeks to set aside sales and mortgages, is *ultra vires*. It had never been anticipated that the Courts would take this view, and in pronouncing their decision the Judges have themselves admitted that "the point is not free from difficulty". The Provincial Government have filed an appeal to the Federal Court, which is believed to have some prospect of success.

It seems to me that there was bound to be litigation regarding this Act, unless the opinion of the Federal Court on all possible doubtful points had been taken in advance by means of a reference under Section 213. I may add that this Act was reserved for Your Excellency's consideration and was the subject of considerable correspondence with the Secretary of State,[40] so that it was very fully scrutinised before assent was finally given.

5. No other Act has so far been challenged in this Province on its own merits, but a notification regarding the colourization of artificial "ghi' issued under the Punjab Pure Food (Amendment) Act of 1938 has led to litigation, which is now pending in the High Court. I enclose a brief note[41] (Enclosure II) regarding this litigation. As you will observe, it is the combined effect of the Act and of the notification which has been challenged and not the Act itself. The Ministry were fully warned (I think amongst others by your Commerce Member) that this notification might lead them into difficulties, but they were unwilling to withdraw it.

6. So much for Acts which have been challenged in the courts. But you have also asked to be informed of Acts in which defects have been discovered and corrected without their being actually taken to the courts. I enclose herewith a list[42] of such Acts with a brief note on each (Enclosure III). You will see that in a number of instances defects have had to be corrected; and I understand that another piece of legislation (The Punjab Weights and Measures Bill, 1941), which was reserved for your consideration and is still being examined in your Secretariat, has been found to require considerable amendment.

7. I do not think that there are any Acts which have been found to lead to serious administrative difficulties; but there are of course many Bills enacted by the present Ministry which, owing to delay in framing rules or in getting up the necessary administrative machinery, have not yet come into actual operation. Difficulties may therefore be found to arise in the future.

8. On the whole, the facts so far as this Province is concerned support Your Excellency's view that judicial decision[s] invalidating important Acts have neither been so many nor so extensive as the Secretary of State is inclined to assume. The Punjab Alienation of Land (Second Amendment) Act, 1938, is really the only important measure to be successfully impugned and, as already explained, this measure was very closely scrutinised before assent was given and no change of procedure other than consulting the Federal Court in advance under Section 213 could have prevented what has taken place. At the same time it must be admitted that the Provincial Government have not had at their disposal an adequate supply of expert

draftsmen and well-trained lawyers capable of dealing satisfactorily with legislative work. In this Province, as is understood to have been the case in certain others, the new Ministry came into power obsessed with the idea that most ills could be cured by legislation, and they proceeded to hurry through the Assembly a large number of Bills, thus throwing a strain on the law officers which they were not equipped to bear. With no very great experience of drafting they were required hurriedly to prepare Bills, and, still more hurriedly, to prepare amendments to meet suggestions made during the passage of these Bills through the Assembly. Moreover, the exact significance of many sections of the Government of India Act, 1935, relating to legislative matters, could not immediately be fully appreciated. Experience and the mere passage of time are proving remedies for some of these ills. Furthermore, promising judicial officers are now receiving regular training in the Central Government's Legislative Department and they should in due course largely make good the deficiencies which are at present felt.

9. As regards consultation with the Centre, I consider that this has already been amply provided for in the Home Department letter No. 57/39-Judl. of the 18th of December 1940. Furthermore, after a Bill has been passed by the Assembly there is always an opportunity for further correspondence with Your Excellency before assent is finally given.

10. I need hardly say that whenever a Bill comes to me for assent the first questions considered are whether it is *intra vires* of the Provincial Legislature and whether there is any repugnancy. No doubt mistakes have sometimes been made, but so far no mistake leading to very serious consequences.

Yours sincerely,
B.J. GLANCY

91

GLANCY TO LINLITHGOW

Private and Personal — Government House, Lahore,
D.-O. No. 368-F.L. — *October 21st, 1941*

Dear Lord Linlithgow,

There have been no political developments of any great importance since I sent Your Excellency my last report. The Premier, as you are aware, has of late endeavoured to re-establish his position as a political leader by means of a press statement criticising Mr. Churchill's declaration about India and suggesting that a time-limit should be fixed within which India should attain its legitimate constitutional aspirations.[43] This *démarche* has disturbed the Muslim League, nor has it aroused much in the way of favourable reaction elsewhere. Though the rank and file of the Unionist Party still remain loyal and though the Party is likely to retain a substantial majority for a considerable time to come, there are stirrings of uneasiness in various quarters. The Premier has, I am afraid, become more vulnerable since he yielded to Jinnah at Bombay. The more intelligent amongst the Muslims are obviously doubtful as to whether the Unionist Party can remain indefinitely in the ascendant if it is tied to the wheels of the Muslim League chariot. Hindus and Sikhs have been busy denouncing the Pakistan doctrine and loud in their complaints about alleged communal discrimination. Non-Muslims have formed themselves into a vigilance society to protect their interests. The Sikhs have also set up a committee with a view to setting at rest the grievances of the community. The result of the recent Batala election, in which Sardar Kirpal Singh was defeated by a margin of nearly a thousand votes, is regarded by the Akalis as a triumphant indication of their ascendancy among the Sikh community: the Akalis mobilized their forces on a large scale for the contest which was attended, I am sorry to say, by a good deal of hooliganism and intimidation.

But the war effort of the Province continues undiminished. Sikh recruits have been coming in well of late as compared with the position a few months ago, though the enrolment of Jat Sikhs is still well below requirements. The Akalis are careful to avoid coming into the open in helping to promote war activities, but it seems to be widely recognised that they are in favour of keeping phute [*sic*] Sikh proportion in the Army. The Military exercises that have recently taken place have done something to encourage active interest in the war. The black-out went off successfully despite a good many complaints from various communities. The Demonstration Train which started its career at Lahore on the 17th of this month, proved a distinct success; on the opening day the crowd besieged the train and paid the demonstrators the compliment of smashing a few windows in their eagerness to see what was inside.

Russian reverses have given rise to a good deal of despondency coupled with complaints that Britain should take some sensational action in order to divert the German onslaught on her ally.

Congress activities are still in the trough of the wave so far as the Punjab is concerned.

I enclose the fortnightly report for the second half of September 1941.

Yours sincerely,
B.J. GLANCY

92

GLANCY TO LINLITHGOW[44]

Personal
[Unnumbered]

Government House, Lahore,
November 10th, 1941

Dear Lord Linlithgow,

I have discussed with Sir Sikander the question of the release of *Satyagrahi* prisoners, and I am now writing to Your Excellency personally in reply to your personal telegram of the 7th November.[45]

2. The Punjab Government are ready to fall in with the views of the Government of India and are replying to this effect. They think it would be more graceful and effective to release all *Satyagrahi* prisoners without discrimination as there are none from whom serious trouble is anticipated, though the right to re-arrest any one repeating the offence will of course be reserved. But the Provincial Government while willing to take this action with regard to *Satyagrahi* prisoners, are very genuinely disturbed at the proposal to set up a Committee to examine cases of Deoli detenus many of whom are very dangerous. We are writing about this and earnestly hope that our views will receive all due consideration.

Yours sincerely,
B.J. GLANCY

93

GLANCY TO LINLITHGOW

Private and Personal
D.-O. No. 372-F.L.

Government House, Lahore,
November 22nd, 1941

Dear Lord Linlithgow,

The Sikh community, especially the Akali faction, has of late been rather more clamorous than usual. Their spokesman have been loud in denouncing the Unionist Government, which they accuse of being determined to abase the Sikhs at every opportunity. Wild allegations are made that Sikhs are never given their fair share in the public services and the old thorny problem of *Jhatka* meat is dragged into the forefront. The non-inclusion of a Sikh member in the enlarged Executive Council is ascribed to the machinations of Sikander and his friends, and Akalis and others are never tired of parading this grievance. The appointment of Sardar Dasaundha Singh as a member of the Punjab Cabinet has also become the subject of increasing indignation. This last complaint, I am afraid, is by no means entirely unjustified. The truth is that Dasaundha Singh has certainly not been a success. He has little, if any, influence with his community, his brain movements are glacial in their rate of progress, he finds it very difficult to get through his work and is a sore trial to those with whom it is his business to deal. He is well-meaning enough no doubt, but I sincerely wish that a more effective successor to the late Sir Sundar Singh Majithia had been put forward. The cry of the Sikhs is that in the face of all these affronts any member of the community who adheres to the Unionists can only be regarded as a traitor to the cause, and there is talk of liquidating the Khalsa Nationalist Party, forming a strong opposition with the aid of certain Hindus and a few disgruntled Muslims and turning the present Government out of power. Though the Unionist Party machine creaks rather ominously at times, there are no signs of this programme succeeding in the near future. Some of the more prominent Akalis are fond of saying in the course of conversation that they now realise the folly of their having strayed from the right path a few years ago and made common cause with Congress and come to logger-heads with British high authorities by such indiscretions as discouraging recruitment to the Indian Army: they suggest that they no longer regard "Khalistan" as a practical idea, that the thought of "Pakistan" is of course quite intolerable and that they dislike still more the prospect of a closer union with the Congress party, since this would eventually mean the submergence of their political identity; consequently they would like to make a virtue of necessity and be good friends with the British and so retain an impartial umpire in their differences with rival factions. Many of them, in particular Giani Kartar Singh, have been actively helpful, as far as they deem it expedient, in promoting Sikh recruitment, they confess that this policy is essential for the preservation of the Sikhs as a separate entity, but they maintain that they should be given some recognition for this manifestation of grace and repentance and should be rewarded with high appointments in the Central Government. Another avenue which some of them have been exploring is the possibility of weaning Sikander and his adherents from the Muslim League; various tentative approaches have been made or suggested in this respect, and there has been a certain amount of speculation about the reasons for Sikander's recent visits to Hyderabad and Bhopal. It is suggested that if Sikander would openly abandon the Pakistan theory, and if a Sikh Minister who is truly representative of the Khalsa could be appointed to the Cabinet, then all distrust would happily disappear. It seems very doubtful, however, whether Sikander, whatever his inclinations may be, will be afforded in the near future as good an opportunity of breaking with the Muslim League as he rejected a few months ago. The upshot of all this is that the Sikh community is growing more and more uneasy and there is a feeling that it must move in some direction or other to ensure its survival. But there is much jealousy and dissension in the ranks; the tendency to pass the time by heaping abuse on the Punjab Ministry does not help towards a general reconciliation.

I have been touring of late in several districts of the Province, mainly with the object of holding War Darbars, rewarding those who have done good service and trying to encourage others tó follow their example. The results have, I think, been good. Certainly there, has been a great demonstration of willingness to assist. As far as Jat Sikhs are concerned recruitment has flagged again after its recent improvement, but one reason for this, though it is sometimes overstated, is that, as the Recruiting Officers point out, enlistment always tends to decline when agricultural operations are in progress. Opinion still varies widely as to the effects produced by the Khalsa Defence League, but I think there is no doubt that at least in certain districts it has been of considerable value. It might perhaps be well to give the League some open encouragement on a suitable opportunity, but the Ministers still regard it with a good deal of suspicion. Patiala is here now and I propose to have a talk with him on things in general; he made, as you know, a very helpful speech about Sikh recruiting the other day.

Begum Shah Nawaz and Sardar Naunihal Singh came and discussed with the Premier and myself not long ago their experiences at the first meeting of the National Defence Council. They were much gratified by their reception and by all the trouble that had been taken to provide them with information, and they were particularly enthusiastic about the Commander-in-Chief's lucid exposition of the war situation. They said that the only discordant note was struck by the churlish behaviour of a representative from Sind, but the irreproachable demeanour of all others present instilled into him a more proper sense of decorum before the meeting came to an end. Begum Shah Nawaz had various suggestions to make about the closer association of women in the War effort, but not many of them were very pertinent or practical. She said that some disappointment had been caused because Indian troops as compared with Australians had not been given their fair share in triumphal entries into towns in Syria: let us hope that there are a sufficient number of future triumphs in store to satisfy the aspirations of all.

War news of late has not produced any very sensational effects in the Press. On the whole the public remain calm and often apathetic. Adverse reactions on the part of Muslims to the steps we have taken in Iraq and Iran are steadily dying down: one District Board in a preponderantly Muslim district said in their address to me the other day that they were grateful for the precautions we had taken in this direction. Congress activities still remain scarcely noticeable. Mr. Munshi of Bombay has visited a few places in the Punjab and gone away; his observations on Pakistan led to the inevitable counter-attacks and had a certain, though not a very marked, effect in promoting communal disunity.

I enclose the provincial reports for the first and second halves of October.[46]

Yours sincerely,
B.J. GLANCY

NOTES

1. Lord Linlithgow minuted: 'Delighted'.
2. Lord Linlithgow minuted: 'Too early'.
3. Mr J.W. Hearn.
4. Mr P.L. Orde.
5. Sir Henry Craik sent Lord Linlithgow his promised reply on the traffic in illicit arms in his letter No. 326 of 7 March 1941. Craik made the point that some officers felt more needed to be done to stop the supply of arms within the N.-W.F.P. The Governor considered it was desirable to hold a conference with the N.-W.F.P police authorities and they would try to arrange this as soon as possible. R/3/1/63.
6. The report and letter have not been traced.
7. Mr Amin-ud-Din.
8. Lord Linlithgow minuted: 'I am glad the G[overnor] is taking this course.'
9. In this unnumbered telegram Lord Linlithgow informed Sir Henry Craik that Sir Sikander had told him the previous day that in view of Mr Jinnah's 'continued advocacy of Pakistan as official policy despite understanding he gave Sikander at Bombay that he would not press it, he [Sikander] proposed to resign from the Working Committee of the Muslim League next week.' Linlithgow did not respond to this but made it clear that he had no work for

Sikander at the Centre and his best war contribution was to continue as Premier of the Punjab.

In paragraph 2 of the telegram Linlithgow said he was by no means easy at Sikander's proposed step. Although the Viceroy had strong views as to the arguments against Pakistan, 'there seems a good deal to be said against any avoidable split in the Muslim League more particularly at a time when we are nearing the end of the second stage of the Gandhi *Satyagraha* campaign, and any such spilt would be a great encouragement to the Congress and the anti-war party.' The Viceroy feared that Sikander might play into the hands of his enemies in the Punjab by quarrelling with the League and so weaken his position there or make it impossible.

In later paragraphs of the telegram Linlithgow suggested there was much to be said for Sikander's staying with the League but taking the line in an early speech that he (Sikander) had an open mind on the matter of territorial readjustments and indeed had a scheme of his own. [See *P.P., 1936-1939*, Appendix III.] Sikander might say that he was not wedded to any particular solution but was only concerned to find one in the best interests of all. Linlithgow feared Jinnah might exploit Sikander's resignation to Sikander's disadvantage. R/3/1/63.

10. Lord Linlithgow minuted on this paragraph: 'I take note of Craik's view and await the result of his talk with Sir Sikander.'
11. Only the second resolution is printed in R/3/1/63.
12. Lord Linlithgow minuted: 'The event will show where the greatest advantage lies. I hope very much that all [will] be well.'
13. Not printed.
14. Mr P.L Orde.
15. Mr K.H. Henderson.
16. Mr N.M. Buch.
17. Mr Amin-ud-Din.
18. 'May there be victory upon victory.' (*Urdu.*)
19. Item (*b*) here would appear to have a passage missing. It should presumably read: 'established a convention that any legislation affecting the religious affairs of the Members of the Assembly representing a particular community would be enacted by an absolute majority of the Assembly Members of that community alone.' See Enclosure 2 to No. 65, demand (2).
20. Lord Linlithgow minuted: 'I am truly sorry. He was one of the most charming and attractive Indian gentlemen I have ever met.'
21. This document is taken from MSS. EUR. F 125/109.
22. Ibid.
23. In this telegram Lord Linlithgow referred to an earlier telegram (1028-S of 19 May 1941) in which he had informed Governors that he was likely to suggest to Mr Amery a small expansion of his Executive Council by choosing individuals rather than representatives of parties. He would probably

simultaneously set up the War Advisory Council. Linlithgow was anxious not to provoke Congress nor take on the Muslim League. He was therefore anxious to avoid, by selecting League Muslim representatives for his Council, conflict with the League. MSS. EUR. F 125/109.

24. This document is taken from MSS. EUR. F 125/109.
25. Sir Bertrand Glancy did not send Lord Linlithgow a Fortnightly Report in the middle of July 1941 as he had been in close touch with the Viceroy over developments and did not feel it necessary to put anything in writing. Moon to Laithwaite, 16 July 1941. R/3/1/63.
26. These were to be: Khan Bahadur Allah Bakhsh (Sind), Mr A.K. Fazlul Haq (Bengal) and Sir Muhammad Saadulla (Assam).
27. I.e. the Provincial Cabinet.
28. Lord Linlithgow minuted: 'I think I must check upon this. Ask Ogilvie if he has ever heard of him.' Sir Charles Ogilvie was Secretary, Defence Department, Government of India 1937-45.
29. Lord Linlithgow minuted with regard to this sentence: 'I have long had this in mind, but fear that such a plan would seriously weaken the Defence Council.'
30. In his letter of 3 July 1941 Lord Linlithgow thanked Sir Bertrand Glancy and Sir Sikander for their very full examination of possible Punjab candidates for the National Defence Council which was sent in No. 79. Linlithgow agreed that the Muslim Premiers should serve on the Council qua Premiers. He added that they must 'be at pains to avoid anything which could suggest we were endeavouring to outwit Jinnah'.

    The Viceroy intended that Sikander would serve as the Muslim member from the Punjab but it would not be possible to include a Punjabi Hindu. With regard to the Sikhs, Linlithgow himself would have been very ready to accept either Sir Jogendra Singh or Master Tara Singh. However in the light of the strong views of Glancy and Sikander, the Viceroy was intending to approach Sardar Baldev Singh. Linlithgow did not consider that Sardar Naunihal Singh 'carries the guns'.

    In the outcome the Punjab would have two representatives on the Council. There was a possibility of a third member as Linlithgow wished to add a woman representative and had Begum Shah Nawaz in mind. R/3/1/63.
31. Lord Linlithgow acknowledged this letter later on 6 July 1941. In this acknowledgement Linlithgow said that Mr Amery had authorised the inclusion of Begum Shah Nawaz as a member of the National Defence Council. This would give the Punjab three representatives and no province had more than three representatives. Linlithgow felt that when Sikander knew this, he would realise that the Punjab had been generously treated.

    On 10 July 1940 Linlithgow wrote to tell Glancy that he had talked with Sikander about the National Defence Council. Sikander strongly urged the Viceroy to reconsider the Sikh representation and made a new point which carried weight, namely, that Sardar Baldev Singh had walked out with Congress. Linlithgow remained of the opinion that Nau Nihal Singh would be nothing like the calibre of the other members of the Council. However as Linlithgow was anxious to meet Sikander, and in the light of the new information, he was prepared to agree to the inclusion of Naunihal Singh as the Sikh representative. R/3/1/63.

32. There are no further letters from Sir Bertrand Glancy on the formation of the National Defence Council in R/3/1/63. However the print does include two letters from Lord Linlithgow of 16 and 17 July 1941.

In his letter of 16 July Linlithgow thanked Glancy for having made some progress in 'this difficult business'. The Viceroy then explained the difficulties in reconsidering arrangements made with the King and Mr Amery. Linlithgow asked Glancy to maintain his pressure on Sir Sikander. The Viceroy continued:

'I would only add that, as you realise, it will be quite out of the question for me to go to Raghavendra Rao who, with the Secretary of State's approval, has been offered and has accepted the Civil Defence portfolio, and is at the moment working on it, and suggest for a moment that he should replace Bajpai [prospective Indian Agent-General in the U.S.A.]; or to go to the Nizam who has agreed to make Hydari's services available under some protest and let him know that he will not be needed for another couple of months.'

The first two paragraphs of Linlithgow's letter of 17 July read:

'You have done your best, and I am very grateful to you. I judge that you are not likely to get much further with Sikander, and that indeed further pressure might produce a setback. Sikander has been, and is still being, both weak and silly. But he is necessary to our war effort, and I am not prepared (though he most thoroughly deserves it) to drive him out of office.

'I have therefore entered into negotiations with the Secretary of State for the addition of two further appointments to my Executive Council, and Amery has accepted my proposals. The names are not yet absolutely firm, but they look like being: Firoz Khan Noon [a Punjab representative] and Nalini Sarker (Bengal), i.e., one Muslim and one Hindu.'

The Viceroy was not inclined to inform Sikander of these two extra additions to the Executive Council until the news was made public. He was anxious 'to blur the fact that Sikander's blackmail has been successful' and asked Glancy to tell Sikander at an appropriate time that the extra appointments represented no more than a telescoping of intended plans – 'the complete scheme now, instead of two bites at the cherry!' In the event Sir Firoz Khan Noon was included in the expanded Council as member for Labour and Mr Sarker as member for Education, Health and Lands.

33. This document is taken from MSS. EUR. F 125/109.

34. Lord Linlithgow's statement on the expansion of the Executive Council and

the creation of the National Defence Council had been made on 22 July 1941. See *India and the War: Text of Announcement by the Governor-General of India on the 22nd July, 1941.* (Cmd. 6293.)

35. Only telegram 575-S.C. of 15 August 1941 from Lord Linlithgow is included in R/3/1/63. This gave assessments from Sind, the Punjab, Bengal and Assam of the reactions of the respective Premiers to Muslim League criticism of their action in joining the National Defence Council.
36. Sir Roger Lumley.
37. This telegram (in fact dated 5 September 1941) was sent by Lord Linlithgow to the Governors of Bengal, the Punjab and Assam. Linlithgow asked for views as to the line which should be taken with regard to the prospective vacancies on the National Defence Council resulting from the Muslim League's action.

    In telegram 2455-S of 27 September 1941, Linlithgow told the same group of Governors that, after consulting Mr Amery, they felt the wise course was to take no action in filling vacancies until after the first meeting of the Council. R/3/1/63.
38. This document is taken from MSS.EUR.F 125/109.
39. Not printed.
40. See *P.P., 1936-1939*, Nos. 58 and 76 and noting.
41. Not printed.
42. Not printed.
43. In a statement issued on 1 October 1941, Sir Sikander criticized a recent statement by Mr Churchill on India in relation to the Atlantic Charter. Sikander wished that Churchill's statement had never been made as it created the impression that earlier announcements by H.M.G. and the British no longer held the field. He called upon H.M.G. to make a fresh declaration reaffirming its intentions for India. A few days later Sikander added that if the British did not do this within two or three weeks, he would not hesitate to appeal to the Indian political parties to present a united front.
44. This document is taken from MSS. EUR. F 125/109.
45. Lord Linlithgow's telegram referred to an official telegram from the Home Department of the Government of India. This is not included in MSS. EUR. F. 125/109 but it is clear that it divided existing prisoners into various classes. Only those who were genuinely *Satyagrahis* were recommended for release. The Viceroy was doubtful whether any political advantage would follow from the releases but he felt the gesture worth while. He noted that he had expected the matter to be raised by the expanded Executive Council. MSS. EUR. F 125/109.
46. Lord Linlithgow minuted on this letter: 'Glancy is moving a little towards the Akalis; but is still influenced by the feelings of his ministers and Sikander in particular. I don't think we shall do much with the Sikhs until we do give the Akalis a job or 2.'

CHAPTER 4

Documents for 1942

94

GLANCY TO LINLITHGOW

Private and Personal
D.-O. No. 377-F.L.

Government House, Lahore,
January 1st, 1942

Dear Lord Linlithgow,

Japan's entry into the war and the early successes that she has achieved have produced as yet no very profound impression on the public in this Province. There has certainly been no wave of despondency comparable to the alarm which set in when France capitulated, and the general feeling is that Japan cannot hope for any great length of time to resist the combined forces of Britain and America.

What has interested the man in the street far more than war news has been the increasing rise in the price of foodstuffs and other commodities. Action taken to control the price of wheat has met with general approval, in spite of a Resolution to the contrary effect which was carried in the Legislative Assembly. On the whole District Officers have been successful in their efforts to enforce the orders passed, though there have been in places well-founded complaints that dealers have withheld all but small stocks from the market or have sought to evade control by means of adulteration. A fair number of offenders have been prosecuted and this has produced some salutary result, but the inclination of the ordinary merchant is to part with as little grain as possible in the hope of being able to dispose of the remainder at more favourable rates either by secret transaction or by removal elsewhere. The situation is by no means free from anxiety, as anything approaching a prolonged scarcity of supplies in a particular area may well lead to looting and riots. An experienced Deputy Commissioner has been put on special duty to co-ordinate wheat control in the Province. One of the main problems is the shortage of rolling stock. I understand from the North-Western Railway authorities that the position in this respect is more promising than was the case a little while ago, but it is still far from satisfactory. We shall be grateful for any help which the Central Government can give us in this direction and we shall be glad to know as soon as is possible what other articles, if any, are likely to come under all-India control.

The widespread interest in the grain-control situation has tended to throw into the shade agitation connected with the Marketing Act and Sales Tax Act. Concessions made by the Punjab Government induced the ring-leader of the traders to announce that the *hartal* arranged as a protest against the Marketing Act would be cancelled. It remains to be seen whether his followers will abide by this decision, but agitation has certainly died down to a considerable extent. In other directions also the Punjab Ministry have shown a more conciliatory attitude to the moneyed classes, and have modified various proposals calculated to cause resentment among the urban community.

Congress reactions in this Province to the release of *Satyagraha* prisoners have not been encouraging, but, as you know, the *Satyagraha* movement and Congress activities generally have been at a very low ebb of late in the Punjab. It is represented that the gesture made by Government is of no value in itself and the usual demand is put forward for a "change of heart". The Muslim League will no doubt indulge in a counter-blast to the latest Congress pronouncement, and communal relations, already sufficiently strained, are likely to be further embittered. No definite developments have taken place in the direction of a rapprochement between the Ministry and Sikh leaders; Sardar Baldev Singh, who has announced his intention of forming a new party, is aware that, if he does not take too extreme a line, the Premier will be glad to discuss matters with him; it is possible that a meeting between them may be arranged, and that something tangible may emerge.

A suggestion has been made to me that a special fund should be started to replace the *Prince of Wales* and the *Repulse*. The attention of those concerned has been drawn to the fact that they can earmark, if they wish to do so, any contributions made to the War Purposes Fund.

I enclose the provincial fortnightly report for the first half of December.

Yours sincerely,
B.J. GLANCY

95

ABELL TO LAITHWAITE

Secret

Government House, Lahore,
January 11th, 1942

Dear Gilbert,

As desired in your confidential demi-official letter No. 2448-G.G. of the 17th of June 1938, I forward a note recorded by His Excellency the Governor on the various Punjab Ministers.

Yours sincerely,
GEORGE ABELL

ENCLOSURE TO NO. 95

NOTE BY GLANCY

Secret

Government House, Lahore,
January 11th, 1942

Sir Sikander Hyat Khan is a man of very considerable ability and a most strenuous worker: he is essentially fair-minded, possesses great personal charm and still commands a large measure of respect. But there is no doubt that his unexpected surrender to Jinnah last summer has weakened his position. Non-Muslims have remained quite unconvinced by his explanations of his *volte-face* and tend more and more to regard him as a self-confessed Pakistani. Even among Muslims there are many who have been seriously upset by his abasement at Bombay and regard his manoeuvres there as damaging to provincial prestige. One consequence is, I fear, that he has become less certain of himself. As regards his policy of promoting the war efforts of the Province he has never wavered: he has maintained a steady pressure in all forms of war activity, and for this he is deserving of no little credit.

Sir Chhotu Ram is made of sterner stuff than his leader. He still pursues his ideals persistently and often passionately. But, though his outlook is the same as ever, he has been of late more circumspect in his public utterances. He is an effective and hard-working Minister of marked capacity whose instinct is to ride straight at his fences, whatever their dimensions.

Malik Khizar Hayat Khan Tiwana is maturing in the cask of political experience. He is not free from occasional vagaries, but he does his work shrewdly and adequately. He is a distinct asset to the Cabinet.

Sir Manohar Lal is sound and very pleasant to deal with. He is not sufficiently assertive when he meets with opposition, though he has shown some signs of improvement in this respect.

Mian Abdul Haye can scarcely be described as a very satisfactory member of the team. He is not lacking in intelligence. But he is an indifferent and by no means a single-minded administrator.

Sardar Dasaundha Singh has unfortunately failed to justify whatever hopes may have been entertained regarding his capacity. His intentions are good, but his mental calibre is regrettably low. The assistance which he affords to his colleagues and subordinates is negligible, and he exercises little, if any, influence among his own community.

B.J. GLANCY
Governor of the Punjab

96

GLANCY TO LINLITHGOW

Private and Personal — Government House, Lahore,
D.-O. No. 382 — *February 5th, 1942*

Dear Lord Linlithgow,

Japanese successes in the Far East have given rise to a good deal of uneasiness, but there has been no widespread feeling of alarm comparable to that which manifested itself in the summer of 1940. No serious run on the banks has been reported. Newspapers have behaved reasonably well on the whole, though considerable disappointment has been expressed at successive withdrawals in Malaya and Burma and recent set-backs in Cyrenaica.

Wheat control has been working effectively enough, though there have been complaints about insufficient supplies in various centres from time to time. The shortage of wagons has led to difficulties in regard not only to grain, but to other commodities such as salt and fuel. It is to be hoped that with co-ordinated traffic control the position will improve.

The *hartal* on which shopkeepers have embarked to protest against the Sales Tax Act still continues. As I mentioned to you in Delhi the other day, the Premier interviewed the main organizer of the *hartal*, one Bihari Lal Chanana, about the middle of December last and made two substantial concessions to the traders relating to the activities of Inspectors and an optional method of assessment. Bihari Lal went away apparently content with these concessions, and the Premier was left with the impression that the *hartal* would in consequence not materialize. But Bihari Lal, if he was ever serious in his professions made to the Premier, allowed himself to be overruled by his followers. The *hartal* started on January the 9th and has now been going on nearly a month. The traders have been making a series of further demands and have said at times that they will not be satisfied unless the entire Act is repealed. Responsible merchants would be glad enough to have the affair ended, but they lack the courage to act independently. Small shopkeepers have found it difficult to carry on, and shop employees have been hard hit in places. The public have suffered a considerable degree of inconvenience in many places, though this is frequently overdrawn. The organizers have been busy enlisting the support of the press and various political malcontents. They have collected a fair amount of money and achieved a considerable degree of notoriety. In many rural areas and a certain number of townships there has been virtually no *hartal*, but it has been fairly complete in Lahore, Amritsar and a few other cities, though there has been a good deal of selling through the back door and the European and many Muslim shops have refrained from taking part in the affair. For the last week or so the traders have been indulging in what they call "direct action", which consists in holding meetings where certain individuals, generally of no importance, shout slogans against the payment of the tax. These demonstrations, which amount to little more than what was going on before resort was had to "direct action", have been ignored. If any steps are to be taken, it would seem preferable to deal under the Act itself with selected merchants of prominence for failure to submit their returns. During the Premier's absence[1] Sir Chhotu Ram, who was carrying on in his place, resolutely declined to yield any further, but he was careful to refrain from any unbridled speeches, and the criticisms directed against him on this occasion by the traders and their supporters have been quite unjustified. The Premier since his return has again entered into negotiations with Bihari Lal Chanana and has, I understand, held out various further concessions, mostly of no great value, on which he would be prepared to give way. These negotiations appear to have satisfied all traders except certain piece-goods merchants of Amritsar. It is not unlikely that the *hartal* will be called off within the next day or two. There are many who believe that the same result would have been achieved if the

Premier had taken a firmer line and who would have been better pleased if he had done so.

Sikh politics have been much confused. Tara Singh has established himself as the head of the Shiromani Akali Dal, but has considerable difficulty in reconciling the views of the two main opposing factions among his followers. He is, according to the proverb, "sailing in two boats", and divides himself between veering towards Congress ideas and passively encouraging Sikh enlistment in the Army. Sikh recruitment still falls considerably short of what it should be. Some of the Akalis have of late been making attacks on the Maharaja of Patiala; these appear to be largely inspired by interested persons who seek preferment in the State.

There have been some very useful showers in many parts of the Province and in most places *rabi* prospects are distinctly promising.

Yours sincerely,
B.J. GLANCY

97

GLANCY TO LINLITHGOW

Government House, Lahore,
D.-O. No. 387 *February 23rd, 1942*

Dear Lord Linlithgow,

The Premier has just been round to see me and has asked me to pass on the following suggestions to you in case, as he says he has good reason to believe, a further statement about constitutional developments in this country is likely to be issued in the near future.

He urges that the preamble of any such statement should stress the fact that India has earned by the valour of her soldiers on the field the right to a position of full equality with the Dominions within the Empire.

Secondly, he asks that the part played by those who have actively helped in the War should be given a prominent mention in any announcement about the ultimate intentions of the British Government. He suggests that a statement should be made to the effect that when the War is over the British Government will either establish a constitution for India as devised by the main parties concerned in agreement with one another or, failing that, will set about devising one itself, taking into counsel all those who have bestirred themselves to defend the country in the time of danger.

I do not know whether Sikander is right in thinking that a further announcement is contemplated in the immediate future. If he is correct, I think there is much to be said in favour of making it the occasion for encouraging those who are already helping the Empire's cause and for trying to enlist the support during the remainder of the War of those who have so far done little or nothing in the way of active assistance. But I fully realise the intense difficulties of evolving any statement that is likely to be free from objection from all points of view.

Yours sincerely,
B.J. GLANCY

98

GLANCY TO LINLITHGOW[2]

Telegram

Most Immediate
Secret and Personal
No. 14-G *March 4th, 1942*

Your telegram No. 511-S. of March 3rd.[3] My views on first point namely effect on Punjab of declaration now that India will have right to secede after new constitution are as follows. (Group corrupt) [?Responsible] section of Mohammadans who constitute majority in this Province are quite unshakeable in their view that Britain must hold ropes until a constitution acceptable to their community is devised. They will undoubtedly be worried that constitution framed as now contemplated, whether word "independence" is specifically mentioned or not, will place power in hands of Hindus and that Hindus whom they already suspect of pro-Japanese tendencies will be set on secession. Consequently they will align themselves elsewhere and will be diverted effectually from working for the defence of India as a whole just at a time when this is most essential. One result will be unprecedented intensification of bitterness between Muslims and Sikhs, relations between which communities are already dangerously strained. Recruitment will be very seriously affected as all communities will wish to keep their young men at home to defend their own interests. Disorder will be inevitable and security troops now greatly reduced are likely to be insufficient. Muslim League may be expected to gain great accession of strength in the Punjab and will use their influence ruthlessly for disruption. I anticipate that Premier with most or all of his Ministers will resign. This will further very seriously affect the situation and it would be quite impossible to find any substitute capable of holding Punjab together and helping in war as Sikander has done.

As to second point namely declaration that Provinces will have option of acceding or not acceding this cannot counteract effect of declaration with which first point is concerned. Punjab even if it were able to stand by itself is not homogeneous but made up of communities antagonistic to each other and internal trouble within the Province will be unavoidable. I do not anticipate that the Punjab would accede. Majority community would tend to form a block with Moslem neighbours elsewhere.

Repeated to Secretary of State.

99

GLANCY TO LINLITHGOW[4]

Telegram

Most Immediate
No. 15-G *March 4th, 1942*

I have sent you a copy of my telegram to the Secretary of State dealing with specific points but I cannot too strongly stress my conviction that a declaration on the lines contemplated will be completely disastrous and will mean that Indian elements who have hitherto played their part in the war will be utterly dumb founded and will cease to co-operate. I most earnestly plead that farthest His Majesty's Government should go is to say that immediately after the war they will accept any constitution on which main parties will agree and that failing this they will devise if necessary with assistance of dominions or America a constitution calculated to give all parties a fair deal in participating in government of the country with right to secession should they so desire. Nothing will convince Muslims that framing of a constitution as contemplated in proposed declaration will not amount to a betrayal. The effect on I.C.S. and other services will also be most serious. I have not of course consulted Sikander and I do not know whether he has been sounded to any extent while at Delhi but even should he have indicated his willingness to accept move now proposed I shall be intensely surprised if he resists temptation (group omitted) to resign. Such resignation will be a serious set back and I respectfully ask that you emphasise this point and if you see fit (group corrupt) view that I have expressed. Would [it] not be possible before this momentous decision is made to hold a Governors' meeting at Delhi, postponing action till then?

100

GLANCY TO LINLITHGOW

Private and Personal
D.-O. No. 388

Government House, Lahore,
March 5th, 1942

Dear Lord Linlithgow,

It is idle to deny that public morale has seriously deteriorated during the last few weeks as the result of bad news from Malaya, the Dutch East Indies and Burma. There is no actual panic, but there has been an increasing amount of defeatist talk and defeatist articles in newspapers. As danger approaches the relations between Muslims and Sikhs are becoming more and more strained, and each community is eyeing the other with growing mistrust.

Recruiting has so far continued to be good but some of the main sources have been heavily drained and are beginning to show clear signs of exhaustion. Unfavourable war news will also affect recruiting adversely; many classes, for instance Dogras, have suffered severe casualties and there is a natural feeling of anxiety about the fate of sons and brothers serving overseas, though I must say that the attitude of old soldiers with relations in the field has been magnificent wherever I have met them.

The chief item of provincial interest is that the *hartal* organized as a protest against the Sales Tax Act has, at least for the time being, come to an end. It lasted for seven weeks, which must have greatly surprised even those responsible for its organization. The Provincial Government made many concessions to the shopkeeping class and after various amendments had been incorporated no one could say that the particular legislative measure was in any way harsh or offensive, especially as it was plain that the ultimate incidence of the tax would fall on the consumer: possibly if the Premier had been less accommodating before he left India for Iraq at the beginning of the year the agitation would have died down, as there would have been less reason to believe that whatever demand was put forward by the shopkeepers would be conceded. The main cause, however, of the *hartal* continuing so long was the pent-up resentment of townsmen against the whole series of enactments adversely affecting the urban classes which the Punjab Government brought into force a year or two ago. Coupled with this was a feeling of exasperation aroused by intemperate speeches made in particular by the Revenue Minister, in which *banias* and tradesmen were held up to derision and abuse: it must, however, be admitted that the Minister in question has for several months back been far more restrained in his public utterances. The shopkeepers undoubtedly had the sympathy of the great majority of city-folk, and one of the results of this was that they allowed themselves to be stampeded beyond their better judgement: their union or *Beopari Mandal* came to be controlled largely by people who were not really representatives of the trading community, and consequently negotiations became increasingly difficult. Various party organizations, including sections of the Congress and the Akalis, took a hand in keeping the agitation alive: though the actual hardship inflicted on the population in general was exaggerated, a considerable degree of inconvenience was caused and a great additional strain was imposed on District Officers and on the police. In spite of all attempts to avoid making martyrs, minor clashes with the police became in some places unavoidable, and feelings were certainly running very high. It was a great relief to all when the *hartal* at last collapsed. Some of the unruly elements are still trying to revive it, but I doubt whether they will succeed in view of the desire of genuine traders to recoup themselves for the losses caused by their prolonged inactivity: many of them are now indulging in "Spring Sales", for which they must have prepared well in advance of the end of the *hartal*. Let us hope that one good result will come out of the affair – and that is that the Provincial Government will feel less temptation to press forward further legislation of an anti-urban variety.

Rabi prospects are distinctly encouraging. There has been sufficient rain in most parts of the Province, and bright sunshine is now required if there is, as we hope, to be a bumper crop. Meanwhile, until the new harvest comes into the market, we shall have great difficulty in making wheat supplies go round in the Province: arrangements are being made to mix wheat with coarser grains in order to eke out existing stocks.

Yours sincerely,
B.J. GLANCY

101

GLANCY TO LINLITHGOW[5]

Government House, Lahore,

[Unnumbered] *March 7th, 1942*

Dear Lord Linlithgow,

Will Your Excellency kindly refer to your letter of February the 17th, and subsequent telegram of March the 3rd about the National Defence Front, which is now to be called the National War Front.

2. We are getting on with our arrangements in spite of the fact that the actual inauguration of the Front has been postponed. In the circumstances of the Punjab the only possible choice for the leader seems to be Sir Sikander himself. If we try to find a non-party man, we are left with a selection of nonentities. Sir Sikander has stood so whole-heartedly for the war effort and the Opposition has done so little that the choice seems inevitable. We propose, however, to associate with him a small committee of deputy leaders, including Raja Narendra Nath, Sardar Bahadur Mohan Singh and Begum Shah Nawaz. Thus all the main communities as well as the women of the Province will be represented. As Secretary we propose to appoint Eustace, an I.C.S. officer of over 12 years' service, who while working in Kangra district has shown great keenness and ability in arranging village publicity. As soon as the date of inauguration is announced we will call a meeting of the War Board to inaugurate our Provincial War Front. I think the scheme has great possibilities and we will do our utmost to make it a success in the Punjab. The funds made available for each district will be particularly valuable, but I am afraid that we shall have some problems to face over urban publicity in the Punjab, as the urban population is strongly resentful of the policy of the Unionist Party and relations have been embittered by the recent *hartal*. As most of the rumours start from the towns where many people listen regularly to enemy broadcasts, this is certainly unfortunate.

3. I think it will be desirable to have a badge for those who enrol themselves as members of the Front.

Yours sincerely,
B.J. GLANCY

102

GLANCY TO LINLITHGOW

Telegram

Most Immediate
No. 16-G *March 9th, 1942*

Your telegram No. 575-S.[6] I am not entirely clear about the precise wording of the proposed announcement as now revised but it appears to me to contain elements which will make it less disturbing than the original draft to the majority in the Punjab though their apprehensions will certainly not be wholly allayed. I think therefore that the revised draft is definitely to be preferred to the original. At the same time I anticipate that prominence given to elected constitution-making body will result in very strong protest from the Muslim League which is likely to have serious repercussions in the Punjab and may well lead to collapse of Ministry with grave effects on the war effort. If on receipt of the full amended text I have any further comments I will telegraph again.

Above is text of message sent to Secretary of State. I am not in position to speak for Congress strongholds in India but I doubt whether any material satisfaction will be caused by an announcement which will obviously be interpreted in various ways. I again suggest definite advance on previous announcements might be provided by declaring that if main parties in India fail to reach common agreement then other parts of the Empire who have already attained Dominion Status and possibly also America will be asked to devise fair solution either (*a*) in collaboration with the British Government or (*b*) without such collaboration. This might serve to counter Congress propaganda that Britain will never willingly part with power. It might also help in steadying world opinion. This suggestion seems outside terms of present reference made to me but I ask you if you see no objection to pass it on to His Majesty's Government.

Repeated to Secretary of State.[7]

103

GLANCY TO LINLITHGOW

Telegram

Immediate
No. 17-G *March 10th, 1942*

I am still[8] most gravely apprehensive of the results which proposed announcement will produce. Whether Congress party will be in any way satisfied appears to me extremely doubtful and still more doubtful whether any kind of material help can be expected from them in consequence. But I feel convinced that effect on minorities and particularly on the Punjab will be disastrous and subversive of all war effort. Minorities can surely derive no satisfaction from promised provision for protection unless they are assured as to way in which such a promise can be implemented.

I am not sure whether guarantee to the Army is to be mentioned in the main announcement[9] but it seems preferable that it should be included now rather than be left over for subsequent announcement. Guarantee to consider other services, fulfilment of financial and other obligations also require inclusion. If minorities and other interests concerned are not to be utterly confounded I would endeavour (group corrupt) that instead of mere mention of provision for protection the announcement should state that transference of responsibility will depend on adequate arrangements being made for protection of such interests and on His Majesty's Government being convinced that these arrangements will be duly carried out in practice.

104

GLANCY TO LINLITHGOW

Telegram

Important
No. 18-G *March 13th, 1942*

Your telegram No. 607-S. of March 11th.[10] Punjab are willing to do what they can to help but wheat situation here is extremely serious. Our entire visible stocks of wheat do not exceed four lakhs maunds including stocks pledged to banks and already requisitioned. Against that weekly requirements for urban populations are six lakhs maunds. Orders have already issued for supply of 10,000 maunds to Delhi. We are intensifying our efforts to discover concealed stocks but at present there are no indications that such stocks are considerable. Should we succeed unearthing any substantial concealed stocks we will inform Government of India immediately but Your Excellency will understand supreme importance of avoiding riots in the Punjab. We have introduced barley mixture in Lahore and have been urging Wheat Commissioner and Supply Department that standard mixture should be adopted for military needs which seems most important.

105

GLANCY TO LINLITHGOW

Telegram

Important
Secret and Personal
No. 19-G *March 16th, 1942*

Your telegram No. 655-S. of 16th March.[11] I suggest Tara Singh, Jogendra Singh and Kirpal Singh to meet Cripps. Kirpal Singh is son of Sir Sundar Singh Majithia and President of Khalsa College, Amritsar.

I understand that it would be convenient for me to arrive 21st March morning. This will suit me as I have engagements. I would prefer to keep on [sic] previous days though if necessary I will of course come earlier. I could stay over till 23rd March if conversation with Cripps impossible on 22nd.

106

GLANCY TO LINLITHGOW

Confidential Government House, Lahore,
D.-O. No. 390 *April 14th, 1942*

Dear Lord Linlithgow,

I am not troubling Your Excellency with a general report just at present as we have discussed the Punjab and all-India affairs so recently at Delhi. But there is one point arising out of Sir Stafford's mission[12] which I should like to emphasize especially as it appears to me to be of the greatest importance if the general war effort is not to be impaired.

One of the main reasons which led to the breakdown of the negotiations was no doubt the fact that party leaders were for the most part only interested to a minor extent in co-operating with Sir Stafford in his endeavour to find a practical solution of the constitutional problem: their main interest appeared to lie in using the opportunity to manoeuvre their own particular parties, and in some cases themselves individually, into as prominent and unassailable a position as possible. As to the rank and file, now that no positive result has been secured, there are certainly a great many people of various persuasions who are unaffectedly disappointed. But this feeling is of course by no means universal and it would be futile to deny that there are considerable sections of the population who are unfeignedly relieved at the thought that a settlement on the lines proposed has at least been deferred. Those who subscribe most strongly and most genuinely to this latter point of view pertain largely to minority communities the interests of which appeared to be adversely affected by the solution in prospect; perhaps the most prominent of all were the Sikhs. From the outset the Sikh community were very seriously perturbed by the potentially fissiparous nature of the War Cabinet's proposals. The Sikhs were outspokenly apprehensive lest the Punjab should decline to accede to the all-India confederacy and should carry off the whole Province into the outer darkness of Pakistan. They regarded themselves as being in danger of everlasting subjection to an unsympathetic and tyrannical Muhammadan Raj. Unrest increased very markedly among the community and the danger to internal security became definitely more pronounced. We are doing what we can to deal with the situation. It is possible that, as things have turned out, those who have been making for trouble amongst the Sikhs will be less active or at least less successful in their attempts to represent the community as being threatened with extinction. But, if there is to be a real chance of things settling down in the Province while we get on with the war, surely it is essential to avoid giving any impression that the ultimate solution of India's problem will necessarily follow the same lines as those laid down in the recent formula. I see that the London *Times* is quoted in Reuter's Government summary of yesterday as having said that the "permanent plan for India once set forth in this authoritative form remains the foundation of British policy". If you agree with the views that I have expressed,[13] may I suggest that a warning of the consequences involved by this kind of statement should be given without delay where it is due and that all possible steps should be taken forthwith to avoid including in any official or semi-official or inspired pronouncements, either in India or at home, words which can be taken to imply that the terms of the offer, now they have been rejected, will inevitably be renewed? It seems well that there should be a breathing space while those who genuinely desire to think things out can be given an opportunity of doing so, and while attention can be concentrated to the maximum extent possible on the war.

Yours sincerely,
B.J. GLANCY

107

GLANCY TO LINLITHGOW

Private and Personal
D.-O. No. 393

Government House, Lahore,
May 1st, 1942

Dear Lord Linlithgow,

The apparent slowing down of the Japanese advance on India has gone some way to arrest defeatism, and the urban population are showing less signs of despondency than was the case a week or two ago. The Commander-in-Chief's admirable broadcast has also had a distinctly heartening effect. There has been a noticeable move on the part of students and communists to take an active interest in the defence of the country, and we will do what we can to turn this to good account. The organization of A.R.P. and Civil Defence is making material progress, though a very great deal has still to be done in this direction. We have taken steps, which I hope will be effective, to relieve District Officers of much of their routine work, so that they may devote as large a portion of their time as possible to their extra duties connected with the war. Recruiting, considering the extent to which the Province has already been tapped, has on the whole been going on successfully, but there is likely to be a material drop for some weeks to come on account of harvesting operations.

Newspapers and attempts to engineer political meetings are two disturbing elements. As regards the Press, the Punjab Government have passed an order of pre-censorship in the matter of news affecting war work in respect to the *Partap*, which has been one of the worst offenders amongst the local periodicals. The result has been that the *Partap* has stopped publication as a protest; the order issued has evoked the professed indignation of the Press in general and of those who lose no opportunity to oppose the Unionist Government. But it is to be hoped that other newspapers will profit by the example that has been made. As to political meetings, many efforts are being made in various quarters to organize discussions on as large a scale as possible of the merits or demerits of "Pakistan". The question of prohibiting all such meetings in the interests of tranquillity for a specified period is under consideration. The Akalis and the Mahasabha have advertised a combined anti-Pakistan meeting to take place at Amritsar on the 13th of June. Action has been taken to point out to the organizers that this will infallibly provoke retaliation and that they will stand to gain nothing by providing Mr. Jinnah and his followers with a further supply of free ammunition. So far the Akalis have shown less indication of absorbing this advice than the Mahasabha leaders.

The Sikhs although, as I have recently told you, they are undoubtedly relieved by the rejection of the offer brought by Sir Stafford Cripps, are still feeling distinctly restive. Master Tara Singh and his Lieutenants have found it an easy matter to stir up communal feeling at the alleged danger of the Sikhs being subjected to Muhammadan rule in the Punjab, and they are loath to cease from exploiting this opportunity. They will no doubt derive some degree of comfort from the sympathetic references made to Sikhs in the debates which have just taken place in Parliament, but it is to be hoped that these expressions of sympathy will not go to their heads and lead them to believe that "Khalistan" is regarded in responsible quarters as a practicable proposition. As you are well aware, the practical objections to "Khalistan" are even greater than those which lie in the path of Pakistan. Apart from the upheaval that would be caused by tearing out a large section of territory from the vitals of the provincial body politic, it is worth remembering that there is not one single district in which the Sikhs command a majority. Another illustration of the complexity of the problem is to be found in the Punjab States Agency. Little reliance can be placed on the results of the last Census owing to the determination of all communities to inflate their own figures, but it is true that a few years ago, though there are half a dozen Sikh States in the Agency, there was only one State, the Muslim State of Malerkotla, where the majority of the population were Sikhs.

The obvious course for the Sikhs to pursue is to seek a satisfactory basis for combining with the major community in the Province. The Sikhs are still clamouring for what they profess to regard as their due representation on the Governor-General's Executive Council and in the Punjab Cabinet. The names most commonly mentioned as suitable candidates for elevation to the Executive Council are those of Sir Jogendra Singh, now Prime Minister of Patiala, and Sardar Baldev Singh, and occasionally Sardar Buta Singh, C.B.E., of Amritsar. For inclusion in the Punjab Cabinet, which is of course from the practical point of view a matter of far greater moment to the Sikh community, the name most persistently put forward is that of Sardar Baldev Singh. Baldev has recently met the Premier and a meeting seems likely to take place between the Premier, Baldev Singh and Master Tara Singh. So a compromise on these lines is still a possibility. There are two ways in which this could be brought about, firstly by the retirement of Sardar Dasaundha Singh, whose appointment has never ceased to give umbrage to the Sikh community, and, secondly, by inflating the Cabinet by the inclusion of some four additional members; I have told the Premier that in my opinion this latter alternative is definitely to be deprecated, as, apart from additional expense, it would undoubtedly give rise to useless multiplication of work. The appointment of a member of the Cabinet whom the Sikhs in general would regard as reasonably representative would, I consider, be of great value, and this move could be made use of to settle various outstanding problems, such as the relaxation of restrictions now placed on the use of *Jhatka* meat – an issue which is by no means as simple as might appear and has recently been again dragged into the forefront of the battle by the Akalis. It is scarcely necessary to say that Master Tara Singh and his immediate associates would not altogether appreciate these developments, as they naturally prefer to appropriate to themselves all credit for services rendered to the community. It is possible that if Baldev Singh came into the Cabinet and succeeded in making himself prominent, the Akalis might find it expedient to disown him altogether. But it is clearly preferable to strengthen the position of a new Sikh Minister as a unifying factor rather than to let him dance to the tune of an outside party directorate.

The traders' revolt against the Sales Tax Act appears now to have spent itself and most of the responsible merchants are submitting their returns under the Act where they had not already done so. They show signs of realising that they have been misled and they seem inclined to try and ensure that the power to control their business activities will not in the future be left in the hands of self-interested politicians.

The agricultural situation is favourable. High winds and hailstorms, which gave great cause for anxiety a fortnight or so ago, are reported to have done only sporadic damage to the crops and a wheat harvest well above the normal is expected.

Yours sincerely,
B.J. GLANCY

108

GLANCY TO LINLITHGOW

Private and Personal
D.-O. No. 396

Government House, Lahore,
May 26th, 1942

Dear Lord Linlithgow,

Communal tension has shown some occasional symptoms of abatement during the last few weeks, but the situation is by no means free from anxiety. Deputy Commissioners have been empowered to impose a ban on political meetings which appear likely to give rise to serious ill-feelings between rival communities, and in Jullundur a Pakistan meeting has lately been prohibited. The anti-Pakistan demonstration staged to take place in the Amritsar district next month has now been called off by the Sikhs and the Mahasabha.

One reason for this prudent decision on the part of the Sikhs is that approaches between the Premier and Akalis' sympathisers were a short time ago progressing very successfully. Statements of reconciliation had been drafted and agreed to by Sikander on the one hand and Baldev Singh on the other. Their purport was to indicate that the Punjab Government had decided to adopt a more liberal policy in the matter of allowing *Jhatka* meat in official institutions, extending the use of the Gurmukhi language in Government schools and taking pains to see that a due share in Government services was given to the Sikh community, for all which marks of grace Baldev Singh on behalf of his party expressed his most grateful appreciation. These draft pronouncements were seen and blessed by Master Tara Singh and his Chief Lieutenant, Gyani Kartar Singh, but suggested that the credit for the happy results attained was due to Baldev Singh himself rather than to the Akali High Command, so the decision was reasonably satisfactory. The publication of these statements has been held up pending a definite decision on Baldev Singh's part as to whether he would accept a seat on the Provincial Cabinet. Baldev Singh has gone off to Tatanagar to ask for his father's consent to his taking this step, and since then nothing decisive seems to have been heard from him. It is hoped that the projected arrangement will go through, but there are various people who conceive that their interests will suffer if the programme is carried out and are now engaged in throwing obstacles in the path.

The case in which certain European soldiers were recently accused of man-handling a girl in Lahore has now been withdrawn, as no evidence of the alleged misdemeanour has been forthcoming. The whole affair appears in fact to have been a "frame-up" and strenuous efforts are being made to bring the organizers to book. Unfortunately the principal delinquent who incited the mob to attack the soldiers concerned seems to be mentally deficient, and it is difficult to extract any useful information from the statements he has made.

Pandit J. L. Nehru has passed through the Punjab and has indulged in a few speeches. He announced on his return from Kulu that his visit to the Himalayas had cleared his brain of confusion, though this was not altogether apparent from the tenor of his remarks. Incoherent and unconvincing though his speeches may have been, they have certainly tended to stir up ill-feeling against the British Government and Europeans in general. The same is true of many of Mr. Gandhi's recent utterances, and it is commonly believed that the Mahatma will before long resort to some sensational adventure in order to restore his position to the full glare of the political limelight.

With the communal undercurrents as treacherous as they are, we are distinctly apprehensive about the proposal to relax the restrictions imposed on the Khaksars and to modify the orders which confine their leader to the Madras Presidency. The Khaksar movement has shown itself in the Punjab to be an uncontrolled and highly dangerous organization. The Allama is known beyond all doubt to be entirely irresponsible and untrustworthy. If any further latitude is shown to the Khaksars and their leader, this is bound to have a most disturbing effect on other communities, who will certainly be inspired to organize rival movements with the same dangerous potentialities. So we are hoping that at this time when communal reactions need the most vigilant watching any such experiment will be postponed.

The Punjab Government are moving up to Simla in a few days' time and according to present intentions are likely to remain there for about two months. The original idea was that Ministers and Secretaries should recess in Simla by turns, but it has been found that this would lead to considerable delay and dislocation in the disposal of work and would give rise to difficulties in the matter of Cabinet meetings.

Yours sincerely,
B.J. GLANCY

P.S. – I enclose the provincial fortnightly report for the first half of May.

109

GLANCY TO LINLITHGOW

Government House, Lahore,
D.-O. No. 397 *May 28th, 1942*

Dear Lord Linlithgow,

I think I should write to Your Excellency at this early stage about the question of a successor to our Chief Justice, Young, who reaches the age of 60 on April the 7th, 1943, and will then be due to retire. He tells me that he has no desire to retire at an earlier date unless the war should come to an end before then, in which case he would like to be relieved of his office as soon after the termination of the war as possible.

In the circumstances of the Province I think it is definitely desirable to have another European Chief Justice if this can be arranged, and I know that the Premier strongly concurs in this view.[14] The senior European Puisne Judge of the Punjab High Court is Monroe, who will be 60 on the 7th April 1944. His age is against him and in any case it would hardly be possible to recommend him. The other European Judges are Blacker, Sale and Beckett, who are respectively 7th, 9th and 10th on the list. They are too junior to be appointed without causing friction in the High Court. It seems therefore that an attempt should be made to find a suitable European either from another High Court or from home. Young's own suggestion is that Goodman Roberts, the Chief Justice of Burma, should be considered.[15] Neither Young nor I know him personally, but he would appear to be a distinct possibility.

2. In spite of the preference I have expressed for a European Chief Justice, Your Excellency will wish me to mention the claims of the senior Indian Judges. The senior Puisne Judge, Tek Chand, is due to retire on the 26th August 1943. Dalip Singh, No. 2, retires in June 1945 and would therefore only be able to serve for two years if appointed. He is moreover quite unsuitable, as he has not the strength of character to administer the High Court with success. This was pointed out by Emerson in his letter to Lord Willingdon of December 24th, 1930, and the criticism is still true. The next Indian Judge is Bhide, who will be 60 in February 1943, that is before Young's retirement. We then come to Abdul Rashid, an ex-Barrister, who has been a Judge since 1933, but certainly does not carry the guns for a Chief Justice. The remaining, two Indian Judges are Din Muhammad and Ram Lal neither of whom would be in the least suitable.

3. You will remember your correspondence with my predecessor about Sir Muhammad Zafrullah's desire to become Chief Justice. Whether Zafrullah still retains this desire, now that he has gone to the Federal Court, I do not know, but I agree with what Craik said in his letter of November 25th, 1938.[16]

Yours sincerely,
B.J. GLANCY

110

GLANCY TO LINLITHGOW

Private and Personal
D.-O. No. 399-F.L.

Barnes Court, Simla,
June 10th, 1942

Dear Lord Linlithgow,

Morale in the towns shows signs of growing steadier. An increasing interest is being taken in A.R.P. and Civil Defence. The tone of the Press, thanks largely to the action taken against the *Partap* newspaper, has been more satisfactory. Mr. Gandhi's lucubrations in the *Harijan* have, however, been exercising an unsettling effect, and those who have been helping in the war effort and wish to continue doing so not infrequently express surprise at the latitude that is allowed to the Mahatma and Pandit J.L. Nehru.

Negotiations between the Premier and S. Baldev Singh have made further progress. Baldev has now obtained his father's consent to his accepting a seat in the Cabinet, he is to meet Sikander at Lahore in a few days' time and the forecast is that he will take over charge as a Minister before the end of this month. Wild speculation has been rife all over the Province as to the changes to come, and Master Tara Singh who has been subjected to a good deal of questioning and criticism has given out some sadly inaccurate accounts of what the Sikh community can expect from the deal. It is open to doubt how long the alliance between the Unionist Party and the Akalis will continue. Baldev has himself been professing that he has been forced into a political career against his own wishes and that he bitterly regrets the turn that events have taken. But, though he is scarcely a model of stability and his past record cannot be said to be by any means irreproachable, it is to be hoped that a position of responsibility will sober him down and that he will show himself to be of some positive value both in the Cabinet and outside. On the whole the impending move has been well received by Muslims and Sikhs, though there are some, especially Hindus, who regard it with considerable misgiving. Sikander has taken his more important Ministers into his confidence, and I understand that their reactions have been favourable.

We have released a fairly large number of communists though not so many as Teja Singh and his lieutenants would like. The behaviour of the ex-detenus has on the whole been satisfactory, but it is difficult to know how far they can be trusted; they are not content to accept Roy's line of action and their allegation is that they can make no headway with the masses unless they dilute their war Gospel with attacks on the British Government. The Akalis view the enlargement of Sikh communists with obvious disapproval; they are afraid that a rival party may acquire influence and rob them of their control over Gurdwara funds, so they roundly accuse the communists of all forms of wickedness from atheism downwards.

A "Guerilla War Training Camp" for students, which has been set up in the grounds of the Forman Christian College, Lahore, is going surprisingly well. There are about three hundred students in the Camp including small contingents from Bengal, the United Provinces, Bombay, &c. They are working for long hours with great enthusiasm under qualified instructors and the organizers are to be congratulated on their success.

Yours sincerely,
B.J. GLANCY

111

GLANCY TO LINLITHGOW

Private and Personal
D.-O. No. 399

Barnes Court, Simla,
June 25th, 1942

Dear Lord Linlithgow,

I am writing to let Your Excellency know that the Sikander-Baldev Singh pact[17] appears to have finally gone through. Many attempts were made by Congress and other interests to wreck the negotiations and only a few days ago it looked as if there was no prospect whatever of success. Sikander deserves, I think, the greatest credit for his perseverance and patience. Let us hope that Baldev, who is to be sworn in as a Minister tomorrow, will prove himself to be a worthy servant of the Province.

As to Dasaundha Singh, his behaviour has been commendable. He made a most praiseworthy speech at the Lahore meetings, in which he said that he was entirely ready to subordinate his interests to those of the Punjab and that he would continue loyally to follow Sikander's lead in any capacity. He has now put in his resignation. Sikander says that he feels in honour bound to do his utmost to provide for Dasaundha Singh and he has asked me to enquire whether there is any prospect of his late colleague being given a seat on any Central Committee on a salary of Rs. 1,500 per mensem or so. I should be grateful if you would be good enough to let me know whether there is any such possibility, but I have told Sikander plainly that I fear the chances of this are extremely remote. Dasaundha Singh has certainly not been a success as a Minister and his ability, though he rates it highly himself, is distinctly meagre; still he is, I believe, straightforward and loyal and not a mischief-maker. Failing any accommodation at the Centre, the only alternative that I can see is for me to give the late Minister a seat on the Provincial Public Services Commission when a vacancy occurs early next November. He is scarcely an ideal selection for this, but with a good Chairman I dare say that he would be adequate. With the kind assistance of Thorne[18] and Hallett[19] I am in strong hopes of securing the services of Marsh, now Adviser in the United Provinces, as Chairman when the present incumbent relinquishes his office.

Yours sincerely,
B.J. GLANCY

112

GLANCY TO LINLITHGOW

Private and Personal
D.-O. No. 400-F.L.

Barnes Court, Simla,
June 30th, 1942

Dear Lord Linlithgow,

News of the set-backs in Libya and Egypt has, as is only natural, been exercising a very disheartening effect though it has not produced the same degree of consternation as an immediate threat to India from the East. Another factor which is persistently lowering the morale of certain classes is Mr. Gandhi's pernicious writings in the *Harijan*. From his latest lucubrations there would seem to be some grounds for believing that he is now thinking better of indulging in the particular form of anti-Government activity which he originally contemplated. But there is a general belief that he will before long resort to some spectacular variety of mischief designed to restore the prestige of Congress and to focus the lime-light on himself. The advice that he gives to the public, illogical and confused though it may be is undoubtedly disseminating poison, and there are many, both among officials and non-officials, who express no little surprise that the Congress campaign to undermine the war effort is allowed to continue. I have no hesitation in agreeing with Hallett's view that if Gandhi oversteps the mark, we cannot on this occasion afford to give him any interval of grace.

The Khaksars have been showing signs of renewed activity and we have been considerably perturbed by the Home Department's last letter in which it suggested that Provincial Governments, other than the Punjab and the North-West Frontier Province, should consider lifting the ban against this movement. With our bitter experience of the Khaksars' criminal proclivities and the complete irresponsibility of their leader no one in the Punjab believes that their intentions are anything but sinister. We should consequently much prefer that the Khaksar organization should continue to be treated on an All-India basis as has been the case during the last year. If the ban against the Khaksars is lifted in any Province adjoining the Punjab, I see very little prospect of our being able for any length of time to avoid similar action. And once we are driven to this there will be an inevitable tendency on the part of other communal organizations to bring themselves into prominence, and the general peace will be severely threatened.

The negotiations between the Premier and Sardar Baldev Singh have, as I have already separately reported, come to a successful issue. Sardar Baldev Singh has now taken his seat on the Cabinet, but it is too early as yet to gauge how adequately he will fill his part. On the whole there is a genuine feeling of relief throughout the Province, but there have been many attacks, both on Sikander and Baldev Singh, in the Press and elsewhere and each of them has been roundly accused of selling the fort and gaining nothing for his community. Master Tara Singh has given out that the Akalis as such are no party to the pact,[20] which is of a purely communal nature, and that they will persist in opposing the Unionist or any other party on political issues. There is nothing very surprising in this announcement considering the difficulties with which the Akalis have to contend.

The attack on the Simla-Kalka Rail Motor, which was reported to the Home Department early on the morning after it occurred, was a most dastardly affair and has resulted in the loss of six valuable lives. Squadron-Leader Hogg, who had rendered such invaluable services to the Boy Scout movement, is universally regretted and will be an extremely difficult officer to replace. A special officer has been appointed to investigate this outrage and a very large reward has been offered, but I am afraid that the culprits will be hard to trace. I am not inclined to give any credence to the theory that the dacoity was inspired by political motives, the intention being to kill off European officers; there were two officers in uniform in the Rail Motor neither of whom received any injuries. It appears to be more likely that the attack was made merely to rob the passengers; it is true that the mail bags were not opened and that no great trouble was taken to secure all that was in the passengers' possession, but this may have been due to the perpetrators being in a hurry to get away. We will certainly spare no effort to bring the criminals to book.

Yours sincerely,
B.J. GLANCY

113

ABELL TO LAITHWAITE

Confidential
D.-O. No. G.S.-573

Barnes Court, Simla,
July 4th, 1942

My dear Gilbert,

The six-monthly report on the Ministers required by your confidential D.-O. No. 2448-G.G., dated the 17th June 1938, is now due. His Excellency asks me to say that he has really nothing of importance to add to the notes about the other Ministers forwarded with my demi-official of the 11th January 1942, but as a result of the recent change of Ministers he asks me to send the enclosed note about Sardar Baldev Singh. He has taken over the portfolio of Development from Sardar Dasaundha Singh who has resigned.

Yours sincerely,
G.E.B. ABELL

ENCLOSURE TO NO. 113

NOTE BY GLANCY

Undated

Sardar Baldev Singh has become a member of the Council of Ministers as a result of a rapprochement between the Unionist Party and the Akalis.

The family was not distinguished until his father, Sardar Indar Singh, who was the son of a small Jat landlord of the Ambala district, qualified as an engineer, became a contractor for Tatas and made a fortune. Sardar Indar Singh has now a very substantial interest in the various Tata businesses and is an extremely wealthy man. Sardar Baldev Singh was also assisting in the control of his father's various business interests and sometimes suggests that he has become a politician against his will. It has however come to notice that he has been financing the Akalis and other more dubious agencies. He was elected unopposed to the Punjab Legislative Assembly in 1937, was unseated as a result of an election petition and was re-elected in 1938. It is said that he has never yet opened his mouth in the Assembly.

Sardar Baldev Singh is 39 years of age and was educated at the Khalsa College, Amritsar. It is impossible at this stage to gauge his personal ability or the amount of support that he will be able to retain in the Akali Party or amongst the Sikhs generally. It is however clear that he is a very much more representative choice than Sardar Dasaundha Singh and carries a great deal more influence.

114

GLANCY TO LINLITHGOW

Confidential
D.-O. No. 401

Government House, Lahore,
July 10th, 1942

Dear Lord Linlithgow,

Your Excellency will be interested in seeing the enclosed note which Sikander gave me just before we left Simla, setting forth his tentative formula for the solution of the communal problem. The proposal amounts, as you will see, to a scheme that in the absence of a 75 per cent. majority of members of the Punjab Legislative Assembly in favour of either accession or non-accession to the Indian Federation, the Muslim community should by means of a referendum be given an opportunity of deciding on non-accession and that, if they so decide, the non-Muslim portions of the Punjab should by a similar referendum be accorded the right to cut themselves adrift from the Province as constituted at present. If it actually came to the point of non-Muslims deciding to break adrift, this would mean that, assuming the unit concerned to be a district, the Ambala Division and a large part of the Jullundur Division and also the Amritsar District would cease to belong to the Punjab. If a smaller unit such as a tahsil, as is, I gather, Sikander's idea, is taken, at least a very large part of the areas I have mentioned and possibly certain others would disappear from the Province. In either case a disastrous dismemberment of the Punjab would be involved. The underlying idea of the scheme is therefore to bring it home to all reasonably-minded men that Pakistan should it ever eventuate, would smash the Province as it now exists.

Sikander's position is that he has now succeeded in bringing about a rapprochement with the Sikhs, he has in hand a proposal for placating the urban population by means of further concessions relating to the Sales Tax Act, and the only other remaining menace which he fears as being likely to impede the War effort of the Province is the controversy for and against Pakistan. He believes that his present formula has a good chance of relegating the Pakistan issue to the background until the War is over; the action for which the formula provides would not come into operation until the Central constitutional issue has been decided; Sikander hopes that during the next few years his formula will have the effect of laying the Pakistan controversy to rest.

Sikander has asked me to let you know what his intentions are, so that you may judge, before he takes action, whether the move which he now contemplates would be likely to prove an embarrassment in the light of the all-India political situation. Should you see no objection to his proceeding with his plan, he would in the first instance consult the Muslim members of his party, after that he would lay the proposal before the Sikh members of the party, then he would consult the party as a whole and, if the reactions remain favourable, the Provincial Assembly would be invited to pass a resolution endorsing the scheme.

The formula evolved by Sikander appears to me, as I have told him, to have much to commend it so far as those who are inclined to be reasonable and fair-minded are concerned. Unfortunately the proportion of reasonable men is lamentably low, and I am very doubtful as to the effect which the scheme is likely to produce on Jinnah. Sikander agrees with me that Jinuah's personal feelings will be seriously offended, because the scheme does not emanate from himself as the head of the Muslim League. I am inclined to think that, apart from his personal feelings, Jinnah may be genuinely opposed to the whole idea as amounting in effect to an exposure of the weaknesses of Pakistan. Whether Jinnah genuinely believes in Pakistan as a practical proposition may be open to doubt; but he appears to be consistently reluctant to explain its detailed workings, and the term "Pakistan" has become so sacred and mystic that any attempt to analyse and define its consequences would appear to be little short of profanity. Sikander is disposed to the view that Jinnah will not oppose the scheme, as he is already committed to the principle of self-determination; I doubt this personally, since many people, like for instance the inhabitants of southern Ireland, are liable to hold inconsistent opinions as regards the doctrine of self-determination when applied to themselves and when applied to others. Sikander also thinks that Jinnah may be inclined to regard the scheme as indicating that Pakistan is thereby proved to be a practical proposition in regard to one of the most vital and important parts of India, thus strengthening Jinnah's chances of pressing for a high proportion of Muslim representation at the Centre. Here again I have my doubts; it appears to me not unlikely that Jinnah may look upon this exposure as a detraction from the value of the Pakistan bogy designed for the terrorisation of Congress and the British Government. There would seem to be a distinct possibility that Jinnah may raise the cry that Sikander's formula places Islam in danger and that confusion may become worse confounded. But I must admit that Sikander knows Jinnah a great deal better than I do, and I can make no kind of pretence to be able to fathom the workings of Jinnah's mind. If Sikander's plan of campaign is carried out, Jinnah will presumably come to know, through the Nawab of Mamdot (the head of the Provincial Muslim League) or through other informants, what is afoot as soon as the Muslim members of the Unionist Party have been approached; it is difficult to say in this event how long it would take him to make his reactions plain.

I shall be grateful if Your Excellency will be good enough, as soon as you conveniently can, to let me know whether you would prefer Sikander to proceed with his intentions or to hold his hand.[21]

Yours sincerely,
B.J. GLANCY

ENCLOSURE TO NO. 114

NOTE BY SIKANDER HYAT KHAN

Confidential

A tentative formula for solving the communal problem

(*a*) If not less than 75 per cent. of the total strength of the elected members of the Punjab Legislative Assembly pass a resolution either in favour of or against non-accession to the Indian Federation, that verdict shall be regarded by all the communities of the Punjab as final and binding.

(*b*) If neither a resolution advocating nor a resolution negativing non-accession is moved, or if such resolution, when moved, fails to be passed by the majority indicated in (*a*) above, but a demand for non-accession continues, then the wishes of the Muslim community as a whole shall be ascertained by means of a referendum in which all the Muslim electors on the electoral roll of the Punjab Legislative Assembly shall have the right to vote provided such a referendum is claimed in a formal resolution passed by the vote of not less than 60 per cent. of the Muslim members of the Punjab Legislative Assembly.

(*c*) If as the result of a referendum suggested in (*b*) above the Muslim community gives its verdict in favour of non-accession, Indian non-Muslims will, for the ascertainment of the wishes of their community as a whole, have the right to claim, whether with a view to accession to the Indian Federation or formation of a separate sovereign State by themselves or in mutually agreed upon combination with other contiguous territories bordering on the east, a referendum, in which all the non-Muslim Indian electors on the electoral roll of the Punjab Legislative Assembly shall have the right to vote, for the separation from the present Punjab Province of those contiguous portions of it in which non-Muslims constitute a majority provided that such a referendum is claimed in a formal resolution passed by the vote of not less than 60 per cent. of the total strength of the non-Muslim Indian members of the Punjab Legislative Assembly.

115

GLANCY TO LINLITHGOW[22]

Telegram

Immediate
Private and Personal
No. 33-G *July 15th, 1942*

Your private and personal telegram No. 2085-S., July 14th.[23] We are replying today to Home Department telegram No. 4425 of July 12th and am sending a copy direct to Secretary of State.

Though effects of Congress move may be less embarrassing in the Punjab than in other Provinces it appears that the situation is becoming increasingly dangerous and that positive action will soon be unavoidable. Publicity is Gandhi's main weapon and there would seem much to be said in favour of minimising this: (*a*) by imposing pre-censorship order on Congress pronouncements and on *Harijan* and any similar publications, and (*b*) intensive counter-propaganda at home and abroad. It might be salutary to point to Rajkot parallel[24] in which Gandhi resorted to sensational and quite unjustifiable action mainly in order to distract attention from dissensions in the Congress ranks. Use might also be made of Gandhi's open admission before his retreat from Kathiawar that his fast had been a sinful departure from the path of non-violence.

116

GLANCY TO LINLITHGOW

Private and Personal — Barnes Court, Simla,
D.-O. No. 402 — *July 17th, 1942*

Dear Lord Linlithgow,

Sikander has asked me to bring to Your Excellency's notice a further suggestion which he has evolved for the constitutional advance of India with reference to the composition of the Governor-General's Executive Council. His idea is that for the period antecedent to the final framing of the all-India constitution the Governor-General should continue to exercise full control in the matter of choosing his Councillors in respect to Defence, Finance, Customs and External Affairs, and that all other Members of

Council should be selected by the Governor-General from a panel of names to be put forward by the existing Provincial Legislative Assemblies.

The object of this suggested manoeuvre would be to show that the Central Government is being made more representative and responsible, and thus to take the wind out of the Congress sails. Apart from dislocations and embarrassments which the manoeuvre would involve, I am very doubtful, as I have told Sikander, whether it would have any substantial effect; it would not, as Sikander admits, be acceptable to the Congress, and I should have thought that, as far as reasonably minded men are concerned, the Congress leaders have already shown themselves to be so utterly intransigent that a concession such as that contemplated would be superfluous.

Sikander appears to be seriously disturbed by the possibility that Gandhi if he fails to induce the British Government to yield to his demands, may make terms with Jinnah by an out-and-out offer of Pakistan and then present a united front to Government. It seems to me that, even if Jinnah were amenable, it would be very difficult for Gandhi with all his political agility to adopt an attitude which has brought Rajagopalachariar into such complete disrepute with the orthodox Congress party. Sikander, however, has a strong suspicion that the split between Gandhi and Rajagopalachariar was prearranged by the Congress leaders; I have myself seen no evidence of this.

Sikander is also disturbed by the fact that there are now only three Muslim Members on the Executive Council; he would like to see the proportion of Muslims amongst the Indian Members of Council adjusted to at least one-third, in order to prevent Jinnah and others from making capital out of this deficiency. I think there is a good deal to be said in favour of such an adjustment when it becomes practicable.[25]

Yours sincerely,
B.J. GLANCY

117

GLANCY TO LINLITHGOW

Private and Personal
D.-O. No. 403

Barnes Court, Simla,
July 18th, 1942

Dear Lord Linlithgow,

Many thanks for Your Excellency's letter of the 16th July.[26] I am very glad to hear what you have been good enough to tell me about the discussion that took place in Council, and I entirely agree about the value of counter-propaganda.

I should not think that there will be any lack of articles in various sections of the Indian Press strongly condemning the attitude which the Congress has adopted. Jinnah has been sufficiently outspoken not long ago in the *Dawn* and elsewhere conveying his warning to the British Government of the consequences which they are to expect if they yield to Congress demands; it seems scarcely likely that the Muslim Press in general will adopt a different line. I see that the *Eastern Times* of Lahore, which describes itself as the "premier Indian Muslim journal and leading English organ in northern India" contained quite a helpful article in yesterday's issue about "Wardha's ultimatum"; it ended up with the remark that Mr. Gandhi's recent performance was "undoubtedly the greatest and most unashamed attempt at blackmailing in history". Sikh newspapers may be less downright than this, but they are likely to have a good deal to say on the subject. We will collect extracts from various newspapers and send to Delhi anything that is likely to be of assistance by way of propaganda in case it may not have come to notice.

I am getting into touch today with Sikander who has not yet returned from Lahore. As to Jogendra Singh, I am arranging to try and get into contact with him, but, as you are so well aware, he will have to be talked with considerable caution. Master Tara Singh and his Akalis are notorious for their habit of "sailing in two boats" and, in spite of the Sikander-Baldev Singh pact,[27] they have by no means severed their connection with the Congress. I am doubtful whether either prominent Akalis or Jogendra Singh, who takes his cue from them, will be as outspoken as one would like. However, I will see what can be done.

Yours sincerely,
B.J. GLANCY

118

GLANCY TO LINLITHGOW[28]

Secret
D.-O. No. 404

Barnes Court, Simla,
July 26th, 1942

Dear Lord Linlithgow,

Will Your Excellency please refer to your telegram No. 2120-S. of July

18th in which you asked to be kept in the closest touch with Provincial reactions to the resolution of the Congress Working Committee?

2. It has never seemed likely that the Working Committee's demands would meet with any general support outside Congress circles in this Province. Punjabi Muslims of almost all shades of opinion subscribe to the criticisms voiced by Jinnah, Firoz, Sikander and others. The Muslim Press in Lahore is unanimously hostile, using such expressions as "blackmail", "hypocrisy" and "ludicrous demand". The Qadiani paper *Sunrise* takes the same line. Sikander said in a meeting at Lyallpur: "If the British quit India, chaos will follow and no ordered Government will be possible."

3. The Punjab Congress party is fortunately at a low ebb and its leaders are continually at loggerheads with each other. The two main groups led by Dr. Gopi Chand Bhargava and Dr. Satyapal will both be inclined to follow Gandhi's lead, but the Satyapal group will hesitate to do anything that may increase the prestige of Gopi Chand. The Congress Communists cannot well support a movement of the kind contemplated and may be forced out of their alignment with the Congress. The Congress Akalis will be in an awkward position in view of the recent Akali-Unionist rapprochement and of their serious internal differences and, though individuals may join a civil disobedience movement, it is scarcely conceivable that there will be any unanimity on the subject.

4. It is significant that the Lahore Hindu Press, which ordinarily supports the Congress, has shown no great enthusiasm for the resolution. The *Tribune* while resenting outside criticism has refused to advocate a mass movement. The *Daily Herald* has said that "it would be much better if the Congress instead of demanding the withdrawal of British rule had made some start with the facilities granted by the Government to prepare India to meet all eventualities." The *Hindu* asks "how the Congress when it has no scheme for maintaining [?attaining] independence can hope to ensure that India will enjoy *swaraj*."

5. The Sikhs generally are better disposed to Government than for some time past as the result of the Sikander-Baldev pact and the appointment of Sir Jogendra Singh to the expanded Council. Sir Jogendra Singh and Sardar Baldev Singh made distinctly satisfactory speeches at a tea party last Tuesday which I attended. Baldev Singh's remarks included the following:

"Let me again make it clear that while I stand steadfastly to safeguard the interests of my community, I will be failing in my duty if I do it at the expense of any other community or do something which will embitter the communal situation.... Our country is threatened with evil forces of aggression and it should be the duty of every true Punjabi to get ready to make any sacrifice to meet internal disorder, and to defeat the forces of external aggression. My community has already played its part well and I have no doubt whatsoever that it will excel its tradition by answering the call of the hour and mustering in thousands to repel the evil forces that are threatening the democracies of the world."

The speech was reported in the Press. In the *Tribune* of yesterday there is a statement by Sardar Naunihal Singh, Sardar Jogendar Singh Mann, Sardar Bahadur Gurbachan Singh and Sardar Raghbir Singh Sandhanwalia. The first two are M.L.As., Naunihal Singh being also of course a Member of the National Defence Council. Sardar Bahadur Gurbachan Singh is Deputy Speaker of the Punjab Legislative Assembly, while Sardar Raghbir Singh Sandhanwalia is President of the Khalsa Defence League of India. This statement definitely criticises the Congress proposals, though it is not as outspoken as one would like: I append a copy[29] for ready reference. As I anticipated, Sir Jogendra Singh and Sardar Baldev Singh have hesitated to come out into the open on the subject of the Congress Working Committee's resolution. Nevertheless there are gratifying signs that the Sikhs will be sensible and the Congress proposals have been criticised in Sikh newspapers of the Punjab. It is difficult to be sure that professional agitators among the Sikhs would not create a certain amount of disturbance if the movement really got going elsewhere. There are always a good many Sikhs who are temperamentally "agin the Government", but the bond between the Akalis and the Congress is not so strong as it was, and Gandhi can certainly not rely on any general Sikh support in the early stages of a mass movement.

6. As we reported yesterday to the Home Department, there are signs that the vernacular Press is being used by the Congress to broadcast veiled instructions for a mass movement, and even the Indian News Agency yesterday published a long report from Bombay giving the comments of Mr. Mehrally, Mayor of Bombay, in support of the proposed movement. It seems most unsatisfactory that the Indian News Agency should be used for what amounts in effect to Congress propaganda. More stringent action to control the Press and Press agencies seems well worth considering.

7. The Congress in the Punjab is, I think, lukewarm about launching a movement and ill-equipped to do so, but disturbances in other parts of India can hardly fail to give rise to some degree of trouble in this Province.

Yours sincerely,
B.J. GLANCY

119

GLANCY TO LINLITHGOW[30]

Telegram

No. 36-G *July 29th, 1942*

Your private and personal telegram No. 2208-S.[31] My personal inclination is in favour of deportation as likely to provide the more effective deterrent. But Punjab Government is not so intimately concerned as some other Provinces and few if any will qualify for deportee category from Punjab.

120

GLANCY TO LINLITHGOW[32]

Telegram

No. 37-G *July 29th, 1942*

Your Excellency's telegram No. 2157-S, dated July 22nd about state and morale of police force. The sanctioned strength of the Punjab Police is now 9,000 more than the pre-war strength. The standard of recruits has naturally gone down somewhat owing to military recruiting but the number of unfilled vacancies in the regular police is very small. The Additional Police are however considerably below strength owing to the fact that the men taken are of the same type as those accepted for garrison duties in the army. The force as a whole is working under considerable strain and we are short of experienced officers but I think the morale is as good as ever and my Inspector-General[33] is satisfied that provided no extra large scale internal security measures are required simultaneously the force will be able to tackle a mass movement by the Congress. I agree with his estimate.

121

GLANCY TO LINLITHGOW[34]

Telegram

No. 40-G *August 5th, 1942*

Your telegram No. 2274-S, August 3rd.[35] We are instructing Deputy Commissioners to explain to District War Committees which are of course quite distinct from the War Front the way in which Congress have taken action designed to betray the country. This would seem to be an effective way of rallying the opinion of those who are well disposed. District Officers will no doubt take other opportunities of putting across the Government's point of view and this can be done with good effect in interviews.

2. It has been suggested that a special effort might be made to induce the Russian radio to give out useful propaganda at the critical time. I hand on this suggestion to Your Excellency for consideration.

122

GLANCY TO LINLITHGOW

Private and Personal
D.-O. No. 407

Barnes Court, Simla,
August 21st, 1942

Dear Lord Linlithgow,

I have not thought it necessary to send Your Excellency a periodical letter for some time past, as we have been in constant touch over recent political developments.

Up to the present reactions in the Punjab to the Congress campaign of disorder have been remarkably mild, and it is to be hoped, though I fear it is by no means altogether certain, that this state of affairs will continue. One fortunate feature is that colleges and schools are on vacation till the end of September and consequently the organizers of Civil Disobedience have not been able to make use of students for their own nefarious purposes. So far there have been no serious outbreaks of lawlessness and we have not had to resort to firing. Congress, as you know, has never taken a very firm root in the Punjab, and has been continually weakened by dissensions within the ranks.

Muslims, except for a small number of unrepresentative individuals, have shown no sympathy for Mr. Gandhi and his "non-violent" outbreak of fanaticism. Muslim papers continue to expose Congress insincerity in no uncertain terms; I append to this letter a typical extract[36] from the *Eastern Times*.

Hindus in rural areas have not been substantially affected. Urban Hindus, though they are largely attracted by the Congress movement and may be ready to afford financial assistance, are for the most part disinclined to go to the length of open and active support on any considerable scale.

Shopkeepers have had a sufficient taste of trade-dislocation last winter to make them chary about indulging in a prolonged *hartal*; also their nerves have been steadied of late by the more conciliatory attitude which the Punjab Government has adopted.

Normally the champions of Congress would look to the Akalis to provide the most unruly and determined element in provincial disorders. There is a general consensus of opinion, however, that Akalis are less liable today to be led into anti-Government demonstrations than they were a little while ago, and for this the credit is mainly due to the Premier for his wisdom and perseverance in carrying through the "Sikander-Baldev pact".[37] There is no doubt that this move has gratified the Sikhs in general, but the Akalis are still a notoriously unstable section of the population. One might suppose that, having recently achieved two of the main objects for which they had been clamouring – the inclusion of a Sikh Member in the Governor-General's Council[38] and the appointment of Baldev Singh as a Minister in the Punjab – the Akalis would now be content to rest on their laurels and be careful to refrain from any active participation in Congress vagaries. But Master Tara Singh has come out with a statement that he will not oppose any adventures on which Congress may embark. We have taken steps to point out to him and his friends that any continuance of this form of response to the favours which the Sikhs have lately received from Government must make it increasingly difficult for those who sympathise with the community to espouse their cause. Tara Singh and his confederates, however, are habitually loath to commit themselves, and their conception of the rôle of a leader is a resolute refusal to give a lead in any definite direction. Amritsar, the stronghold of the Akali party, still remains the danger centre, and, as I write, I have just received news that a goods train has been derailed in the neighbourhood. Details have not yet been reported. Railway security measures have been introduced in this part of the Punjab.

Congress socialists show signs of going underground and require careful watching. Communists, in spite of the encouragement that has been given them, have not been behaving satisfactorily, and tend to stress increasingly their opposition to the British Government and to submerge their support of war activities. It is difficult to repose any confidence in their assurances.

The progress of the Congress campaign elsewhere in India is of course bound to have an important effect on the peace of the Punjab. I do not want to give any unnecessary trouble, but I should be very grateful if I could be supplied with as much information as is practicable about events outside the Province – particularly in regard to the extent of sabotage on the railway line leading from the coalfields through Bihar and the United

Provinces to the Punjab, and any indication as to the date on which normal communications can be expected to be resumed. Our coal-supplies are running dangerously short.

Recruitment, notwithstanding unfavourable war news and internal commotions, has been going on remarkably well. One very satisfactory feature is a marked increase in the number of Jat Sikhs coming forward to join the Army.

Monsoon rain has been abundant in most parts of the Punjab, particularly in the south-eastern tracts which have been afflicted by famine and scarcity in the last few years. It is to be hoped that the favourable prospects for the *kharif* harvest will have some effect in steadying the prices of food grains.

Yours sincerely,
B.J. GLANCY

123

GLANCY TO LINLITHGOW

Private and Personal
[Unnumbered]

Barnes Court, Simla,
August 27th, 1942

Dear Lord Linlithgow,

In Your Excellency's letter of July 20th[39] on the subject of Pakistan and Sikander's suggestions for a future constitution you said that you felt pretty clear that His Majesty's Government would be most unlikely to consider any further move during the war unless there was some marked change in circumstances having regard to the fate of the Cripps Declaration.

2. Two of my Ministers, Sir Chhotu Ram and Sardar Baldev Singh, in conversation have particularly asked me to urge that no declaration on the subject of Pakistan should be made by His Majesty's Government as a result of the recent resolution of the Muslim League.[40] They feel that the one thing that would certainly cause extensive trouble in the Punjab would be any such declaration, and I agree with them. I realize that in view of what Your Excellency has said it is extremely improbable that any such declaration will be considered, but I think I should pass on to Your Excellency what these two Ministers have said. Sikander, who is still in Egypt, would, I am sure, agree, and has been doing his best to stop down all propaganda whether pro- or anti-Pakistan.[41]

Yours sincerely,
B.J. GLANCY

124

GLANCY TO LINLITHGOW[42]

Barnes Court, Simla,
D.-O. No. 408 *September 1st, 1942*

Dear Lord Linlithgow,

In your telegram No. 2494-S. of August 18th, 1942, Your Excellency mentioned the importance of collecting evidence to prove the responsibility of Congress and of Gandhi in particular for the campaign of violence.

As the Punjab has fortunately been far removed, up to now, from the centres of disturbance and as there are no important Congress leaders in the Punjab, we are not well placed here to collect the evidence required, and there is little I can say of which Your Excellency is not already very well aware. Our C.I.D. are, however, very much on the look-out and if anything of importance turns up, I will of course inform you at once.

A C.I.D. agent from the Punjab went to Bombay for the All-India Congress Committee meeting. He got in touch with Birla and Seth Amba Lal Sarabhai of the Calico Mills, Bombay, and they handed on certain information which they claimed to have received direct from members of the Working Committee. According to them, Gandhi explained to the Working Committee that this would be the last Congress movement directed by him. Though he was still a strong believer in non-violence, he realized the impossibility of conducting the campaign on non-violent lines and he gave it as his opinion that the destruction of railway lines, telephone and telegraph wires and other Government property was not an act of violence, because these things were being used by a foreign Government to keep India in perpetual slavery. Although he disliked loss of life, he would not hold any of his followers responsible for committing acts of violence if during the struggle with Government some lives were lost. He even went on to say that he was in favour of a form of guerilla warfare aimed at crippling the Government.

A communist observer who interviewed Gandhi in Delhi said: "Gandhi considers that those who held to non-violence not as a belief but as an expedient should not desist from helping [?fighting] the enemy even by violent means if they are true to themselves." This is on record with the Intelligence Bureau.

Then there is the alleged saying of Gandhi quoted in the weekly report of the Director, Intelligence Bureau,[43] dated August 22nd, "Do not kill. All else is non-violence."

Mohan Lal Saxena, M.L.A. (U.P.), is reported to have said in Lahore that Gandhi had allowed members of the Working Committee and indeed Congressmen in general complete liberty of action and initiative to organize "every possible measure" against the British Government. Although Gandhi's own instructions were based on non-violence, he appears in fact to have provided his followers with "dispensations" allowing them full licence to issue such instructions on their own authority as they thought fit.

Mangal Singh, M.L.A. (Punjab), when he reached Delhi from Wardha early in July and gave his impressions to local Congressmen on arrival, said that the prevailing feeling was that there should be a revolt against the British at all costs. The Congress High Command was not afraid of general chaos, terrorism, communal riots, &c.

All this can scarcely be described as direct evidence suitable for publication, but Gandhi's reference to "open rebellion" and Maulana Azad's statement in Delhi on July 17th "we will not be responsible for the masses who may turn violent" are already public property. The Madras Government have now published the instructions of the Andhra Congress Committee and there would perhaps be no harm publishing the fact that the All-India Congress Committee's instructions include the following: "Put thanas and tahsils and later district headquarters out of action through non-violence." When such instructions are issued with a slogan "Do or Die" and special emphasis on the duty of students to be in the forefront of the battle, violence is inevitable and neither Gandhi with his experience of Chauri Chaura[44] nor any of his lieutenants can possibly have been behind to the consequences. Nor does it seem credible that the careful planning of sabotage against communications in different parts of India could have been the work of any less extensive organization than the Congress.

Gandhi has stated more than once that a free India can only emerge out of chaos, and in the *Harijan* of August 9th Mahadev Desai published an article on "ways of non-violent non-co-operation", which described German unarmed resistance to the French in the Ruhr and specifically mentioned "stray acts of violence, e.g. derailment of running trains, bombs placed on running trains by saboteurs and so on". It is difficult to believe that this article was not intended to serve as a guide to those who were prepared to follow the path of violence.

Yours sincerely,
B.J. GLANCY

125

GLANCY TO LINLITHGOW

Private and Personal
D.-O. No. 411-F.L.

Government House, Lahore,
September 30th, 1942

Dear Lord Linlithgow,

There has been nothing of any great consequence to bring to Your Excellency's notice since I sent my last report and since we discussed matters in Simla a few weeks ago. So far the Punjab has happily continued to be free from serious disorders. Students came back to their various colleges a few days ago and have been giving a certain amount of minor trouble; we thought at one time of postponing the beginning of term, but decided that this would inflate the students' ideas of their own importance and might give rise to increased trouble later on. Muslim students have been behaving commendably, but attempts have been made with varying success to get at Hindus and Sikhs. A few colleges at Lahore and Amritsar are still out on strike and those concerned have been trying to contaminate others elsewhere. The majority of the strikers are mainly interested, it appears, in prolonging the holidays, and the more serious-minded have up to the present been deterred by an increased number of police from indulging in undue activities. A small number of ring-leaders have been arrested, and the heads of colleges have been reminded of their responsibilities and of the consequences that may befall them if they let their institutions get out of hand. We are trying to use the opportunity to tighten up educational control, but it is not altogether easy to find an effective solution.

The situation as regards the Sikh community is much the same as before. Master Tara Singh still continues to maintain his balance between pro-Congress and anti-Congress Akalis. His own proclivities and those of Giani Kartar Singh, one of his principal lieutenants, are towards peace at home and support for the Army, but he is reluctant as always, to show his hand. His speeches tend to be constructed on the Gandhi model – a series of discrepant statements between which the audience can take their choice according to their inclinations. A few Congress-Akalis have been courting arrest by shouting slogans, but so far it does not look as if the situation will change for the worse. This state of affairs may, however, alter considerably if we are driven to lift the ban which is now imposed on the Khaksars, as this is bound to have an unsettling effect on other communities.

Baldev Singh, the Sikh Member of the Cabinet, has shown signs of late of taking an independent line. He was indiscreet enough to subscribe, without consulting Sikander, to a statement criticising Mr. Churchill's recent speech about India. And he has been giving out questionable remarks about the principles of the Land Alienation Act – a subject which is regarded in Unionist circles as altogether too sacred to admit of any expression of heretical opinion. There is in consequence a certain feeling of uneasiness in the Cabinet, but it is to be hoped that the "Sikander-Baldev Singh Pact", which has undoubtedly done much to stabilize the communal position in this Province, will prove capable of surviving these symptoms of disruption.

Recruiting, as Your Excellency is aware, has not suffered any material set-back from the Congress campaign and is going on most admirably.

Fine weather has now set in after an abnormally heavy monsoon. Accounts of damages caused by floods seem on the whole to have been exaggerated, the *kharif* crop is doing well up to the present and prospects for the next *rabi* harvest can be regarded as favourable. This should have a reassuring effect on the prices of food grains; in this respect the situation is somewhat easier than a little time ago, but there are still complaints from various places of inadequate supplies and profiteering.

Yours sincerely,
B.J. GLANCY

126

GLANCY TO LINLITHGOW[45]

Telegram

Immediate
No. 75-G *October 1st, 1942*

Your telegram No. 373-S.C., 30th September.[46] I agree that it is most important that Secretary of State should avoid giving impression that our troubles are over. In the Punjab a potential source of trouble is Sikhs. It might perhaps be suggested that Secretary of State should avoid any discussion of Pakistan issue which would arouse Sikh feeling and embarrass Provincial Government. Specific mention of Sikhs should however be avoided as there are many pitfalls.

127

GLANCY TO LINLITHGOW

Private and Personal
D.-O. No. 417-F.L.

Government House, Lahore,
November 13th, 1942

Dear Lord Linlithgow,

There is little of any great importance to bring to Your Excellency's notice since we met at Rawalpindi last month. Any active support of Congress appears to be on the decline, though there have been a few minor demonstrations on the part of students and others from time to time. The Sikh community as a whole has wisely continued to abstain from any participation in the Congress crusade. There is no doubt that the "Sikander-Baldev Singh Pact" has been a powerful factor for good, and that it has exercised a distinctly pacifying effect on the Sikh community. There are signs that Baldev Singh is inclined to attach increasing value to his appointment as a Minister and that he is less likely to run out of the ropes. Communal relations have on the whole been less strained and social gatherings have been held at Lahore on the occasions of the Id and the Diwali with the object of bringing the various communities together; the Sikhs are about to organize a similar event in commemoration of Guru Nanak's birthday. This happy state of affairs is in danger of disturbance when Mr. Jinnah pays his forthcoming visit to the Punjab. Lyallpur, Jullundur and Lahore are included in his programme, and it is only to be expected that his tour will give rise to further disquieting cries for "Pakistan" and counter-attacks on the part of non-Muslims. Sikander, who would of course be much relieved if Jinnah's visit were cancelled, has chosen this time to float his scheme, of which I have already informed you, for the possible dismemberment of the Province. The main object of his exposition is to point out the practical difficulties that lie in the way of partition, and in this he has not been without success. The scheme has not been popular with Muslims and it is of course intensely disliked by Hindus. Sikh leaders have been professing to take the idea seriously and some of them have been attempting negotiations with Jinnah, the intention being apparently to see whether they can get more out of Jinnah or Sikander; steps have been taken to point out to some of them in the course of friendly discussions that they are not likely to secure any practical benefit from dealings with Jinnah and that the various elements in the Province would be better advised to try and settle their difficulties among themselves. I do not think that responsible reasonably-minded Sikhs have any serious desire to see the Province dismembered as long as they are likely to be given a fair deal.

There has been some endeavour to revive agitation on behalf of the Khaksars. The Premier in answer to questions in the Assembly made it plain that the Punjab Government would only be willing to see the ban on the Khaksars removed provided that Allama Mashriqi would issue instructions that all drilling, all spades and other emblems are to be given up and that the activities of his followers are to be confined to social service on the part of individuals. This, as you know, is what we represented to the Government of India some time ago. I see that according to the Press, Allama Mashriqi has given out that he is prepared to accept this condition. I think that it would be only prudent before the ban is finally removed, if that is ever to take place, to see that he supplies the Central Government with a copy of the instructions that he proposes to issue to his flock in this behalf and also to warn him clearly that any breach of these instructions is likely to result in the ban being reimposed. We intend addressing the Central Government to this effect.

Recruiting has, I am sorry to say, declined rather markedly of late. The main cause of this, apart from agricultural operations, has been the severe malaria epidemic, which it has been very difficult to control in the absence of an adequate supply of quinine. We are doing what we can to cope with the epidemic, which is now far less severe than it was, and I hope that recruitment will soon revive. The events that have taken place in the north of Africa should go a long way to improve the morale of people in the towns. So far as the villagers go, there is no cause for complaint. Your Excellency's recent Durbar at Rawalpindi has certainly had a striking effect and has made a deep impression in the Division. Since we met I have been touring in the Salt Range where I was struck by the dearth of young men, large numbers of whom have gone off to the Army; at almost every village I was met by a most heartening collection of fine old soldiers who were, I am convinced, quite genuine in their expressions of friendliness and loyalty.

I enclose the Provincial fortnightly report for the second half of October.

Yours sincerely,
B.J. GLANCY

128

GLANCY TO LINLITHGOW

Private and Personal
D.-O. No. 419-F.L.

Government House, Lahore,
November 28th, 1942

Dear Lord Linlithgow,

The best thing to be said about Jinnah's tour in the Punjab is that it has come to an end; it was throughout a success for the Qaid-i-Azam, but it has certainly not tended to improve communal relations. At the beginning of his crusade at Jullundur, Jinnah made a pointed attack on the author of a certain new formula devised for the solution of India's difficulties; he was obviously referring to Sikander's "partition scheme", though he did not mention the Premier by name. A day or two later Sikander found it expedient to attend the Muslim League meeting at Lyallpur and to make his obeisance to the Qaid-i-Azam. In return for this Jinnah was kind enough to express his approval of the Premier and to say that at Jullundur he had not been alluding to Sikander's formula, which he had not had time to study. Sikander was undoubtedly in an embarrassing position and he could scarcely have been expected to risk an open rupture with Jinnah, but in proclaiming that he saw eye to eye with the champion of "Pakistan" he has to a considerable extent weakened the "Baldev Singh-Sikander Pact" and undermined whatever confidence other communities have reposed in his assurances. The Sikhs in particular are feeling injured and bewildered. Master Tara Singh has been freely criticizing both Jinnah and Sikander. Giani Kartar Singh appears to be still groping for some means to satisfy the separatist ambitions of his community. In a speech at Nankana he made bold to say that Sikhs should work for the unity of India as a whole, but should aim at an appropriate partition of the Punjab. One of the suggestions is that this partition should be based not on population, but on landed interests, as this would lead to results more favourable to the Sikhs. Among the Muslims there is a definitely increasing number shouting for "Pakistan", without for the most part any serious attempt at analysing what it means. The general atmosphere is more uneasy than it was and it looks as if cleavages would grow more pronounced.

Another Communal Reunion Party took place yesterday and I was among those present. This time the occasion was the anniversary of Guru Nanak's birthday and the host was Baldev Singh, who showed up well throughout and seems to be gaining self-assurance. The usual speeches were made and every one appeared very friendly but there was a certain air of unreality about the proceedings.

Chakwal in the Salt Range has been the scene of a War Front rally on a fairly large scale. Portraits of Their Majesties were given a prominent place and loyal sentiments were expressed on all sides. The Premier and the Ministers attended the gathering, which also served to promote the cause of the Unionist Party.

As regards the Khaksars, I do not think that Sikander or the Provincial Government can be charged with inconsistency. The position of the Punjab Government has been for some time past that if the Allama would give out that the movement was to be completely demilitarized, then the removal of the ban need not be opposed. It may seem surprising that the Allama has been ready to give the assurance required. It appears doubtful whether on his past form he has any serious intention of abiding by his undertaking, and I think that before orders are issued it should be very firmly instilled into him that if his followers do not adhere to his instructions, the ban will have to be reimposed; it would seem well that this warning should be widely made known throughout the country.

Morale in the urban areas continues to improve in consequence of the good news from the various War Fronts. Fear that India may be invaded appears to be disappearing. One of the effects of this will no doubt be a declining interest in A.R.P. endeavours.

I enclose the provincial fortnightly report for the first half of November.

Yours sincerely,
B.J. GLANCY

129

GLANCY TO LINLITHGOW

Secret
D.-O. No. 420

Government House, Lahore,
December 22nd, 1942

Dear Lord Linlithgow,

I am sorry to add to Your Excellency's troubles, but I think I should send you without delay a copy of an "interception" which was brought to my notice yesterday.

Though the writer of the letter to Colonel Shamsher Singh[47] is described as signing his name illegibly, I fear there is no doubt whatever that the author is Moon, now Deputy Commissioner of Amritsar. Moon, as you know, is in normal times an excellent officer – both in the Secretariat and in the Executive line. He has been doing admirable work in his present post. But he has always been highly strung, he suffers from intellectual exhibitionism, and the strain on his nerves has evidently been too much for him. I knew that he was distressed at what he regarded as the harsh treatment meted out to Congress prisoners, particularly as he was a close personal friend of Amrit Kaur and her family, and I did what I could to smooth him down: still I would never have believed, until I saw this interception, that he would have so far lost control of himself as to send a copy of a confidential[48] official letter to a private individual and to express the sentiments to which he has given vent in such a quarter.

I have discussed the affair with Sikander. Though we both of us have a strong personal regard for Moon, we are agreed that the only thing to do now is to let him go from the service as quickly and as quietly as possible. I cannot of course guarantee that Moon's letter will not be given publicity and used as propaganda by the Amrit Kaur family or will not leak out through the censor staff employed by the Superintendent of Police, Simla. But I hope this will not occur. I propose therefore to send for Moon, to confront him with the interception and to advise him to ask for permission to retire and then to go home as soon as he can. The reason to be assigned, if, as I hope, he will agree to this, should be his indifferent health: he has not been keeping well of late, and is manifestly in need of rest and change.

I shall be grateful if Your Excellency will be good enough to let me know as soon as you conveniently can whether the action which I propose to take has your approval.

Yours sincerely,
B.J. GLANCY

ENCLOSURE 1 TO NO. 129

MOON TO SHAMSHER SINGH
Intercepted Letter

Amritsar,
December 11th, 1942

Dear Shammy,

After nearly a month I have received a reply to my letter[49] and I enclose a copy for your own private information.

I do not know what your reaction will be. I experienced mingled feelings of amusement, astonishment and disgust. I was astonished, because I really did not think that Government would have the nerve to deal out to me such pitiful claptrap. It is [an] insult to one's intelligence besides being a reflection on their own.

I have not had time to think the matter over thoroughly and decide on my course of action. You will understand the difficulty of serving loyally a Government with such standards of value and above all, of intellectual honesty. As regards the prisoners – or rather to avoid any misnomer the "rebels" – the release of a considerable number is now contemplated (so perhaps after all they are not rebels). I have recommended that about half of those from here should be let out. The question of their treatment therefore to some extent falls into the background. And I believe there has been some improvement. But it is a shameful story. I hope Amrit is regaining her strength and spirits, and that all of you are well. I have no time for move [more].

Yours —,
(Sd.) ILLEGIBLE

ENCLOSURE 2 TO NO. 129

BOURNE[50] TO MOON
Intercepted Letter

D.-O. No. 18710-B.D.S.B *December 9th, 1942*

Your confidential letter No. 320-S.T., dated the 13th November 1942, on the subject of the treatment of civil disobedience prisoners, 1942, [?was] received just as orders [?were] issued making certain modifications in the treatment authorised for such prisoners. I am to say that no further concessions are contemplated.

2. Government considers that you are labouring under a misapprehension of the position. Though these prisoners are called "civil disobedience prisoners", events elsewhere have shown that the movement fostered by Congress amounted to open rebellion and the [?that] civil disobedience in the old sense is an entire misnomer. Sympathisers with any such movement in Britain would have [?been] recommended [?for] far more severe punishment than it has been possible to give in the Punjab, the reason being that India is still nominally a subject country. In any Free Country

the only punishment for rebellion in times of War is a firing squad. Though the rest of India may not see eye to eye with the views of the Punjab, that Province, having [?only] a handful of urban politicians, considers the War to be its own war and public opinion, among those who really count, would not tolerate the grant of the easy conditions of jail life accorded in prisons [?to] so-called agitations [?agitators], and would regard this as incommensurate with the heinousness of the offence, actual or contemplated, which is no less than the destruction of the country's cause and the maintaining of the safety of the lives, honour and property of its people including 15 million relatives of the fighting men in the Indian Army.

130

GLANCY TO LINLITHGOW

Secret
D.-O. No. 422

Government House, Lahore,
December 28th, 1942

Dear Lord Linlithgow,

Nothing could have been more tragic than the sudden death of Sikander[51] an hour or two after he had been as cheerful and charming a host as ever to a large number of guests including myself at a party arranged to celebrate the marriage of three of his children. I have conveyed Your Excellency's gracious message to the eldest son,[52] who was one of the bridegrooms so shortly before, and have also released it to the press.

Sikander's loss is one that we shall feel grievously and public opinion about the most suitable successor has not yet settled down. I propose therefore to wait for a few days before forming my conclusion as to the person most likely to command a stable majority in the Legislature.

In the meantime I propose to carry on with the present Ministers, in much the same way for all practical purposes as on the occasions when the late Premier left India on visits to the Middle East.

When a decision has been reached about the person to be consulted in forming a new Ministry, I think it might be well, though there is nothing that I can find specially enjoining this procedure, to arrange for all existing Ministers to resign, and to reappoint the same day those who will continue. This might be of value in indicating that the Ministers command the confidence of their new leader: also it might be of service in establishing a precedent for future cases in which resignations of Ministers in similar circumstances may be in point of fact more necessary than in the present instance. It does not at present appear likely that there will be more than the minimum amount of change in the Ministry, but I cannot yet be certain about this.

Yours sincerely,
B.J. GLANCY

131

GLANCY TO LINLITHGOW

Private and Personal
D.-O. No. 423-F.L.

Government House, Lahore,
December 29th, 1942

Dear Lord Linlithgow,

Sir Sikander's tragic death within the last few days has overshadowed all other events in the Punjab. Apart from his outstanding services to the province and his skill in keeping the Unionist Party together, he was an extremely popular figure, and his loss is likely to be felt all the more keenly as the days go by. As Your Excellency can imagine, there is already a good deal of log-rolling going on in regard to his successor. The sooner this comes to an end the better it will be, and I hope that it will soon be a little more obvious than it is at present which of the possible candidates is likely to command the most stable majority in the Legislature.

So far as I can judge, Baldev Singh is not likely to break away from the Ministry in consequence of Sikander's death, but the Akalis show signs of becoming restive again, and Tara Singh evidently considers that he should take steps to bring himself into a more prominent position. The Akalis are still threatening an attack on the Kapurthala State on the plea that the Maharaja does not conform to Sikh principles and that the Durbar are trampling on the rightful claims of the community. Whether anything will actually materialize from these threats it is difficult to say, but we are watching the situation carefully. The Akalis received a set-back at Amritsar the other day in the election for the post of President of the Khalsa College Council when the candidate supported by their party and also heavily backed by the Maharaja of Patiala was defeated by Kirpal Singh, the son of the late Sir Sundar Singh Majithia. By the exercise of a considerable degree of ingenuity Kirpal Singh succeeded in securing a majority amongst the electors and the rival party walked out of the meeting. Left to themselves

Kirpal Singh and his supporters then proceeded to replace the Maharaja of Patiala by the Raja of Faridkot as Chancellor of the College. It is said that the rules of the institution precluded the Maharaja of Patiala from continuing in office any longer. I have sent for the rules to see whether this contention is correct; but even if it is so, a good deal of bad blood is likely to arise from what has occurred.

We received good showers of rain in almost all parts of the Punjab within the last fortnight. This should help considerably in *rabi* prospects. I hope that it may have some effect in bringing down the price of grain. We have certainly got into a highly anomalous and embarrassing position and personally I doubt very much whether the fixation of maximum prices will ever prove really effective. I sincerely hope that the reports of additional shipping being available to carry wheat from Australia to this country are correct, as this would appear to provide by far the readiest practical solution,

We have managed to get over our difficulty about the appointment of a Sikh member on the Public Service Commission. It has been found possible to recognise the services of Dasaundha Singh in another way, and I have given the appointment to Sardar Bahadur Mohan Singh, lately an Adviser at the India Office, who should, I think, do well.

Thanks to the good war news, morale remains high. I took the chair at two War Front meetings on tour the other day. They were well organized and resulted in a good display of enthusiasm which, I hope, will be translated into more active support.

Yours sincerely,
B.J. GLANCY

132

GLANCY TO LINLITHGOW

Private and Personal
D.-O. No. 424

Government House, Lahore,
December 30th, 1942

Dear Lord Linlithgow,

Many thanks for Your Excellency's letter[53] of December the 26th about Moon.

When the Congress leaders were arrested in August it was decided to treat all détenus and all political convicts in the same way. There was to be none of the A and B classification which used to enable many such prisoners to enjoy considerable comfort. On the other hand they were not to live in as Spartan a way as ordinary C class prisoners. Diet was to cost Re. 0-6-3 per head per day as against the C class average of Re. 0-3-6 and prisoners might wear their own clothes or B class prison clothes whichever they preferred. They were, however, to be allowed to write only one letter and to receive only one in two months, were not to supplement their diet from outside and were not to be allowed newspapers. No interviews were permitted.

On October 13th revised orders were issued applying to détenus only, which improved conditions a good deal. Diet was to cost Re. 0-9-3 per day. Charpoys instead of the usual berths were to be provided as soon as possible where not already provided: these had already been ordered in every case, but supply had proved most difficult owing to shortage of materials. In future a letter might be written and one received each month. Approved newspapers in English and Indian languages were to be provided and suitable books might be presented to jail libraries for the use of prisoners.

On November 13th Moon put in a protest of which I enclose a copy; this appeared to refer to the original rules. The Chief Secretary replied referring to the new conditions in his confidential demi-official letter No. 18710-S.B., dated the 9th of December 1942, of which Moon sent a copy to his correspondent in Simla.

I may add that several women détenus including Amrit Kaur were confined together in the Ambala jail so that they should not lack company, and of this Moon was aware.

I think Your Excellency will agree that though the détenus were certainly not pampered in the Punjab, conditions were at no time so harsh as to warrant an accusation of cruelty or vindictiveness, and after the orders of October 13th they were still less open to objection.

I entirely agree that if Moon is to retire, he should go straight home, and, should events take the course which we expect, I will do my best to ensure that he does so.

As regards proportionate pension, I am strongly in favour of treating Moon, who has done splendid work during his service, with all possible generosity, and I have every hope that our new Premier, whoever he may be, will accept this point of view. Moon will have earned about £600 a year, I think. A medical certificate may not be obtainable, but in fact Moon is at the moment a sick and overstrained man as any layman can see, and he badly needs a rest.[54]

Yours sincerely,
B.J. GLANCY

ENCLOSURE TO NO. 132

MOON TO WACE

Confidential
D.-O. No. 320 S.T.

Deputy Commissioner's Office, Amritsar,
November 13th, 1942

Dear Mr Wace,

I am writing to you on the subject of the treatment of civil disobedience prisoners, 1942, about which for some time several officers including myself have felt considerable disquiet. The questions recently asked in the Assembly show that the treatment meted out to them has aroused a good deal of criticism. This criticism can hardly be said to have been satisfactorily met by Government spokesmen. My impression is that Government would be well advised and can well afford to reconsider their policy in this matter. I, therefore, venture to address you on the subject and request you to bring what I have to say to the notice of Government.

2. I understand that with very few exceptions all civil disobedience prisoners detained under Rule 129 or Rule 26 are being treated so far as diet, accommodation, amenities, &c., are concerned very much in the same way as C class convicts. Many of them are persons of education, position and refinement. We are unfortunately compelled in the public interest to keep them for a time out of the way so that they may not imperil the safety of the State. This we must do; but any harshness over and above this can only be justified on the ground that it is necessary in order to deter others. For clearly these people, however, perverse or misguided their opinion may be, are not likely to be *reformed* by punishment. Nor, I imagine, do we really wish to punish them *retributively* – indeed many of them have not actually rendered themselves liable to punishment by wrong doing. It is only therefore as a deterrent to others that harshness in their case can be justified.

3. It might at one time have been argued that leniency in the treatment of civil disobedience prisoners might induce others to come forward and embarrass Government by courting arrest, while a certain display of

severity would effectively discourage many who might otherwise have joined the movement. This argument no doubt had some validity in other provinces and perhaps even in the Punjab at the outset. But whatever validity it may have had then it has none now. The civil disobedience movement (which in my opinion never was and was never likely to be a serious menace here) has admittedly now collapsed in the Punjab and short of some startling and unforeseen changes in the general situation I see little prospect of its recrudescence. Potential participants are deterred from coming forward not by any thought of the treatment which they are likely to meet but by a realization of the hopeless futility of their activity in this Province.

4. It seems to me, therefore, that the only justification there was for treating these civil disobedience prisoners with the same sort of harshness as we use towards criminals, has gone. The continuance of such harshness can therefore only increase resentment without bringing any compensating advantage. It is surely a grave error to add gratuitously even a pie to the legacy of bitterness which recent events must inevitably leave behind. Especially would it seem unwise to do so in this Province. It so happens that the majority of the civil disobedience prisoners are Hindus and it is unfortunately a fact that the great bulk of the Hindu population, whatever their political views, tend to sympathise with their brothers in jail and feel resentment at their ill-treatment. Government in the Punjab has to reconcile strong communal antagonizms. It is surely therefore a mistaken policy to persist in a course of action which by increasing the resentment of one community will certainly increase the difficulty of a future reconciliation.

5. Finally on quite general grounds I would urge a reconsideration of treatment meted out to these prisoners. They are not convicted criminals and some of them only joined the movement out of loyalty to Congress – loyalty which however misguided is entitled to some respect. Yet these people are being confined with a rigour which smacks of the concentration camp and is in sorry contrast to the principles of freedom for which we are supposed to be fighting this War.[55]

6. I would, therefore, very earnestly urge that this matter be reconsidered. Government can afford to be generous. We are in the fortunate position here of having always had the situation well in hand. There is no reason why we should not calmly and deliberately decide to be generous. I would suggest that each case should be dealt with now on merits and each internee given the treatment to which his social status and education entitles him. If this is done we shall, I believe, be losing nothing. We may even gain by

diminishing ill-will; and we shall, at any rate, have the satisfaction of bringing our practice more into accord with our professions.[56]

Yours sincerely,
E.P. MOON

NOTES

1. Sir Sikander Hyat Khan visited Indian troops in Iraq at the start of 1942.
2. This document is taken from MSS. EUR. F 125/110.
3. In this telegram Lord Linlithgow drew Sir Bertrand Glancy's attention to some key points in the first draft of the 'Cripps' Offer'. The Viceroy stated that it contained two main features:

   '(*a*) a clear implication that India will be promised the right to secede if she wishes after the new constitution; and (*b*) that local option of Provinces to accede or not to accede is contemplated.'

   The Viceroy added that 'the Declaration goes so far as regards secession that from the purely internal point of view His Majesty's Government might well use the actual word "independence"'. MSS. EUR. F 125/110. See also N. Mansergh et al. (eds.), *The Transfer of Power, 1942-7*, London: H.M.S.O., 1970-83, Vol. I, Nos. 194, 197, 200 and 226.
4. This document is taken from MSS. EUR. F 125/110.
5. Ibid.
6. In this telegram of 8 March 1942 Lord Linlithgow sent Sir Bertrand Glancy a substantial portion of a revised version of the 'Cripps' Offer'. MSS. EUR. F 125/110. See also Mansergh, *Transfer of Power*, Vol. I, Nos. 265 and 286.
7. This refers only to the first paragraph of the telegram.
8. Since the despatch of No. 102, Lord Linlithgow had sent Sir Bertrand Glancy the full text of the 'Cripps' Offer' as it stood at that date in telegram 576-S of 8 March 1942. MSS. EUR. F 125/110.
9. The last sentence of telegram 576-S reads: 'As regards the Army, it would be proposed in any case to send round order to troops explaining that their position and rights remain fully guaranteed.'
10. In this telegram Lord Linlithgow said that the wheat position had reached a stage of acute crisis in the North-West Frontier Province, Delhi and United Provinces' towns with several weeks remaining before the new crop could come on to the market. However the Punjab had issued export prohibition and requisitioning orders under emergency powers delegated by the Centre. The Viceroy was unable to agree to the proposition that the use of these powers should result in a very unequal distribution of such stocks as were available. He hoped Sir Bertrand Glancy would convince Sir Sikander of the soundness of his attitude and secure that at least half the visible stocks (including those already requisitioned by the Centre) were made available for consumption in areas outside the Punjab. R/3/1/64.

11. In this telegram Lord Linlithgow said that Sir Stafford Cripps would wish to see, among others, two Sikhs from British India. The Viceroy, himself, felt that perhaps Cripps ought to see three. He asked Sir Bertrand Glancy to send him two or three names he could recommend. Linlithgow added that Cripps would be seeing the Maharaja of Patiala. R/3/1/64.
12. Sir Stafford Cripps had arrived in India on 22 March 1942 for his discussions with Indian leaders and he left on 12 April following the failure of his mission. The 'Draft Declaration' or 'Cripps' Offer' was announced on 30 March. It was published as Cmd. 6350 and is also to be found in Mansergh, *Transfer of Power*, Vol. I, No. 456. From the viewpoint of the Punjab the critical provision in the 'Offer' was to be found in clause (c). Part of this clause reads:

    'His Majesty's Government undertake to take accept and implement forthwith the Constitution so framed subject only to:
    (i) the right of any Province of British India that is not prepared to accept the new Constitution to retain its present constitution position, provision being made for its subsequent accession if it so decides.

    With such non-acceding Provinces, should they so desire, His Majesty's Government will be prepared to agree upon a new Constitution, giving them the same full status as Indian Union, and arrived at by a procedure analogous to that here laid down.'
13. Lord Linlithgow minuted: 'P.S.V. – S./S. & H.M.G. are entitled to know the Governor's views.' Linlithgow added: '(i.e. the essential difference between an offer and a declaration.)'
14. Lord Linlithgow minuted: 'I agree.'
15. Lord Linlithgow minuted: 'This does not fit with what I have heard. I know nothing of the C.J. personally.'
16. See *P.P., 1936-1939*, No. 66.
17. See Appendix for the text of the Sikander-Baldev Singh Pact.
18. Sir John Thorne was Secretary to the Governor-General (Public) at this date.
19. Sir Maurice Hallett was Governor of the United Provinces at this date.
20. See Appendix.
21. In his reply of 17 July 1942, Lord Linlithgow said that in his judgement the 'Cripps' Offer' had been withdrawn by H.M.G. and that Glancy should not encourage Sir Sikander to promote a plan which made an unjustifiable assumption as to the future policy of H.M.G. The Viceroy entirely agreed with Glancy's criticizms of Sikander's formula. R/3/1/64. See also Mansergh, *Transfer of Power*, Vol. II, No. 280.
22. This document is taken from MSS. EUR. F 125/110.
23. On 14 July 1942, the Congress Working Committee, meeting at Wardha, passed the momentous 'Quit India' resolution calling for the immediate ending of British rule in India. On 8 August the All-India Congress Committee, at its meeting in Bombay, approved and endorsed the Working Committee's

resolution. In addition it sanctioned 'the starting of a mass struggle on non-violent lines on the widest possible scale'. Early on 9 August Mr Gandhi and the Congress leaders were arrested and imprisoned. The 'Quit India' resolution was published in Cmd. 6430. See also: Mansergh, *Transfer of Power*, Vol. II, No. 470.

When he sent telegram 2085-S, Lord Linlithgow had not seen the full text of the Wardha 'Quit India' resolution. He said he did not intend to reach a final conclusion until the terms were available. He also drew Sir Bertrand Glancy's attention to the Home Department telegram referred to in this paragraph which requested information on denial policy. MSS. EUR. F 125/110. See also Mansergh, *Transfer of Power*, Vol. II, No. 261.

24. See *P.P. 1936-1939*, Nos. 81 and 82.
25. Lord Linlithgow replied on 20 July 1942. He agreed with Sir Bertrand Glancy's criticisms of Sir Sikander's latest idea. The Viceroy felt that H.M.G. was unlikely to consider any further move during the war unless there was some marked change of circumstances. Linlithgow shared Glancy's scepticism that Mr Gandhi might make a united front with Mr Jinnah. The Viceroy was left with a feeling that Sikander felt a shade out in the cold and was anxious to keep himself near to the spotlight. R/3/1/64. See also Mansergh, *Transfer of Power*, Vol. II, No. 294.
26. In his letter of 16 July 1942, Lord Linlithgow thanked Sir Bertrand Glancy for No. 115. The Viceroy said that a useful discussion on denial policy had taken place in Council the previous day. There was general solidarity on the point that if the All-India Committee of Congress ratified the 'Quit India' resolution (see note 23 above), they must be prepared to take immediate action. The members of Council were very emphatic on the importance of propaganda both at home and abroad. The suggestion was also made that they must mobilise, so far as possible, those individuals and parties in the country who did not agree with Congress and Mr Gandhi.

    Linlithgow pointed out that one of the elements that needed mobilising was the Sikh community. He asked Glancy to do what he could with Sir Jogendra Singh to try to get the Sikhs to come out in reasoned criticizm and opposition to Congress. In addition anything Sir Sikander could say would be of real value. The Viceroy agreed that they might have to consider the *Harijan* position. R/3/1/64. See also Mansergh, *Transfer of Power*, Vol. II, No. 276.
27. See Appendix.
28. This document is taken from MSS. EUR. F. 125/110.
29. Not printed.
30. This document is taken from MSS. EUR. F 125/110.
31. In this telegram of 27 July 1942, Lord Linlithgow said he was considering whether to deport Congress leaders or whether to hold the Working Committee in detention in India. MSS. EUR. F 125/110.
32. This document is taken from L/P&J/8/609: f 406.

33. Mr P.L. Orde.
34. This document is taken from MSS. EUR. F 125/110.
35. In this telegram Lord Linlithgow stressed the importance of making clear to the public of the provinces the reasons why they were going all out to deal with the Congress menace and also to hearten the man in the street. He imagined it would be important to give District Officers a line and to consider the possibility of fairly active propaganda in the towns. The Viceroy felt they had probably gone as far as they could with the National War Front if they were to avoid the suggestion that they were making it political. MSS. EUR. F 125/23.
36. Not printed.
37. See Appendix.
38. Sir Jogendra Singh had joined the Governor-General's Council on 29 July 1942.
39. See note 25 above.
40. The resolution, passed by the Muslim League Working Committee at Bombay on 20 August 1942, condemned the decision of Congress to launch an 'open rebellion'. It reiterated the League's offer to co-operate with the British Government during the war on the basis of a real share and responsibility at the Centre without prejudice to the political issues involved in the framing of the future constitution. It was of the opinion that the Muslim masses could only be roused to intensify the war effort if they were assured that this would lead to the realisation of the goal of Pakistan. See Mansergh: *Transfer of Power*, Vol. II, No. 598.
41. Lord Linlithgow acknowledged this letter on 28 July 1942. He said he was forwarding a copy of it to Mr Amery. The Viceroy agreed that it was wise to avoid committing themselves in either direction on the subject of Pakistan. R/3/1/64.
42. This document is taken from MSS. EUR. F. 125/110.
43. Mr D. Pilditch.
44. Early in 1922, during Mahatma Gandhi's civil disobedience campaign, a mob set fire to a police station at Chauri Chaura, a village in the United Provinces. Twenty-two police constables were killed. It was this incident that led Gandhi to call off the civil disobedience campaign.
45. This document is taken from MSS. EUR. F. 125/110.
46. Lord Linlithgow's telegram reported that it was understood that a House of Commons' debate on India would take place on 6 October 1942. Linlithgow asked Governors whether they had any points that they wished him to make to Mr Amery. MSS. EUR. F 125/110.
47. Colonel Shamsher Singh was a brother of Rajkumari Amrit Kaur, herself Secretary to Mahatma Gandhi.
48. Although the file copy in Lahore of Mr Bourne's letter was marked 'Confidential' the original letter as received by Mr Moon was not so marked. On 19 January 1943 Moon wrote to Sir Bertrand Glancy:

'Though I don't lay any great stress on the point myself, still, as you laid some emphasis yesterday on the fact that Bourne's letter to me was "confidential", I may mention for the sake of accuracy that it was not so marked and was received here in a cover addressed to me not by name but by designation, which was opened by my office. I have verified this by reference to the original letter.'

Enclosure in Glancy to Linlithgow, 20 January 1943. R/3/1/65.

49. See Enclosure to No. 132 for the text of Mr Moon's letter to Government. Moon had written to the Punjab Home Secretary (Mr Wace) but he received a reply from the Chief Secretary (Mr Bourne).
50. In his interview with Sir Bertrand Glancy on 18 January 1943 Mr Moon said he had concluded, from the style of Mr Bourne's letter, that it must have been based on the instructions of Sir Sikander Hyat Khan. Glancy to Linlithgow, 19 January 1943. R/3/1/65.
51. Sir Sikander died suddenly before midnight on 26 December 1942.
52. Major Shaukat Hyat Khan.
53. In this letter Lord Linlithgow said he would be submitting the papers concerning Mr Moon to Mr Amery. The Viceroy asked what precisely was the treatment of prisoners to which Moon objected. He also wondered whether Moon had made previous protests and how they had been dealt with. R/3/1/64.
54. On 19 January 1943 Sir Bertrand Glancy sent Lord Linlithgow an account of his interview with Mr Moon the previous day. During the interview Moon had said that 'if Government chose to read his private correspondence, this was no fault of his.' Glancy reported that 'Moon assured me that he was very sorry if he had caused us anxiety, particularly as he could now have no chance of setting himself right with Sikander, to whom he had been considerably attached. But as regards what he has done Moon continued to try and justify himself and declined to admit that he had been to blame. It was evident, however, in the course of the interview that he was not far off a break-down.' R/3/1/65.

    Correspondence concerning the Moon case continued until the end of April 1943. At one stage Mr Amery suggested that Moon should be employed outside the Punjab but Glancy did not think this a practicable solution. During an interview with Glancy on 29 April 1943, Moon said that he felt the correct course for Government was to dismiss him. Glancy, however, persuaded him to apply for six months' leave and for permission to resign from the Indian Civil Service. Moon resolutely refused to apply for a proportionate pension. *Ibid.*
55. Lord Linlithgow minuted against this sentence: 'Rot!'
56. Lord Linlithgow minuted: 'Bar a silly sentence Moon's letter is v[ery] sensible. But I am afraid there can be no forgiveness for the breach of faith. No Gov[ernmen]t can stomach betrayal by a Senior C[ivil] S[ervant].'

CHAPTER 5

Documents for 1943

133

GLANCY TO LINLITHGOW

Secret
D.-O. No. 425

Government House, Lahore,
January 2nd, 1943

Dear Lord Linlithgow,

Will your Excellency kindly refer to my telegram No. 80-G. of the 30th of April [December] 1942[1] about the selection of a successor to fill the place of Sir Sikander? This is to give you some account of what has been happening here in the last few days.

It appeared to me from the beginning that there were only two candidates whose claims need be seriously considered – Khizar and Firoz. But other people had different ideas, and every wire within reach was pulled more and more vigorously as the days went by. The Khattar faction, to which of course Sikander himself belonged, were anxious that his mantle should fall on a member of the same tribe, their nominees being his elder brother Liaqat [Hyat Khan] or Muzaffar [Khan], a close relation. Another coterie who began to interest themselves actively were Muslim Leaguers, and a deputation was sent to interview Jinnah at Delhi but found that he had gone back to Bombay. Various agents set to work to collect signatures from M.L.As. in favour of one candidate or another.

One of the first to come and see me was Manohar Lal, the Finance Minister. He said that he and two other Ministers, Abdul Haye and Baldev Singh, strongly supported Khizar. Chhotu Ram, the Revenue Minister, was still away on tour and had not yet expressed his views beyond announcing that he was not a candidate himself. Manohar Lal had evidently a poor opinion of all competitors other than Khizar: he said that the course was clear and that in order to put an end to intrigue it would be advisable to decide the issue at once. This was on Monday, December 28th, the day after Sikander's funeral. I pointed out that, though I had a high regard for Khizar, it seemed necessary to wait for a few days in order to make reasonably sure that he was most likely to command a really stable majority.

Firoz had a long interview with me not long afterwards. He made it plain that he had no desire to stand for the Premiership himself. He pointed out that he was already entrusted with an extremely responsible office from which he could scarcely be released. He also realized that if he did become Premier this would mean that Khizar, who is a great personal friend of his, would have to retire from the Cabinet: it would be impracticable to allot two out of the three Muslim Ministerships to a Noon and a Tiwana, as the two tribes are so closely connected. Firoz was strongly in favour of Khizar and he also pressed for a very early decision. He said that the other candidates, whom he regarded as quite unworthy, were canvassing and creating dissensions: Khizar on the other hand was taking no steps to rally his supporters and, if he did so, they would begin bargaining and cause difficulties later on.

I saw Chhotu Ram as soon as he was available, on the morning of December 30th. He confirmed his announcement that he was not competing himself. He said that Sikander had in the past suggested to him that he might succeed to the Premiership, but he realised that no one except a Muslim could hope to retain this office for any length of time. I told him that, the communal situation being unfortunately as it is, there appeared to be no disputing this conclusion. Of the various candidates he considered that Khizar was the best. He said that in this he was sure of the support of his own block in the Assembly, and the main thing was to keep the Unionist Party together. I think he has behaved very well throughout.

Khizar with whom I next discussed the position was refreshingly frank and free from any coyness or false modesty. He gave me to understand, without actually saying so, that he considered himself as the right man to succeed: he reminded me that Firoz who might have been a serious rival to Sikander some years ago had withdrawn and accepted the High Commissioner's post in England. Since then he had himself loyally served under the late Premier on the Cabinet, and, though he had never anticipated that an opportunity would occur so soon, he had naturally had his expectations. He was quite ready to take on the appointment if I had confidence in him and he was confident himself that he, or for the matter of that, any other prominent Muslim once nominated would have the support of practically the entire Unionist Party, and they would fall into line behind him.

Later in the day I sent for Muzaffar. I had heard from two or three sources that, though he had given out that he had no wish to become Premier, he was in reality out for the appointment, and was likely to try and advance his own claims once his kinsman, Liaqat, was held to be unsuitable. We had a perfectly friendly conversation, he said he was strongly in favour of keeping the Unionists together, and he thought on the whole that Liaqat was the best choice. He declared that he was not competing himself and that he was quite content with a seat on the P.S.C. to which he had just been appointed. I could not avoid a feeling that, if I had pressed him, he would have modified what he told me about his own ambitions, but I had no intention of doing so. I do not think he would have been a success: he is 63 years of age and, though he has much the same charm of manner that Sikander possessed, I do not believe that he would have proved sufficiently energetic or determined: also there are a fair number of Unionists who would have been unwilling to serve under his banner on account of certain incidents in the past. Muzaffar assured me that he would do his best to see that the party remained intact and stood behind whoever was selected.

I did not see Liaqat. His appointment was in my opinion out of the question. He has been away from the Punjab for, I should think, some twenty years, he has not got a seat in the Assembly, and I do not believe that he would have had a firm following. One of those most active in pressing Liaqat's claims was our old friend, Maqbool Mahmood: Maqbool, as Your Excellency knows, was Sikander's brother-in-law and his daughter has recently married Sikander's eldest son. He is well-known in the Punjab as an intriguer of the first water, and I was warned on all sides that he was only playing for his own hand, and required watching by day and night.

In the evening of the same day I sent for Khizar again and told him that my mind was made up: I considered that he was the right man for the appointment and as it appeared that he would command adequate support it was desirable to make the announcement without delay. I asked him whether he intended to suggest any change with regard to the four other remaining members of the Cabinet. He said that for the present he would prefer that they should all be retained. Though there is one member who might, I think, be replaced without any serious loss, I consider that Khizar was right in the view that he expressed. The rest of the Cabinet came round to Government House not long afterwards: they all confirmed their willingness to serve under Khizar and they said they were all glad that he was being appointed. I told them that, though there was no rule providing expressly for their resignation and reappointment, it seemed to me that this procedure would be in accordance with the spirit of the Instrument of Instructions and would also serve to show that they enjoyed the confidence of the new Premier and that they were a united team. They all agreed that this action was highly desirable. Their resignations were there and then written out and their reappointment order was signed by me just afterwards. As Your Excellency is aware, the announcement was given out to the Press the same night and appeared in the papers the following morning (December 31st).

So far the reactions have been favourable. I hope they will remain so. For the present the rival groups are concentrating their attention on the vacant Ministership and other minor appointments such as Parliamentary Secretaryships. I believe that Khizar will do well. He is a man of strong character and he has very considerable ability and is not afraid of work. He has not got all Sikander's affability, but he is very obviously a man of good breeding and good address. He is aware that his seniors in age will expect to be treated with deference, and I think he should get on well with them. I have never heard him speak in public: I believe he is moderately good at this and no doubt he will improve with practice: he is certainly lucid enough in explaining his views in Council Meetings.[2]

I apologise for the length of this letter. There is only one sequel that I might mention. The Provincial Head of the Muslim Leaguers, the Nawab of Mamdot, asked for an urgent interview with me. No doubt he was acting under the guidance of Mr. Jinnah. I put off seeing him till early on December 31st just after the appointment had been announced. He said when he came that the urgent need for the interview had now gone by, but that he and his friends had arranged for a meeting to take place on January 6th to discuss their line of action. He is not a very bright young man himself and he admitted that much intrigue would have taken place if the appointment had been delayed as long as he had contemplated. This would undoubtedly have been the case, and I think that the solidarity of the party might have been seriously undermined if any suggestion of the necessity for Muslim League approval had been allowed to come to the fore.

Yours sincerely,
B.J. GLANCY

134

GLANCY TO LINLITHGOW

Secret
No. 430

Government House, Lahore,
January 24th, 1943

Dear Lord Linlithgow,

The new Premier, Malik Khizar Hayat Khan, has discussed with me on various occasions the question as to who should be selected to fill the vacant seat on the Punjab Cabinet. The man selected will of course have to be a Muslim. There is no candidate who can be described as outstanding, in fact the field of competitors is regrettably poor. There are a few individualists with no kind of backing who have put forward their own names: among them are one or two who possess distinct ability as parliamentarians, but are universally held to be lacking in other essential qualifications. Apart from these the "possibles" are now reduced to three:

(1) Sir Muhammad Jamal Khan a wealthy Tumandar from the Dera Ghazi Khan District.
(2) Major Ashiq Hussain, a scion of the Qureshi family of Multan.
(3) Major Shaukat Hayat Khan, the eldest son of the late Sir Sikander.

No. 1 is a man of very considerable importance in his own part of the Province, but he has only a very small handful of followers in the House. He has been an M.L.A. for several years, but is said to have never opened his mouth in the course of a debate. He has not been too staunch a supporter of the late Premier. Also, though he is a shrewd man and pleasant enough to meet, he has the reputation of being very sensitive and touchy: he has an undue capacity for making enemies.

No. 2 belongs to an old and revered family. Whatever backing he might have would be effectually neutralised by party faction. As to capacity I fear there is no doubt that he is definitely below par.

As to No. 3, there are certain obvious criticisms that can be made. He is only 28 years of age, he has had no political experience, and his appointment may strike a good many people as an attempt at introducing the hereditary principle where it does not belong. All the same the Premier is strongly inclined to back him, and I think that, considering the quality of other aspirants, the choice is in the circumstances as good as any that can be made. Shaukat is an attractive, well-educated and intelligent young man. He was wounded and taken prisoner in Eritrea and has, I believe, done well as a soldier. It is claimed that the inclusion in the Cabinet of one who has so recently served in the Army will help the Punjab's War Effort. There is certainly a fairly strong feeling in certain quarters in his favour – more sentimental than logical though it may be. The Khattar faction all give out that they are prepared to sink whatever personal ambitions they may have and lend their support to Shaukat. They have sounded Shaukat who tells me that, though he feels extremely loath to leave the Army, he realises that now that he has the responsibility of being the head of the family he would in any case have to give up his profession when the war is over: he has, I gather, told his friends and enquirers that, if it is thought he would be rendering more valuable service as a Minister than as a serving soldier, he would be willing to fall in with their wishes and to leave the Army provided that the Military Authorities agree to let him go.

This is the position and I think the Premier should be allowed to have his way. He has not yet given out his intentions and does not mean to do so until the lie of the land is clear. He appears to have the Party well behind him for the time being, and no danger of a landslide is discernible at present.

If Shaukat is to be selected, various steps will have to be taken. He will have to be placed on the Electoral Roll, on which apparently his name does not figure at present, and he will of course have to be elected to the Assembly within six months of his appointment: in this there should be no great difficulty. The most immediate action required will be to secure his release from the Army. If Your Excellency sees no objection, I should be most grateful if you would be good enough to let me know whether the Higher Military Authorities are likely to raise any difficulty about this. On hearing from you I will pass the word to the Premier and, if all is well, Shaukat will then put in a formal application.[3]

Yours sincerely,
B.J. GLANCY

135

GLANCY TO LINLITHGOW[4]

Governor's Camp, Punjab,
February 12th, 1943

[Unnumbered]

Dear Lord Linlithgow,

Will Your Excellency please refer to your letter of February 3rd[5] about food grains.

The gravity of the food situation and the need of the full assistance and co-operation of every official were stressed at a conference held recently in Lahore and attended by a number of Deputy Commissioners.

We will do all we can both to spare surplus grains of the 1942 *kharif* harvest and to increase our production of rice and millets in the 1943 harvest. As regards the latter we have reason to hope that we may exceed the 'target' figure of acreage set us by the Government of India.

Yours sincerely,
B.J. GLANCY

136

GLANCY TO LINLITHGOW

Private and Personal — Camp, Jullundur,
No. 432 — *February 13th, 1943*

Dear Lord Linlithgow,

I am afraid it is some time since I sent Your Excellency my last periodical report, but I have had the benefit of discussing various matters with you at Delhi last month and we have been corresponding on a good many different subjects.

Economic problems are still very much to the fore in this Province. The price of wheat shot up soon after the control rate was removed to over Rs. 13 a maund, but has now fallen to something under Rs. 11. Some people profess to think that there will be a marked drop in the price of grain when the new crop, of which the prospects are most encouraging, comes on to the market. It is, I think, unwise to make any definite prophecy about this unless and until it becomes known that substantial shipments of wheat are actually coming in from overseas. At present the tendency is to believe that this plan is only a paper project. A fair amount of wheat is now finding its way into the towns, but the poorer classes are in great difficulties in making both ends meet. We are eking out our grain reserves as well as we can to meet the requirements of poor citizens in larger towns: action taken for seeing that only the deserving benefit by these arrangements has on the whole been very successful, and in many cases A.R.P. wardens have been of great help in this direction. Our reserves should last us on a modest scale of distribution until the *rabi* crop begins to trickle in, but there are many difficulties still ahead of us.

Complaints about salt have for the most part come to an end, and I am very grateful to Your Excellency for the help you have given us in seeing that satisfactory arrangements are brought into force. I wish that the position as regards sugar was equally satisfactory: we are still hoping that, as in the case of salt, sugar consignments will be sent to the nominees of District Magistrates. And we are eagerly looking forward to the arrival of good supplies of Standard Cloth.

Mr Phillips[6] paid a visit of several days to Lahore. He appeared to enjoy his programme, various outings in the countryside were arranged for him, he came with me to a few social entertainments given by prominent Indians and he gave a fair number of interviews to different people. He was commendably cautious in expressing his views, and a good many people commented with regret on his reticence. He in his turn complained that several Indian personalities with whom he came in contact were not as forthcoming as they might have been. We were careful not to ride him off going where he liked or meeting any one whom he desired to see, and this I think he appreciated. He appeared to be anxious to help towards a solution of India's problems, but he was very far from certain as to the manner in which he could be of practical assistance.[7] When he has visited other Provinces no doubt his ideas will become more clear.

Sikander's son, Shaukat, has taken over charge as a Minister, his main departments being Public Works (Roads, Buildings and Electricity) and Local Self-Government. As I told Your Excellency, his selection was scarcely an ideal choice, but was perhaps as free from criticizm as any other that could have been made. The Premier has shown no signs of regretting his preference, and says that Shaukat is settling down well. On the whole his appointment has met with a favourable reception: there are various disruptive elements, instigated to a certain extent by professed, though not always cordially acknowledged, adherents of the Muslim League, but for the time being the Unionist Party seems to be getting on as harmoniously as could be expected.

Akalis have been restive again and have been concentrating their attention on the Kapurthala State where they say the "Patit" [*sic*] Maharaja has been ignoring the rightful claims of the Sikh community. We have been doing whatever we can to prevent this campaign from reaching serious developments, and it is to be hoped that before long it will subside.[8] Akali leaders are, however, likely to search out other avenues for activity in order to keep up their influence with their followers.

I enclose the provincial fortnightly report for the second half of January 1943.

Yours sincerely,
B.J. GLANCY

137

ABELL TO LAITHWAITE

Confidential — Camp,
D.-O. No. G.S.-118 — *February 15th, 1943*

My dear Gilbert,

I am desired to make the usual six monthly report on the Ministers as required by your confidential D.-O. No. 2448-G.G., dated the 17th June 1938.

2. Since the last report was sent Sir Sikander Hyat Khan has died and the resultant vacancy has been filled by the appointment of his eldest son, Major Shaukat Hyat Khan.

3. I attach a note by His Excellency about Major Shaukat Hyat Khan and an addendum for the note on Sardar Baldev Singh forwarded with my last D.-O. No. G.S.-573 of July 4th, 1942.

4. There is nothing new to say about the remaining Ministers.

Yours sincerely,
GEORGE ABELL

ENCLOSURE TO NO. 137

NOTE BY GLANCY

Confidential — *February 13th, 1943*

Major Shaukat Hyat Khan has been appointed to the Cabinet in the vacancy caused by the death of his father. He is only rising 28 and has had no political experience, but he has done well in the Army, was wounded and taken prisoner in Eritrea and was on the staff of the Indian Division in the Middle East. He was educated at the Muslim University School at Aligarh, Government College, Lahore, and the Indian Military Academy. It was largely a sentimental feeling on the part of those who had great admiration for his father that procured his inclusion in the Cabinet. Another factor was the failure of political opinion to combine and support any strong rival. In order to remain a Minister Major Shaukat Hyat Khan will have to obtain election to the Assembly within six months.

Sardar Baldev Singh in much of his work has shown promise as a

Minister. He continues to be satisfactory in the representative sense, as there is a considerable body of Sikh opinion behind him. On the other hand he has been on occasions too easily swayed by certain prominent members of the Akali party and he has shown a tendency to dabble in various matters which he would be better advised to leave alone.

B.J. GLANCY
Governor, Punjab

138

GLANCY TO LINLITHGOW[9]

Telegram

Immediate
Personal
No. 11-G *February 19th, 1943*

Your telegram No. 484-S. about Gandhi's fast.[10] We are taking such precautions as appear appropriate and are in touch with military authorities. So far as we can gauge situation we hope to be able to cope with developments without further outside assistance.

139

GLANCY TO LINLITHGOW[11]

Telegram

Immediate
Personal
No. 12-G *February 20th, 1943*

Your telegram No. 483-S., 18th February, about Gandhi's fast.[12]

Contents have been communicated only to Premier and very limited number of officers whom it is essential to inform.

Arrangements for closure of public offices. I am strongly of opinion that this or any similar action would be of no value and would be regarded as mere hypocrisy apart from being greatly resented by certain communities. I am glad to know that Hope and Twynam share Your Excellency's views in this matter and sincerely trust that all other Governors will agree.

I am also strongly opposed to relaxation of orders regarding processions and meetings in this Province. Processions have been banned for the last two years in all important towns. As to meetings District Magistrates have recently been told to prohibit for period of one month any meetings in public places designed to further Congress objects. This will be interpreted as covering condolence meetings, &c., but no reference will be made in orders issued to Gandhi's fast or death. We consider such meetings will inevitably lead to breaches of the peace and that consequently prohibition is necessary. If any persons wish to express condolence or resort to customary forms of mourning they can hold meetings in religious buildings or organize *hartals*.

140

GLANCY TO LINLITHGOW

Private and Personal — Government House, Lahore,
No. 442 — *March 15th, 1943*

Dear Lord Linlithgow,

Nothing of any outstanding importance has been happening in the Punjab since I sent you my last report. Mr Gandhi's fast gave rise to very little excitement in this Province, though Hindus in the towns were mostly in sympathy with his manoeuvre and many were genuinely distressed by the thought that his demonstration might lead to fatal results. The rest of the population were either indifferent or in some cases derisive, and I think there is no doubt that, if Government had surrendered, their prestige would have been seriously impaired.

The prospects for the coming harvest continue to be most encouraging. The removal of the controlled price for wheat is generally welcomed, grain has been coming into the Mandis in pretty large quantities and the food situation is considerably less alarming than was the case at this time last year. Wheat prices have fallen to about Rs. 9 a maund and it looks as if they will be appreciably lower when the new crop is ready, provided that nothing occurs in the meantime to disturb the market. There are still some who believe that Government intend to reimpose controlled prices and I have seen Press reports of Central Assembly proceedings which rather tend to confirm this impression. If the market is to steady down, it seems to me of great importance that this impression should be removed; I have addressed the Food Department about this point.

There is a fairly strong demand that we should increase our dearness allowance for low-paid Government Servants. We should like to conform as closely as we can to the standard set by the Central Government, from whom we are awaiting an answer to a reference we have made.

The position as regards law and order is on the whole satisfactory. Serious crime has been showing a distinct tendency to decrease and the Police have of late achieved some remarkable successes in the campaign against dacoity in the neighbourhood of Ferozepore.

The Premier has, as you are aware, been attending a Muslim League meeting at Delhi, where he had none too easy a time. Mr. Jinnah would like the Muslim League to have a much greater degree of control over Punjab politics, and he and his lieutenants complain that the Unionist Party in this Province have hitherto only been paying lip service to the League. The Premier acknowledged the general leadership of the Qaid-i-Azam amongst the Muslims of India and referred him to the Jinnah-Sikander Pact[13] – a loosely worded document the purport of which is to the effect that in all-India politics the League is to be regarded as supreme and that the Unionist Party is more or less free to take its own line in the Punjab. Khizar affirmed his adherence to this pact and for the time being this has been accepted. A proposed resolution advocating more active interference by the League in Punjab politics was withdrawn. The Premier has succeeded for the present in blocking the attack, but it seems evident that there are rocks ahead. Jinnah had also some kind words to say about the Punjab Governor's alleged violation of constitutional procedure in failing to consult Muslim Leaguers before taking steps for the appointment of a Premier, and he appears to have been disagreeably surprized when his attention was drawn to the text of the Governor's Instrument of Instructions.

I enclose the provincial fortnightly report for the second half of February.

Yours sincerely,
B.J. GLANCY

141

GLANCY TO LINLITHGOW

Private and Personal
No. 444

Government House, Lahore,
April 17th, 1943

Dear Lord Linlithgow,

Gandhi's fast has receded ingloriously into the background so far as this Province is concerned and minor attempts to work up enthusiasm for Congress manoeuvres have met with no success. I agree entirely with everything that Your Excellency has said on this subject in your private and personal letter of March the 19th. There is no doubt that your firm handling of the situation has had the effect of markedly depressing the level of Congress shares and correspondingly strengthening those of Government. There have been no unfavourable service reactions in the Punjab as far as I am aware, and no difficulties with Hindu officers of the I.C.S. have been brought to my notice.

2. The main threat to our political tranquillity comes from Jinnah and the Muslim League. Shaukat tells me that you were good enough to see him at Delhi just after his interview with Jinnah, and he is most grateful for the encouragement you gave him. Jinnah appears, as you will have gathered, to have been extremely rough and overbearing in his dealings with Shaukat, whom he advised to return to the Army and give up the idea of a Muslim League ticket for the Punjab Assembly, which he could only hope to secure by means of cajolery and underground activities. Jinnah said that Shaukat's appointment as a Minister was an insult to democracy. He seems to have made one curious assertion and that was that according to his information the Governor had been anxious to refer this matter to the Muslim League, but that Khizar and his friends had objected. This balloon was obviously intended to draw Shaukat's fire, but Shaukat, so he tells me, was discreet enough to refrain from comment. Shaukat was not favourably impressed by Jinnah's tirade. He has decided now to stand for the constituency in his own district, Attock, vacated by his kinsman Nawab Muzaffar Khan on appointment to the Provincial Public Services Commission. Shaukat has accordingly applied, in accordance with the terms of the Sikander-Jinnah Pact, for a Muslim League ticket for the constituency concerned. I doubt whether he has been wise in the decision, as the Khattar faction have many enemies in Attock and an election there

is likely to be a costly and uncertain affair; he would have been more prudent in my opinion to have tried for a safer seat which could have been placed at his disposal. Jinnah would seem to have aroused his fighting spirit. The next question is whether the Muslim League Working Committee, to whom Shaukat has sent in his application, will give him the ticket for which he has asked. This Committee, which has taken the place of the Parliamentary Board mentioned in the Sikander-Jinnah Pact, consists of the Nawab of Mamdot as President of the Provincial Muslim League and twenty others – largely men of no importance – whom he has nominated. Most people seem to think that Shaukat will secure his ticket from this strangely constituted body. If he does so, an appeal against the decision will, it appears, lie to Jinnah. The prevalent belief is that Jinnah would not go to the length of turning down a decision of the Committee in favour of Shaukat, but Jinnah's performances are never easy to predict. If Jinnah should take this step, it looks as though an open rupture would be unavoidable. Sir Chhotu Ram is convinced that in this case not more than about a dozen Muslim members would desert the Unionist Party and the position would still remain secure. Khizar is not so sanguine as to the result of a battle with Jinnah unless the point of difference can be narrowed down to a War issue. There is no doubt that the "Pakistan" slogan is gaining in volume, and I fear that there are a fair number of politicians in the Province who would sell the Unionist fort for their own personal advantage. One of the difficulties, as I have mentioned in my last letter, is the loose wording of the Sikander-Jinnah Pact, the more I study this document the less I like it. Unfortunately it is easier for Jinnah to twist the Pact to suit his own convenience than for the Unionist Party; it contains no satisfactory enunciation of the doctrine that the Central Muslim League authorities are expected to refrain from interference in Punjab politics.

3. The Akalis have been somewhat quieter of late. I have had a long talk with Master Tara Singh, who complained that the Sikander-Baldev Singh agreement was not being honoured in the matter of extended facilities for the use of *Jhatka* meat. I told him that action was being taken in this direction in various Government institutions, but that if he pressed for an open pronouncement on the question, he would rouse a counter agitation on the part of Muslims for greater liberty in the matter of beef and would thus defeat any prospect of success. He did not dispute the truth of this, but his main anxiety is to keep himself and his friends in the lime-light and he is also nervous lest some of the Sikh detenus may reproach him for his lack of initiative when they emerge from jails in which *Jhatka* facilities

have not been forthcoming. I also told Master Tara Singh that the Kapurthala campaign was bringing him no credit and that if he went to the length of organizing a *morcha*, the Punjab Government would undoubtedly take firm action. The Kapurthala affair has now been compromised and I hope that it will not break out again; the Maharaja of Kapurthala has not by any means been discrete in all his actions, particularly in paying a rather provocative visit to preside over the prize-giving ceremony at the Khalsa College, Amritsar, when the trouble was at its height. He has been spoken to plainly about this both by the Resident[14] and myself. Akali influence in Patiala has been severely shaken by the removal from office of the Home Minister, Raghbir Singh, and the Inspector-General of Police, Gurdial Singh Dhillon; they are said to be on leave, but unlikely to return. Kirpal Singh Majithia is jubilant about these developments; he is making renewed overtures to the Maharaja of Patiala and says he hopes to build up resistance against the Akalis both in the States and in British India.

4. We have released of late a good many more communists, but their behaviour has been far from satisfactory up to date. The Premier regards them with unqualified distrust, and I must confess that his attitude seems to be well justified.

5. *Rabi* prospects continue to be good, though we have been harrowed by frequent storms and high winds. So far I have heard of no serious damage on a widespread scale. Harvesting has begun, and the yield, if all goes well, should be unusually favourable. The price of wheat now stands at a little over Rs. 9 a maund in the mandis. There should be a further fall before long. Sugar supply arrangements are working more effectively than was the case a little time ago. There are continual clamours for a more liberal supply of standard cloth. Prices of nearly all commodities have been ranging very high and low-paid Government Servants are finding it increasingly difficult to maintain themselves and their families. We have been unable to avoid raising our dearness allowances, but in deference to the wishes of the Central Government we have not extended the benefit to those drawing more than Rs. 100 a month.

6. I enclose the provincial fortnightly report for the second half of March.

Yours sincerely,
B.J. GLANCY

142

GLANCY TO LINLITHGOW[15]

Private and Personal — Government House, Lahore,
[Unnumbered] — *April 26th, 1943*

Dear Lord Linlithgow,

I have seen the reference from the Food Department to which you have alluded in your private and personal letter dated the 18th April.[16] I can assure Your Excellency that the Punjab fully realises its responsibility in this matter and will co-operate in every possible way in reaching and, if possible, exceeding the export targets.

2. I can also assure Your Excellency that I shall keep a careful watch over the scheme in order to ensure the maximum results. Your Excellency will realise that the Punjab has many local difficulties to overcome not the least of which is the leakage of foodgrains through the adjoining States. This falsifies our figures and causes undue strain to the officers who administer our arrangements. I have no doubt that the Food Department will give this matter the attention which it deserves.

Yours sincerely,
B.J. GLANCY

143

GLANCY TO LINLITHGOW

Barnes Court, Simla,
D.-O. No. 448 — *May 15th, 1943*

Dear Lord Linlithgow,

Will Your Excellency kindly refer to your letter of the 7th of May 1943 about the proposal that the Punjab and the Delhi Province should be treated as one territory so far as concerns the movement of grain? I have not yet seen the papers about the modified free trade scheme relating to Bengal, Assam, Bihar, &c., but have asked that they should be put up to me as soon as they are available. As regards the Delhi proposition, I have been inclined to think that the best hope of preventing acute difficulties in the matter of supplies from arising in Delhi later on in the year would have been afforded by keeping as close as possible check on all grain moving into Delhi and on the subsequent activities of dealers. At present, apart from smuggling, a large quantity of grain is moving into Delhi carried by private travellers, who are allowed to take with them as much as 2½ maunds; until recently the limit was as high as 5 maunds. Both these limits were fixed, I am told, by the Central Government authorities without reference to the Punjab, and I should have thought that even the lower figure was considerably too high. I fear that the employment by the Punjab of an inspection establishment working in Delhi would not be likely to produce any practical results. However, I will discuss the matter with the Premier as soon as he comes to Simla. He is expected to arrive here in a day or two and would have come earlier but for the election campaign in Campbellpur. I have been considerably disturbed by the extent to which the price of wheat has risen during the last few days. The most recent quotation that I have seen from Lyallpur ranges from Rs. 11-8-0 to Rs. 11-12-0 a maund. This question I will also discuss with the Premier. I must confess that I had not expected this development, and the solution will be by no means easy.

Yours sincerely,
B.J. GLANCY

144

GLANCY TO LINLITHGOW

Telegram

Immediate
Personal
No. 17-G

May 18th, 1943

Your telegram No. 1193-S. of 17th May about Chhotu Ram's speech.[17] I take same view as Your Excellency of his statements as reported and had marked the case for discussion with Premier as soon as he arrived. He is due to reach here today and after seeing him I will send for Chhotu Ram and speak to him very severely. It is possible that certain sections of the Press may for their own reasons have distorted his remarks but he should in that case have issued repudiation.

145

GLANCY TO LINLITHGOW[18]

Most Secret
D.-O. No. 449

Barnes Court, Simla,
May 20th, 1943

Dear Lord Linlithgow,

Will Your Excellency kindly refer to your most secret letter of the 7th instant about pro-Japanese activities. The only officer whom I have thought it necessary to consult so far is the D.I.G., C.I.D.[19] I will take an opportunity of discussing the question in strict confidence with the Premier and, should he have any views differing from my own, I will let you know without delay. Speaking for myself, I welcome generally the proposals that have been made.

I am in favour of steps being taken to confiscate the property of individuals known to be helping the enemy, and also to stop the payment of family allotments and allowances to dependents in India of men believed to be traitors, provided of course that there are solid grounds for such belief. As to the danger of advertising the existence of the I.N.A., it seems to me that we must reconcile ourselves to the fact that the existence of this so-called Army is widely known through the Japanese Radio, and I do not see that we need hesitate to mention it, provided we stress the fact that it is a term invented by the Japanese for their own nefarious purposes and is very far from representing in fact what it purports to convey.

As regards the penalty for tampering with the loyalty of members of the Services, I think that the maximum penalty should be death. It has been suggested to me that death should be the only penalty. I doubt whether this is practicable, but the wide publication of instances in which the extreme penalty has been exacted should produce a salutary effect. The question of setting up a special Tribunal for the disposal of such cases seems to be worth considering in order to ensure that there is no undue leniency.

I also concur in the proposal that publicity should be given outside the Services, in recruiting areas particularly and in India generally, to punishments inflicted on members of the Services convicted of traitorous conduct.

I am very strongly in favour of an intensified campaign on the part of the National War Front and any other suitable agencies against the Japanese and any who support them. In this Province the public seem to be becoming more and more complacent and they require to be woken up. I think that there would be considerable advantage to be gained from giving as wide publication as possible to instances of Japanese brutality to Indians, both soldiers and civilians, and of the Japanese desecration of places of worship and their other insults to religion.[20]

Yours sincerely,
B.J. GLANCY

146

GLANCY TO LINLITHGOW

Telegram

Immediate
No. 19-G *May 23rd, 1943*

My telegram No. 17-G., May 18th, about Chhotu Ram's reported remarks to Chamars. I have spoken to him and pointed out highly objectionable nature of statements ascribed to him. He says that he has been deliberately and grossly misrepresented by his old enemy the *Tribune* followed by other papers of the same persuasion and that he had contemplated issuing repudiation but did not do so as more correct account of his vernacular speech had appeared in press elsewhere. Premier (group corrupt) told him that it is clearly necessary for impression created to be counteracted and for European members of services to be reassured. He will take occasion when speaking at Tarn Taran in four or five days time to give out that *Tribune's* version is perverse and will do what he can to set the matter right and to assort [?assure] those whose feelings have been injured. He will be accompanied by publicity agent who will send his own version to press. I think this is the best course he can adopt at this stage.

147

GLANCY TO LINLITHGOW

Private and Personal — Barnes Court, Simla,
D.-O. No. 451 — *May 29th, 1943*

Dear Lord Linlithgow,

Tunisia Day was celebrated with much enthusiasm throughout the Punjab.

There was an impressive parade in Lahore and there have been genuine rejoicings in all the main centres in the Province. There is a general feeling of confidence in the forthcoming defeat of the enemy, though Congress-minded papers persist in publishing gloomy articles about the danger from Japan.

The economic situation, however, continues, naturally enough, to arouse considerably more interest than the prosecution of the war. A bumper *rabi* crop has now been gathered in; there were no reports of any serious shortage of agricultural labour, a point about which Your Excellency enquired in your private and personal letter of April the 22nd. But in spite of an excellent harvest my expectation that the price of wheat would fall below Rs. 9 a maund has been far from justified. Just when the price should normally have fallen it advanced to about Rs. 12 a maund at Lyallpur. Since then there has been a slight decline and the market rate is now fluctuating between Rs. 10 and 11. As long as there is a demand for wheat at much higher prices from other parts of India and the belief is held that there is an all-India shortage of grain, there seems little prospect of the Punjab wheat market dropping substantially below its present level. Wheat is, however, now moving into the Mandis in large quantities and we are doing what we can to encourage the flow to continue. There have been loud complaints of high prices in urban areas, where poor people on more or less fixed incomes are finding it increasingly difficult to subsist. At Amritsar there have been demonstrations and considerable restlessness has manifested itself in other places. There is still a marked scarcity of small coin and a persistent clamour for cheap cloth, which we hope will soon be at least partially satisfied. Action taken by the Government of India has led to a sharp fall in the price of gold and silver at Amritsar; speculative stocks have also declined. The National War Front is organizing an intensive war savings campaign.

Locusts have appeared in large numbers, particularly in the north of the Province where we are co-operating with the North-West Frontier authorities in dealing with this menace. No serious damage has so far been reported.

The Muslim League has done nothing sensational during the last month by way of bringing further pressure on the Punjab Ministry. But the "Pakistan" slogan is gaining momentum and there is a general feeling of uneasiness abroad. There has been a considerable amount of discussion in the Press as to whether Jinnah was justified in suggesting that the Punjab Cabinet is a League Ministry. The Nawab of Mamdot (the Provincial Muslim League Leader) has sought to improve the occasion by a Press statement that the Sikander-Jinnah Pact has come to an end, the implication being that more active interference by the Muslim League in Punjab politics is to be expected. As the Punjab Premier announced recently in Delhi that he adhered to the Sikander-Jinnah Pact, and this announcement drew no criticism from Jinnah, the justification for the Nawab's statement is not apparent. He gives out, I am told, that he wrote to the Press entirely on his own initiative, but it seems very doubtful whether this is the truth. The withholding of Gandhi's letter to Jinnah[21] has not caused any great sensation in the Punjab, nor, in view of Jinnah's statement,[22] is this to be expected. Papers like the *Tribune* have naturally done their best to incite Jinnah to regard Government's action as an insult and a direct challenge; they must be disappointed by the results which have attended these manoeuvres up to date. Shaukat, as Your Excellency will have seen, has just been declared successful in the Attock election. He won by a little over 3,000 votes, which coincides almost exactly with his anticipations. It is almost certain that there will be an election petition.

The Khaksars have been making themselves gradually more prominent of late. Though they have not gone to the same length in the Punjab as in certain other Provinces in the matter of parading with *belchas*, they have persisted in wearing badges and appearing in something which closely approaches uniform. It seems clear enough that the Allama has no intention of abiding by his undertaking and that definite action will have to be taken. We are addressing the Government of India on the subject.

The Akali party has been giving us a certain amount of trouble. Master Tara Singh is feeling uneasy and insecure. He has written to the Premier saying that the Sikander-Baldev Singh Pact has not been observed as it should have been and that he contemplates repudiating it altogether. His main grievance relates to *jhatka* meat, though he knows well that facilities in this matter are being extended. The Premier has given Master Tara Singh a soft answer and I much doubt whether the Master Ji has any serious intention of denouncing the Pact. But the Akalis continue to bring pressure to bear on Baldev Singh, which he finds it at times difficult to resist; the result is the obtrusion of communal considerations in matters in which they should be left in the background.

The Police have achieved further notable successes in rounding up dacoits. We are anxious to secure the arrest of a notorious offender called Birju Singh, who conducts his operations largely from Rajputana, and we have written to the Political authorities and asked for their co-operation.

Yours sincerely,
B.J. GLANCY

P.S. – I enclose the Provincial fortnightly report for the first half of May.

148

GLANCY TO LINLITHGOW[23]

Telegram

Immediate
Private and Personal
No. 21-G *May 31st, 1943*

Your private and personal telegram No. 1260-S., May 26th.[24] Withholding of Gandhi's letter to Jinnah has aroused no unfavourable reactions in this Province apart from Congress-minded press which has tried unsuccessfully to stir Jinnah to take offensive. In certain quarters the action taken is welcomed as likely to deflate Jinnah.

149

GLANCY TO LINLITHGOW

Personal
No. 453

Barnes Court, Simla,
June 8th, 1943

Dear Lord Linlithgow,

Will Your Excellency kindly refer to your personal letter of May the 26th, 1943[25] about Khaksar activities? I mentioned this matter briefly in my private and personal letter of the 29th of May, which crossed the letter now under reply. My views are entirely in accordance with those which you have expressed. It is true that in the Punjab Khaksar recrudescence has been comparatively mild and that so far the Allama's most objectionable form of action is to allow his followers to wear circular red badges: a very clear warning has been given him that this practice is a violation of his undertaking and that serious consequences are likely to ensue if it persists. But in some other Provinces, judging by reports received, the Khaksars have gone considerably further and in certain places they have not hesitated to parade with *belchas*. We have written officially to the Government of India on the 29th of May urging that Mashriqi should be told that "the observation of *all* conditions laid down by the Government of India must be enforced by a fixed date in *all* Provinces throughout India and that the penalty for non-observance in *any* Province would be the imposition of an all-India ban."

The Allama has in my opinion shown quite clearly that he has no inclination whatsoever to abide by his promises and he is now trying to manoeuvre himself and his followers into their old position. He has, it would appear, shown no desire to lean up against the Muslim League; in fact he has lost ground with certain Muslim elements by his tendency to admit Hindus and Sikhs into the Khaksar fold. But it is quite possible that he may reorientate his position, should it suit him to do so, in which case it may be considerably more difficult to avoid trouble in dealing with the movement later on. The effect on other communities of allowing this dangerous organisation to regather its strength is also a matter that deserves very serious consideration. I am strongly in favour of firm action without further delay.

Yours sincerely,
B.J. GLANCY

150

GLANCY TO LINLITHGOW

Barnes Court, Simla,
June 18th, 1943

No. 455

Dear Lord Linlithgow,

Will Your Excellency please refer to your letter of the 16th of June about Sir Chhotu Ram's activities in relation to food.[26] I have been equally upset by his alleged statements on this subject, which appear to represent an unholy bid for his own popularity. Several days ago when I first saw the cutting which you have enclosed about there being no possibility of the arrival of Australian wheat, I handed it over to the Premier and said that this advice from Sir Chhotu Ram, if it was correctly reported, was greatly to be deprecated. I told the Premier that apart from other considerations these remarks were quite irreconcilable with an announcement which was recently published to the effect that 64 thousand tons of wheat had arrived in Calcutta; I said that any suggestion that further arrivals were impracticable was calculated to mislead all concerned and might give cultivators very serious cause for regret later on. The Premier said that he would pass this on to Sir Chhotu. The result has been a communication from Sir Chhotu to the vernacular press. I enclose a free translation of an article which appeared in the *Inqilab* of the 13th of this month. Sir Chhotu's advice as embodied in this article, though less outrageous than his remarks as previously reported, is still in my opinion very definitely objectionable. The most mischievous part is his suggestion that zamindars should keep their wheat at home or bring it in minimum quantities to mandis. The concluding portion of his advice is likely to increase the friction between the rural population and those who live in the towns and cities. It would have been more appropriate if Sir Chhotu had said that Government, both at the Centre and in the Province, were giving due consideration to the interests of growers, that a good price was now obtainable, and that growers should not hesitate to bring their grain to the market; any tendency to hoard would detract from the Punjab's War effort and would mean that cultivators could expect little sympathy from any one in hard times to come.

Sir Chhotu is expected to arrive in Simla today and I intend to speak to him together with the Premier tomorrow and point out the error of his ways.[27]

Yours sincerely,
B.J. GLANCY

ENCLOSURE TO NO. 150

CUTTING FROM THE *INQILAB* (LAHORE) OF 13TH JUNE 1943

IMPORT OF WHEAT, PRICES AND CONTROL

Lahore, 11th June 1943 – Sir Chhotu Ram, Revenue Minister, has sent the following statement to the Press:

Some press correspondents and newspapers have a particular mentality and are fond of misrepresenting my speeches. My recent speeches in regard to wheat have been treated in this manner. I therefore wish to give the following correct summary of these speeches:

(1) The Punjab Government has always tried to do its best for the benefit of the zamindars and this policy has been followed in the matter of control (of prices).

(2) The position of the Government of India is that they will not impose any direct control on the price of wheat in mandis, but the purchase of wheat on behalf of other Provinces and of the Military authorities will be carried out through authorized agents. Although no restrictions are imposed on the purchase of wheat by private individuals, export to places outside the Province will only be permitted through these agents.

(3) In special circumstances efforts will be made to import wheat from outside, as was recently done when wheat was brought to Calcutta from Australia. Still in present shipping conditions it does not seem likely that it will be possible to make arrangements for the import of wheat from outside on any large scale.

(4) Until any authoritative announcement is made by Government no reliance should be placed on newspaper headlines regarding import of wheat from Australia and a consequent drop in the prices, as it is just possible that such news may be given by selfish dealers or their agents in order to buy wheat at cheaper rates from the zamindars and sell it to Government and others at higher prices.

(5) If it is possible for the ordinary consumer to purchase wheat at cheap rates, then the zamindar will to a certain extent have the satisfaction of having sold his wheat to poor people, but if the zamindar sells his wheat at cheap rates (to traders) and the consumer has to pay a higher price, then in that case neither the zamindar nor the private consumer nor Government benefits; the benefit goes to the traders.

(6) Sometimes it so happens that when the zamindar takes his cart loaded with wheat into a mandi, a rumour is set afloat that the price of wheat has dropped; consequently the poor zamindar is obliged to sell his wheat at a price lower than the ordinary rate, so that he may be saved the trouble of taking his wheat home. Further, the unnecessary commission, &c., charged in the mandis has not yet been stopped and the old false weights have not yet been replaced; in view of this zamindars would be well advised to sell their wheat at their own homes. Alternatively, there should be some mutual arrangement whereby the despatch of wheat to mandis could be regulated and there was no abundance of it in Mandis, e.g. if only 5 maunds are required in a particular mandi and the quantity sent is 10 maunds, this will naturally tend to reduce the price.

(7) There is little in the agitation carried out by the ordinary wheat consumer, for 80 per cent of the population of this Province are producers of wheat. Among the remaining a majority could afford to purchase wheat at any cost.

Low-paid Government servants or employees of local bodies or factories should be given suitable dearness allowances and able-bodied men should all be able to find work somewhere. Special arrangements should be made for those who are really poor or are unable to work – in villages the zamindar should set apart one seer for each maund of wheat, and in cities rich men like big *Sahukars*, traders, contractors, &c., should contribute to a charity fund, out of which District Officers should purchase wheat and sell it to the poor at reduced rates.

But if any one wishes that the whole burden should be thrown on zamindars, that would be most unreasonable and unjust.

151

GLANCY TO LINLITHGOW

Confidential
No. 456

Barnes Court, Simla,
June 19th, 1943

Dear Lord Linlithgow,

Will Your Excellency kindly refer to my letter of yesterday's date about Sir Chhotu Ram's reported speeches concerning the grain situation?

I had a talk today with the Premier and Sir Chhotu and pointed out that any advice of the kind which Sir Chhotu had been accused of tendering was much to be deprecated, that cultivators in the Punjab had been treated with marked consideration by the Central Government authorities, who had not only agreed to our proposition that grain purchasing transactions should take place to the greatest extent possible in the earlier months of the year so that producers should get the largest measure of benefit, but had expressed their willingness to come to the assistance of cultivators if the price of wheat fell below a certain level; I said that, if cultivators in the Punjab were encouraged to take undue advantage of the present situation, they must naturally expect to suffer from a lack of sympathy when times were bad. I also said that the importation of wheat in large quantities from Australia was, as far as I was aware, by no means an inherently impracticable proposition, but that it would naturally mean a decrease in the amount of shipping available for the transport of war material, &c.; it appeared to me to be quite possible that if the price of grain continued to rise inordinately and the danger of trouble in main centres and war factories grew more acute, Government would decide to bring in wheat from overseas in much greater quantities, but this would detract from the war effort in general and would be far from creditable to the Punjab. Sir Chhotu said that, as usual, he had been sadly misrepresented in the Press. Anything that he had said was due to his desire to prevent cultivators from being cheated by traders who, apart from certain malpractices still continuing in mandis, had spread consistent rumours that wheat was coming from overseas in enormous quantities and that Government purchasing agents no longer desired to buy any more wheat in India. What he had said about Australian wheat was that, though its arrival was quite possible in moderate quantities, he saw no prospect of any very large importations unless circumstances changed. And what he had said about the disposal of grain was by no means intended to discourage growers from selling; he had not suggested to them that they should not place their produce on the market, but merely that they should dispose of it to banias in their own villages unless they had reason to believe that they would get a sale for it in neighbouring mandis. As to prices he had, he said, expressed the opinion in public that anything from Rs. 10 to Rs. 12 a maund would be a reasonable price (he pointed out that the Hapur rate now quoted is well in excess of Rs. 12), and that if they tried to sell at anything exceeding Rs. 12 a maund, this would amount to "positive looting" on their part. With this latter proposition put forward by Sir Chhotu the Premier was inclined to disagree. He expressed the view that any attempt to suggest a reasonable price might have reactions in the contrary direction, and he thought that, while any move to dissuade cultivators from selling was obviously highly objectionable, the market, being a sensitive affair, had best be left to regulate itself; he was inclined to think that any direct call to the growers to bring their produce into mandis might make them suspicious and tend to adopt the contrary course.

Sir Chhotu assures me that he will say nothing and do nothing to discourage cultivators from placing their grain on the market.

Sir Chhotu maintained that, if Government had gone in for forward purchases direct from cultivators before the *rabi* crop was ready, they would have been able to purchase what they liked at not more than Rs. 9 a maund. This system of advance purchases was, as Your Excellency knows, the method that we adopted in Kashmir. Sir Chhotu says that he firmly believes it would be quite practicable in a future year. I think personally that it is at least worth considering.

Yours sincerely,
B.J. GLANCY

152

GLANCY TO LINLITHGOW

Personal
[Unnumbered]

Barnes Court, Simla,
July 3rd, 1943

Dear Lord Linlithgow,

Will Your Excellency kindly refer to my personal letter No. 453 of the 8th of June 1943 about Khaksar activities? The Khaksars have now gone to further lengths in the Punjab in violation of the Allama's assurances. They have recently held a camp in the Sheikhupura district, where they have paraded openly with Belchas and have indulged in military drill and sham fights. Also, we have evidence that the Khaksars have been trying with some success to establish a "cell" in the Police force in the west of the Punjab. We have come to the conclusion that the time has gone by for a further warning to be given to the Allama, as we had originally recommended, and that an all-India ban should be reimposed on the Khaksar movement without delay. We have addressed the Central Government in this sense three days' ago – on the 30th of last month.

I trust that this recommendation will meet with Your Excellency's approval. There is one point that I should like to emphasise, and that is that it seems to me very important that Government should present a firm and united front against the Khaksars. As we have shown in the correspondence with the Central Government, the Khaksars have until recently gone back on their undertakings more flagrantly in other Provinces than in the Punjab. I do not know what the attitude of other Local Governments may be, but I sincerely hope that their views will coincide with ours. Should this unfortunately not be the case, it appears very necessary to avoid giving any impression that one particular Province, or Provinces, is more insistent than others on the suppression of Khaksar activities.[28] If such an impression were to get abroad, the position of the Province or Provinces that have recommended suppression would be most embarrassing; not only would those responsible for the organisation of the movement give trouble, but, as I said in my letter of the 8th of June, it is quite possible that other parties, for instance the Muslim League, might see fit to make use of the occasion. Also the position of the Central Government is likely to be weakened if the Khaksars and their friends are given an indication of the place or places against which the spearhead of their attacks can be best directed.

The recrudescence of the Khaksar movement is causing no little anxiety to other communities, and, unless very early action is taken against them, the effect on the tranquillity of the country and on the War effort is in my opinion likely to be deplorable.

Yours sincerely,
B.J. GLANCY

153

GLANCY TO LINLITHGOW

Private and Personal
No. 457

Barnes Court, Simla,
July 6th, 1943

Dear Lord Linlithgow,

The price of wheat has remained more or less constant during the last few weeks and now stands in the neighbourhood of Rs. 10 a maund. Firms purchasing wheat on behalf of the Central Government have acquired considerably more than the railways seem able to handle. A possible solution of the transport difficulties, so far as moving grain to eastern India is concerned, might perhaps lie in the extended use of river transport on the Ganges, &c.; I have asked our representatives, who are attending the Food Conference at Delhi, to make a suggestion to this effect. Another possible, though more expensive, alternative means of transport might conceivably be found in the diversion of military motor transport learners who are now driving lorries in all directions in the Punjab. We are getting on with the acquisition of Provincial wheat reserves.

The decision of the Central Government to control cloth has resulted in a fall in prices by some 20 to 30 per cent. in the wholesale market in the Punjab, though the drop in the retail market is by no means so pronounced. There are complaints from a good many districts of a shortage of sugar and small change. The supply of fuel also constitutes a serious problem and the outlook in this Province is distinctly depressing, as it appears that we are to lose a whole quarter's allotment.

The Punjab Government propose to increase the dearness allowance for provincial Government servants, the main modification being a 20 per cent. allowance for those drawing pay between Rs. 75 and Rs. 250 a month. We have asked for the views of the Government of India about this. Complaints from provincial Government servants are universal and, as their basic pay is considerably less than that drawn by Central Government servants, it is very difficult to ignore their demand. Pensioners have also been clamouring to be given a dearness allowance; they are certainly in a bad way and there is a precedent for what they ask. We addressed the Government of India in this matter a considerable time ago and have been hoping for a reply.

2. There is a considerable amount of uneasiness in political circles about the intentions of the Muslim League. The Nawab of Mamdot, the head of the Provincial Muslim League, has been down to Karachi to interview Jinnah. He has not given out what was the result of the meeting, but he has paid a visit to Simla and tried without success to induce the Premier to issue another statement making obeisance to the Qaid-i-Azam. The newspapers are full of all manner of reports, including a story that Captain Shaukat Hyat Khan has ambitions to conspire with Mamdot to win the Premiership for himself; I have no reason to suppose that this rumour is in any way well-founded. The orthodox members of the Unionist Party are tired of Mamdot's manoeuvres, and there is some chance of his being replaced by a more trustworthy successor when the Provincial Muslim League election takes place in the autumn; this idea, which it was intended to keep secret, has leaked out in the Press. Mamdot is certainly a nuisance; he is very far from being bright, but there is no doubt that he is mischievous and ambitious. I doubt, however, whether there will be any serious chance of his being replaced, should Jinnah see fit to take an active interest in the provincial election. Jinnah's henchmen are reported to be still trying to acquire a house for him in Lahore.

3. A good deal of unrest and uncertainty prevails in Akali circles. Master Tara Singh has met with opposition from various quarters and Giani Kartar Singh has ceased to be Secretary to the Shiromani Gurdwara Parbandhak Committee. The Akali campaign against Kapurthala continues in rather a desultory way. I have been in touch with the Resident[29] about this and hope that the Maharaja will take a firmer and more consistent line in future.

4. Recruiting for the Army has been deteriorating for some time both in quality and quantity. This is due mainly to exhaustion in the best recruiting areas and also to preoccupation with agricultural pursuits. With prices as they are at present the pay of a sepoy has lost a good deal of its attraction.

5. The Police have been maintaining their successes in the campaign against dacoits and the Faridkot and Nabha Durbars have been co-operating satisfactorily, for which we are duly grateful.

6. I have written a separate letter to Your Excellency about the Khaksars. They are evidently out to give trouble and we are firmly of the opinion

that it will be unwise to defer the reimposition of the ban against this dangerous movement.

7 General Auchinleck's appointment as Commander-in-Chief has met with universal appreciation in the Punjab. The appointment of Lord Wavell as Viceroy has aroused misgivings in Congress circles, who profess to regard this move as a foretaste of repression.

Yours sincerely,
B.J. GLANCY

154

GLANCY TO LINLITHGOW

Barnes Court, Simla,
No. 458 *July 16th, 1943*

Dear Lord Linlithgow,

Will Your Excellency kindly refer to your letter of the 12th of July about the interview which you gave to Shaukat a few days ago? I feel that I must apologise for Shaukat's having troubled you in this way. I think that it was inexcusable for him to raise the subject of the proposed all-India memorial to his father in its present nebulous condition, and the ambitions of Abdul Salim Khan to be appointed to the Political Department. What is still more unforgivable is his having led you to believe that he had come to see you on either of these two matters with my knowledge. I had no knowledge that Shaukat was seeking an interview with you, or I would not have failed to let you know in advance. I have also ascertained that the Premier had no knowledge of Shaukat's intention to ask for an interview at Delhi. Shaukat has, I am sorry to tell you, been developing of a late a most disquieting disregard for the truth and he has been giving us no little anxiety by the indiscretions in which he has indulged. He has just returned to Simla and I am going to speak to him very severely.

I entirely agree with Your Excellency that the Sikander memorial scheme, as it appears to stand at present, is certainly deserving of no backing from the Viceroy. Neither the Premier nor I are in possession of any details as to what is contemplated.

I know nothing of the merits of Abdul Salim Khan, but I am told that he is an Extra Assistant Commissioner on the North-West Frontier cadre. It seems to me quite outrageous that Shaukat should have ventured even to mention this matter in the course of his interview.

Yours sincerely,
B.J. GLANCY

155

GLANCY TO LINLITHGOW[30]

Most Secret and Personal
[Unnumbered]

Barnes Court, Simla,
July 19th, 1943

Dear Lord Linlithgow,

With reference to your most secret and personal letter, dated the 15th July 1943,[31] regarding the possibility of a further fast by Gandhi, I think as regards his detention that any deviation from the course adopted when he last fasted would be undesirable. It would greatly weaken Government's position with non-Congress elements in the country. I further feel that it would be preferable to keep Gandhi where he is rather than move him to Ahmednagar.

2. The question of publicity is more difficult, but I favour controlled publicity from the start. The publicity on the last occasion was, if anything, excessive and I suggest for Your Excellency's consideration that the regular bulletins on Gandhi's state of health which were broadcast on the radio should be omitted if the fast is repeated. I think that these radio broadcasts raise more excitement than the newspaper reports.

Yours sincerely,
B.J. GLANCY

156

GLANCY TO LINLITHGOW

Confidential
No. 460

Barnes Court, Simla,
July 20th, 1943

Dear Lord Linlithgow,

Will Your Excellency kindly refer to your confidential letter of July the 16th, 1943,[32] about suggestions that have been made to the effect that the Punjab Government is now inclined to give preferential treatment to

Muslims at the expense of members of other communities? In my opinion there is no justification whatsoever for any such insinuation, nor so far as I am aware, is there any ground for holding that the Governor, however much he may try to carry the Premier and the Ministry with him, has tended to shirk his special responsibilities in regard to the protection of minorities. It is of course true that there are attempts on the part of the Muslim League to exercise increased pressure on the Ministry and that Khizar is in some respects in a weaker position than his predecessor. But for this, as Your Excellency is aware, Sikander is very largely to blame, as the surrenders which he made, sometimes unnecessarily, to Jinnah have left his successor an unpleasant heritage. It is also true that comments in the Press from time to time seek to give the impression that a particular community is being treated with unfairness or injustice; Hindu, Sikh and Muslim newspapers all like to indulge in this habit, however flimsy the excuse. I do not know whether Your Excellency's interviewers have made any specific allegations, but should this be the case, I will of course be glad to supply any information that may be required. My own experience leads me to the view, which I have reason to believe is shared by senior European officers in the Punjab, that Khizar has shown no kind of communal partiality in regard to appointments. I think in fact that he is singularly free from communal bias. Perhaps it is worth while mentioning one instance, the only occasion on which, so far as I remember, I have had any serious difficulty in regard to an undue preference shown by the Ministry for a Muslim candidate. This instance occurred in Sikander's time towards the end of last year. A very senior appointment in the Irrigation Branch was about to fall vacant and Chhotu Ram in sending up the file to Sikander suggested that they should both talk over the matter in the usual way with the Governor. Sikander, however, chose, strangely enough, to content himself with a discussion with Chhotu, and the result was that the papers came to me with a note saying they had come to the conclusion that the appointment should go to a certain Muslim officer. There was no doubt that this particular officer was unfitted for the post and I had to have a serious talk with Sikander on the subject. The question had not finally been decided by the time Sikander died. When Khizar took over, there was no further difficulty; both he and Chhotu Ram agreed readily to the appointment of a European officer, who was obviously the right man for the post. I am not suggesting that Sikander was communally-minded, but I fear that his better judgement was at times overborne by pressure from outside.

As to the nervousness caused among Sikhs and other minority

communities by the 'Pakistan' slogan, I fear there is no doubt that a certain degree of uneasiness does exist both in non-official and official quarters. We have been very considerably embarrassed of late by certain untoward remarks made by Shaukat Hyat Khan in regard to "Pakistan" and the Muslim League in the course of his recent tour; he has now been recalled to Simla and taken very sternly to task by Khizar, and he is now publishing an explanation in the Press which, though I am afraid it does not ring convincingly, may go some way towards counteracting the mischief that he has done.

I am sending you an appreciation[33] of the various members of the Ministry in which I have touched on this unpleasant incident.

Yours sincerely,
B.J. GLANCY

157

BRANDER TO LAITHWAITE

Secret
D.-O. No. G.S.-441

Barnes Court, Simla,
July 21st, 1943

Dear Gilbert,

As desired in your confidential d.-o. letter No. 2448-G.G., dated the 17th June 1938, I enclose a note recorded by His Excellency on the Punjab Ministers.

Yours sincerely,
G. BRANDER

ENCLOSURE TO NO. 157

NOTE BY GLANCY

Secret

Barnes Court, Simla,
July 21st, 1943

Lieut.-Colonel Malik Khizr Hayat Khan Tiwana: He has now worked as Premier for about six months and he has had an extremely difficult row to hoe. The untimely death of his predecessor, Sir Sikander, and the reconstruction of the Cabinet naturally caused considerable dislocation and gave rise to not a little disappointment and heartburning among certain members of the Unionist Party who aspired to a post in the Ministry. In Muslim circles, both inside and outside the Punjab, the slogan of Pakistan has been gradually gaining ground: Jinnah is more anxious than ever to dominate the politics of the Punjab and is constantly on the watch for a chance to disrupt the Unionist Ministry: a fair number of Muslim Unionists are ready from personal motives to enrol themselves under Jinnah's banner and give trouble to the Premier. Khizr has been blamed in other quarters, because he attended the Muslim League meeting at Delhi and made his bow to the Qaid-i-Azam. But he went no further than his predecessor in his professions and all that he conceded in effect was his adherence to the "Sikander-Jinnah Pact",[34] a document which, in spite of its deplorable looseness, appears to have been designed to prevent Jinnah from active interference in provincial politics, while acknowledging the supremacy of the League in all-India affairs. It is not apparent that Khizr could have done less than this unless he was prepared to challenge the Qaid-i-Azam to open conflict. Khizr's considered view is that he might successfully do battle with Jinnah if he could choose his own battle-ground, for instance the War Effort, or if Jinnah should make a patently false move, but that it would be unwise at present to provoke a clash without very good reason: the danger of Jinnah's professing to unfurl the green flag of Islam is obvious and it is very doubtful how many of the Unionist Muslims would have the hardihood to resist the pressure of this manoeuvre. One of Khizr's main difficulties of course is the absence of any convincing battle-cry with which to rally his followers. He has no inclination to imitate Congress tactics and clamour for the independence of India, nor to abase himself to Jinnah and cry aloud for Pakistan. The pro-zamindar campaign of the Unionist Party with its concomitant agrarian legislation has for the present more or less exhausted itself: this is not on all accounts to be deplored, but whatever cohesive effect it has exercised on the majority of the Party has been gradually evaporating. The War Effort and the interests of Punjabi soldiers still help to provide the machine with a certain amount of fuel, but, as danger from the enemy has receded, this factor has become less potent than before.

There is no denying that Khizr lacks the experience and political agility of his predecessor, but he is in many respects a firmer character. He has a most attractive personality and he is very pleasant to work with. He is shrewd, even-tempered and blessed with a sense of humour. Though he is at heart an aristocrat and something of a reactionary, he keeps his prejudices in the background and is in my opinion essentially fair-minded. He has shown no signs of communal bias. His application to business is apt to flag at times, but this is largely due to his health which is not all that one could desire.

Sir Chhotu Ram: There is little to add to what has already been recorded. He is unquestionably a man of great ability and he has continued to work devotedly for the advancement of the agricultural classes. He has controlled effectively the departments in his charge. He was born a zealot, and a zealot he will die. His dislike of Banias and moneylenders is quite ineradicable. He has little, if any, regard for the feelings of others, and in his public speeches, which on normal occasions take the form of vernacular harangues lasting for several hours, he is frequently indiscreet and gratuitously offensive. This is unfortunately an inherent defect in his composition, and though there appeared at one time to be some hope that he would endeavour to cultivate a greater degree of self-control, his recent performances have belied this expectation. He has lately incurred wide-spread and well-justified criticism, because the advice which he has given to cultivators has been calculated to make them discontented with the high prices now prevailing and to withhold their grain from the market. He has undertaken to abstain from tendering such advice in future, and it is to be hoped that he will do so. There is this much to be said in explanation of his conduct that when it was authoritatively announced by the Central Government last year that the basic maximum price for wheat would remain at Rs. 5 until the new harvest was ready, Sir Chhotu advised cultivators to sell in accordance with this declaration: when conditions became unhappily complicated, eventually leading to the abolition of controlled prices, Sir Chhotu came in for considerable criticism from those who had reason to regret their acceptance of his advice.

Sir Chhotu Ram is naturally in favour of the survival of the Unionist Party. When Sir Sikander died last December he was not misled by any personal ambition into seeking the Premiership for himself. His behaviour was helpful and correct and he has loyally supported the leader of the Ministry.

Sir Manohar Lal: He continues to prove a highly successful Finance Minister, though he can scarcely claim the credit for bounteous rains and abnormally favourable prices. A courteous and benevolent gentleman by nature, his tendency is to avoid all unnecessary controversy, and retire from the scene of action when storms are threatening. Of late this tendency has, I am glad to say, been less marked. Since the new Premier has assumed office he has made a habit of consulting Sir Manohar informally on frequent occasions, and the Finance Minister shows signs of becoming less diffident in the expression of his views.

Mian Abdul Haye: There is nothing new to say about this Minister. He is intelligent enough, but his administration of his departments is erratic and inspires no great degree of confidence. He has little, if any, political backing. But, so far as I can judge, he has been loyal and helpful in supporting his Premier against assaults from without: if the Unionist Party were to collapse, there would be no serious chance of his finding a seat in another Ministry. His health has recently given some cause for anxiety.

Sardar Baldev Singh: He has a fair measure of natural sagacity combined with the experience of a successful businessman. But it cannot be said that he has yet found his feet as a Minister. Though not a professed Akali himself, he owes his seat on the Cabinet to the support of the Akali party and he is seldom able to stand up against the dictation of Master Tara Singh and his henchmen, even when he knows that their injunctions are ill-advised. In consequence he is in effect the most communally-minded of all the Ministers; he allows communal considerations to obtrude themselves when no kind of regard should be paid to them, and, when challenged, he has no hesitation in saying that he will find it hard to defend himself from personal criticism if he pursues a different line of action. He is still young and he appears to be taking a greater interest in his work. It is to be hoped that he will develop a greater sense of independence.

Captain Shaukat Hyat Khan: He owes his present position to the fact that he is the son of the late Premier: there was unfortunately no competitor of outstanding merit for the post of Public Works Minister which fell vacant when Sikander died and Khizr succeeded to the Premiership, and it appeared that the selection of Sikander's son would cause the minimum of disruption in the Unionist Party. But Shaukat has done nothing so far to justify his choice. He has shown himself to be foolish, conceited and strikingly prone to prevarication. Though he was roughly treated by Jinnah, he appears now to have concluded that complete subservience to Jinnah gives him the best chance of a successful career. His speeches in the course of his recent tour, from which he has been summarily recalled, have caused grave embarrassment to the Premier and given rise to much uneasiness in the minds of Minority communities. Shaukat is only 28 years old, and he has only been a few months in office. Perhaps it is too early as yet to judge him, but it will be a matter for surprise if he ever makes good. There are some who explain his conduct by the fact that he is both the nephew and the son-in-law of Mir Maqbul Mahmud, a political acrobat who is perhaps more universally distrusted than any other of his kidney in the North of India.

B.J. GLANCY
Governor of the Punjab

158

GLANCY TO LINLITHGOW

Barnes Court, Simla,
No. 462 *July 23rd, 1943*

Dear Lord Linlithgow,

Many thanks for Your Excellency's letter of the 20th of July about Shaukat. I have spoken to him very severely about his vagaries and so has the Premier. As to his interview with you, he asserted that I had misunderstood him and that he had really told me that he meant to seek an interview with you; I have no recollection whatsoever of his ever having mentioned the subject. He also said that you had misunderstood him about the Sikander memorial and that all that he had asked you to do was to subscribe to the memorial as a private individual.[35] It was fairly apparent from what he said afterwards, however, that he was prevaricating. The trouble about Shaukat, as Khizar remarked the other day, is that everyone who talks to him is represented as having misunderstood what he says. As to the Sikander memorial, he seemed uncertain whether the target he was aiming at was a crore or 50 lakhs; the object in view is, he says, to fund the proceeds and distribute the annual interest to deserving soldiers or their families. Until the project is defined and it is known how the money is to be administered, it is clearly inadvisable to encourage the idea.

As to the other subject which he mentioned to you, his excuse is that his father had discussed with you the desire of Shaukat's brother-in-law to be taken into the Political Service; I have no knowledge whether Sikander ever actually mentioned this matter to you. I have made it clear to Shaukat that it was improper of him to have mentioned either of these subjects in his interview with you. I do not think that he will expect anything in the nature of a reply from you.[36]

Yours sincerely,
B.J. GLANCY

159

GLANCY TO LINLITHGOW

Barnes Court, Simla,

[Unnumbered] *July 29th, 1943*

Dear Lord Linlithgow,

Will Your Excellency kindly refer to your letter of the 12th of July in answer to mine of July 6th? I have been meaning to write to you about paragraph 2 of your letter, which relates to the Food Conference recently held in Delhi, but the official record[37] of the Conference seems to have taken some considerable time to prepare, and I have only seen a copy a few days ago. Possibly the proceedings have been watered down, though they purport to be a verbatim account of what was actually said, but from the record as it stands I have not been able to find the reference to any outspoken protest which Sir Chhotu Ram's remarks elicited, nor indeed any proposal of his that the very maximum prices should be ensured for the grower. Sir Chhotu gave me to understand that what he tried to press for was that the grower should be given a "fair" price, though not by any means the maximum; in conversation with me he has maintained again that he thinks that anything exceeding Rs. 12 a maund would be an excessive price for the grower to obtain, though he certainly appears to have given no kind of indication at the Conference that this was his view. His equilibrium appears to have been upset by the fact that the wheat price in the United Provinces just across our border has been ranging at something approaching 50 per cent. higher than the Punjab market rate. Also I see that he raised certain rather embarrassing questions (page 39 of the proceedings) with reference in particular to the policy which seems to have been adopted by the Government of Bengal. It was, I see, admitted by Mr. Suhrawardy[38] that the Bengal Government were selling at Rs. 15-8-0 to their mills. But the information given to me, not exclusively by Sir Chhotu Ram, is to the effect that this did not represent the whole story and that at about the time when the Conference took place the Bengal Government were allowing as much as Rs. 4 a maund for milling charges and that after a further addition of Re. 1 or so a maund they were giving out wheat to the consumer at not less than Rs. 20 a maund. Sir Chhotu Ram was apparently bitten with the idea that, if such practices were regarded as permissible elsewhere, an additional benefit might perhaps be arranged either for the Punjab grower or the Provincial Government.

In discussion with me after the Conference took place he was disposed to argue that the action of the Bengal Government represented a loss to the Punjab cultivator. I have pointed out to him that, even assuming his information is correct, the sufferer is not the up-country grower but the Bengal consumer. I believe that he now realises that this view is correct.

I have not been able to understand what General Wood[39] meant by his remarks recorded at page 51 of the Conference proceedings: "My view of the recommendations about price control is that price control is easy when we have physical control over the stocks. *Let us not repeat the mistake that the Punjab made last year.*" So far as I am aware, the Punjab did its best to carry out the policy laid down by the Central Government last year, and the main difference between the action taken by the Punjab Government and that adopted by certain other Provinces was that in the Punjab we continued to keep our authorised rates at the Lyallpur Centrally-fixed Rs. 5 a maund plus freight, whereas in certain other Provinces authorized rates were allowed to rocket.

As regards the main result of the Conference, my own personal view is that the decision to abstain from a further modification of the system of control over movements was eminently sound. I feel little doubt that if the "free trade" areas had been expanded, there would have been a tidal wave of high prices up the Ganges and up the Jumna, giving us all grave embarrassment up-country without any lasting benefit to deficit Provinces. I have very considerable sympathy with the plea with which Sir C.P. Ramaswami Iyer concluded his remarks (page 8 of the Conference proceedings). Sir Chhotu Ram, I see, expressed views in favour of what he called "Qualified" free trade; he does not appear from the proceedings to have been asked for an explanation of what he meant, but he tells me that his idea was that the existing restrictions on the movements of grains from one province to another should continue, but that permits might be granted more freely to private traders. Personally I think that Government should be very chary about granting any such permits unless they are sure where the grain is going and for what purpose it is going to be used.

Also I am very strongly inclined to adhere to the recommendation which I urged at Delhi in January last about the importation of wheat from overseas. It appears to me that such import would provide the most hopeful means of reducing the price of grain in the country generally to a reasonable level. I do not think it would be necessary to import on anything approaching a gigantic scale, but a well-advertized demonstration or series of demonstrations that Government were in a position to build up and increase supplies in this manner should, I think, help very materially in inducing both growers and dealers to moderate their ambitions. It would no doubt be regrettable that shipping, which might otherwise be reserved for purely military material, should be diverted in this way, but in the long run this would, it appears to me, be preferable to a serious risk of stoppages in factories and possible outbreaks of unrest.

The last thing I have to say, before apologizing for the length to which this letter has run, is that Sir William Roberts, who has been helping the Punjab Government in an honorary capacity over our food and price problems during the last year, has, he tells me, written to General Wood offering, now that his work with us is coming to an end, to place his services free of charge at the disposal of the Government of India. It appears to me that this offer is well worth considering. He has been of very great help to the Punjab and has in a private capacity gained experience of market conditions over a large number of years.

Yours sincerely,
B.J. GLANCY

160

GLANCY TO LINLITHGOW

Private and Personal
No. 465

Barnes Court, Simla,
August 6th, 1943

Dear Lord Linlithgow,

Increased activities by Muslim Leaguers have led to further uneasiness in Ministerial and political circles. Captain Shaukat Hyat Khan's unpardonably indiscreet references to "Pakistan" in the course of his recent tour came near to bringing matters to a head. His perambulations, as you are aware, have now been brought to an abrupt conclusion, but he has done enough to show that little, if any, reliance can be placed on his loyalty to his Leader. He has not entirely made up his mind whether to pose as the Repentant Sinner or the Injured Innocent: in the latter role he is sadly unconvincing and has met with no official applause. League newspapers, incited by Shaukat's vagaries, clamour more loudly than ever for a declaration that the Unionist Party is at an end, and a mischievous and unedifying controversy has been raging round the question whether the party in power is a creation of the League or a Coalition or a combination or merely a Union. There is a general demand that the Premier should come out into the open and make his position clear. It seems likely that he will be driven to do so as the result of the forthcoming Muslim League meeting at Delhi. The Premier is, I gather, determined to take his stand on the Sikander-Jinnah Pact and to insist on retaining the term "Unionist" or "Unionist Coalition" (both of which expressions figure in the Pact) as the correct designation of his Party. His intentions are likely to be indicated to Jinnah before the meeting takes place. If Jinnah adopts a moderate line and decides not to force the issue, the existing truce may continue indefinitely. But, if he is set on pressing for outright subservience to the Muslim League, it is quite on the cards the Premier will conclude that his correct course is to resign, rather than see his Muslim followers gradually fading over into opposition under stress of promises and threats. I most sincerely hope that Jinnah's intransigence will not bring matters to this pass. It may be unlikely enough that his supporters could at present succeed in working up a majority in the Punjab Assembly, but each of the main communities as represented in the House contains a fairly large proportion of unstable elements, and in many cases it would be rash to assume that public interest would prevail over personal considerations. Even if it be taken for granted that the deadlock would be of short duration and would eventually result in the return of stragglers to the Unionist fold, it is disquieting to think that a pre-eminently Muslim Government, which, whatever its defects, has carried on for so many years with reasonable efficiency, should now collapse through the machinations of the Qaid-i-Azam and be replaced by a system of administration set up under Section 93 of the Act.

2. The Congress party have shown very little liveliness of late and there is not much prospect of their successfully staging any serious disturbances in the Punjab on the approaching anniversary of last year's sensational adventure. Precautions have, however, been taken, and Railway security measures are being brought into force in the south-east of the Province. The Hindu Press has naturally displayed considerable anxiety about the chances of the Ministry subordinating themselves to the Muslim League, and there have been various attempts to effect a better understanding between Hindus and Sikhs.

3. The Akalis have been busy defending their position against assault. Master Tara Singh and Giani Kartar Singh have visited Simla and I have had a fairly long talk with them. It appears that, in spite of their almost incessant complaints that the Sikander-Baldev Pact is being disregarded, they realise that much has been done in fulfilment of its intentions. A statement has been made by Master Tara Singh that his party will have

nothing to do with a Muslim League Ministry, but it is a matter of opinion how far he would abide by this declaration if offered a substantial inducement to march in the opposite direction. His main interest is centred at present in a Bill for the Amendment of the Gurdwaras Act whereby he hopes that he and his associates on the Shiromani Gurdwara Parbandhak Committee will acquire control of revenues now in the hands of various Local Committees and will be allowed in the alleged interests of the Panth an increased degree of latitude in the general disposal of religious funds.

4. Khaksar activities have not by any means subsided. Allama Mashriqi has given his followers instructions purporting to indicate his intention to take heed of the warning recently conveyed to him, but it is sufficiently evident that he still means to preserve his irregular army as a distinctive organization ready at any favourable opportunity to menace and disrupt the peace of the country. The Khaksars have of late fallen further from grace with the Muslim community in general because of their manoeuvres to bring about an understanding between Gandhi and Jinnah, and because the miscreant who is reported to have made an attempt on Jinnah's life was a former adherent of the Khaksar cause. It seems unlikely that drastic action against the Khaksars would at the present juncture arouse any appreciable degree of resentment in other quarters.

5. The economic situation remains substantially unchanged. The price of wheat in the main centres shows a slight, though not a marked, tendency to rise; it is still some 40 to 50 per cent. below the price in the United Provinces. Large quantities of grain are lying in the Mandis, but difficulties in the matter of railway transport have not yet permitted of export to anything like the extent contemplated by the Food Department. We have agreed to our rice exports being increased beyond the quota originally fixed. There appears to he a fairly widespread belief in certain quarters that the Punjab is largely to blame for the scarcity prevailing in other parts of India. I see, for instance, that Mr. Haridas Madhodas the President of the Indian Merchants Chamber, is reported in the *Civil & Military Gazette* of the 5th of August to have levelled against Sind, the Punjab and the U.P. accusations of profiteering or of adopting a policy of reprehensible selfishness. The same issue of this periodical contains a brief statement aimed at refuting these charges so far as the Punjab is concerned. This statement goes on to make allegations against the Bengal Government which, so far as I have been able to ascertain, approximate to the truth. I have written separately to Your Excellency about this matter and we are also in correspondence with the Central Government. If it is correct that the Bengal Government have been making a profit of some 6 or 7 rupees

a maund on wheat supplied to the public, it seems to me to be highly advisable that this practice should be stopped. Apart from any question of morality, there is an obvious danger of contagion. If it is known or believed that one Provincial Government is adding to its revenues through the sale of grain produced elsewhere, there is bound to be a clamour that others further afield should be given a share in such dubious transactions, and in this way the general situation may deteriorate still further.

6. We hope in the course of the next few weeks to receive our share of standard cloth for the last three months. Prices of cloth are easier than they were. Fuel difficulties are disquieting and in this respect the outlook both in the immediate future and from a long-range point of view is distinctly gloomy.

7. Serious crime in the Province continues to show a welcome decrease. The Police have been commendably successful in their campaign against dacoits and deserters. Birju, the notorious dacoit who has been responsible for a large number of offences, has recently been arrested in the Jaipur State; it is to be hoped that on this occasion he will not fail to receive his due reward.

8. The monsoon started late, but during the last week or two has been doing its best to make up for lost time. In most parts of the Province agricultural prospects are favourable.

Yours sincerely,
B.J. GLANCY

161

GLANCY TO LINLITHGOW

Private and Personal
No. 467

Barnes Court, Simla,
August 25th, 1943

Dear Lord Linlithgow,

Will Your Excellency kindly refer to your private and personal letter of the 17th of August 1943 about the wheat position?[40]

We will do our best to help in setting right the situation, and I entirely agree that no useful purpose will be served by indulging in recriminations about the past. Transport arrangements have, I am glad to say, very markedly improved and despatches are now taking place on a very considerable scale. We are enlarging our staff. Khizar, as you will no doubt have seen has come out with a statement urging all growers, both large and small, to bring their grain to market. I hope that this appeal will assist in producing the desired effect.

There are two points which regard to the future which I venture to press again. Firstly, I continue to believe that nothing will produce so steadying a result throughout the country as a well-advertized series of demonstrations that grain can be brought in from overseas in large quantities, and I sincerely hope that it will be possible to make some announcement about this before long. Secondly, I hope very earnestly that if the Bengal Government have not already been deterred from making a profit out of grain supplied from upcountry, very early steps will be taken in this direction and that the public will be informed. I have pointed out repeatedly to all and sundry that the sufferer from such manoeuvres is not the upcountry grower but the Bengal consumer. It may be said that this is logically a sufficient argument, but the fact remains, as I have said before, that if any Government is known or believed to behave in this way, the temptation to others to follow suit is difficult to remove. It would, I am convinced, produce a very wholesome effect if the public could be assured that such highly questionable practices had been brought to an end.

Yours sincerely,
B.J. GLANCY

162

GLANCY TO LINLITHGOW

Private and Personal — Barnes Court, Simla,
No. 468 — *September 7th, 1943*

Dear Lord Linlithgow,

Accounts of the distress prevailing in Bengal have awakened a markedly sympathetic response in all sections of the Press in this Province and several moves have been made by charitable associations and others to organize relief. The Premier in response to the first appeal which he issued on behalf of Bengal sufferers received a long telegram from Suhrawardy of the Bengal Ministry, conveying his thanks and quoting figures calculated to prove that the Bengal Government were no longer making any kind of profit from the sale of food grains; this was followed up by a letter giving further information. Though the figures were not convincing in all respects, the Premier has agreed to issue a further appeal to the effect that the Bengal authorities have expressed their gratitude and have given an assurance that no profit now accrues to official agencies through the sale of food grains: consequently doubts should now be dispelled, and there should be no hesitation in bringing grain to the market. It is to be hoped that this further appeal will help in producing the desired effect. I think it would be of considerable assistance if the Central Government would come out with a clear statement saying that they have satisfied themselves that the sale price in Bengal is reasonable and admits of no profit to the Provincial Government. About 120 wagons of grain, mostly wheat, have lately been leaving the Punjab daily, and efforts are being made to increase the flow. The amount of wheat (excluding "wheat products") which under the Revised Basic Plan we are still due to despatch for *Civil Requirements* elsewhere is, according to the latest figures available, some 185,000 tons. Out of this amount 59,000 tons have been purchased. The quantity still to be purchased for Civil Requirements outside the Province thus comes to 126,000 tons. Practically no purchases have been effected lately and it looks as if the Ceiling Price should be raised by eight annas[41] or so a maund if the flow is to be maintained. Prices have been rising slightly, but not markedly. As to *Military Requirements*, the amount still to be purchased stands, according to the latest figures available, at 339,000 tons. A limiting factor in speeding up military transactions is the capacity of the mills with which the military purchasing agents deal: they can only cope with about 1,200 tons a day and storage is a serious difficulty.

2. One of the consequences of the Cotton Cloth and Yarn Control Order is that dealers have become apprehensive that they will be put to loss by Standard Cloth transactions. The Provincial Government have now guaranteed agents and retail dealers against any such losses. The intention is to distribute cloth through retail dealers appointed by Government agency for the next period.

3. The Nawab of Mamdot and certain other Muslim Leaguers have been working to maintain pressure on the Unionist Government to accept the ascendancy of the League. The Premier hopes to make informal contact with Mr. Jinnah in the course of the next few days and to ascertain whether he is determined to force the issue when the meeting of the Central Muslim League takes place next month.

4. The Khaksar movement shows tendencies of going underground; it is by no means dead and still remains a menace to peace. Allama Mashriqi has been indulging in a series of unbridled statements scarcely calculated to conciliate Mr. Jinnah. His latest fantasy is a declaration that he has good reason to suppose that the attack on the Qaid-i-Azam was organized by the Unionist Party. Bahadur Yar Jang, who passed through the Punjab

the other day, has openly expressed the opinion that Allama Mashriqi is too irresponsible to control the Khaksar organization and that he should resign. There appear to be many others who hold the same view and it seems not unlikely that the Allama's resignation may actually take place.

5. Sikh politics have become, if possible, more confused than ever, Master Tara Singh and his main lieutenants have aroused a considerable volume of opposition by their advocacy of the doctrine of "Azad Punjab". This opposition is being voiced in particular by two organizations led respectively by Sant Singh, M.L.A. (Central) and Baba Kharak Singh. But Master Tara Singh and the Akalis are in a strong position owing to their control of Gurdwara funds, and, if the Gurdwara Amendment Bill is passed, the dice will be loaded still more heavily in their favour.

6. Congress supporters are inactive. No serious trouble occurred anywhere in the Punjab to mark the anniversary of last year's upheaval.

7. We have of late released another batch of some twenty members of the Communist Party. The Communists have certainly been behaving more reasonably during the last month or two and it is to be hoped that these releases, though they undoubtedly involve some risk, will be justified by the results.

Yours sincerely,
B.J. GLANCY

163

GLANCY TO LINLITHGOW

Barnes Court, Simla,

No. 469 *September 16th, 1943*

Dear Lord Linlithgow,

Will Your Excellency kindly refer to your letter of the 14th of September 1943, in which you have asked about the outcome of the Premier's talks with Jinnah? From the account which Khizar has given me the meeting can scarcely be described as in any way conclusive. The conversations lasted for hours and hours, but most of the time was taken up by a series of lectures from Jinnah about the services that he had rendered to mankind and by a reconstruction of the attack made on him recently by his Khaksar assailant. Khizar did not succeed for a long time in getting Jinnah to come to the point and even then the Qaid-i-Azam was as evasive as possible. It seems clear that Jinnah is set on obtaining mastery for the League over the

Punjab Ministry as soon as this can be achieved, and one interesting point that emerged was that Jinnah did not seem to be at all perturbed by the possibility of a Section 93 administration in the Punjab; in fact he expressed the view that this might help to rally Muslims in the Punjab, as had been the experience in the North-West Frontier Province. Khizar made it plain, he tells me, that he intended to abide by the Sikander-Jinnah Pact and to maintain the name "Unionist" or "Unionist Coalition" for the Punjab Ministry. Jinnah showed no sign of wishing to denounce the Pact, provided of course that he could interpret it entirely in his own way. He maintained that the Unionist Party had ceased to exist when the Pact was drawn up, and when Khizar pointed out that he himself was returned to the Assembly on the Unionist ticket, Jinnah was much incensed and the meeting nearly came to an abrupt end. However, they seem to have parted outwardly as friends. It seems fairly clear that Jinnah will stage an attack on the Punjab Ministry before very long, but the precise moment which he will choose is still obscure.

Khizar and Sir Chhotu and Sardar Baldev Singh are proceeding to Delhi today in deference to Your Excellency's wishes to discuss the food problem, but I do not suppose that you will have time to give Khizar a separate interview. The Premier and his colleagues all say that they are ready to do what they can in organizing a campaign to induce growers to bring their grain to the mandis, but they think that they are much more likely to be effective in this direction if by means of action taken by the Central Government the Punjabi can be definitely assured that the Bengal authorities have ceased to make a profit out of the sale of foodstuffs; there is undoubtedly a good deal of strong feeling about this abroad in the Punjab and of this I believe that Sir J.P. Srivastava[42] is fully aware.

Yours sincerely,
B.J. GLANCY

164

GLANCY TO LINLITHGOW

Private and Personal — Barnes Court, Simla,
No. 470 — *September 30th, 1943*

Dear Lord Linlithgow,

Will Your Excellency kindly refer to your private and personal letters of the 27th and 29th instant about the grain position? Since the first of these letters was written I have had the benefit of a further discussion with you and you have given an interview to the Punjab Premier.

As regards the first paragraph of your letter of the 27th, the point that I endeavoured to make is this. The Premier and his colleagues are only too willing to launch a further crusade in amplification of the appeals already made by the Premier urging growers to place their grain on the market. If this crusade is to produce the maximum effect, it seems desirable that it should contain arguments which have not been stressed already. I accordingly suggested that the Ministers should be placed in a position (*a*) to declare on the authority of a statement made by the Central Government that no profit of any kind was accruing to the Bengal Government directly or indirectly on transactions connected with the disposal of grain imported into that Province, and (*b*) to point to the fact that the importation of grain into India from outside was actually proceeding on a definitely substantial scale.

As to (*a*), I am not personally in favour of any official reference whatever being made to the actual profits that Bengal may have secured hitherto. It may be true, as Sir J.P. Srivastava is said by both the Premier and Sir Chhotu Ram to have informed them, that the Bengal authorities admit to having made a profit of Rs. 33 lakhs, apart from milling proceeds, on grain brought in from the North but I cannot see the slightest advantage in giving out sensational and disturbing information of this kind. All that seems to me necessary is a statement by the Central Government that they have satisfied themselves that the Bengal authorities are now making no profit whatsoever on these transactions, but are actually incurring a loss: this might perhaps be coupled with an assurance that any past profits will be more than absorbed by the result of present and future transactions, but this addition might well be omitted or deferred if it is likely to cause delay. A statement of this kind is, I consider, most eminently desirable, because the vagaries of the Bengal Government are the subject of repeated comment in the Press and on every side. They will provide, until it is definitely known that they have come to an end, a most cogent argument for those who say, however, reprehensibly – if Bengal, the seat of the famine, is selling imported grain at a profit, why should the up-country grower and dealer abstain from charging a higher price?

As to (*b*) – the importation of grain into India from outside, I hope that the announcement will not be long delayed. I have, as Your Excellency is aware, been repeatedly urging this policy for a long time back as the most effective method of steadying prices. I do not deny that the diversion of shipping to this purpose is to be regretted, but it seems to me to be unavoidable. Now that India stands deprived of her normal rice supplies from Burma, it would scarcely appear strange that even in wartime such steps as are practicable should be taken to provide a substitute from overseas. Such higher military authorities out here with whom I have been able to discuss matters do not seem inclined to dissent from this proposition. I drew Your Excellency's attention the other day to the advice contained in the Confidential Bi-Weekly Guidance Notes on the War Situation, dated September 25th, 1943, which I have lately received from Delhi – the passage runs: "Point out serious concern of British Parliament over food situation in India and the fact that His Majesty's Government are giving full assistance by way of facilitating import of food-stuffs into India." If this advice is, as I presume, authoritative, a public statement would appear to be free from objection. I am convinced that if this action is taken and if continuous and effective publicity is given to future developments of this policy, the result cannot fail to be beneficial.

There is a third line of approach to the Punjab grower – the suggestion which, as I told Your Excellency the other day, Raisman[43] has mentioned to me: it is to the effect that the Central Government should sponsor some form of insurance against unduly depressed grain prices in the future. This idea has not yet, I understand, taken definite shape and in accordance with Raisman's wishes I have said nothing on the subject to the Punjab Ministry since he spoke to me. But I have frequently pointed to them what may be called the negative aspect of this proposition. I have repeated that if the Punjab seeks to take undue advantage of the scarcity now prevailing, it can look for no sympathy in years to come when prices fall and the grower in northern India appeals for a limitation on foreign imports. I do not suppose that any scheme such as that which Raisman had in mind can be worked out without a considerable expenditure of thought and time. But an announcement of this nature as soon as it can be released in positive and tangible form should act as a very potent leverage. Perhaps it is not too much to hope that a scheme on these lines could be evolved and given out before a campaign, if that idea should find favour, is set on foot for forward purchases in advance of the next *rabi* harvest: the Ministry and I myself are, as I have told Your Excellency, disposed to recommend such a campaign provided that the practicability of imports from abroad has been adequately demonstrated.

Coming now to the second paragraph of your letter of the 27th of September, I need not, I hope, assure you that the Ministry are no less jealous of the good name of the Punjab than Your Excellency and I myself. The whole of the Punjab in common with the rest of India is gravely disturbed by the plight of Bengal and we are all out to help in coming to the rescue of those in distress. I would suggest that very serious thought should be given to the question before any attempt is made to concentrate on the Punjab and on the Punjab Ministry the blame for what has come to pass. I am not fully aware of whatever criticizms may have been directed against the Punjab by Home authorities or by the Press in England. The *New Statesman* is reported to have published an article in the course of which it is stated that as soon as scarcity began to manifest itself in India the Punjab Government imposed an embargo on the export of grain from its territories. In the light of what Your Excellency has been good enough to say about the contribution of the Punjab to the War Effort, I have no doubt that the India Office has gladly availed itself of the opportunity to point out the falseness of this strange accusation. Any challenge thrown out to the Punjab Ministry by way of holding them responsible for the Bengal tragedy is not likely to go unanswered. It is true no doubt that Sir Chhotu Ram was responsible for making remarks in the course of his voluminous speeches likely to induce growers to hold up their stocks in the hope of higher prices. I have never sought to defend him as regards this offence: as Your Excellency is aware, I have taken him to task, he has given me his assurance that he will not err again in this direction, and since then, as far as I am aware, he has kept his word. Since then the Premier has issued two appeals to growers to follow his own example and bring their grain to the market. And Sir Chhotu Ram has on more than one occasion advocated the import of grain from overseas to relieve the situation. How can it be said then that the Punjab Ministry are black-mailing the starving population of Bengal? I have no desire to resort to recriminations about the past. But if it is pertinent to bring up against the Punjab remarks which Sir Chhotu Ram saw fit to make some time ago, it is surely permissible, leaving aside the errors and experiences of last year on which the Punjab Ministry could have much to say, to point out certain conditions now prevailing in other Provinces bordering on the Punjab. On the edge of the Punjab, in the United Provinces – a territory administered under Section 93 of the Act where one might suppose that all-India interests would be given greater and more effective consideration than in a Province where a popular Ministry still functions – the price of wheat is roughly three rupees a maund higher than in the Punjab. The United Provinces is a surplus Province in the matter of wheat. It may be true, as Raisman indicated the other day, the Punjab surplus is materially greater than that of the United Provinces. But Hapur is an important wheat market. Apart from Sind, Hapur in the United Provinces and Lyallpur in the Punjab were the only two markets nominated by the Central Government last year as pivotal points in which the maximum price of wheat was fixed at Rs. 5 a maund. Even assuming that there should be disparity of something from six annas to one rupee in favour of Hapur, there is no obvious reason for the extent of the present discrepancy. If this discrepancy is allowed, as it has been, to continue, can it be expected that the Punjab grower will refrain from embarrassing the Ministry or that the Ministers will find a ready response? It does not appear to me that any practical advantage would result from the suggestion made by Raisman the other day that action should be taken to "suppress" the publication of Hapur prices: these will be widely known even if they are not reported in the newspapers. I do not know whether the United Provinces Government are making any profit out of wheat exports, but the United Press on the 18th of this month gave out the following statement:

"It is learnt that the United Provinces is exporting 40,000 tons of wheat to Bengal at Rs. 16 per maund – F.O.R. Howrah."

I cannot vouch for the accuracy of this statement but I understand from the United Press representative at Simla that to the best of his knowledge no contradiction has been issued. Also it is a fact, as both Raisman and Mehta, the Sugar Controller, are aware, that the United Provinces Government are charging Rs. 3-2 per maund as their fee for a licence to export *gur* from the Province. It is reported that they are adopting the same line of action in the matter of oil-seeds. Apart from the fact that such practices are not easy to reconcile with the provisions of the Government of India Act, do they not furnish a direct incentive to other Provinces to make a profit from the exports of their produce? Is it not to the credit of the Punjab Ministry that they have refrained from following such examples? I have every sympathy with Raisman and the Central Government in their manifold difficulties, but I think Your Excellency will agree that, while not attempting to shield Sir Chhotu Ram or any other offenders for their past misdeeds, I am bound to keep you informed of the Punjab point of view. I could elaborate the argument in various other directions, but perhaps I have said sufficient on the subject. I would only repeat that I am strongly inclined to deprecate both on the grounds of justice and policy a frontal attack on the Punjab Ministry. It seems to me that in this crisis we should abstain from all unnecessary recriminations concerning the past, whether in regard to the Punjab Ministry or other authorities, and concentrate on the present and the future. As I have said, we are all anxious to do our best to assist.

In the matter of inflation I have pointed out on various occasions the inherent danger to the Ministers both individually and collectively, and I shall continue to do my best to keep their attention directed to this factor.

I enclose for your information a copy of the communication[44] issued to District Officers, bringing to their notice the Premier's appeals, the text of which Your Excellency has seen, and urging them to take effective action. We will do what we can to see that their efforts are not relaxed.

There is I think, only one point in your letter of the 29th instant with which I need trouble Your Excellency by adding to the length of this long letter and that relates to the Premier's remarks about cheap cloth. What he tells me he wished to point out was that the effect of the Central Government's campaign to reduce the price of cloth had only manifested itself to a very limited extent so far as the rural community is concerned. This I believe to be correct up to the present, but I am making further enquiries.

I hate to indent further on Your Excellency's time when I know that you are so desperately busy, but perhaps I could be permitted to come and see you one evening – Friday if that would suit you – for a short time before I leave Simla. I will get Brander to ring up Laithwaite and find out whether this would be possible.

Yours sincerely,
B.J. GLANCY

165

GLANCY TO LINLITHGOW

Barnes Court, Simla,
No. 471 *September 30th, 1943*

Dear Lord Linlithgow,

Your Excellency will remember asking me to clear up two points with reference to wheat-supplies. First, the question whether the Provincial Food Department had raised the price limit for wheat purchases on behalf of other Administrations from Rs. 10-4 to Rs. 10-12 without reference to the Government of India and secondly whether purchases were made for the Provincial Reserve of wheat at prices in excess of these limits.

2. As regards the first point, it is not correct that this action was taken by the Punjab without reference to the Government of India. I enclose copies of Christie's demi-official letter No. 47-S of the 30th August 1943, and Wace's reply No. 1075-S.F.S.-43/8378-S dated the 4th September 1943.[45] It will be seen from this correspondence that although the Central

Government did not specifically express their approval to the Rs. 10-12 price limit, they appear to have realized the necessity for the action taken, and since then no protest has been received by the Provincial Government. The action was taken in good faith in order to maintain a flow of supplies. It had been impossible to make any purchases at the previous price limit of Rs. 10-4 since the middle of August. Stocks awaiting transport were shrinking and it was clearly necessary to start purchasing again. If, however, the Central Government consider that this is desirable, it is suggested that precise instructions should be issued regarding the limits, if any, within which the Provincial Food Department are entitled to modify the purchase price limit. Sardar Baldev Singh, the Minister concerned, has been trying and is still trying to get in touch with Sir J.P. Srivastava or Hutchings on this point.

3. As to the second question – purchases for the Provincial wheat reserve – it is true that between the 16th and 20th September 2,500 tons of wheat were purchased at prices varying between Rs. 10-12 and Rs. 11 per maund. This is admittedly open to exception and will not be repeated. No further purchases are to be made on this account. The amount so purchased was not large enough to exercise any considerable effect on the market. It is relevant to state that at the same period when the price limit stood at Rs. 10-12 per maund, the Food Member of the Central Government during his visit to Lahore approved of the purchase of 10,000 tons of wheat at Rs. 11 per maund by the Central purchasing agents. Also that at the same time the Military purchasing agents, Messrs. Owen Roberts, were buying for the Army for October delivery at Rs. 11 per maund, while the North-Western Railway authorities, presumably acting with the approval of the Central Government, were making purchases at rates varying from Rs. 10-12 to Rs. 11-1 per maund in the Mandi.

The Punjab Food authorities have no wish whatsoever to encourage a rise in prices and indeed have made strenuous efforts to keep them down. A striking instance of this occurred recently when the Regional Food Controller, Eastern Area, recommended an export permit for 50,000 maunds of rice, purchased at Rs. 28-4 per maund F.O.R. Calcutta. The Punjab Food Department declined to agree. Our Director of Food Supplies has been buying rice at Rs. 17-14 per maund and his last purchase was as low as Rs. 17 per maund.

Yours sincerely,
B.J. GLANCY

166

GLANCY TO LINLITHGOW

Private and Personal
[Unnumbered]

Government House, Lahore,
October 12th, 1943

Dear Lord Linlithgow,

Will Your Excellency kindly refer to your private and personal letter of the 10th instant about the "freezing" of stocks of foodgrains pledged to certain Banks and the subsequent action which the Central Government wish to be taken?

The matter was discussed here in a Council Meeting yesterday at which I presided, and I am glad to inform you that the decision reached was that the Punjab Government should co-operate as desired. The fact that the Government of India had passed the 'freezing" order themselves without first consulting the Punjab aroused, not unnaturally, a considerable volume of criticizm. It was explained that the original intention of the Government of India was understood to be that the Punjab Government should be asked to issue the "freezing" order, but that owing to leakage of information which had occurred in Delhi, it was considered necessary for the Central Government to take action without delay. It was felt, however, that as Sir Colin Garbett, the representative of the Government of India had reached Lahore before it was decided to pass the "freezing' order, he might well have been given directions from Delhi to get into touch with the Premier, who together with certain other Ministers was also in Lahore, and explain the position in advance. Less opposition would have been experienced if the "freezing" order had been extended to the United Provinces and if the Punjab had not been the only Province in British India affected thereby. I understand from Sir Colin Garbett that the reasons for omitting the United Provinces were: (1) that very little grain was believed to be pledged to Banks in the United Provinces and (2) that available stocks were mostly in the hands of the Provincial Government: assuming that there was no other reason, it is not altogether clear what harm would have resulted from including the United Provinces in the order, and if this had been done it would certainly have made things easier with the Punjab Ministry.

One important point that remains to be determined is the price to be paid for the stocks that are to be requisitioned. Sir Colin Garbett who was asked to come and take part in the Council discussions in order to answer certain questions after the atmosphere had cooled down, said that he had no definite information on this point, but that his own view was that those who had engaged in legitimate transactions should be allowed a reasonable margin of profit and that any penal action should be confined to those found to have been guilty of exceptionable practices. We shall be interested to know whether this view is accepted.

Yours sincerely,
B.J. GLANCY

167

GLANCY TO LINLITHGOW

Private and Personal
[Unnumbered]

Government House, Lahore,
October 12th, 1943

Dear Lord Linlithgow,

Arrivals of grain in the markets have been satisfactory. Apart from the 100,000 tons assigned to Delhi (out of which, according to the District Magistrate's figures, some 55,000 tons have already been received) we now have to despatch *for civil requirements* outside the Province about 1,62,000 tons: of this 58,000 tons have been acquired, leaving a balance of some 1,04,000 tons to make up our civil quota. Wheat products still to be exported stand at about 70,000 tons, and the amount of wheat which the Military agents have still to acquire is, according to their latest returns, something under 2,70,000 tons. I have written to Your Excellency separately about the "freezing" order relating to stocks pledged to certain Banks: the Punjab Government have agreed to take the further action desired.

The fuel position has been growing more acute and is likely to deteriorate further. There are complaints from many parts of the Province about shortages of sugar and kerosene oil. Standard cloth has not yet found its way in any considerable quantity into the villages, but it is to be hoped that the flow will steadily improve. Small coin is still difficult to procure. Action has been taken against hoarders in many cases, but the results have been to a certain extent discounted by the lenient attitude adopted by the High Court on appeal. I was told of a case in Kangra the other day where a man in quite a small position was found to have accumulated no less than Rs. 16,000 in small coin and hard cash. I trust that in this case an exemplary punishment will be awarded.

The *kharif* harvest has been distinctly patchy and the outturn will be substantially less than that of last year. *Rabi* prospects are so far satisfactory.

Politically there is little to report. The eyes of politically-minded Muslims are turned to the All-India League Meeting which is to take place in Delhi on November the 13th and 14th. It is doubtful whether the Punjab Ministry will be subjected to any sensational attack there; it appears more probable that the Qaid-i-Azam will content himself for the time being with his tactics of attrition. It is likely that before the League Meeting occurs in Delhi there will be a session of the Punjab Assembly and that the Premier will take the opportunity of discussing Provincial League machinery with the Muslim members of the party. He is still determined to take his stand on the Sikander-Jinnah Pact and on the continuance of the Unionist Party.

Hindu politics in the Punjab are still suffering from the chronic complaint of frustration. Sikh factions are becoming, if anything, more involved and bewildering. Giani Kartar Singh is reported to be about to make a further contact with Jinnah in order to extort terms from him with a view to a possible Muslim League and Akali coalition and incidentally to ascertain the full implications of Pakistan: he will be lucky if he succeeds.

Yours sincerely,
B.J. GLANCY

168

GLANCY TO WAVELL[46]

Private and Personal — Government House, Lahore,
No. 472-F.L. — *October 30th, 1943*

Dear Lord Wavell,

The question of foodgrain supplies continues to be the outstanding problem and Your Excellency may be glad to have a brief account of the present position. I will not trouble you with figures relating to foodgrains other than wheat, since in regard to them there is broadly speaking no trouble. In the matter of wheat supplies the situation up to a few days ago was that out of our total quota of a million tons we had accounted for the following:

(1) Civil requirements outside the Punjab:	
(a) already exported	1,78,000 tons
(b) purchased, but not yet exported	85,000 tons
(2) Deliveries made for the Army	1,88,000 tons
(3) Wheat moved to Delhi (according to Delhi figures)	60,000 tons
(4) Wheat product permits issued	58,000 tons
Total accounted for	5,69,000 tons

There is not likely to be any serious difficulty in our providing the remainder of our quota for Delhi (40,000 tons) or in the matter of wheat products (61,000 tons). The Army purchasing agents (Messrs. Owen Roberts) have still roughly 2½ lakhs of tons to acquire; they are continuing their purchases, but the extent of their operations is limited largely by the capacity of their millers, who can only handle about 1,200 tons a day, so in the absence of any extensive storage accommodation they do not buy great quantities in advance.

2. As to the balance of our quota for civil requirements outside the Province, this comes in round figures to only 63,000 tons, and this is considerably more than covered by the stocks in the Punjab which were affected by the recent "freezing" order issued to Banks and estimated to amount to 1,35,000 tons. So the position is by no means as depressing as it is sometimes represented to be. Wheat is coming into the market in reasonably large quantities. District Officers have been asked in furtherance of the Premier's appeal to do all they can to encourage the flow of grain into the mandis, and special reports have been called for from important wheat-growing districts. But the situation is – so I gather from Sir Colin Garbett, the Central Government's Regional Commissioner – that the Government of India, in view of the results of the "freezing" order, are not anxious to buy more wheat now in the Punjab for civil requirements in other parts of India, except in the case of offers which are well below the existing ceiling rate, that is to say Rs. 10/- a maund.

3. The Punjab Ministers have not been very easy to handle of late. They continue to be pressed by their agricultural supporters to represent that, with prices ruling as they are just outside the Punjab and elsewhere, this Province has not been given a fair deal. Also the Ministers are resentful of the action taken by the Central Government in themselves issuing the "freezing" order instead of requesting the Punjab Government to take this step; I understand that the original intention was to ask the Punjab to

pass the order, but that this plan was altered on account of a leakage of information at Delhi. It seems a pity that the Punjab Premier was not informally apprised of the situation in advance.

4. I have warned Ministers individually and collectively time and again that they will be well-advised to abstain from making unwarranted or provocative statements about the grain position and to refrain from indulging in accusations against other parties. They have all assured me from time to time that they appreciate the wisdom of this advice and will abide by it, but unfortunately they are often forgetful. The chief offender is the Revenue Minister, Sir Chhotu Ram. Though he is a man of very considerable attainments, he has unhappily very little control over his tongue; he has the habit of delivering speeches lasting sometimes as long as four hours at a stretch and in the course of these orations he is apt to become bewildered by his own verbiage; in addition to this he is often deliberately misrepresented by the Press, as there are few newspapers to whom he has not given cause for offence. The Punjab Assembly is to meet in a day or two and it is to be expected that some hot words will be spoken on the subject of grain supplies and kindred matters. I have cautioned the Ministers to exercise due control in what they say themselves; it remains to be seen how far some of them will remember this admonition.

5. In the matter of Standard Cloth supplies the position is still not satisfactory. The quota which we are due to receive for the period ending next January is 73 million yards and out of this only about 3½ million yards have so far arrived. I hope that, so far as this is possible, deliveries will be speeded up.

6. In the matter of politics there is not very much to report. Attacks made by extremist Muslim Leaguers on the Punjab Ministry have been less virulent than they were some time ago. The position of the Provincial Muslim League is likely to be clarified in the course of party discussions during the period of the forthcoming Assembly session. The general opinion is that Mr. Jinnah is unlikely to engineer a direct assault on the Punjab Ministry at the All-India League Meeting next month.

7. Hindu and Sikh political leaders have made no sensational movements of late. Sikh leaders have, as usual, been quarrelling persistently with each other. The attention of the Akalis is mainly concentrated on a Bill to amend the Sikh Gurdwaras Act; the original Bill has now been split up into two sections and the portion relating to controversial matter is likely to be circulated for public opinion. The late Premier, Sir Sikander Hyat Khan, made an informal agreement with the Akali leaders, known as the "Sikander-Baldev Pact", one of the provisions of which was that in religious matters which concerned one individual community alone it should be

left to the representatives of that community in the Assembly to decide what action should be taken; the Akalis would like this proposed convention to be applied to the Bill in which they are now interested, but it appears doubtful how far this idea will meet with the approval of the House.

8. I am greatly looking forward to meeting Your Excellency in Delhi and still more glad to hear that you are about to pay us a visit at Lahore.

Yours sincerely,
B.J. GLANCY

169

GLANCY TO WAVELL[47]

Secret
No. 474 *November 30th, 1943*

[Dear Lord Wavell,]

Your Excellency will, I hope, have received my telegrams of yesterday and today about the question of an announcement on the subject of price control. The question was discussed in Council this morning and I am glad to say that the Cabinet have now accepted the view that the announcement should be made by the Punjab Government: the more I think of it, the more convinced I am that this course is greatly preferable to the issue of a direction by the Government of India. I enclose for Your Excellency's approval the text of the announcement which the Punjab Government propose to make. Though the draft may appear long-winded and in places verging on the flamboyant, I do not see that it contains anything radically objectionable. The Ministers' difficulties with the Assembly and the elector have to be borne in mind. It is only after protracted discussion that the wording has been agreed upon and, unless you see any reason to the contrary, I would recommend that it may be accepted as it stands.

There are two other main points.

The first concerns the question of requisitioning. The Premier says that in the course of the interview that you gave him Your Excellency assured him that no requisitioning *from the grower* was contemplated. The Ministers feel extremely strongly on this point. They are convinced that any requisitioning which is to take place should, as has hitherto been the case in the Punjab and also, it is understood, in certain other Provinces, be confined to stocks held by traders and middlemen unless there is to be a serious danger of unrest. It is certainly the case that requisitioning from small landholders, who form the vast majority of growers in this Province, would present very great practical difficulties, and it is by no means easy to lay down any satisfactory dividing line between small and big landholders. The Ministers maintain that in their position they could accept no responsibility for an attempt to commandeer grain from growers. So determined were they in this matter that they were most anxious to include a passage to this effect in the draft announcement. They will now be content if Your Excellency will be good enough to confirm the assurance that the Premier says that he received from you. They propose to explain the position accordingly to the grower in due course and they believe that this will help them very materially in the campaign which they intend to launch in order to induce the grower to co-operate.

The second point is that the Ministry regard it as essential that a simultaneous announcement about the impending imposition of maximum prices should be made by all Provinces where this policy is not already in actual operation. If, as I hope, this can be arranged, we should be glad to know the zero hour at which the Punjab announcement should issue.

Though the Ministers are still not fully satisfied with the price to be laid down for wheat in the Punjab, they have made no further attempt to manoeuvre for a higher rate, and I do not think they will revert to this matter provided that, as already agreed, the difference between U.P. and Punjab prices does not exceed six annas a maund. The subsequent announcement laying down details of prices can issue as soon as the Food Department have been able to effect such inter-Provincial co-ordination as is practicable. So far as I am aware, there has been no leakage of information from this end up to date — a distinctly unusual departure.

I shall be grateful to receive Your Excellency's further instructions as soon as possible.

[Yours sincerely,
B.J. GLANCY]

ENCLOSURE TO NO. 169

DRAFT ANNOUNCEMENT BY PUNJAB GOVERNMENT

The Punjab Government have given prolonged attention to the question of India's food supplies. They have done their best to assist in securing the supplies required for the Defence Services and for the Deficit Provinces:

statistics published from time to time will, it is hoped, have shown beyond doubt the very great measure of success that has been achieved. The object of the Punjab Government throughout has been to make grain available to the consumer at a reasonable price and at the same time to ensure a fair return to the grower. One question that has on various occasions been considered not only in the Punjab but throughout India is whether the imposition of maximum prices on the sale of food grains is or is not advisable. As is well known to the public, the Punjab Government have hitherto consistently opposed the policy of prescribing maximum prices, and they have stated plainly their reasons for preferring the adoption of other methods in order to attain the results desired. They have tried to urge with full force the point of view endorsed almost unanimously by the Punjab Assembly. But their arguments have not prevailed. Recently the Punjab Ministry have had the benefit of personal discussion with His Excellency the Governor-General who informed them that in the opinion of his advisers one single co-ordinated policy throughout the country was essential in view of war conditions and the present food crisis unhappily obtaining in Bengal and some other parts of India. He also informed them that the Government of India have definitely reached the conclusion that the most effective method of righting the present position lay in the direction of price control. In the view of the Government of India the high traditions of service and sacrifice which the Punjab has always sought to maintain can best be preserved by conforming to this line of policy. The Punjab Government accordingly, eager as they have always been to co-operate in promoting the successful prosecution of the war and the interests of India in general, have felt constrained to act in pursuance of this advice, though their views of the administrative and economic difficulties in the Province remain unchanged. Now so far as lies in their power they will do their best to make the policy of the Central Government a success and they look to all classes to assist them in this behalf. It will still be their object to secure as far as possible a fair price both for the consumer and the grower; though it can obviously not be expected that all conflicting interests will be completely satisfied, Government hope that all classes will endeavour to reconcile themselves to the decision which has been reached in conformity with what is considered by the Central authorities to be essential in the interests of India as a whole. The intention is that the maximum price not only of wheat but of all principal foodgrains shall be prescribed in all the Provinces of India. In the case of wheat and other *rabi* produce the price will take effect from the time when the next *rabi* harvest comes on to the market. The intention of the Central Government is that the Punjab grower shall not be placed in an unfavourable position in the matter of grain prices as compared with growers in other parts of the country. The Central Government have also given their assurance that they will use every possible endeavour to make available in sufficient quantity consumer's goods and to lower simultaneously, if not earlier, the level of their prices: in this matter the Punjab Government will not fail to make such further representations as may in their view become necessary. The maximum prices to be laid down will be announced as soon as it is possible to arrive at detailed decisions in consultation with the Central Government and with other Provinces.[48]

170

GLANCY TO WAVELL[49]

Private and Personal
No. 475

Government House, Lahore,
December 8th, 1943

Dear Lord Wavell,

I am afraid that it is some time since I sent Your Excellency my last periodical letter, but since then we have had the opportunity of discussing various subjects both at Delhi and Lahore.

2. The food problem is still the main preoccupation. The Punjab Government's announcement accepting food-control, the text of which you have already approved, will issue as soon as our Food Department are informed by the Government of India of the date on which similar and simultaneous announcements are to be made by the U.P. and the North-West Frontier Province. The Punjab Government communiqué will conclude with a brief paragraph saying that the principle of rationing has also been accepted and will be brought into force in the main cities of the Province as soon as arrangements can be completed. The Premier, as I have told Your Excellency, will also be issuing a statement of his own for the edification and reassurance of his constituents. This is likely to contain a certain amount of criticism of the Central Government's direction in the past and is designed to explain and justify the line taken by the Punjab hitherto. It is also likely to contain a passage saying that, while the Premier and his colleagues will do their best to make control a success, they do not propose to include in their contemplated programme of procurement the

requisitioning of grain from the "homes of growers". This expression is favoured by the Premier as an attempt at indicating that, while village to village requisitioning cannot be regarded as a practical proposition, large land-holders need not expect the same treatment, since it is not their practice to store grain in their homes. The Premier assures me that he fully intends to co-operate and I believe he means what he says. The price of grain has been falling fairly markedly, but there has been a slight upward tendency within the last few days: this may be due to the growing belief that control is not actually to be brought into force until the next *rabi* harvest comes on to the market. Rain is badly needed in nearly all parts of the Province and unless it comes soon *rabi* prospects will be materially affected.

3. There have been no striking developments recently in provincial politics. The Premier continues to maintain the firm attitude which he took up at the Muslim League meeting at Delhi. The Committee appointed by Jinnah to examine the Provincial Muslim League constitution have written to say that they would like to come to Lahore and hold discussions with Muslim M.L.As. The Premier has countered this by saying that he was given to understand that the object of the Committee was to advise as to whether the Provincial League constitution contained anything at variance with the principles of the All-India League, and he docs not see how this purpose is likely to be served by the discussions now contemplated. The next move lies with Jinnah.

4. Sikh leaders have been quarrelling steadily with each other. The Akalis' approach to Jinnah has not led to any sensational results as yet. It is clear enough that both parties distrust each other thoroughly.

5. Communists have been active in various directions, and there are indications that they will do their best to exploit any agrarian dissatisfaction aroused by the policy of control.

6. Crime has been showing some increase of late. The Kalka Rail-Motor outrage which created so much stir the summer before last has now been worked out. The principal culprit, who was a Pathan employed as a fitter in the Kalka railway shops, committed suicide in the course of an encounter with the police at Bhatinda. His brother, who also took part in the Kalka outrage, has been arrested in the N.W.F.P. and has made a confession before a Magistrate. But he is almost certain to retract this and there is very little else in the way of positive evidence against him.

7. Coal shortages are worrying us very considerably and a serious situation has arisen in regard to the supplies of the Lahore Electric Company. These are now reduced to one day's reserve of coal and it has

been necessary to shut off the industrial load. For any help that Your Excellency can give us in securing more regular coal supplies I shall be most grateful.

Yours sincerely,
B.J. GLANCY

1. Not printed.
2. In a letter of 6 January 1943, Sir Bertrand Glancy told Lord Linlithgow that Malik Khizar Hyat Khan had agreed to become Provincial Leader of the National War Front. This position was vacant following the death of Sir Sikander. R/3/1/65.
3. In telegram 6-C of 5 February 1943, Sir Bertrand Glancy informed Lord Linlithgow that Major Shaukat Hyat Khan's appointment to the Ministry was now definite and was likely to be announced that day. R/3/1/65.
4. This document is taken from L/E/8/3310.
5. The text of this circular letter from Lord Linlithgow to all Governors, stressing the gravity of the food situation, is on L/E/8/3310.
6. Mr William Phillips had arrived in India in January 1943 as Personal Representative of President Roosevelt.
7. Lord Linlithgow minuted: 'It has not much to do with him.'
8. Lord Linlithgow minuted: 'I hope the Punjab Govt. may set its face firmly against this & give all possible protection to the Ruler & Government of Kapurthala.'
9. This document is taken from MSS. EUR. F 125/111.
10. Mahatma Gandhi had begun his fast on 10 February 1943 and concluded it on 3 March. Lord Linlithgow's telegram dealt with security preparations should Mahatma Gandhi die while fasting. MSS. EUR. F 125/111.
11. This document is taken from MSS. EUR. F 125/111.
12. This telegram considered arrangements should Mahatma Gandhi die while fasting. MSS. EUR. F 125/111.
13. See *P.P. 1936-1939*, Appendix I.
14. Mr C.L. Corfield, Resident for the Punjab States.
15. This document is taken from MSS. EUR. F 125/111.
16. This letter informed Governors that they would shortly be receiving the decision of the Executive Council as to the quantities of foodgrains which surplus areas would be expected to surrender to deficit areas during the following twelve months. MSS. EUR. F 125/111.
17. On 13 May 1943 the *Tribune* reported a speech Sir Chhotu Ram had made at a public function of the Chamars held in the Lahore Cantonment. Chhotu Ram was alleged to have said: 'If the British Government remains in India, no one will ever be happy.... Englishmen are not angels sent by God on earth.... It is due to our own differences that they are ruling in this country....

If you [the Untouchables] demand your share first and stand in the way of India's getting independence, you will also be the losers.'

In telegram 1193-S, Lord Linlithgow told Sir Bertrand Glancy that he took a serious view of Chhotu Ram's remarks. He asked the Governor to admonish him strongly. The Viceroy preferred to see Chhotu Ram leave the Government than that he made such a statement. R/3/1/65.

18. This document is taken from MSS. EUR. F 125/111.
19. Mr E.W.C. Wace.
20. In a subsequent letter, No. 450, of 24 May 1943, Sir Bertrand Glancy reported that he had discussed this subject with Malik Khizar Hyat Khan who concurred with the views expressed in the present letter. However Khizar was 'inclined to doubt the advantage of giving publicity outside the Services, particularly in recruiting areas, to punishments inflicted on members of the Services convicted of traitorous conduct. He thinks that such action, at least so far as the Punjab is concerned, is likely to be unnecessary and that it might give rise to misrepresentations.' There was, Glancy felt, a good deal to be said in favour of Khizar's view. MSS. EUR. F. 125/111.
21. See next document and its note 24.
22. In a statement issued on 28 May 1943, Mr Jinnah said that Mr Gandhi's letter could only be construed as a move on his part to embroil the League into a clash with the British Government for the purpose of helping his release.
23. This document is taken from MSS. EUR. F 125/111.
24. In this telegram Lord Linlithgow informed Governors that: '[f]ollowing on Jinnah's speech last month to Muslim League Gandhi has sent Home Department a letter to Jinnah saying that he has noted his speech and inviting Jinnah to come and see him. Letter is entirely non-committal as regards Pakistan and expresses the hope that Jinnah will take Gandhi as he finds him.' After discussion in Council and consideration by Cabinet it had been decided that Government should stick to its policy of refusing to facilitate any contacts between Mahatma Gandhi and the outside world. Gandhi and Jinnah had been told of the decision but no indication was given to Jinnah as to the contents of the letter. MSS. EUR. F 125/111.
25. In this letter to Governors, Lord Linlithgow said he had always taken the view that the Khaksars were, potentially, a most serious organization and he had no doubt that efforts which appeared to be afoot to revive the military character of the organization must be very firmly resisted. An additional reason why they should be particularly careful was that they could not altogether exclude the possibility of a collusion between the Khaksars and the Muslim League and its leader. It was true that Jinnah had so far betrayed no special interest in the Khaksars and it was possible that Mashriqi regarded himself as a rival rather than a willing colleague of Jinnah. But there had been signs, both in the Muslim League volunteers and among the Khaksars, of the kind of sabre-rattling which they would do well to suppress at the outset. Linlithgow sought Governors' views on the matter. Ibid.

26. Lord Linlithgow had drawn attention to press reports of Sir Chhotu Ram's speech to a gathering of 30,000 zamindars at Lyallpur a few days previously. R/3/1/65.
27. Lord Linlithgow minuted: 'Sir B.J. Glancy had better know that in my opinion, Sir Chhotu Ram's attitude, if persisted in, is likely to lead in the not distant future to a Section 93 position in the Punjab. Such ruthless political opportunism is impossible to reconcile with the general food position in India and the overriding calls of war.'
28. Lord Linlithgow minuted: 'And particularly, of course, a popular Ministry.'
29. Mr C.L. Corfield.
30. This document is taken from MSS. EUR. F 125/111.
31. In this letter to Governors, Lord Linlithgow said he had been considering with Sir John Colville, the Governor of Bombay, the possibility of a further fast by Mahatma Gandhi to mark the twelve months' anniversary of his detention. Colville had replied that he had no information to suggest a fast was imminent. However Linlithgow sought Governors' views on the policies they should adopt if Gandhi were to fast again. MSS. EUR. F 125/111.
32. In this letter Lord Linlithgow observed that it seemed as if Malik Khizar Hyat Khan lacked the political ability and experience of Sir Sikander to stand up effectively against Mr Jinnah. The Viceroy had a feeling that: 'under the stress of the League's growing influence in the Punjab, the Muslim members of the Ministry and their hangers-on have been tempted to show themselves more Muslim than the League itself' so that 'the government is tending to become Muslim rather than "Punjabi".' Lord Linlithgow stressed that in order to safeguard the minorities and services, there must be no doubt as to the Governor's responsibilities or his intentions to discharge those special responsibilities. He asked whether, in Sir Bertrand's time or earlier, there had been any 'blurring of the dividing line between matters in relation to which you and your predecessors acted on advice and those which you had had to decide in your individual judgement or discretion.' R/3/1/65. See Mansergh, *Transfer of Power*, Vol. IV, No. 49.
33. See Enclosure to next document.
34. See *P.P., 1936-1939*, Appendix I.
35. Lord Linlithgow minuted: 'He was lying. He wanted my name at the head of the list and said so!'
36. Lord Linlithgow minuted at the end of this letter: 'He seems to have been well sat on all round!'
37. The record of this Food Conference has not been traced in the India Office Records.
38. Mr H.S. Suhrawardy was Member for Civil Supplies (including Food), Government of Bengal at this date.
39. Major-General E. Wood was Secretary, Food Department, Government of India at this date.
40. In this letter Lord Linlithgow said that the success or failure of India's food administration depended very largely on the Punjab. He added: 'To put it

quite clearly I mean that the procurement of the necessary surplus wheat from the Punjab is more important than any political considerations, any interests of the Ministers, and even, in the last resort, the continuance of Provincial Autonomy in the Punjab.' R/3/1/65.

41. [Note in original:] Action in this direction has just been taken.
42. Sir J.P. Srivastava was Food Member of the Viceroy's Executive Council at this date.
43. Sir J. Raisman was Finance Member of the Viceroy's Executive Council at this date.
44. Not printed.
45. Neither of the letters referred to in this sentence is printed.
46. This document is taken from L/P&J/5/246: ff 32-4.
47. This document is taken from L/E/8/3311: ff 101-3.
48. Lord Wavell replied to this letter on 2 December 1943. He said that it had been considered in the Executive Council that morning and the draft announcement had been accepted as it stood and Council expressed their appreciation of the helpful attitude of the Punjab Government in this important matter. Lord Wavell then conveyed other aspects of the Council's conclusions:

    (*a*) It was agreed that while requisitioning from the small grower should not form part of the procurement plan, Council considered the Punjab Government would be most unwise to make any announcement to restrict their legal right to requisition. Wavell added: 'While I agreed with the Premier that village to village requisitioning from small growers in the Punjab would be impracticable, I certainly did not intend the Punjab Government to give a public undertaking that they would not requisition in any circumstances, and Council's view on this point appears to me to be sound.'

    (*b*) It would be difficult to arrange immediately for a simultaneous announcement by all Provinces which had not yet introduced statutory price control.

    (*c*) Council did not think there would be any great difficulty in the coordination of prices in Sind, the N.W.F.P., Punjab and U.P.

    (*d*) It was noted that the draft announcement did not mention rationing. Particular importance was attached to the early introduction of urban rationing.

    (*e*) Council pointed out the importance of adequate administrative action to ensure price control worked. Lord Wavell asked for everything possible to be done to ensure this machinery was ready for *rabi* 1944.

    Lord Wavell added: 'Please let the Premier know that I very much appreciate the way he and his Ministers met me; and that I am clear that their action will have a most beneficial effect on India's problems; I am sure that they will carry out their undertakings wholeheart lly and loyally.' L/E/8/3311: ff 96-7.
49. This document is taken from L/P&J/5/246: ff 12-13.

APPENDIX

Sikander-Baldev Singh Pact[1]

Lahore,
June, 1942

The terms of the Pact which has been arrived at between Sardar Baldev Singh, leader of the United Punjab Party and Sir Sikander Hyat Khan, were announced by the Premier at a press conference held at Lahore on the 15th June 1942.

The terms, which are embodied in a letter addressed by Sir Sikander Hyat Khan to Sardar Baldev Singh, relate to facilities for *Jhatka*, teaching of Gurmukhi, legislation regarding religious matters, service under the Punjab Government and Sikh representation at the Centre. The terms are so formed as to apply equally to all communities in the Punjab.

DETAILS OF THE PACT

In connection with the question of *Jhatka*, Sir Sikander Hyat Khan proposes, with the approval of the Cabinet, to issue instruction that in Government institutions where separate kitchens exist or can be provided for Muslims, Hindus and Sikhs, and where facilities exist for obtaining meat, every community should be free to cook and use meat slaughtered according to their own rites, subject only to such restriction as may be necessary to avoid injury to the feelings of the other communities.

As regards the teaching of Gurmukhi as second language in schools, Sir Sikander Hyat Khan says that it will not be possible to give effect to this suggestion forthwith, but he agrees that there should be no objection in adopting and giving effect to it as soon as may be possible. Any formula in this connection will, of course, apply to [all] communities alike.

As for legislation relating to religious matters, Sir Sikander Hyat Khan has agreed to set up a convention that in matters which exclusively concern a particular community, that community alone should have the right to decide if the matter, when it comes before the House, should be proceeded with or not. It can be left to the members of that community to take a decision at all stages of such legislation.

As regards recruitment to the Services, Sir Sikander Hyat Khan states that the Government has already fixed the proportion for various communities, including the Sikhs, who have been allotted 10 per cent share. It is the duty of every Minister to see that no departure from this formula is countenanced.

As for Sikh representation at the Centre, the Premier has assured Sardar Baldev Singh that if and when an expansion or change in the present Executive Council is contemplated, the Sikh claim will, as hitherto, have his full sympathy and support. He shall also be glad to support the Sikh claim for due share in the Central Services.

NOTE

1. This text is taken from N.N. Mitra (ed.), *Indian Annual Register*, January-June 1942, pp. 344-5, Calcutta: Annual Register Office, [1942].

Index

Certain terms, such as Hindus, Muslims, Sikhs and Punjab, occur in almost every document and have therefore not been indexed. For the same reason there are no index entries for Lord Linlithgow and Lord Wavell while they were Viceroy nor for Sir Henry Craik and Sir Bertrand Glancy while they were Governor of the Punjab. Footnotes are indexed under the document to which they are attached.

The index entries refer to document numbers